PRENTICE HALL

HISTORY OF MUSIC SERIES

H. WILEY HITCHCOCK, editor

MUSIC
IN THE UNITED STATES:
A Historical Introduction

third edition

MUSIC IN THE UNITED STATES:
A Historical Introduction

H. WILEY HITCHCOCK
Distinguished Professor of Music,
City University of New York
and
Director, Institute for Studies in American Music
at Brooklyn College

PRENTICE HALL, ENGLEWOOD CLIFFS, NEW JERSEY 07632

Library of Congress Cataloging-in-Publication Data

Hitchcock, H. Wiley (Hugh Wiley), date
   Music in the United States.

   (Prentice-Hall history of music series)
   Includes bibliographies and index.
   1. Music—United States—History and criticism.
I. Title.   II. Series.
ML200.H58   1988   781.773   87-14496
ISBN 0-13-608407-9

Cover art: The Banjo Player by William S. Mount (1807–1868)
Courtesy of the Detroit Institute of Art

Printed in the United States of America
20   19   18   17   16   15   14   13   12   11   10

 ©1988, 1974, 1969 by Prentice Hall
A Division of Simon & Schuster
Englewood Cliffs, New Jersey 07632

PRENTICE-HALL INTERNATIONAL (UK) LIMITED, *London*
PRENTICE-HALL OF AUSTRALIA PTY. LIMITED, *Sydney*
PRENTICE-HALL CANADA INC., *Toronto*
PRENTICE-HALL HISPANOAMERICANA, S.A., *Mexico*
PRENTICE-HALL OF INDIA PRIVATE LIMITED, *New Delhi*
PRENTICE-HALL OF JAPAN, INC., *Tokyo*
SIMON & SCHUSTER ASIA PTE. LTD., *Singapore*
EDITORA PRENTICE-HALL DO BRASIL, LTDA., *Rio de Janeiro*

FOREWORD

Students and others interested in the history of music have always needed books of moderate length that are nevertheless comprehensive, authoritative, and engagingly written. The Prentice-Hall History of Music Series was planned to fill these needs. It seems to have succeeded: revised and enlarged second editions of books in the series have been necessary, and now a new cycle of further revisions exists.

Six books in the series present a panoramic view of the history of music in Western civilization, divided among the major historical periods— Medieval, Renaissance, Baroque, Classic, Romantic, and Twentieth-Century. The musical culture of the United States, viewed historically as an independent development within the larger Western tradition, is treated in another book; and one other deals with music in Latin America. In yet another pair of books, the rich folk and traditional musics of both hemispheres are considered. Taken together, these ten volumes are a distinctive and, we hope, distinguished contribution to the history of the music of the world's peoples. Each volume, moreover, may of course be read singly as a substantial account of the music of its period or area.

The authors of the books in the Prentice-Hall History of Music Series are scholars of international repute—musicologists, critics, and teachers of exceptional stature in their respective fields of specialization. Their goal in contributing to the series has been to present works of solid, up-to-date scholarship that are eminently readable, with significant insights into music as a part of the general intellectual and cultural life of man.

H. WILEY HITCHCOCK, *Editor*

PREFACE

The Preface to both the first and second editions of this book began with these sentences: "Surely no lengthy justification is needed for a historical survey of American music and musical life. For reasons suggested in Chapter Three of this book, we know less about our own music than about that of western Europe. . . ." Happily, for this third edition I can amend this beginning as follows:

Since the publication of the first edition of this book, almost twenty years ago, general knowledge of, and interest in, the music and musical life of the United States have vastly increased. But still, no lengthy justification is needed for publishing yet another edition (the third, following a second in 1974). Not only have there been major developments in American music in the past decade and a half (these being considered in my completely new Chapter Twelve); there has also been an extraordinary upsurge of American-music scholarship—and by that term I mean to suggest not only writings about the American musical past (up to yesterday) but also editions and recordings of American music, through a very wide spectrum of genres and periods. My own conception of our musical history has been altered, inevitably, by the passage of time—but also, in significant ways, by this scholarship: the third edition of *Music in the United States* (*MinUS*), although obviously a revision and not a new book, reflects this development on virtually every page.

I am still unhappy about the continued tendency of many persons— musicians as well as music lovers—to downgrade American music, especially "serious" American music, vis-à-vis that of Europe (though their number continues to diminish). I am equally unhappy about the resistance of many to the enjoyment of *all kinds* of American music—to be exclusive in their tastes. Those tendencies have prevented us for a long time from enjoying, to the fullest, our musical heritage. My own attempt is still (as I have written here before) to view our music in the round, believing that pop songs as well as art-songs, player pianos as well as piano players, rock as well as revival hymns, minimalism as well as minstrelsy are important parts of the American musical experience. I also attempt to view it head-on, to measure it in its own terms, and to seek the "why" behind the "what" in our musical history.

This new edition has two huge advantages over the previous ones. First, it has been able to capitalize on several major recording projects of the past decade: the more than one hundred albums of New World Records' *Recorded Anthology of American Music* (*NW*) and the boxed sets *The Smithsonian Collection of Classic Jazz* (*SCCJ*)* and *The Smithsonian Collection of Classic Country Music* (*SCCCM*), to all of which I frequently refer; and the fifteen-disc series *Folk Music in America* from the Library of Congress, not to mention the earlier, invaluable AAFS series drawn from the library's Archive of Folk Song. Second, it has also been able to capitalize on the work of the nearly 1000 contributors of the 5000-odd entries in *The New Grove Dictionary of American Music* (*TNGDAM*), the first comprehensive scholarly encyclopedia of the music of the United States. The many dates, statistics, and other details that differ in this edition of *MinUS* from those in earlier editions reflect this new authoritative resource, as do larger matters of fact and opinion. I occasionally refer specifically to entries in *TNGDAM*, but *only* occasionally; let me remind readers that for almost every topic touched on in this book a *TNGDAM* entry exists, usually with a helpful bibliography.

My approach to nineteenth-century American music has focused on what I call "cultivated" and "vernacular" traditions. In dealing with the latter, as with secular music in the Colonial era, I discuss much music now considered "folk music"—but in its function as the *popular* music of its time

---

* A revised edition of this set was issued in 1987, just too late for references to be made to it in this book.

(as I explain in Chapter Three); American folk music as such is considered more broadly by Bruno Nettl and Gerard Béhague in their companion volume in the Prentice-Hall History of Music Series, *Folk and Traditional Music of the Western Continents*. In discussing American music since World War I, I have emphasized the principal stylistic trends and the predominant musical attitudes. Many fine composers and performers have thereby gone unmentioned; they have had to make way, with my regrets, for those who seem to me to be the ones in whose work the major issues of twentieth-century American music have been addressed most clearly, boldly, and influentially. I make no apologies for devoting an entire chapter of a rather brief book to Charles Ives: his thought and his music continue to stand as provocative, stimulating, and fertile challenges to American musical evolution.

This is a book based on primary sources: almost without exception I have studied the scores or listened to performances of the music cited herein (or done both). My debts to other scholars, however, are many; I have acknowledged these in bibliographical notes, at the end of each chapter, which will help readers reach out beyond this book to other sources; and in footnotes I have attempted to cite primarily works that can serve as useful further references. Whenever appropriate and possible, I have quoted composers on their own music. Two resources to which I do not refer, but which every reader should be aware of, are the unique, massive *Resources of American Music History: A Directory of Source Materials from Colonial Times to World War II*, eds. D. W. Krummel et al. (Urbana: University of Illinois Press, 1981), and the exceptionally valuable annotated bibliography by David Horn, *The Literature of American Music in Books and Folk Music Collections* (Metuchen, NJ: The Scarecrow Press, 1977); a supplement to Horn's bibliography is to be published. Also scheduled for publication is the much-revised third edition of Gilbert Chase's *America's Music* (Urbana: University of Illinois Press); and two other surveys should be cited here—Daniel Kingman's *American Music: A Panorama* (New York: Schirmer Books, 1979; rev. ed. in progress) and Charles Hamm's *Music in the New World* (New York: W. W. Norton, 1983). Essential complements to these histories, and to this one, are the second edition of Eileen Southern's *The Music of Black Americans* (New York: W. W. Norton, 1983)—vastly improved over the first (1971), which was a landmark achievement in its own right—and *American Music Recordings: A Discography of 20th-Century U.S. Composers*, ed. Carol J. Oja (Brooklyn: Institute for Studies in American Music, 1982).

Valuable series of earlier American music in facsimile-reprint and fresh editions have proliferated. I refer from time to time to specific volumes in a number of these; let me here just enumerate them by series title. Series with volumes in print include Dover Publications in American Music, Earlier

American Music (*EAM*), and Recent Researches in American Music (*RRAM*); series with volumes yet to appear include the Smithsonian Library of American Music, Garland Publishing's Three Centuries of American Music, and Garland's American Musical Theater Series.

In the first two editions of this book I acknowledged the support and help of many students, colleagues, and friends, to whom I remain most appreciative. For this edition I was helped in many different ways by others, especially William Bolcom, Anne Carley, Sidney Cowell, Richard Crawford, Charles Dodge, Paul Echols, Susan Feder, Betty Freeman, Emily Good, Charles Hamm, Barbara Heyman, Charlotte Kaufman, Kathleen Mason Krotman, Judith Kuppersmith, Leslie Lassetter, Minna Lederman, Daniel Lentz, William Lichtenwanger, R. Allen Lott, Jessica Lowe, Carol Oja, Nancy Pardo, Vivian Perlis, Kathleen Preston, Roger Reynolds, John Rockwell, Ellen and David Rosand, William Schuman, K. Robert Schwarz, Alyn G. Shipton, Nicolas Slonimsky, Stephen Spackman, Mark Tucker, and Martin Williams.

Once again, I am indebted to many libraries, especially the New York Public Library and its Music Research Division; the Music Division of the Library of Congress; and the music libraries of Brooklyn College, New York University, the University of California at Los Angeles, and Yale University.

The work toward this revision of *MinUS* was largely done in Santa Monica, California, where I was privileged to be among the first group of Getty Scholars (1985–86) at the Getty Center for the History of Art and the Humanities. To the library and support staff of the center; its director Kurt W. Forster; and Herbert H. Hymans, head of the Getty Scholars program, I am very grateful indeed. And it would be ungracious of me not to thank Macmillan (London) and Grove's Dictionaries of Music (New York) for having engaged me, as co-editor of *The New Grove Dictionary of American Music*, to immerse myself, for what turned out to be five years, in the very deepest and broadest oceans of American music.

My final acknowledgment remains essentially as before: To my wife, Janet, I am grateful for many things, among them the model of her own impeccable scholarship; her contribution to whatever accuracy and grace of expression may be found herein; and her cheerful sufferance, for several years (but now it's many), of my humming, whistling, singing, playing through, and listening to three and a half centuries of American music.

The first edition of this book was dedicated to my parents. This new and very different third edition, written with an acute sense of how fast things change in American musical life and one's views of its history, I dedicate to my grandchildren, John Wiley Watkins and Alison Jarvis Watkins, hoping they will be interested some day in knowing what it was like, way back when.

H. W. H.

CONTENTS

ABBREVIATIONS

ACS   *The American Composer Speaks*, ed. Gilbert Chase (Baton Rouge: Louisiana State University Press, 1966)

AM   Gilbert Chase, *America's Music* (rev. 2nd ed.,; New York: McGraw-Hill Book Company, 1966)

EAM   *Earlier American Music*, ed. H. Wiley Hitchcock (New York: Da Capo Press, 1972–)

ISAMm   I.S.A.M. monograph (Brooklyn: Institute for Studies in American Music, 1973–)

MinA   *Music in America: An Anthology from the Landing of the Pilgrims to the Close of the Civil War. 1620–1865*, ed. W. Thomas Marrocco and Harold Gleason (New York: W. W. Norton & Co., Inc., 1964)

MM   *Modern Music*, ed. Minna Lederman (1924–46)

MMEA   Irving Lowens, *Music and Musicians in Early America* (New York: W. W. Norton & Co., Inc., 1964)

MQ   *The Musical Quarterly* (1915–)

NW   *Recorded Anthology of American Music* (New York: New World Records, 1975–)

OAM   John Tasker Howard, *Our American Music* (4th ed.; New York: Thomas Y. Crowell Company, 1965)

PNM   *Perspectives of New Music* (1962–)

RRAM   *Recent Researches in American Music*, ed. H. Wiley Hitchcock (Madison: A-R Editions, Inc. 1976–)

SCCCM   *The Smithsonian Collection of Classic Country Music*, comp. Bill C. Malone (Washington: Smithsonian Institution, 1981)

SCCJ   *The Smithsonian Collection of Classic Jazz*, comp. Martin Williams (Washington: Smithsonian Institution, 1973; rev. ed. 1987)

TNGDAM   *The New Grove Dictionary of American Music*, ed. H. Wiley Hitchcock and Stanley Sadie (London: Macmillan Press Limited and New York: Grove's Dictionaries of Music, Inc., 1986)

part one

The Colonial and Federal Eras (to 1820)

ONE

SACRED MUSIC IN NEW ENGLAND AND OTHER COLONIES

In his poem *The Gift Outright*, Robert Frost remarked that "the land was ours before we were the land's./She was our land more than a hundred years/Before we were her people." Acknowledging that there was an "American music" of long standing among the native American Indians; that French Huguenots sang psalms on their arrival in Spanish Florida in 1564; that Englishmen under Sir Francis Drake sang psalms in Spanish California in 1579; and that there is evidence of the use of trumpets and drums, popular and religious song, in Virginia long before the colonization of New England, we still must recognize that the heart of "our land . . . before we were her people" was New England. It is with the music of early New England that our historical introduction must begin.

The musical world left behind by the earliest English-speaking American colonists was a rich one, perhaps the richest England has ever known. At court and in the mansions of the British peerage was heard elegant and sophisticated music of many kinds—madrigals, balletts, ayres, canzonets, and other part-songs by such Renaissance masters as William Byrd, Thomas Morley, Thomas Weelkes, and John Dowland; variations, dance pieces, preludes, and other fanciful works for harpsichord by Elizabethan virginalists like Orlando Gibbons, John Bull, and Giles Farnaby; fantasies and suites for ensembles of viols and other instruments. The music at the Chapel Royal and in the great cathedrals was no less elaborate and magnificent: both Catholic and Anglican services were permitted under Elizabeth I, and choirs of good size performed intricate and resonant motets and Mass-settings in the one, anthems and great services in the other.

The American colonists, however, could hardly maintain such kinds of music in the New World. Almost none of them were of the wealthy aristocracy that had created and supported such music in England. The leisure necessary to enjoy such purely artistic music was, needless to say, not their lot. Cargo space was at a premium on the tiny colonial ships, and large instruments like organs or harpsichords could not be accommodated. Thus, the colonists could and did enjoy only music that was quite simple and fully functional: social music and worship music. Of the former we have few specific details; of the latter we know more. The history of "American music," in the first century of British colonization, may best begin with New England worship music, specifically the psalmody, sung in religious meetings and at home, that had originated in mid-sixteenth-century Protestant sects of western Europe.

PROTESTANT BACKGROUNDS

John Calvin, austere leader of the Swiss-French Protestant movement, believed that the only proper music for the church had to be based on the lyric poetry of the Bible, the Psalms. Like Martin Luther, Calvin encouraged a congregational music in the language of the people, not a choral music in the ecclesiastical Latin of the Roman Catholic Church. But, unlike Luther, Calvin thought that polyphonic music, instruments, hymns, and other non-biblical texts were too much associated with Catholicism; he replaced them with the unaccompanied congregational unison singing of psalms, translated into metrical French verse. By 1562 the Calvinists had published in their center at Geneva the complete psalter in translations by Clément Marot and Théodore de Bèze (Beza, in Latin), with melodies composed or adapted by Louis Bourgeois. Similar psalters for congregational use were prepared by Dutch Protestants; in the same year as the Geneva psalter, the London printer John Day published a complete English psalter, with translations of the psalms by Thomas Sternhold and John Hopkins and with melodies partly of English origin, partly of continental—the latter brought back, after Queen Elizabeth's ascendancy, by English Protestants who had sought asylum in Geneva during the reign (1550–58) of Mary, a Catholic.

The music of these Protestant psalters was adapted from a variety of sources. Some melodies were derived from popular songs of the day; some were older hymn tunes; some were altered versions of Catholic chants. They must have been sung with fervor and gusto: apparently because of their sprightliness, the French Huguenot psalms were dubbed "Geneva jigs" and "Beza ballads"; Shakespeare, in *The Winter's Tale* (Act IV, scene 3), has the clown say, "Three-man song men all [i.e., singers of part-songs], and very good ones . . . but one Puritan amongst them, and he sings psalms to hornpipes!"

In view of the character of this music and considering the popularity of part-songs in the sixteenth century, it should not surprise us that polyphonic arrangements of psalm tunes, for enjoyment and edification at home, were soon forthcoming. In England Daman's psalter of 1579 ("to the use of the godly Christians for recreatying them selves, in stede of . . . unseemly ballades") contained four-part settings, and in 1592 Thomas East enlisted the aid of prominent composers of the day (John Dowland, Giles Farnaby, Michael Cavendish, and others) to provide polyphonic settings for his psalter. Two later and very popular collections of harmonized psalm tunes were Richard Alison's of 1599 and Thomas Ravenscroft's of 1621.

EARLY NEW ENGLAND PSALMODY

That the fiercely devout New England colonists regarded the singing of psalms as an integral part of life is suggested by a comment of one of the little group of Pilgrims that sailed from Delftshaven, Holland, in 1620:

> They that stayed at Leyden feasted us that were to go at our pastor's house, [it] being large; where we refreshed ourselves, after tears, with singing of Psalms, making joyful melody in our hearts as well as with the voice, there being many of our congregation very expert in music; and indeed it was the sweetest melody that ever mine ears heard.[1]

The "joyful melody" sung by "many . . . very expert in music" was doubtless a group of the psalms collected, translated, and published in 1612 for his congregation by the pastor of the English Separatists at Amsterdam, Henry Ainsworth. Ainsworth's psalter included both prose and poetic translations, copiously annotated, of the entire Book of Psalms; it also included 39 melodies borrowed by Ainsworth from "our former Englished Psalms [and from]

---

[1] Edward Winslow, *Hypocrisie Unmasked* (1646), quoted in Waldo Selden Pratt, *The Music of the Pilgrims* (Boston: Oliver Ditson Company, 1921), p. 6.

the French and Dutch Psalms." In variety of length, meter, and rhythm Ainsworth's choices were remarkable: compare, for example, the lilting asymmetry of Psalm 21, which is of English origin and which Ainsworth probably got from Daman's psalter, with the powerful, stomping regularity of Psalm 44, a Huguenot tune first printed in Genevan psalters, then taken over in the Sternhold-Hopkins English psalter (Example 1-1).

EXAMPLE 1-1. Psalms 21 and 44 (first verses of text only) from Ainsworth's psalter (1612), after the Amsterdam edition of 1618: *The Psalmes in Metre* (no author, place, or publisher given). Their music duplicates that of the first edition: H[enry] A[insworth], *The Book of Psalmes: Englished both in Prose and Metre. With Annotations . . .* (Amsterdam: Giles Thorp, 1612).

Used by the Pilgrims of the Plymouth colony and also by settlers at Ipswich and Salem, Ainsworth's psalter was finally replaced in the 1690s by another one that came to be universally known as the Bay Psalm Book (its real title: *The Whole Booke of Psalmes Faithfully Translated into English Metre*). This was the first book-length work to be printed in the British colonies (at Boston, in 1640) and was a product of the Massachusetts Bay Colony. The thirty-man committee of Puritans that compiled it sought to make "a plain and familiar translation" of the psalter more accurate than the Sternhold-Hopkins version they had brought with them from England. Also called the "New England version," the Bay Psalm Book originally included no music but directed that most of its verses could be sung either to Ravenscroft's tunes or those of "our english psalm books"—i.e., Sternhold-

Hopkins. Enormously popular, the Bay Psalm Book was published in almost thirty New England editions by 1760. To the ninth edition of 1698 (or possibly to an earlier, missing one) were appended thirteen melodies, with basses as well, which the unknown compiler had borrowed from various editions of John Playford's *Introduction to the Skill of Music* (London, 1667 and later).

That only 13 melodies could suffice for all 150 psalms suggests that the psalms of the Bay psalter were less diverse metrically than those of earlier psalters, and perhaps that the New England congregations of the late seventeenth century were less "expert in music" than their forebears. Indeed, "almost all this whole book of psalmes," declared the Preface of the 1640 edition, was composed in three meters: Common Meter (8, 6, 8, and 6 syllables for the four-line verses); Long Meter (8, 8, 8, 8); and an irregular meter of 6, 6, 8, 6. The decline in the number of psalm tunes regularly sung was a reflection of a general decline in the quality of psalmody in the colonies. By the early eighteenth century, Puritan ministers were raising horrified outcries at the poor singing in their churches; one complained in 1721 that "the tunes are now miserably tortured, and twisted, and quavered . . . into an horrid Medly of confused and disorderly Noises." Precentors, who were appointed to "line out" the psalms for their congregations—that is, to set the pitch and remind their fellows of a psalm tune by chanting it, line by line, echoed by the congregation—were altering the melodies at will: "every Leading-Singer would take the Liberty of raising any Note of the Tune, or lowering of it, as best pleas'd his Ear, and add such Turns and Flourishes as were grateful to him," wrote Rev. Thomas Symmes of Bradford, Massachusetts, in 1720, repelled by what came to be called the "Old Way" of singing—a folkish oral tradition that paid little heed to the notated music on which it was based.

Like clergymen before and after them, the Puritan ministers of New England set out to reform the music in their churches—by encouraging their congregations to replace the Old Way with a new way based on singing the notes as written. In so doing, they created the first music instruction books in America, established a unique kind of musical education, and paved the way for the first school of American composers.

First came sermons, pleading for "regular" singing, by note instead of by rote; one such plea was Symmes's sermon on "The Reasonableness of Regular Singing" (1720). The earliest practical attempt to improve matters, and the first American music textbook, was a small volume by the Rev. John Tufts of Newbury, Massachusetts, *An Introduction to the Singing of Psalm-Tunes*, first published in 1721. Tufts wrote a brief preface explaining the rudiments of music and a new method of musical notation (by letter rather than by note) that he had devised, and he followed these with a collection of English psalm tunes (without texts). The fifth edition of 1726, the earliest extant, includes thirty-seven such tunes, with two other harmonizing parts. Among them is one, *100 Psalm Tune New,* which has not been found in earlier publications and which may perhaps be claimed as the first American composition; whether Tufts wrote it himself we do not know. The little piece (Example 1-2) is worth a brief look: not ungraceful, it has nevertheless an

EXAMPLE 1-2. J. Tufts, *100 Psalm Tune New, An Introduction to the Singing of Psalm-Tunes . . . The Fifth Edition* (Boston: Printed for Samuel Gerrish, 1726), p. 10.

angularity of melody (the Cantus is the principal air) and a predilection for unisons, octaves, and bare fifths—not to mention the parallel fifths at the end of the second phrase—which distinguish it from British psalm tunes of the period. As we shall see, it was precisely such features of style that were to characterize native American music of the later eighteenth century.

At almost the same time that Tufts first published his *Introduction,* another manual appeared, also including a number of psalm tunes with accompanying parts. This was *The Grounds and Rules of Music Explained* (Boston, 1721) by Rev. Thomas Walter of Roxbury, Massachusetts, a nephew of the well-known Cotton Mather and, like Tufts, a graduate of Harvard College. These two "tunebooks" (as such works came to be known, even after they were furnished with texts as well as tunes) were eminently successful: Tufts's went through eleven editions between 1721 and 1744, and Walter's was still in print (as part of another book) almost a half century after it was first published. They marked the beginning of a significant movement in American music, that of the *singing-school* (to which we shall turn in a moment), and were the first of almost 350 American tunebooks that were to be printed by 1810.

The same period saw an expansion in the nature and sources of texts for Protestant American worship music. Calvin had limited the texts of church song to biblical psalms in metrical vernacular translations. The other great leader of the Protestant Reformation, Luther, had not been so restrictive; from the beginning he had permitted, and even composed himself, original hymns. Hymnody flourished under Lutheranism, and even before the eighteenth century it found its way into the English Puritan services. The first significant writer of English hymns was the Rev. Dr. Isaac Watts (1674–1748). In 1707 he published his first major collection, *Hymns and Spiritual Songs* (including such still-popular hymns as "When I survey the wondrous Cross" and "There is a land of pure delight"); in 1715, his *Divine Songs* (the first children's hymnbook); and in 1719, *The Psalms of David Imitated* (including "Our God, our help in ages past" and "Jesus shall reign"). For more than a century Watt's works were the most popular sources of texts for English and American congregational worship music. A further impetus to hymnody was provided, from the 1730s on, by the evangelical movement of Wesleyanism and by the series of "awakenings" and "revivals" which, beginning with the "Great Awakening" of 1735, studded the evolution of American Protestantism.

THE SINGING-SCHOOL MOVEMENT

As we have seen, agitation among Puritan ministers for better singing in their churches resulted in the first American music instruction books. At their call, too, was instituted the first kind of American music school. Rev. Symmes asked in 1720,

> Would it not greatly tend to promote singing of psalms if singing schools were promoted? . . . Where would be the difficulty, or what the disadvantages, if people who want skill in singing, would procure a skillful person to instruct them, and meet two or three evenings in the week, from five or six o'clock to eight, and spend their time in learning to sing?

That is precisely what happened. As early as March 1722, Boston had a Society for Promoting Regular Singing, with a core of about ninety who had learned to read music. From that time on, the singing-school, convened to learn, practice, and demonstrate the skill of reading music at sight, became an important institution in the colonies, social as well as musical. Although originally begun in an attempt to improve church music, and although their music was for the most part religious, the singing-schools were as much secular institutions as sacred, as much social outlets as pious assemblies.

One student at Yale, for example, wrote to a friend with characteristic under-graduate querulousness:

> At present I have no inclination for anything, for I am almost sick of the World & were it not for the Hopes of going to the singing-meeting tonight & indulging myself a little in some of the carnal Delights of the Flesh, such as kissing, squeezing &c. &c. I should willingly leave it now.[2]

In a society that recognized no split between religion and everyday life, the singing-school was a popular meeting ground for both. Not only in New England but also in the more southern colonies, singing-school instruction became popular in the eighteenth century: we hear of it in South Carolina in 1730, Philadelphia in 1753, New York in 1754, and Maryland in 1765.

A broadside or a newspaper advertisement would alert a community that a singing-school was to be organized. Arriving on the scene, the singing master would enroll students for classes once or twice a week for a month or more. Their texts were sometimes manuscript copybooks, into which they laboriously wrote the music they were learning to sing, or sometimes printed tunebooks, partly composed by the singing master, partly borrowed from other sources. (Copyright was nonexistent until late in the eighteenth century, and piracy was as common among literary landlubbers as on the high seas.)

Characteristically oblong (thus sometimes called an "end-opener") and headed by some sociable title like *The Chorister's Companion, The American Singing Book, The Rural Harmony,* or *The Easy Instructor,* the typical tunebook was a how-to-do-it manual, containing an introduction to the rudiments of music theory and notation, and also a what-to-do anthology, with a collection of psalm tunes (and later in the century, of hymn tunes, anthems, and even secular songs) harmonized in three or four parts for men's and women's voices. No instrumental accompaniment was provided; the old Calvinist suspicion of instruments as belonging not to the Lord but to the Devil (or the Catholics) died hard, and the prejudice was only gradually given up during the eighteenth century.

The classes of a singing-school would typically culminate in a "singing lecture"—essentially a choral concert embellished by a sermon from the local minister—or a "singing assembly," without the sermon. Having taught his pupils to sing accurately by note, having enlarged his reputation and the use of his tunebooks, and probably having got in a few licks for some other business interest (most of the singing masters were veritable prototypes of the Yankee peddler or worked at some trade), the singing master would move on to another community to begin a new singing-school.

---

[2] Quoted in *MMEA,* p. 282.

In this way the first group of American composers developed. They forged a distinctive style of music—rugged, powerful, and homogeneous (if also, as we shall see, awkward-seeming and archaic-sounding to later, more genteel ears).

THE FIRST NEW ENGLAND SCHOOL OF COMPOSERS

Singing-schools of the middle decades of the eighteenth century relied on reprints of earlier tunebooks (like Tufts's and Walter's) and the Bay Psalm Book; the next important new book was published only in 1761—*Urania*, an expansive and "choice Collection of Psalm-tunes, Anthems, and Hymns" compiled by the New Jersey-born James Lyon (1735-94) and published in Philadelphia. Lyon apparently culled most of the ninety-six compositions in the work from various English tunebooks in circulation at the time. Among the seventy psalm settings are some of special interest to us: they are "fuging psalm tunes" with a form and texture that were to be taken up lustily by New England tunesmiths. *The V Psalm Tune* (Example 1-3), borrowed perhaps from Abraham Adams's *Psalmist's New Companion*, 6th ed. (London,

EXAMPLE 1-3. *The V Psalm Tune*, in J. Lyon, *Urania* (Philadelphia: William Bradford, 1761), pp. 42–43.

ca. 1760), is characteristic: beginning with a four-part setting of the tune (in the tenor voice), it reaches a cadence (here on the dominant) in measure 12; then it starts afresh with imitative entries for the individual voices—the so-called "fuge" (fugue) or "fuging section"—which soon lead to a final cadence. Aside from some peculiarities in harmony—for instance, the characteristically British use of cross-relations (F♯ vs. F♮) in measures 1 and 2 and the clash of soprano and alto in measure 16—there is a smoothness about the little piece that betrays its transatlantic origin; American fuging tunes would tend to be simpler in rhythm, more angular in melody, less chromatic in harmony, and in some ways stronger in general effect.

In the 1760s, following the publication of Lyon's *Urania*, the pace of American tunebook publications quickened considerably, and by the 1770s a whole group of composers were busily at work in the Northeast. The First New England School, as the group has been called (see pp. 143ff. regarding a second one), was centered in Connecticut and Massachusetts. Its members consisted of journeyman composers—some have termed them "Yankee tunesmiths"—most of whom, as remarked earlier, practiced other trades or professions. The first to make his mark, and the most prominent of the group, was William Billings (1746–1800), a Boston tanner turned singing-school master and composer—and as such the first American to attempt to make music his sole profession—and one of the most picturesque person-alities in American music. Billings's first tunebook, *The New-England Psalm-Singer; or, American Chorister*, was issued in 1770. It was a landmark; only about a dozen tunes by native Americans had previously been published, and with this collection of more than 120 pieces, all of his own composition, Billings increased the number tenfold. The title page of *The New-England Psalm-Singer* was engraved by Paul Revere, which reminds us of Lexington and Concord, of the colonies versus Britain, of growing national conscious-ness and the spirit of independence during the Revolutionary decade of the 1770s. In his prefatory comments "to all musical practitioners," the twenty-four-year-old composer made no bones about *his* independence:

> *Nature is the best Dictator*, for all the hard dry studied Rules that ever was prescribed, will not enable any Person to form an Air any more than the bare Knowledge of the four and twenty letters, and strict Grammatical Rules will qualify a Scholar for composing a Piece of Poetry, or properly adjusting a Tragedy, without a Genius. . . . I don't think myself confin'd to any Rules for Composition laid down by any that went before me. . . .

Warming to the analogy between music and poetry, Billings went on: "[As I] have often heard of a Poetical Licence, I don't see why with the same Priority there may not be a Musical Licence." Here spoke the rebel-lious, self-confident young American of 1770. Here was a composer with a mind of his own. Nevertheless, despite his stated conviction that "I think it is best for every *Composer* to be his own *Carver*," Billings proceeded to instruct his readers in the rudiments of music, and even to make some qualifications in his eulogy of native genius:

> Perhaps some may think I mean and intend to throw Art intirely out of the Question, I answer by no Means, for the more Art is display'd, the more Nature is decorated. And in some sorts of Composition, there is dry Study requir'd, and Art very requisite. For instance, in a *Fuge*, where the Parts come in after each other, with the same Notes; but even there, Art is subservient to Genius, for Fancy goes first, and strikes out the Work roughly, and Art comes after, and polishes it over.

Many years later—in the preface to his last tunebook, *The Continental Harmony* of 1794—Billings was still the self-confident autodidact, putting his faith not in dry-as-dust rules declared by others, but in himself, and insisting on the pre-eminence of self-expression and of "fancy":

> Musical composition is a sort of something, which is much better felt than described (at least by me). . . . But in answer to your question, although I am not confined to rules prescribed by others, yet I come as near as I possibly can to a set of rules which I have carved out for myself; but when fancy gets upon the wing, she seems to despise all form, and scorns to be confined or limited by any formal prescriptions whatsoever.

The New-England Psalm-Singer contains 108 psalm and hymn settings and 15 anthems and canons for chorus. The four-part canon "When Jesus Wept"[3] is one of Billings's loveliest melodic inspirations; similar to it in style is another *Canon 4 in 1*, "Thus saith the high, the lofty one" (Example 1-4). These canons suggest Billings's flair for graceful melody. But perhaps it was his patriotic pieces that accounted for Billings's early popularity. Among the pieces in *The New-England Psalm-Singer* was one, *Chester*, that so caught the fancy of young America that it became a rallying song of the Revolution. When he published his second tunebook, *The Singing Master's Assistant* (Boston, 1778), at the height of the Revolutionary War, Billings reprinted in it the stirring, stomping, march-like tune and added to its patriotic text (his own) new verses that spoke for—shouted for—his whole generation.

> Let tyrants shake their iron rod,
> And Slav'ry clank her galling chains,
> We fear them not, we trust in God,
> New-england's God for ever reigns.

[3] Reprinted in *AM*, p. 132.

EXAMPLE 1-4. W. Billings, *Canon 4 in 1, The New England Psalm-Singer* (Boston: Edes and Gill, 1770); original a whole tone higher.

Thus saith____ the high,____ the lof - - ty one,

I set up - on mine ho - - ly throne.

My name____ is God,____ I dwell____ on high,

Dwell in____ my own ____ e - ter - ni - ty.

Later verses went on with even more fire and sarcasm:

> Howe and Burgoyne and Clinton too,
> With Prescot and Cornwallis join'd
> Together plot our Overthrow,
> In one infernal league combin'd.
>
> . . .
>
> The Foe comes on with haughty Stride;
> Our troops advance with martial noise,
> Their Vet'rans flee before our Youth,
> And Gen'rals yield to beardless Boys.

The Singing Master's Assistant also includes an address, "To the Goddess of Discord," with a short choral piece, *Jargon*, accompanying it. Billings's reasons for writing these are not clear. Perhaps his first tunebook had been criticized for lacking dissonance, for he begins his manifesto to Lady Discord by saying, "I have been sagacious enough of late, to discover that some evil-minded persons have insinuated to your highness, that I am utterly unmindful of your Ladyship's importance." But if he was retorting to critics, he affirmed his fealty to concord: "I shall be so condescending as to acquaint your uglyship, that I take great pleasure in subscribing myself your most inveterate, most implacable, most irreconcilable enemy." Then follows the notoriously dissonant *Jargon*, a musical joke full of harsh intervals and awkward harmonic progressions. The text is a brief quatrain:

> Let horrid Jargon split the Air,
> And rive the Nerves asunder,
> Let hateful Discord greet the Ear,
> As terrible as Thunder.

Billings gives mock instructions for performance with a rough humor that prefigures some of Charles Ives's salty marginal comments (see p. 167):

> In order to do this piece ample justice, the concert must be made of vocal and instrumental music. Let it be performed in the following manner, viz. Let an Ass bray the bass, let the fileing of a saw carry the Tenor, let a hog who is extream hungry squeel the counter, and let a cart-wheel, which is heavy loaded, and that has been long without grease, squeek the treble; and if the concert should appear to be too feeble you may add the cracking of a crow, the howling of a dog, the squalling of a cat; and what would grace the concert yet more, would be the rubbing of a wet finger upon a window glass. This last mentioned instrument no sooner salutes the drum of the ear but it instantly conveys the sensation to the teeth; and if all these in conjunction should not reach the cause [i.e., suffice], you may add this most inharmonical of all sounds, *"Pay me that thou owest."*

By 1781 Billings had published two more tunebooks. The first, *Music in Minature* (1779; the title referred to its unusually tiny size), included mainly reprints of successful earlier pieces. The second, *The Psalm Singer's Amusement,* had plenty of new pieces, among them two that must have been great favorites in the singing-schools. One, *Consonance,* is a setting of a poem by Mather Byles entitled "On Musick." It begins, "Down steers the Bass with grave majestick air/And up the Treble mounts with shrill career." Billings is at his most melodious as he graphically "explains" each of the lines in a technique of musical word-painting that goes all the way back to the Elizabethan madrigal composers. The other, *Modern Music,* explains several musical matters even more explicitly, commencing with the lines "We are met for a Concert of modern invention./To tickle the Ear is our present intention." The singers chant liltingly that ". . . we all agree/To set the tune on E,/The Author's darling Key/He prefers to the rest," and they go on to present, in various meters, modes, and textures, a naive but engaging demonstration of "modern" American music.

Billings was to offer to the public two more tunebooks, *The Suffolk Harmony* in 1786 and *The Continental Harmony* in 1794. In the Preface to the latter, he exclaimed ecstatically over "fuging music" (which he had been composing since *The Singing Master's Assistant* in 1778):

> There is more variety in one piece of fuging music than in twenty pieces of plain song. . . . The audience are most luxuriously entertained, and exceedingly delighted; in the mean time, their minds are surprizingly agitated, and extremely fluctuated. . . . Now the solemn bass demands their attention, now the manly tenor, now the lofty counter, now the volatile treble, now here, now there, now here again—O inchanting! O ecstatic! Push on, push on ye sons of harmony.

Why was Billings so excited about "fuging music"? The answer lies in the fact that Billings, and after him many other Yankee composers, was rediscovering the pleasures of counterpoint. Their predecessors, the earlier compilers of the pre-Revolutionary period, had been content to offer singers nothing but simply harmonized versions of traditional psalm tunes, and the idea of contrapuntal imitation between the voice-parts seemed to offer a much better world of musical pleasure than had the old "plain song." No wonder Billings called the idea of imitative counterpoint—not a new idea, by any means, but one with which most Americans had lost contact—a "most ingenious and . . . most grateful" one. It may be true, but it is certainly irrelevant, that neither Billings nor, perhaps, any of the other Yankee tunesmiths had the background or the technical skill needed to write real fugues (which is why it is useful to preserve the archaic spelling and thus to distinguish the New Englanders' fuging style from the classical European fugue). What they were after, and what they achieved, was music grateful to perform—music that would give every voice a good tune to sing. It was enough for them that the regular, foursquare chordal texture of the music would occasionally give way to a "fugue," and as put by Billings, each part would seem to be "mutually striving for mastery, and sweetly contending for victory."

Billings has captured the imagination of American music historians by virtue of his colorful personality, his apostleship of artistic freedom and individuality, his sense of humor, and his flair for tuneful melody. If he was not the most original, the most typical, or the most popular of the First New England School, he does symbolize perfectly the cheerful, unselfconscious pride, the honest journeyman excellence of our nation's first composers. Nevertheless, he died "poor and neglected." Other composers, from outside the Boston area, had even more successfully caught the popular fancy in the post-Revolutionary War period. Like Billings, they were singing masters and singing-school tunebook compilers.

Daniel Read (1757-1836) was one of the most active, and gifted composer-compilers. He also ran a general store in New Haven, Connecticut. His immense popularity as a composer can be suggested by the fact that his pieces were pirated time and again by other tunebook compilers; one of his Christmas hymns, for instance, *Sherburne* (*NW* 205:s1/1), was reprinted (with or without permission) no fewer than seventy-one times between 1785, when it first appeared in Read's *American Singing Book*, and 1810 (see Figure 1-1), and others by him—such as *Calvary, Greenwich, Judgment, Lisbon, Russia, Stafford, Windham,* and *Winter*—became staples in the "core repertory" of early American psalmody.[4] Timothy Swan

---

[4] That repertory—the 101 sacred compositions most often printed (and/or reprinted) in America between 1698 and 1810—has been established by Richard Crawford in an exhaustive study of American tunebooks and has been presented by him, in modern editions together with complete "tune biographies," in *The Core Repertory of Early American Psalmody* (*RRAM* XI-XII [in one]).

FIGURE 1-1. Daniel Read's fuging tune *Sherburne* (1785), as printed in shape-notes in an 1802 edition of *The Easy Instructor*. Courtesy of The New York Public Library; Astor, Lenox and Tilden Foundations. Music Division.

(1758–1842) of Worcester, Massachusetts, worked mainly in the Connecticut River valley as a singing-school master (also hatter and merchant); his pieces *Bristol, Montague,* and *Rainbow* were successful enough to figure in the core repertory, though in later life he was termed "poor, proud, and indolent" by his neighbors. Supply Belcher (1752–1836) was a tavernkeeper in Stoughton, Massachusetts, before he moved to the northern frontier, published his *Harmony of Maine* (1794), and came to be known as the "Handel of Maine." Justin Morgan (1747–98) is perhaps best known as breeder of the Morgan horse; he was also known in West Springfield, Massachusetts, and later in Vermont as a schoolmaster, tavernkeeper—and singing master. Andrew Law (1749–1821) was a minister, with several college degrees, but eventually all his energies went to organizing singing-schools and to engaging in endless angry correspondence with musical pirates who were, he claimed, "pillaging my books." Other flourishing composers and compilers of music for the singing-schools (and a few of their representative tunebooks, most of them anthologies including compositions by others as well as by themselves) were Jacob French (1754–1817; *New American Melody*), Jacob Kimball (1761–1826; *The Rural Harmony*), Samuel Holyoke (1762–1820; *Harmonia Americana, The Columbia Repository*), Jeremiah Ingalls (1764–1838; *The Christian Harmony*), Oliver Holden (1765–1844; the last three editions of *The Worcester Collection*, 1787–93), Stephen Jenks (1772–1856; *The New-England Harmonist, The Harmony of Zion*), and many others.

The kind of piece the New Englanders liked best was the fuging tune; about one-quarter of their total production is made up of this characteristic type—which, as we have seen, was modeled on English fuging psalm tunes

EXAMPLE 1-5. L. Edson, *Greenfield,* as originally printed in Simeon Jocelin's tunebook *The Chorister's Companion* (New Haven, CT: T. and S. Green, 1782), p. 18.

of the sort Lyon had borrowed for *Urania*. The typical American fuging tune usually proceeds like this: beginning like a choral hymn, in three-part or four-part harmony with the principal air in the tenor voice, it gives way about halfway through to a series of staggered entrances by each of the voice parts (the fuging section), which are then led to a full close; then the "fuge" is repeated. A good example, and one very popular during the Federal era (it was "borrowed" for reprinting some 101 times before 1810, after its initial publication in 1782) is *Greenfield* by Lewis Edson (1748–1820) of Bridgewater, Massachusetts. Example 1-5 gives the piece one whole tone lower than its original pitch, to facilitate comparison between the Yankee musical style in fuging tunes and the style of their British prototypes, as represented in Example 1-3.

Some fuging tunes are strophic settings of metrical psalms or hymns; the same music serves for each of the poetic stanzas. Similarly strophic are "plain tunes," which are syllabic settings of one poetic stanza, with three-part or four-part harmony throughout, no fuging section, and the principal air in the tenor voice; see, for example, Billings's *Conquest*, Read's *Windham*, or Swan's *China* (see Example 1-6). The New Englanders essayed larger types of works also: the set piece, a through-composed setting of poetry longer than a single stanza, and the anthem, a through-composed setting of a prose text, often from Scripture. Whereas the set piece is typically chordal throughout, like an extra-long plain tune, the anthem is characterized by varied textures—now a chordal passage, now a fuging section, now individual voice parts in alternation. These longer pieces are not always successful: the Yankee tunesmiths had a very limited vocabulary of harmony and virtually no concept of modulation, and their attempts to build larger formal structures often become tedious for lack of harmonic variety.

The melodies of all this music are apt to be of a folkish quality, now simple and flowing, now angular and rhythmically powerful, if somewhat rigid. They derived partly from the Anglo-Celtic folk-song tradition, and indeed in many of the tunes can be heard echoes of such airs as *Greensleeves* and *Lord Randal*. One of the most striking is that of Swan's *China*, a piece that so caught the fancy of New Englanders that it was sung at funerals "down East" for about a century after it first appeared in 1790. Example 1-6 gives the entire piece; the air is, of course, in the tenor voice.

The harmony of the Yankee fuging tunes and other works is perhaps the most characteristic feature of their style. Abounding in open fifths, parallel fifths and octaves, modal inflections, and surprising dissonances, it seems almost a throwback to an earlier style of European music, long before the development of the highly organized tonal syntax of the century of Handel and Haydn. Yet the Americans were consistent in their taste, and their music is perfectly homogenous stylistically; in its own terms, it is as "stylish" as the more complex and sophisticated European music of its time.

EXAMPLE 1-6. T. Swan, *China* (1790), after the version printed in William Little and William Smith, *The Easy Instructor* (Albany, NY: Websters & Skinner and Daniel Steele, 1809), p. 99.

In performing these choral pieces, some women usually doubled the leading tenor part in a higher octave; conversely, some men might double the trebles an octave lower. Thus the New England style often resulted in an organ-like sonority of six parts. Sometimes, if the composer wrote "choosing notes" (more than one note to a part), the texture was even richer; Billings's *Chesterfield* (termed by Richard Crawford in his liner notes for NW 255 a "boulderlike drone of a piece") is an especially powerful example. Billings emphasized the desirability of a really solid bass: he complained in *The New-England Psalm-Singer* that "in most Singing Companies I ever heard, the greatest Failure was in the Bass," and he cautioned that "in order to have good Music, there must be Three Bass to one of the Upper Parts. So that for instance, suppose a Company of Forty People, Twenty of them should sing the Bass."

Most of the texts found in the Yankee tunebooks are, of course, religious. Isaac Watts was by far the most popular source for the hymns and fuging tunes. His doughty translations and paraphrases of the psalms fit the rough-hewn, forthright New England music perfectly, and on occasion he could rise to greatness; witness a stanza of his that was set as a hymn by Justin Morgan under the title *Amanda:*

> Death, like an overflowing stream,
> Sweeps us away; our life's a dream;
> An empty tale; a morning flow'r,
> Cut down and withered in an hour.

Watts employed the meters of balladry in his "imitations" (for which read "paraphrases") of the psalms; thus, in his hands Psalm 90, which in the King James Bible begins "Lord, thou hast been our dwelling place in all generations," turns into the rock-firm, memorable Common-Meter quatrain:

> Our God, our help in ages past,
>   Our hope for years to come,
> Our shelter from the stormy blast,
>   And our eternal home.

Nahum Tate and the Wesleys were also favorite poets, and so was John Newton, whose *Olney Hymns* (1779) were full of powerful (some said extravagant) imagery and emotionalism.

Patriotism and religion were often intermingled. One can imagine the political overtones that singing-schoolers must have read into Supply Belcher's lusty *Jubilant,* set to a text by Charles Wesley and published not long after the United States was proclaimed a new constitutional republic:

> Blow ye the trumpet, blow
>   The gladly solemn sound;
> Let all the nations know,
>   To earth's remotest bound:
>   The year of jubilee is come,
>   Return, ye ransom'd sinners, home!

Stephen Jenks voiced the same sentiments even more directly in his fuging tune *Liberty:*

> No more beneath the oppressive hand
>   Of tyranny we groan,
> Behold the happy, smiling land
>   That freedom calls her own.

In 1775, Andrew Law found appropriate verses for *Bunker Hill*— which may be of his composition but is more likely by Sylvanus Ripley— in a poem, "The American Hero," written just after the outbreak of the Revolution by the American-born Nathaniel Miles:

> Why should vain mortals tremble at the sight of
>   Death and destruction in the field of battle,
> Where blood and carnage clothe the ground in crimson,
>   Sounding with death groans.
>
>   . . .
>
> Life, for my country and the cause of freedom,
>   Is but a trifle for a worm to part with;
> And if preserved in so great a contest,
>   Life is redoubled.

We may find Billings's paraphrase of Psalm 137 (*NW* 276:s1/1) amusingly presumptuous, but certainly it was no smiling matter to him when, remembering the siege of Boston, he wrote,

> By the Rivers of Watertown we sat down and wept,
>   when we remember'd thee, O Boston. . . .
> God forbid! Forbid it Lord, God forbid that
>   those who have sucked Bostonian Breasts
>   should thirst for American blood!

Such a piece as the last-mentioned, Billings's anthem *Lamentation Over Boston* (1778), points to one of the most appealing aspects of the singing-school music of the Yankee tunesmiths: this was a music completely in tune with the society for which it was written. These journeyman composers had a secure and respected function in Colonial- and Federal-era life in general; viewed historically from a point two hundred years later, theirs was a sort of golden age of musical participation in which teachers, composers, singers, and populace in general worked together fruitfully. If ever there was truly a popular music, the music of the New Englanders was popular: it arose from deep, old traditions of early America; it was accessible to all and enjoyed by all; it was a plain-spoken music for plain people; and assessed on its own terms, it was a stylistically homogeneous music of great integrity—really the first indigenous music of the United States.

Diffusion of the Yankee idiom outside of New England was aided not only by the peripatetic singing masters—Andrew Law, for instance, conducted singing-schools throughout his native New England and in New York, New Jersey, Pennsylvania, Maryland, and even the Carolinas—but also by the evangelistic revival movements, like the "Great Revival" of 1800. It may also have been encouraged by the development of new systems of music notation, especially the "shape-note" notation of William Smith and William Little, in whose *Easy Instructor* (Albany, NY, 1801) the musical notes were shaped differently according to their position in the scale (see Figure 1-1). At that time, instead of *do, re, mi, fa, sol, la, ti, do,* the syllables *fa, sol, la, fa, sol, la, mi, fa* were used; hence, four shapes sufficed to distinguish the syllables: ◺ *(fa)*, ○ *(sol)*, □ *(la)*, ◇ *(mi)*. Little and Smith's invention, reminiscent of other less successful American attempts (e.g., Tufts's) both earlier and later to make easier the task of learning to read music, had the simplicity of genius. Their four-shape notation was widely adopted in other tunebooks: it would seem that Andrew Law, who claimed shape-notes as his own idea, borrowed them from *The Easy Instructor* for his *Art of Singing* (4th ed., 1803), and other tunebook compilers followed suit, especially those who favored the New England style of music.

But not every post-Colonial American did favor it. With the new wave of immigration that followed the successful establishment and consolidation of the United States of America came a new wave of foreign influence in American music. In the cities along the eastern seaboard, wealth began to accumulate, and so did a taste for European standards of culture—and cultural models as well. The tendency of more-or-less aristocratic Americans to look to Europe for "lessons in living well" had been latent for some time; it was reinforced as Americans, at least those in the eastern cities, sought increasingly to act "urbane." Ironically, in the very place that had seen its beginning, and for the same reason—cultural improvement—the Yankee music began to be attacked. One articulate spokesman for reform was John Hubbard, a sometime musician himself but also professor of mathematics and natural philosophy at Dartmouth College in New Hampshire. Hubbard's *Essay on Music* (1808) was a harsh criticism of the New England style and its artisan composers. It attacked the "common fuge" as a music that "can never be of more consequence than an oration well pronounced in a foreign language," and as for the tunesmiths,

Almost every pedant, after learning his eight notes, has commenced author. With a genius, sterile as the deserts of Arabia, he has attempted to rival the great masters of music. On the leaden wings of dullness, he has attempted to soar into these regions of science, never penetrated but by real genius. . . . [5]

[5] John Hubbard, *An Essay on Music* (Boston: Manning & Loring, 1808), pp. 17-18.

Elias Mann, whose tunebook *The Massachusetts Collection of Sacred Harmony* appeared in 1807 in Boston, made a point of saying in its preface that he had included "none of those wild fugues, and rapid and confused movements, which have so long been the disgrace of congregational psalmody." Andrew Law, after a lengthy career as partisan of the native style, turned his back on it completely. Increasingly, as his knowledge of the "sublime and beautiful compositions of the great Masters of Music" grew, he sought to substitute "serious, animated, and devout" music for "that lifeless and insipid, or that frivolous and frolicksome succession and combination of sounds" which the New Englanders had created. Even Daniel Read, perhaps the most gifted of the Yankee composers, felt the impact of the new wave. Read never became, as did Law, a self-styled reformer; nevertheless, in some oddly touching words written in his old age, he confessed to changed musical values:

> Since studying the writings of such men as D'Alembert [and others], since carefully examining the system of harmony practically exhibited in Handel's *Messiah,* Haydn's *Creation,* and other similar works . . . my ideas on the subject of music have been considerably altered; I will not say improved.[6]

In later chapters, we shall see how the music of the First New England School was submerged beneath the new wave of musical taste in the eastern United States—but not drowned out completely, by any means.

SOUTH OF NEW ENGLAND

If the British colonists of the New World must, because of their predominance among the early settlers, be considered the mainstream of early American culture, there were nevertheless important minority groups very early. In general, these groups—notably German Pietists in Pennsylvania and Moravian brethren in Pennsylvania and the Carolinas—were culturally insular; their communities tended to remain "foreign" enclaves even in a land of immigrants. Nevertheless, their musical cultures deserve brief mention.

A number of Protestant German sects settled in Pennsylvania for religious motives. Each differed in its worship-music practice, but all were alike in their emphasis on congregational song, especially chorales. To Germantown in 1694 came a group of Pietists under the leadership of Johannes Kelpius (1673–1708). Known as the Hermits of the Ridge (or Wissahickon Mystics or True Rosicrucians), they sang hymns, psalms, and anthems and

---

[6] Quoted in *MMEA*, p. 175

apparently used instrumental accompaniment. Kelpius compiled for his flock a hymn book with the Pietist title *The Lamenting Voice of the Hidden Love at the Time when She Lay in Misery and forsaken* (the manuscript is now at the Historical Society of Pennsylvania), containing ten hymn tunes, seven with basses, of a harmonic richness unknown to the New England Puritans.

Conrad Beissel (1691–1768), who emigrated to Pennsylvania in 1720, founded in 1732 a semi-monastic community at Ephrata, in what is now Lancaster County, 65 miles from Philadelphia. Urging on his band an active musical seventh-day observance, Beissel turned from Pietist hymns and traditional chorales to original compositions, some of great length and in as many as eight voices. In 1747 he published in Ephrata a massive collection of sacred texts for choral singing, with a German title that may be translated as *The Song of the Lonely and Forsaken Turtle Dove, namely the Christian Church*, the pages of which give some idea of the uniquely mannered notation of Beissel, even better viewed in the beautifully illuminated manuscripts that emanated from the cloister.[7] Beissel's music is purposely ultra-consonant, avoiding any dissonant harmony on accented text syllables, which produces a monolithic if somewhat tedious result only slightly relieved by occasional antiphonal treatment of the choristers, who are said to have numbered twenty-five, fifteen women and ten men.

The richest and most sophisticated musical culture in colonial America was that of the Moravians in Pennsylvania and the Carolinas. They came from German-speaking Bohemia for the most part, members of the Unitas Fratrum, the first independent Protestant sect, founded in Bohemia and Moravia in the mid-fifteenth century. The first Moravians to reach America came to the West Indies in 1732; a sizable community settled in Bethlehem, Pennsylvania, in 1741. Other Moravian centers were created at Lititz and Nazareth in Pennsylvania and at Salem (now Winston-Salem) in North Carolina.

The musical life of the Moravian brethren was extraordinarily intense. Theirs was the first concerted sacred music in America: instruments joined soloists and choirs in anthems, sacred arias, motets, and chorales. At the major Moravian musical centers, Bethlehem and Salem, brass ensembles serenaded the communities of brethren and played for weddings, christenings, funerals, and other solemn occasions. Collegia Musica—groups meeting regularly to practice music, especially instrumental music—were organized, and substantial libraries of European music of the seventeenth and eighteenth centuries accumulated. Some of this country's earliest and best instrument makers helped to supply the Collegia; especially notable is the organ builder David Tannenberg (1728–1804), who designed and construct-

---

[7] The largest and most stunning of the manuscript versions, once possessed by Benjamin Franklin, is in the Library of Congress.

ed more than forty for Lutheran and Roman Catholic as well as Moravian churches.

Like most of the Yankee composers to the north, many of the Moravian composers were occupied in other tasks for a living. Indeed, some might never have composed at all had not a demand for new music existed. Jeremiah Dencke (1725–95) arrived from Germany in 1761 as pastor and business manager in Bethlehem. He was the first in America to compose sacred music with instruments, notably three sets of sacred songs for soprano, strings, and organ, among them the sturdy chorale *Meine Seele erhebet dem Herrn* (NW 230:s1/1) and the lovely aria *Gehet in dem Geruch Seines Bräutigams-Namens* (NW 230:s1/5), both written for a festival of young girls (Mägden-Fest) in 1767. Johannes Herbst (1735–1812) came to Pennsylvania in 1786, was pastor at Lancaster and later Lititz, and pastor and bishop at Salem in the last year of his life. The most prolific of the Moravian composers, Herbst wrote some 145 sacred songs and about 180 anthems (see NW 230:s1/6-8, s2/1-2). John Antes (1740–1811), American-born, was a string-instrument maker who was later ordained a pastor and sent to Egypt as a missionary. There, between 1770 and 1781, he composed three trios for violins and cello, the earliest chamber music written by an American. Johann Friedrich (John Frederick) Peter (1746–1813) was probably the most gifted of the Moravian composers: more than one hundred works, mostly anthems and sacred arias but also six string quintets (Salem, 1789), reveal him as a sensitive and highly expressive minor master of the early Classic style.[8] David Moritz Michael (1751–1825), a German who was in Pennsylvania from 1795 to 1815 in various administrative posts, put his first-hand knowledge of woodwind instruments to good use in sixteen *Parthien*—suite-like works—for wind sextet; he is also notable for having conducted the first performance of Haydn's *Creation* in America (in 1811, at Bethlehem).

The Moravian culture was essentially insular: although it was known and spoken of admiringly by other Americans in the eighteenth century (Benjamin Franklin, for one), it had little influence outside the Moravian communities themselves. On the other hand, the music of the American Moravians has a special stamp, the result of the New World environment. One specialist in their music cogently describes the source of this "American" quality:

> The Moravians were devout people. Colonial life for them had a religious purpose and religious ideas dominated their activities. This gives their music a special character. In Europe, the average late 18th century composer wrote an occasional piece of church music between the symphonies, sonatas, operas, and other secular works which were his chief concern. To the Moravian musi-

---

[8] The sacred aria *Leite mich in Deiner Wahrheit*, perhaps Peter's earliest work (first performed in 1770 a few months after his arrival in the New World), is recorded on NW 230:s1/4.

cians in America, however, church music was the most important expression
of their inner lives. Their music therefore is better suited to the purpose and
more touching than most religious music written in Europe during the same
period.[9]

The story of sacred music in the middle Atlantic and southern British
colonies is less well documented than in the German-speaking communities
or in New England. The German immigrants maintained and even enriched
their European musical life; thanks to the singing-school movement, the
New Englanders created a whole repertory of published sacred-secular music.
Little is known, however, of sacred music in the Quaker center of Philadelphia until the 1760s; Virginia, almost wholly an agricultural colony, has
left us almost no colonial music; and South Carolina, especially its largest
city, Charleston (Charles Town at the time), had an active secular music life
that has somewhat obscured any special activity in sacred music.

Two native-born composers (the first Americans securely identifiable
as such) figured in the sacred music of Philadelphia in the early 1760s. These
were James Lyon and Francis Hopkinson (1737–91; see pp. 39–41). Lyon
began the history of Philadelphian music publishing in 1761 with *Urania*
(see p. 9). He indicated in the Index that six of the pieces in it were "completely new" (and thus the earliest publications of new compositions by an
American composer); some of these may have been composed by Lyon
himself, but the music for *The 23d Psalm* (Example 1–7) is by Hopkinson,
better known as a cultivated dilettante specializing in secular music. One of
the hymns in *Urania, Whitefield's,* is a setting of a text from the 1757 *Hymn
Collection* of the famous British Methodist revivalist George Whitefield; its
music is the first American publication of the tune *God Save the King,* later
(1831) to be used as the melody for Samuel Francis Smith's "My Country
'tis of Thee."[10]

Charleston, by 1775 the largest city south of Philadelphia, was a
brilliant center of church music, as it was of secular. Free from the restrictions on instruments observed in Puritan New England, Charleston's Anglican
churches of St. Philip's and St. Michael's allowed organs to be heard, and
peals of bells. Organist at St. Philip's from 1737 to 1750 was Charles Theodore
Pachelbel (1690–1750), son of the famous Nuremberg organist Johann Pachelbel. Of Charles Theodore's music we have a fine *Magnificat* for two choirs
and organ—written, however, before the composer left Germany for America.

[9] Hans T. David, ed., *Ten Sacred Songs*. Music of the Moravians in America . . . No.
1 (New York: New York Public Library, 1947), p. v.
[10] The tune has been put to various uses by Americans; one version from the Federal
period begins with the words "God save great Washington," another with "God save America."

EXAMPLE 1-7. F. Hopkinson, *The 23d Psalm Tune*, in J. Lyon, *Urania* (Philadelphia: William Bradford, 1761), p. 50, measures 1-12. The cut-time signature reversed indicates a quick tempo$\frac{2}{2}$.

BIBLIOGRAPHICAL NOTES

Richard Crawford has published invaluable writings on much of the material in this chapter; see in particular his "A Historian's Introduction to Early American Music," *Proceedings of the American Antiquarian Society*, LXXXIX/2 (October 1979), 261–98 (with an accompanying soundsheet), and for citations of other writings by him, the Bibliography appended to his essay *Studying American Music* (ISAM Special Publications No. 3) (Brooklyn: Institute for Studies in American Music, 1985). Irving Lowens's important contributions, especially a group of seminal bibliographical studies, are reprinted, in revised versions, in *MMEA*. Robert Stevenson's *Protestant Church Music in America* (New York: W. W. Norton, 1966), is also a rich reference source.

Nicholas Temperley's *The Music of the English Parish Church*, 2 vols. (New York: Cambridge University Press, 1979), is a detailed study of the British antecedents of early American psalmody; complementing it, in dealing with the American repertory, is his article "Psalms, metrical" in *TNGDAM*. Richard Crawford's "Psalmody," also in *TNGDAM*, is a masterly summary.

The music of Ainsworth's psalter is reproduced in facsimile and transcribed in Lorraine Inserra and H. Wiley Hitchcock, *The Music of Henry Ainsworth's Psalter (Amsterdam, 1612)* (ISAMm 15 [1981]). Chapter 2 of *MMEA* considers "The Bay Psalm Book in 17th-Century New England." A facsimile reprint of the first edition of the Bay Psalm Book has been published (New York: Artemis Books, n.d.). Zoltán Harazti's *The Enigma of the Bay Psalm Book* (Chicago: University of Chicago Press), also published with a facsimile of the psalter, discusses it from the textual standpoint; Richrd G. Appel's *The Music of the Bay Psalm Book (9th Edition* [1698]) (ISAMm 5 [1975]) contains facsimiles and transcriptions of the tunes as first printed in New England.

Alan C. Buechner's Harvard University doctoral dissertation of 1960, *Yankee Singing Schools and the Golden Age of Choral Music in New England, 1760–1800*, remains the best source on its subject. Allen P. Britton's paper for the 1961 Congress of the International Musicological Society, "The Singing School Movement in the United States," and the discussion that followed it, are printed, respectively, in volumes I (1961) and II (1962) of the *I.M.S. Congress Report*.

Richard Crawford, with David McKay, has written the definitive monograph on Billings, *William Billings of Boston: Eighteenth-Century Composer* (Princeton, NJ: Princeton University Press, 1975), and, alone, that on Law, *Andrew Law, American Psalmodist* (Evanston, IL: Northwestern University Press, 1968; repr. New York: Da Capo Press, 1981).

The Complete Works of William Billings, eds. Hans Nathan and Karl Kroeger (n.p.: American Musicological Society and Colonial Society of Massachusetts, 1977-), notable as the first scholarly edition of an American composer's complete works, is in progress. Facsimile editions have been issued of Billings's *The Psalm Singer's Amusement (EAM* 20) and *The Continental Harmony* (Cambridge, MA: Belknap Press of Harvard University, 1961), and also of Supply Belcher's *The Harmony of Maine (EAM* 6) and Ingall's *The Christian Harmony* (*EAM* 22).

Make a Joyful Noise: Mainstreams and Backwaters of American Psalmody 1770–1840 (NW 255) has a good representation of music by composers of the First New England School. *White Spirituals from the Sacred Harp* (NW 205) includes pieces by Billings, Read, and Ingalls in twentieth-century folkish performances that may come closer to the "Old Way" of psalmody than the more polished choral performances on NW 255. *The Flowering of Vocal Music in America*, Vol. 1 (NW 230) includes a number of sacred songs by American Moravians.

TWO

SECULAR MUSIC IN THE NEW WORLD

We have very little hard evidence of secular music-making in the Colonial period, at least until the mid-eighteenth century and even later. As Oscar Sonneck commented in his monumental bibliography of American secular music to 1800, "Before 1790 practically nothing but psalm and hymn books were published, with here and there an issue of secular character as in the various 'Almanacks' and literary periodicals—also a very few songsters with music" (as opposed to the great majority, which were simply printings of song texts).[1] But it is impossible to believe that the colonists, for all the strictures of Puritan and Calvinist mores, did not enjoy secular songs and dances along with psalmody (and, much of the latter, as we have seen, was put to secular, social use in the singing-schools, although it was ostensibly

[1] Oscar George Theodore Sonneck, A *Bibliography of Early Secular American Music (18th Century)*, revised and enlarged by William Treat Upton (Washington: The Library of Congress, Music Division, 1945), p. 575.

sacred). And, in fact, there is plenty of circumstantial evidence that they did.

BRITISH-AMERICAN FOLK AND POPULAR SONG

To begin with, there is the large repertory of Anglo-Scottish-Irish "folk songs" that have come down to us. These were, of course, the "pop songs" of the day—a living music of everyday use by all. During the Colonial period, virtually none were written down: not only were they part of an ages-old tradition whereby popular music was transmitted orally from performer to performer and from one generation to the next, but also the press, in early America, was almost entirely in the control of the clergy, and the clergy had no interest in propagating or memorializing secular music. Nevertheless, that the "underground" popular culture of the American colonies was a very lively one indeed is suggested, for instance, by the fact that about 100 of the 300-odd traditional British ballads—the "Child ballads," so called after Francis James Child (1825-96), their great collector and commentator— have been traced (and are still sung) in this country—more than in living British tradition. The colonists were selective: older songs on themes irrelevant to the Colonial experience (e.g., courtly or chivalric) tended to be dropped; and many that were preserved have to do with sexual rivalry as seen through feminine eyes (*Barbara Ellen, The Gypsy Laddie, Little Musgrove, Jimmy Randall*) or relate directly to the New World experience (*Captain Kidd, The Golden Vanity*). The colonists of course changed the details of many British songs in terms of the American context and developing character. One example is a song from southern England (known also in Ireland), "My Jolly Herring" or *The Red Herring Song*, which was transformed into a tale of Yankee resourcefulness and thrift (with a comic note) as "The Sow Took the Measles."[2] Another is *The Foggy Dew*, of which the original explicit sexuality ("I rolled my love all over the foggy dew") was tempered by Puritan sensibility ("The only thing I did that was wrong/Was to keep her from the foggy dew").

Against the background of this British ballad tradition, Americans of course created their own popular ballads. The earliest that can be dated with certainty is *Springfield Mountain*, a re-creation in song of the death by snakebite on August 7, 1761, of Timothy Myrick of Springfield Mountain (now Wilbraham), Massachusetts (Example 2-1).[3]

---

[2] For some of these points and the specific example of this song, I am indebted to Alan Lomax, *The Folk Songs of North America in the English Language* (New York: Doubleday & Co., Inc., 1960) pp. xv-xxii.

[3] Ibid., p. 6; verses 2–7 of this version of the song, not given in Example 2–1, are found in Lomax, p. 13.

EXAMPLE 2-1. *Springfield Mountain,* as collected by Alan Lomax in Townshend, Vermont (1939); stanza 1 of text only. From *Folk Songs of North America* by Alan Lomax. Copyright © 1960 Alan Lomax. Copyright © 1960 Cassell & Co., Ltd. Reprinted by permission of Doubleday & Company, Inc.

In addition to British ballads and other songs brought to the New World and preserved through oral tradition, the colonists also had copies of various British publications containing popular and traditional songs and tunes. One was Thomas Ravenscroft's three-part collection of 1609-11: *Pammelia . . .* (the earliest British-printed collection of catches and rounds), *Deuteromelia* (which includes the first published version of "Three Blind Mice"), and *Melismata. Musicall Phansies.* Others were John Playford's *The English Dancing Master* (1651; many more editions, as *The Dancing Master,* through 1728), our largest single source of ballad tunes; Thomas d'Urfey's six-volume collection, *Wit and Mirth; or Pills to Purge Melancholy* (London, 1719-20); John Watt's *The Musical Miscellany,* also in six volumes (London, 1729-31); and John Walsh's *The Compleat Country Dancing Master* (London, 1731).

Examples from one or two of these printed collections of British popular tunes can suggest the sturdy musical stock from which sprang early American secular songs and dances. *Newcastle,* from Playford's *English Dancing Master,* is a bold stomping tune with a short-long iambic syncope ("x" in the example) which we shall meet again in several later kinds of American popular music (Example 2-2 [a]). The traditional *Packington's Pound* tune is the basis for anonymous verses about the "gallants of Newgate"—denizens of London's most infamous prison—which were printed in Watts's *Musical Miscellany;* the tune alternates between minor and modal flavor (now using E♮, now E♭) and at one point broadens out marvelously from $\frac{3}{4}$ to to $\frac{3}{2}$ meter (bracketed in the example) (Example 2-2 [b]).

With Example 2-2 (b), which relates textually to the subject matter (London's underworld) of the first popular English "ballad opera," *The Beggar's Opera* (1728) of John Gay and Christopher Pepusch (and whose tune is actually the basis of Air XLIII, in Act III), we approach a more formal kind of secular music than the ballads of oral tradition: music that was heard in concert and on stage in the eastern seaboard American cities, from about 1730 on. These cities had developed remarkably in size and wealth during the first three-quarters of the eighteenth century. If by 1590 substantial towns had been established at Boston, New York, Philadelphia, Charleston,

EXAMPLE 2–2. (a) *Newcastle*; my transcription from John Playford, *The English Dancing Master* (London, 1651 [recte 1650]), No. 77; the original is a minor third higher. (b) "Newgate's Garland," anonymous verse to be sung to the tune *Packington's Pound*, John Watts, *The Musical Miscellany* (London, 1729–31), V, 42.

and elsewhere, by 1774—on the eve of the Revolution—they had mushroomed into real cities, which grew even more rapidly in the next quarter century. The following table[4] shows the growth during this period.

	1690	1774	1800
New York (founded 1625)	3900	25–30,000	60,000
Boston (founded 1630)	700	20,000	25,000
Charleston (founded 1672)	1100	10,000	18,000
Philadelphia (founded 1682)	4000	40,000	70,000

4 Adapted from Charles A. and Mary R. Beard, *A Basic History of the United States* (Philadelphia: The Blakiston Company, 1944), p. 44, and from Russell B. Nye, *The Cultural Life of the New Nation, 1776–1830* (New York: Harper & Row, 1960), p. 124.

Other growing cities were Salem, Providence, New Haven, Perth
· Amboy, Baltimore, Richmond, and Savannah. Although the population of
these cities was only a fraction of the total population of the colonies, their
concentration of wealth and of social, political, and intellectual activity made
them the cultural centers of the new land. As commerical cities, they tended
to reflect the artistic life of similar European cities with which they had close
contacts. Thus, among other kinds of art, art-music gained its first Anglo-
American expression in the cities, where from about 1730 we have records
of concerts, operas, and other secular music.

THE RISE OF CONCERTS AND OPERA

The New World was hardly behind the Old in the establishment of
a secular music culture based on public concerts. This would be a matter
for nationalistic pride were it not for the fact that public concerts in Europe
were a reflection of the rise of the middle class as patron of music, in contrast
to the traditional aristocratic and churchly patronage; lacking a true aristocratic class, America's was basically a middle-class culture from the beginning,
and it was natural that some of its musical energy was directed very early
into public concerts. Thus—even disregarding such isolated events as the
music performed publicly in Philadelphia in 1700 at the consecration of the
Gloria Dei church, or a "consort at Mr. Broughton's" in New York noted
by the Rev. John Sharpe in his journal in 1710—genuine public concerts
are reported as beginning as early as the late 1720s. The first of these we
know about was announced in the Boston *Gazette* of February 3, 1729, as
a "Consort of Musick [to be] performed on sundry Instruments, at the
Dancing School in King-Street."[5]
    Opera, too, was heard in America from the 1730s, not of course the
lavish, costly, and aristocratic Baroque opera but English ballad operas, those
plays-with-songs that had captivated London's public with the immensely
sucessful run in 1728 of *The Beggar's Opera*. To Gay's text, which satirized
the social, political, and musical establishment, Pepusch adapted well-known
popular songs and ballad airs—also, with tongue in cheek, some music from
Handel's Italian operas. (The satiric thrust of *The Beggar's Opera* and its

---

[5] See Cynthia Adams Hoover, "Epilogue to Secular Music in Early Massachusetts,"
Music in Colonial Massachsetts 1630–1820, Vol. II, ed. Barbara Lambert (Boston: Colonial
Society of Massachusetts; distributed by The University Press of Virginia, 1985), pp. 715–868;
the notice in the *Gazette* is reproduced on p. 410. This concert was presented more than two
and a half years before the one most commonly cited (at Boston, in "Mr. Pelham's great room,"
in December 1731), after O. G. T. Sonneck, *Early Concert-Life in America* (Leipzig: Breitkopf
& Härtel, 1907), p. 251.

many immediate imitators, and their use of pre-existent music, were gone from English operas later in the eighteenth century; they were largely sentimental or comic dramas with newly composed songs interpolated in them.) New York audiences heard *The Beggar's Opera* in 1750 and 1751, as produced by a company of "comedians from Philadelphia." But the record of ballad opera in America had begun even before that with *Flora, or Hob in the Well* (abbreviated from the British work of 1729 with text by Colley Cibber and musical interpolations arranged by John Hippisley); this opera was produced at Charleston in early 1735 during the first theatrical season in that city, and produced in 1736, also at Charleston, was Coffey's *The Devil to Pay* of 1731. Other English ballad operas that were to become popular in America included Cibber's *Damon and Phillida* (1749), Henry Carey's *The Honest Yorkshireman* (1736), and Henry Fielding's *The Mock Doctor* (1732). Probably the most popular opera of the entire Colonial and Federal eras was *The Poor Soldier* (1784), a ballad opera with a text by the Irishman John O'Keeffe (and some original music by William Shield).

The operatic centers of America in the eighteenth century were the cities from New York south: at Boston, the anti-theater blue law of 1750 had put an effective check on the establishment of ballad opera there. By the end of the eighteenth century two major opera companies were renowned. One was William Hallam's London troupe, which started its American career in 1752 at Williamsburg, moved to New York, named itself the American Company (and later the Old American), went back to England during the Revolution, then returned after the war to New York. The Old American Company's rival was the New Company founded in 1792 at Philadelphia by Thomas Wignell, English actor and singer, and Alexander Reinagle (see p. 36). The Wignell-Reinagle company played in the celebrated New Theatre on Chestnut Street, a handsome hall with a stage 36 feet wide and 71 deep and with some 2000 seats, 900 of them in two tiers of boxes, above which was a large gallery.

Early American concerts and ballad operas were understandably dominated by immigrant professional musicians, unlike the singing-schools, which, arising from a long native tradition, were led by American-born journeyman composers. The cities could support these emigré "professors" of music, particularly in the post-Revolutionary Federal period of economic and commercial consolidation between 1783 and 1812, and indeed their standards and taste were to have a shaping influence on American musical culture in general. They were aided by, in fact they led, the remarkable development in the late eighteenth century of music publishing in America. In little more than a half century before 1820, American publishers issued an estimated 15,000 separate works in sheet-music editions, plus more than 500 different "songsters"—pocket-size collections of song texts. Instrument manufacture was also on the rise; the simpler instruments had probably been made in

America almost from the beginning, but as early as the 1740s we learn of a harpsichord builder, Gustav Hesselius of the Old Swedes' Church in Philadelphia, and of piano builders from 1775, when John Behrent of Philadelphia announced the manufacture of "an extraordinary instrument, by the name of the pianoforte, in mahogany in the manner of a harpischord."[6]

Concerts and opera performances in the cities were paralleled by a dramatic rise of secular music in the urban home. "Almost every young lady and gentleman, from the children of the judge, the banker, and the general, down to those of the constable, the huckster and the drummer, can make a noise upon some instrument or other, and charm their neighbors with something which courtesy calls music," wrote a correspondent in the Philadelphia *Mirror of Taste and Dramatic Censor* in 1810.[7] Even if professional musicians could not make a living solely by performing, they could eke out an existence by hanging out a shingle as teachers or as proprietors of music stores—"magazines" or "repositories," as they were more often called. In short, secular music was becoming a real business in America as the eighteenth century closed and the nineteenth opened.

We should not, however, expect to find in the secular music of eighteenth-century America anything to match the scope or seriousness of purpose of, say, the music of Vienna, Rome, or Paris. The American ballad opera was an unpretentious entertainment with simple songs, enjoyable to all. The American concert was a mixture of short instrumental pieces delivered by a few performers and songs or duets of no great dimensions. The American music publishers addressed themselves mainly to amateurs: like the singing-school tunebooks, the thousands of music sheets and songsters aimed to satisfy the modest abilities of music makers at home, to offer them practical or topical sources of mild diversion. It remained for a later generation to distinguish between such "popular" music and a more self-consciously high-flown "classical" music with serious artistic pretentions.

Representative of the socially useful and surprisingly diversified output of our early publishers is a collection of the 1790s with the informative title page *Evening Amusement, Containing fifty airs, song's, duett's, dances, hornpipe's, reels', marches, minuett's, &c., &c., for 1 and 2 German flutes or violins. Price 75 cents. Printed & sold at B[enjamin] Carr's Musical repositories, Philadelphia and New York, & J[oseph] Carr's, Baltimore.* Published in 1796, this potpourri of pieces designed for "evening amusement" typifies the kinds of secular music enjoyed by American townspeople of the early Federal period. In it, traditional popular songs (we would call them folk songs today) of the English, Scottish, and Irish past are well represented, among them *Soldier's Joy, The Irish Washerwoman,* and *O Dear, What Can the Matter Be?* Newer songs, many of them from operas,

---

[6] Arthur Loesser, *Men, Women and Pianos* (New York: Simon & Schuster, Inc., 1954), pp. 442–43.

[7] Quoted ibid., pp. 456–57.

are present, like *What a Beau your Granny Was*, *Thou Softly Flowing Avon*, and *How Happily My Life I Led* (the last taken from the comic opera *No Song No Supper* of British composer Stephen Storace). Patriotic songs furnished tunes for several of the items: *God Save Great Washington*; *Yankee Doodle*; Reinagle's *America, Commerce, and Freedom*; and *The Marseilles Hymn*. A variety of dance tunes appears—several hornpipes, a highland reel, a "minuet de la cour," *Mrs. Fraser's Strathspey*—and so do marches, including *General Washington's March*, *The Duke of York's March*, and a march from *The Battle of Prague* by the Czech-English composer Kotzwara. Haydn is represented by a minuet and "airs" from two symphonies.

Here, then, is what our early urban secular music comprised: martial and patriotic music, traditional songs and opera airs, dance tunes, and a smattering of programmatic or absolute instrumental music.

MARCHES AND PATRIOTIC SONGS

As we might expect, both the Revolutionary and Federal periods produced their share of military music, including marches and patriotic songs. Sometimes both were combined, as in *Hail! Columbia*. The poem by Joseph Hopkinson (son of Francis) was written in 1798 to be sung to the tune of *The President's March*; the latter, a sturdy foursquare tune, was the work of Philip Phile, who may have composed it after George Washington's inauguration as president of the new United States in 1789, but did not publish it until 1793 or 1794. It was very popular: arrangements for two flutes and for piano duet appeared, as well as many other versions adapted from Phile's original piano setting. *Hail! Columbia* was first published in Philadelphia by Benjamin Carr "for the Voice, Piano Forte, Guittar and Clarinet"; Ezekiel Goodale's *The Instrumental Director* of 1819 honors it by placing it first among the sixty instrumental pieces in that volume.

Yankee Doodle has all the earmarks of a march, too, and in fact, the earliest known separate edition of the song, published in England in the 1780s, carries the mocking title *Yankee Doodle, or (as now Christened by the Saints of New England) The Lexington March*. A subtitle instructs: "NB. The Words to be Sung thro' the Nose, & in the West Country drawl & dialect"—a jibe at the rural, plebeian backgrounds of most English emigrants to America. Popular here even before the Revolution,[8] *Yankee Doodle* appeared

---

[8] It is mentioned in the libretto of *The Disappointment: or, The Force of Credulity* (New York, 1767), as the tune for Air IV of that ballad opera (which seems to have been the first actually written in America). The work, with music realized by Samuel Adler, is published in *RRAM* III–IV. The Preface therein should be read in the light of Carolyn Rabson's later research, published as "*Disappointment* Revisited: Unweaving the Tangled Web," *American Music*, I/1 (Spring 1983), 12–35; II/1 (Spring 1984), 1–28.

in 1797 or 1798 with bold new words from the press of James Hewitt, leading New York composer in the post-Revolutionary period.

The song destined to become the national anthem was anything but patriotic to begin with. Addressed "to Anacreon in Heav'n," the tune later sung as *The Star-Spangled Banner* originated as a British drinking song, celebrating the twin delights of Venus and Bacchus. Taken up by Americans, it was given new patriotic words in 1798 by a (not *the*) Thomas Paine, who sang of "Ye sons of Columbia, who bravely have fought/For those rights, which unstained from your Sires had descended." The *Star-Spangled Banner* text, which was composed in 1814 by Francis Scott Key after the bombardment of Fort McHenry by the British, was applied to the old tune, and the resulting song was made the national anthem in 1931.

OTHER SONGS AND OPERA AIRS

The song *America, Commerce, and Freedom* found in *Evening Amusement* has a patriotic text, but it originated as a theater air. The composer was Alexander Reinagle (1756–1809), who came to New York in 1786 from his native England but soon moved to Philadelphia, where he dominated the musical scene for over two decades. An indefatigable composer, pianist, arranger, conductor, and impresario, Reinagle typified the immigrant professional musicians of the Federal period. A competent if not extraordinary composer, he wrote many of the airs for the operas produced at the New Theatre on Chestnut Street, where he was musical director. (Its opening concert of February 2, 1793, offered an elaborate program of overtures, concertos, symphonies, songs, a quartet, and glees.) *America, Commerce, and Freedom* was composed for the "ballet pantomine" *The Sailor's Landlady*; lusty and virile, it is one of Reinagle's best songs. Example 2-3 gives the beginning of the verse and the sturdy refrain.

More characteristic of the American opera air than *America, Commerce, and Freedom* was a tender, lyrical effusion in the tradition of English or Irish love songs, modeled on the pleasant if somewhat effete airs of the middle and late eighteenth-century English composers of light operas and songs for the "pleasure gardens" of London, like Thomas Arne (1710–1778), Charles Dibdin (1745–1814), James Hook (1746–1827), William Shield (1748–1829), and Stephen Storace (1762–96). Reinagle surely contributed many of this kind to Philadelphia productions, although few of his airs are extant today since virtually all his music was lost in a fire that consumed the New Theatre on April 2, 1820.

The general nature of the "tender" airs, and of their usually vapid poetry, is well seen in *Why, Huntress, Why?* composed by Benjamin Carr

EXAMPLE 2-3. A. Reinagle, *America, Commerce, and Freedom* (Philadelphia: B. Carr, 1794), measures 9-16, 29-42.

(1768–1831) for an opera on the tale of William Tell (*The Archers; or, the Mountaineers of Switzerland*), produced by the Old American Company in New York in 1796. Carr, who came to New York from London in 1793, established with his brother and his father a chain of music stores in Philadelphia, New York, and Baltimore and was a prolific publisher as well. He also had a nice, if modest, talent as a composer of songs, as suggested by his *Hymn to the Virgin* ("Ave Maria"), No. 3 of *Six Ballads from the Poem of "The Lady of the Lake"* (Philadelphia, 1810), to texts from Sir Walter Scott's popular work; some nine minutes long, with an accompaniment stylishly written for harp, the "Ave Maria," though not perhaps bearing comparison with Schubert's well-known setting, is one of the most impressive American songs before Foster's (*NW* 231:s1/1–4). On a much smaller scale is Carr's sensitive little setting of the "Willow Song" from Shakespeare's *Othello*. It is so inconclusive, however, as to suggest that it was not intended as an independent work but as an interpolation in the play (Example 2-4).

Lacking a lyric theater tradition, New England did not produce a large body of secular song in the eighteenth century, at least not of the sort I have been discussing. The Yankee singing-school tunebooks served, as noted previously, for secular diversion even though their contents were mainly sacred; and into them, as the eighteenth century neared its close,

EXAMPLE 2-4 B. Carr, "Shakespeare's "Willow,' " *Musical Journal*, Vol. I, Vocal Section (Philadelphia: Carr and Schetky, 1800), p. 22.

secular texts crept more frequently. Supply Belcher's *The Harmony of Maine* (Boston, 1794) included no fewer than eight secular, nonpatriotic songs to texts in the English lyric tradition and was intended for use in both "singing schools and musical societies." Belcher meant by the latter term those urban rivals of the singing-schools that were beginning to be organized in the cities—choral or instrumental groups established (usually under immigrant professional musicians) to perform the "new, scientific" music of Europe. The most famous of these was Boston's Handel and Haydn Society, organized in 1815 by Gottlieb Graupner (1767–1836), who, born in Germany, emigrated first to London; then to Prince Edward Island, Canada; to Charleston, South Carolina; and finally settled in Boston early in 1797; there he became an influential entrepreneur of concerts and musical organizations. The invitation to the organizational meeting of the society was explicit about its aim: " . . . cultivating and improving a correct taste in the performance of sacred music, and also to introduce into more general practice the works of Handel, Haydn, and other eminent composers."

Organist of the Handel and Haydn Society was the well-trained, mature, and magisterial British immigrant George K. Jackson (1757–1823), deemed the most learned musician of Boston. Composer of an affecting *Dirge for General Washington* with a complementary *Dead March* for instruments, Jackson also wrote "songs, serenades, cantatas, canzonetts, canons, glees, &c., &c.," as we read in the subtitle of his undated collection *New Miscellaneous Musical Work.* One of its songs, *Cancherizante*, suggests he was indeed musically learned: planned as a demonstration of *cancrizans* or retrograde melodic technique, it is, as Dr. Jackson pedantically explains at the head of the music, "a song to be sung forwards & then backwards beginning at the last note & ending with the first." Pedantic or not, the little song comes off rather well, its music matching nicely the gentle pastoral text (Example 2-5). His setting, for vocal trio, violin, and piano, of Alexander Pope's "celebrated ode" *The Dying Christian* (ending "Oh, grave, where is thy victory?/Oh, death, where is thy sting?")—also set by Billings as an anthem—shows Jackson in a more dramatic vein (*NW* 231:s2/4).

Gilbert Chase has neatly pinpointed (in *AM*, Chaps. 5 and 6) the two kinds of musicians who fostered eighteenth-century urban secular music: immigrant professionals and "gentleman amateurs." Among the latter, best known are Thomas Jefferson, who if not a practicing musician or composer was still an aristocratic patron of art-music; Benjamin Franklin, who was a practicing musician on the guitar, harp, and musical glasses—in fact, he invented an improved version of the glasses, which he called an "armonica"—and who may have composed (although probably not the string quartet sometimes claimed to be his); and Francis Hopkinson. According to John Adams, Hopkinson was a "pretty, little, curious, ingenious" man, "genteel and well-bred." He was something of a poet (his *Battle of the Kegs* is well

EXAMPLE 2-5. G. K. Jackson, *Cancherizante, New Miscellaneous Musical Work* (n.p., n.d. [after 1800]), p. 9.

known) and a political figure (his signature is on the Declaration of Independence, and he was our first Secretary of the Navy). Hopkinson's interest in music extended beyond performance and composition to mechanical improvements for the harpsichord (somewhat belatedly, since the instrument was already being superseded by the pianoforte).[9] In 1788 Hopkinson dedicated a set of *Seven Songs for the Harpsichord or Forte Piano* to George Washington (an eighth was added after the title page was set in type), remarking in the dedication (reprinted in *ACS*, pp. 39–40) that "I cannot, I believe, be refused the credit of being the first native of the United States

[9] In March 1771, Jefferson wrote to his agent in Philadelphia, sending a list of purchases to be made in Europe. Nine weeks later he wrote again to the agent, who was by then in England, correcting the list to include a piano: "I have since seen a Fortepiano and am charmed with it. Send me this instrument instead. . . ." Quoted in O. G. Sonneck, *Suum cuique* (New York: G. Schirmer, Inc., 1916), p. 51.

who has produced a musical composition." Hopkinson probably knew the music of the New England Yankee tunesmiths, some of whom doubtless antedated him as native-born composers, but he must have adjudged his genteel songs for the "republican court circle" of Philadelphia as *real* music, compared to the folkish singing-school tunes of his northern contemporaries. Nevertheless, the first composition we can unequivocally attribute to a native American is a manuscript song by Hopkinson dated 1759, *My Days Have Been So Wondrous Free.* The music does not quite live up to the charm of its first verse line; it is a bit stiff, if innocuously pleasant. The *Seven Songs,* written (or at least published) almost thirty years later, show hardly any advance in style or technique, although one of them, *My Gen'rous Heart Disdains,* is a lilting rondo of considerable verve and wit; Example 2-6 is its refrain.

Song and instrumental music were combined in a special way in a few turn-of-the-century theater works that mingled the English ballad-opera

EXAMPLE 2-6. F. Hopkinson, *My Gen'rous Heart Disdains, Seven Songs . . .* (Philadelphia: Thomas Dobson, 1788), No. 7, measures 21-48.

tradition with the descriptive incidental music of French and German "melodrama," a term at that time denoting a play with background music. Such a mélange was the historically interesting "operatic melodrame" *The Indian Princess* by the American playwright James Nelson Barker and the British-born actor-composer John Bray (1782–1822), produced at the Chestnut Street Theatre in Philadelphia in 1808. The first surviving play on the story of Captain John Smith and Pocahontas, *The Indian Princess; or, La Belle Sauvage* contains an overture, solo airs, choruses, and vocal ensemble numbers in the manner of ballad opera; it also has snippets of instrumental music sounding in the background of the spoken dialogue to underscore the drama and heighten its emotional impact. Open-ended, to be repeated as many times as needed during a given scene, these mood-music miniatures are the precursors of later American background music for drama and films, and they point to the dawning Romantic era's impuse to exaggerated emotionalism (to "melodrama" in the later sense) and to a programmatic, narrative musical aesthetic. (The vocal numbers and instrumental mood music of *The Indian Princess* are recorded on NW 232:s1.)

DANCE MUSIC

One of the least-studied areas of early American music is that of the dance. Yet the colonists, even the earliest ones, were great dancers. Hawthorne's tale of *The Maypole of Merry Mount* is partly legendary, but its essence is confirmed by William Bradford's contemporary account (1647) of the revels at the Merry Mount settlement, where ". . . they also set up a May-pole, drinking and dancing about it many days together." Throughout the Colonial and Federal periods, journals and letters are full of references to dancing. The eminent justice Samuel Sewall of Boston refers in his diary in 1685 to "a Dancing Master who seeks to set up here and hath mixt dances";

by 1716 the *Boston News-Letter* was advertising instruments, instrumental instruction books, and ruled paper (presumably music paper) "to be sold at the Dancing School of Mr. Enstone." Eighteenth-century concerts often concluded with a march, which served then to introduce a post-concert ball.

The main reason, of course, that the actual music of early American dances is not better known is that little of it was published or even written down: like most of the world's dance music, it was not transcribed but improvised by musicians according to the needs of the moment, elaborating upon, extending or shortening, repeating or varying the current repertory of dance tunes. Popular dancing, moreover, is traditionally done to the accompaniment of whatever instruments and/or voices are at hand. Thus when dance music *is* written down, it usually appears as a bare-boned skeleton, to be given flesh and blood in actual performance; the written music is often merely a cue sheet for the musicians. Ultimately, a composer may base a fully realized work on a well-known tune, a dance rhythm, or a typical dance form; but his music presents a somewhat flossy and stylized, if artistically valid, image of a particular dance.

By the late eighteenth century, nevertheless, American dance music found its way into manuscript and even printed music sheets. Some of the pieces are stylized versions for pianoforte of well-known dance types, e.g., the "Tempo di Menuetto" movement of a *Sonata for the Pianoforte with an Accompaniment for the Violin* (1797?; recorded with its other movement, an Andante, on NW 299:s1/6) by Rayner Taylor (1745–1825), a teacher of Alexander Reinagle and active in Philadelphia's musical life from 1793. Many, however, are practical dances written out, usually in abstract format, on treble and bass staves (although often just the treble tune is given), to be fleshed out by actual instrumentation and improvisation on the spot.

The dances in the *Evening Amusement* collection of 1796 mentioned earlier suggest the types favored by the late eighteenth century: hornpipes, reels, minuets, strathspeys, and marches. To these might be added the gavotte, the allemande, the country dance, the cotillion, the quadrille, and (the great novelty of the period) the waltz. The music of a "line dance," like the country dance (or "contra dance"), was often the same as for a "square dance," like the cotillion or the quadrille: hornpipes, reels, cotillions, strathspeys served equally well for these dances of British origin. On the other hand, the minuet, gavotte, and allemande, introduced from France, each had its own tempo, steps, and rhythmic character.

Cotillions and country dances were the most popular in the late eighteenth-century American cities. The music comes as a surprise to present-day listeners since it is obviously the forerunner of square-dance and other "country" music that we think of as rural, not urban. It is not hard to hear *Harriet's Birthday* or *Jefferson's Hornpipe* (Example 2-7)—both published by James Hewitt about 1802 in *A Collection of the Most Favorite Country Dances*—as lusty, ongoing fiddle tunes, pattering along in running

EXAMPLE 2-7. Two country dances, from James Hewitt (compiler), *A Collection of the Most Favorite Country Dances* (Philadelphia: J. Hewitt, 1802), pp. 5, 17.

(a) Harriet's Birthday

(b) Jefferson's Hornpipe

eighth notes until, at the phrase endings, they land stompingly on repeated cadence chords. *Fitz James* (Example 2-8) is a lively dance tune from a collection of "the most favorite cotillions" published in Philadelphia about

EXAMPLE 2-8. *Fitz James* ("First Set, No. 1"), from *A Collection of the most favorite Cotillions . . . (Philadelphia: G. E. Blake, 1804), p. 2.*

1804. The collection is interesting not only for the verve and unpretentious excellence of its tunes but also for its arrangement in "sets" showing the actual order that the dances followed, and for the "figures" (directions for the dances) that follow each tune. *Fitz James* turns out to be a miniature group of variations on its first strain, which then returns at the end to round out the form neatly. The "figure" for this dance is

GRAND ROUND—NB. The Change must be danced at the beginning of every Cottillion—

The leading couples chassez to the right—back again—chassez across each couple with your partners and back again—right and left.

Simple as such dance music is, it has a vitality, an infectious appeal, and a kind of rawboned integrity that transcend much other music of the period.

OTHER INSTRUMENTAL MUSIC

Aside from marches, dances, and some opera overtures, very little instrumental music was published in colonial America. With the Revolution and the stimulus provided by the embryonic bands attached to units of the military, more began to appear in print, and the Federal era saw rather extensive publication of independent instrumental music, mostly by European composers: by 1825, American presses had issued some 170 works by Mozart, almost 80 by Haydn, over 50 by Handel, and about 30 each by Beethoven and Weber. More highly favored than sonatas or even the flowery sets of variations coming into favor in the late eighteenth century were programmatic pieces of all kinds, especially "battle" pieces. The prototype among these, at least in terms of the number of American editions published, was *The Battle of Prague* by František Kočžwara (d. 1791), described as late as 1879 by Mark Twain as "that venerable shivaree" in a hilarious account of its performance by one young lady (*A Tramp Abroad*, Volume II, Chapter 3). Originally a piano work, *The Battle of Prague* (1789) was rearranged constantly by American musicians to fit their instrumental resources; one Boston program in 1810 proudly announced that its version would include "double-basses, cymbals, French horns, kettle drums, trumpets, cannon, etc." (The tiny "Turkish Quickstep" section is performed by winds and a field drum on NW 299:s2/2.) Other battle pieces were also popular: Bernard Viguerie's *Battle of Maringo* [sic] came out in an American edition (1802) as "a military and historical piece for the piano forte," with cannon shots (expressed by the symbol $\otimes$) to be produced "by stretching the two hands

flat on the three lower octaves in order to sound indistinctly every note."
Like other battle pieces, *The Battle of Maringo* is an episodic work, its
various sections entitled "March," "Word of command," "Trumpet call,"
"Cries of the wounded," and such. The whole work ends with a gigantic
⊗ .

One American composer of battle pieces was James Hewitt (1770–
1827), who came to New York in 1792 as "leader of the band" for the Old
American Company. The first concert he organized in New York (September
21, 1792) included not only an overture by Haydn, a quartet by Pleyel, and
a flute quartet by Stamitz but also his own *Overture in 9 movements, expressive of a battle* and an *Overture in 12 movements, expressive of a voyage
from England to America* by Joseph Gehot (born in Brussels in 1756), who
had indeed just made such a voyage, having immigrated to America with
Hewitt a short time before. Hewitt also composed a *Battle of Trenton* (1797;
dedicated to George Washington), which he enlivened with quotations from
Washington's March and *Yankee Doodle.* This was not the first Americn
publication of *Yankee Doodle* in instrumental guise, for three years earlier
Benjamin Carr had included it along with the *Marseillaise, Ça ira, O Dear,
What Can The Matter Be?* and other popular tunes in a patriotic potpourri
called *The Federal Overture.* Carr, whom we have met as an able songwriter,
could also write a graceful Haydnesque miniature for keyboard, if the six
sonatas in *A New Assistant for the Piano-Forte or Harpsichord* (Baltimore
and Philadelphia, 1796) attributed to him are indeed his (Example 2-9).

EXAMPLE 2-9. B. Carr (?) *Sonata 1, A New Assistant for the Piano-Forte or Harpsichord*
(Baltimore, Philadelphia: B. Carr, 1796), second movement.

Carr's tiny sonata movements were aimed to instruct (the fingerings of Example 2-7 are those of the original edition). Much more lengthy and probably written for his own performance are four sonatas left in manuscript by Alexander Reinagle. One of these may have been played by Reinagle at a concert in June 1787, heard and noted in his diary for June 12 by George Washington, then in Philadelphia as a delegate to the Constitutional Convention. Example 2-10 shows the beginnings of the movements of Sonata III, a charming if somewhat over-extended essay in the style of C. P. E. Bach.

Musical education up to this time had been almost completely limited to the classes of the singing-schools; instrumental training, if done at all, was on an informal tutorial basis. But the rise of instrumental music was reflected in the publication also of the first American methods for learning to play instruments. One of the most significant was Samuel Holyoke's *The Instrumental Assistant* of 1800 (followed in 1807 by a second volume); it contained "instructions for the violin, German flute, clarionett, bass viol and

EXAMPLE 2-10. A. Reinagle, Sonata III, beginnings of the three movements (after *RRAM* V, ed. Robert Hopkins).

hautboy" and also "a selection of favourite airs, marches. &c."—sixty-five of them, culminating in a sonata—set as duets and trios in open score. A similiar tutor is Joseph Herrick's *The Instrumental Preceptor* (1807; printed, like Holyoke's volumes, at Exeter, New Hampshire). Two other collections of 1807 are *Martial Music*, by the former Revolutionary War bandsman Timothy Olmstead (1759–1848), and *For the Gentlemen*—"written chiefly in four parts, viz. two clarionetts, flute and bassoon, or two violins, flute and violincello"—by the leading musician of Providence, Rhode Island, the blind Oliver Shaw (1779–1848).

BIBLIOGRAPHICAL NOTES

Charles Haywood's *Bibliography of North American Folklore and Folksong*, 2nd ed. (New York: Dover Publications, 1961), and Ray M. Lawless's *Folksingers and Folkways in America*, rev. ed. (New York: Duell, Sloan and Pearce, 1965), are basic guides to music once popular, now folk. Alan Lomax's book on North American English-language folk songs (see footnote 2) includes the music of 317 songs.

Besides Francis Child's own basic work of 1883—*English and Scottish Popular Ballads* (reprinted New York: Folk Lore Press, 1957)—two other studies of British ballads are important: B. H. Bronson, *The Traditional Tunes of the Child Ballads*, in four volumes (Princeton, NJ: Princeton University Press, 1959–72), and Claude M. Simpson, *The British Broadside Ballad and Its Music* (New Brunswick, NJ: Rutgers University Press, 1966). Cecil J. Sharp and Maud Karpeles, *English Folk Songs from the Southern Appalachians* (1932), 2nd ed. (London: Oxford University Press, 1952), is a classic.

Several of the seventeenth- and eighteenth-century British publications of popular music are available in modern editions. Ravenscroft's *Pamelia, Deu-*

teromelia, and *Melismata* have been reprinted in facsimile (Philadelphia: American Folklore Society, 1961). Playford's *Dancing Master* is similarly reprinted, with an introduction and notes by Margaret Dean-Smith (London: Schott, 1957); a transcription of the music has been made by Leslie Bridgewater and Hugh Mellor (London: H. Mellor, 1933). D'Urfey's *Wit and Mirth* was published in a new edition in 1876; a facsimile of that edition, with an introduction by Cyrus L. Day, is published in three volumes (New York: Folklore Library, 1959). The most extensive discussion of popular songs of this period—and for that matter, to the 1980s—is Charles Hamm's *Yesterdays: Popular Song in America* (New York: W. W. Norton, 1979).

Good studies of musical life in American regions and cities are all too few. Two that are rich in material relevant to the present chapter are Charles Kaufman's *Music in New Jersey, 1655–1860* (Rutherford, NJ: Fairleigh Dickinson University Press, 1981) and H. Earle Johnson's *Musical Interludes in Boston, 1795–1830* (New York: Columbia University Press, 1943). Another long-neglected area of research, that of music publishing, has been boldly invaded by Richard J. Wolfe in *Early American Music Engraving and Printing: A History of Music Publishing in America from 1787 to 1825 with Commentary on Earlier and Later Practices* (Urbana: University of Illinois Press, 1980).

The national songs of America (plus many, many others) are presented engagingly, with accounts of their origins and publication histories, in James J. Fuld's *The Book of World-Famous Music: Classical, Popular, and Folk*, 2nd ed., rev. and enl. (New York: Crown Publishers, 1971). Vera Brodsky Lawrence's *Music for Patriots, Politicians, and Presidents* (New York: Macmillan, Inc., 1975) is full of superb illustrations. The origins of the tune of *The Star-Spangled Banner*, which eluded researchers for a long time, were tracked down by William Lichtenwanger, who describes them in "The Music of the Star-Spangled Banner," *College Music Symposium*, XVIII (1978), 34–81.

NW 283:s1/3–4 offers dance music of the period: Thornton Hagert's liner notes for the album are exceptionally informative.

The two basic sources on the early development of American concert music and opera, still unsurpassed though written many decades ago, are by Oscar Sonneck, *Early Concert-Life in America* (Leipzig: Breitkopf & Härtel, 1907; repr. New York: Musurgia, 1949) and *Early Opera in America* (New York: G. Schirmer, Inc., 1915); repr. New York: R. Blom, 1963). The grass roots of American instrumental ensemble music, in the field music of the Revolution, are the subject of Raoul Camus's *Military Music of the American Revolution* (Chapel Hill: University of North Carolina Press, 1976). Sonneck's *Bibliography of Early Secular American Music* (Washington, DC: Library of Congress, 1905) was revised and updated by W. T. Upton (Washington, DC: Library of Congress, 1945; repr. New York: Da Capo Press, 1964). Taking up where Sonneck–Upton leaves off is Richard J. Wolfe's three-volume bibliography, *Secular Music in America 1801–1825* (New York: New York Public Library, 1964).

For two opposing views of the authorship of a famous string quartet, see W. Thomas Marrocco, "The String Quartet Attributed to Benjamin Franklin," *Proceedings of the American Philosophical Society*, CXVI/6 (December 1972), 477–85; and M. E. Grenander, "Reflections on the String Quartet(s) Attributed to Franklin," *American Quarterly*, XXVII/3 (March 1973), 73–87.

Battle music is dealt with in an article so titled by J. Bunker Clark, in *TNGDAM*.

Several volumes of *EAM* are relevant to this chapter: Belcher's *Harmony of Maine* (*EAM* 6); *The American Musical Miscellany*, a 1798 collection of more than 100 songs (*EAM* 9); *The Indian Princess* (both Barker's play and Bray's music) (*EAM* 11); *Riley's Flute Melodies* (Vol. I, 1814–16; II, 1817–20), containing more than 700 tunes (*EAM* 18); and Benjamin Carr's *Musical Miscellany in Occasional Numbers* (1812–25), which includes more than 80 vocal and instrumental pieces (*EAM* 21). Eve R. Meyer has selected and edited a fine selection of more than 20 songs by Carr in *RRAM* XV.

part two

The Romantic Century
(1820–1920)

THREE

CULTIVATED AND VERNACULAR TRADITIONS, AND THE IMPACT OF ROMANTICISM

Americans distinguish colloquially between two broad categories of music: they speak of "classical" and "popular" music. The terms may be poor ones, especially the former (because of its several meanings), but they bespeak a common realization of the existence of two major traditions in American music. These I shall call the "cultivated" and the "vernacular" traditions, and I shall explain what I mean by these terms in a moment. There is, of course, yet another great category of American music: folk music. This body of music, whether as a legacy of older musical tradition still to be found in cultural backwaters (and at times taken up somewhat self-consciously by the more sophisticated) or as traditional communal music made by various immigrant or ethnic minority groups, is not treated, as such, at any length in this book—not by any means because this music is unimportant in American cultural history but because it is dealt with by Bruno Nettl and Gerard Béhague in a companion volume in the Prentice-Hall History of Music Series: *Folk and Traditional Music of the Western Continents*, 2nd ed. (1973).

However, as we have observed (see p. 29), whether one speaks of a certain music as "folk" or "popular" often depends on the time being considered. The British ballads of the Colonial era and the songs and dances of the Federal era were in every sense *popular*, not "folk" music; many of them still survive, but *now* as folk music (in the first sense described). Conversely, some folk music occasionally becomes popular: think of "folk singers" or country-music performers in recent decades and the music they have diffused so widely—nationalized, in effect—that it has become truly a "popular" music, a music of the populace. For that matter, some "classical" music may also become a kind of popular music: in Germany and Austria, this has happened to some of Schubert's melodies; in the United States, to some of Stephen Foster's. The rapidity with which such shifts in social function and "status" of various music have occurred in the United States is one of the most striking things about our dynamic musical culture (reflecting, of course, our culture at large)—in fact, as far as I know, unique.

To return to cultivated and vernacular American-music traditions: I mean by the term *cultivated tradition* a body of music that America had to cultivate consciously, music faintly exotic, to be approached with some effort, and to be appreciated for its edification—its moral, spiritual, or aesthetic values. By *vernacular tradition* I mean a body of music more plebeian, native, not approached self-consciously but simply grown into as one grows into one's vernacular tongue, music understood and appreciated simply for its utilitarian or entertainment value.[1]

As America entered the nineteenth century, a distinction between cultivated and vernacular traditions was hardly visible. The music of the ballad operas at New York and Philadelphia was also the music of broadsides and songsters, as it was of the popular products of sheet-music publishers. The fuging tunes of the New England Yankees aimed to improve church singing and thus to be spiritually edifying, but they served also as a popular social music for secular entertainment. The Alexander Reinagles of the late eighteenth century brought a cultivated professionalism to the New World, but they wrote and played and sang to the populace at large as well as to the gentlemen and gentlewomen.

However, as the nineteenth century unfolded we can distinguish with increasing clarity two bodies of American music, two attitudes toward music: cultivated and vernacular traditions become visible; an eventually profound schism in American musical culture begins to open up. On the one hand there continued a vernacular tradition of utilitarian and entertainment music, essentially unconcerned with artistic or philosophical idealism; a music based on established or newly diffused American raw materials; a "popular" music

---

[1] My terms *cultivated tradition* and *vernacular tradition* are derived from similar terminology (relating mainly to other aspects of American culture) in John Kouwenhoven's *Made in America. The Arts in Modern Civilization* (New York: Doubleday & Co., Inc., 1949).

in the largest sense, broadly based, widespread, naive, and unself-conscious; and a music whose "success" was measured not by abstract aesthetic standards but by those of the marketplace. On the other hand there developed a cultivated tradition of fine-art music significantly concerned with moral, artistic, or cultural idealism; a music almost exclusively based on continental European models, looked to rather self-consciously; an essentially transatlantic music of the pretenders to gentility; a music by no means widespread throughout all segments of the populace but one that its advocates hoped was sophisticated; and a music that in general could not and did not pay for itself but required, for its very existence, some degree of patronage—for its composers if not its performers.

Many factors worked to create this dualistic musical culture in nineteenth-century America, among them the rapid geographical expansion of the nation and distinctive new immigration patterns. Perhaps most significant were the impact of Romantic attitudes and ideals and the continued growth of public concerts as a primary source of musical experience.

The extraordinary territorial growth of the United States in the nineteenth century accelerated a split between cultivated and vernacular traditions in American music because it diversified the cultural possibilities of American society. Dominating the entire social and cultural situation was the moving frontier, constantly pushing westward and leaving behind it an ever-widening area of newly settled towns, with the older urban centers of the eastern seaboard behind *them*. Necessarily, musical life was different in the pioneer settlements along Horse Creek in Wyoming, between the Mormon and Oregon trails; in a relatively new but well-established and growing town like Pittsburgh, just beyond the Allegheny Mountains (its population increasing between 1810 and 1850 from less than 5,000 to more than 70,000); and in an "old" urban center like New York or Boston. Music of cultivated taste was taken up first in the older eastern cities, which were closest in spirit and space to Europe's centers of an art-music tradition. The music formerly enjoyed in such cities by all levels of society then tended to become both a slightly déclassé "popular" music and part of a vernacular tradition accompanying the westerly push of Americans across the land. By 1853, for instance, a Boston writer remarked of the Yankee singing-school tunebooks, once enjoyed by Bostonians great and small, that "if used at all, [they] have been crowded to the far west, mostly out of sight and hearing."[2]

The frontier settlements had virtually no contact with the developing cultivated tradition of the eastern urban centers. However, the newly established towns in between, rapidly growing in numbers, in population, in stability and ease of life, did have some contact and sought still more. But lacking the urbanity, wealth, leisure, and comforting traditions of the eastern

---

[2] Nathaniel Gould, *Church Music in America* (Boston: A. N. Johnson, 1853), p. 55.

seaboard cities, they were at once envious, fearful, and resentful of the culture "down East." The men, only one step removed from pioneering, viewed any time spent on non-productive, inutile art as wasteful or effete. Land and money needed cultivation, not their sensibilities. Music, the most intangible and "useless" among the arts, had their special disdain and hostility. Leave music to the women or to the immigrant "professors" (most often organists in the local churches who also gave music lessons privately) or to the occasional touring virtuoso performers and ensembles whose number increased steadily from the 1840s on. Thus crystallized an American view of fine-art music as something that was essentially the province of foreigners or females (or effeminates)—a view still common in the twentieth century although it weakened rapidly after World War I.

New immigration patterns during the nineteenth and early twentieth centuries were also of great importance in shaping America's music, particularly that of the cultivated tradition, but ultimately also that of the vernacular. The flow of immigrants was immense—more than 35 million between the declaration of national independence and the imposition of immigration quotas in 1924—spurred on by the land-rich, broadening nation and its manpower-hungry industrialization. The overwhelmingly white, Anglo-Saxon, Protestant population of the early United States (always excepting the native Americans and the Hispanics of the Southwest) was augmented by the main immigrations of the 1820–60 period: some 5 million Europeans, 90 percent of them from England, Ireland, or Germany. By contrast, in the 1860–1920 period, during which about 30 million entered the country, the immigrants were mostly non-English, non-Protestant, and from central and southeastern Europe (Italy, the Balkans, Poland, and Russia). The arrival of large numbers of Germans, in the first of these periods, and of other continental Europeans in the second, was critical in the molding of cultivated American taste because it diluted the traditional mainstream of Anglo-American culture and especially because it occurred at the peak of the Romantic movement in Europe. Early nineteenth-century America was ripe for Romanticism: indeed, someone has said that the American Revolution itself was perhaps the first and greatest example of Romanticism and, as Lewis Mumford has written, "pioneering may in part be described as the Romantic movement in action."[3] Ordinary Americans may not have been aware of the philosophic concepts of Romanticism—idealism, imagination, boundlessness, personal freedom, individualism—but their whole way of life and thought reflected them. And their musical attitudes were no less ready to be shaped along Romantic lines.

Romanticism had its beginnings in both France and England, as well as an early flowering in Germany. Although springing initially from the egalitarian and libertarian ideals of the French Revolution and back-to-nature

---

[3] *The Golden Day*, 2nd ed. (Boston: Beacon Press, 1957), p. 20.

goals as expressed by Jean Jacques Rousseau, Romanticism found perhaps its highest expression and made its greatest impact through German music and musicians. Outside the field of opera, in which Italy maintained a national identity, hardly any kind of nineteenth-century music escaped being touched by German influence; hardly any musician could avoid the impact of Beethoven, Schubert, Schumann, Mendelssohn, Liszt, Wagner. Essentially, the centers of nineteenth-century musical thought were in Berlin, Leipzig, Munich, and Vienna; essentially, the ultimate in fine-art music was considered to be German music.

Even before massive crop failures and the 1848 revolutions brought a huge wave of Germans to the United States, some Americans were shifting their musical allegiance from England to Germany. The influential hymnodist Thomas Hastings spoke for his generation, poised on the brink of submission to German rather than English models, when he wrote in 1822 in his *Dissertation on Musical Taste*:

> We are the decided admirers of *German* musick. We delight to study and to listen to it. The science, genius, the taste, that every where pervade it, are truly captivating to those who have learned to appreciate it: but such, we presume, are not yet the *majority* of American or English auditors or executants.[4]

Hastings was writing as one of the first spokespersons for the cultivated tradition of American music. Terms like *science, genius,* and *taste* bespoke special standards, not for all music but for the *art* of music; not for music as a utilitarian part of everyday life or a pleasant diversion on the surface of life but as an art whose holy mission it was to edify and uplift. "Appreciation" of such music required cultivation. As expressed by the highly respected and pontifical editor and critic of the later nineteenth century, John Sullivan Dwight, the aim of such music and of the other arts was to remedy the defects of a materialistic society by "familiarizing men with the beautiful and the infinite." This was the credo of the cultivated tradition. As the exponents of this attitude saw it, German music more than any other achieved the desired goals. One significant result of this view was a rejection of the American musical past, dominated as it had been not only by popular, "unscientific" taste but also by British backgrounds. Both the friendly, folkish music of the First New England School and the great melodic reservoir of Anglo-American song were spurned as bases for the new "scientific" music of the cultivated tradition.

In their self-conscious, unself-confident striving toward a transatlantic taste for cultivated music, Americans also tended to reject the American *present* as a source of musical subject matter. The very aspects of American

---

[4] *Dissertation on Musical Taste* (Albany, NY: Websters and Skinner, 1822), p. 194.

civilization that were unique had of course no models in Europe; they found scant celebration in American art-music. Europeans of the early nineteenth century were, after all, infinitely disparaging of American culture: "Who, in the four quarters of the globe, reads an American book, or goes to an American play, or looks at an American painting or statue?" asked the British author-minister Sydney Smith in 1820.[5] The European might grudgingly admit to American achievements in industry, technology, and science but considered them, if anything, inimical to art and edification. When the Philadelphia journalist-composer William Fry asked the director of the Paris opera if he might present at his own expense an open rehearsal of his opera *Leonora*, he was refused with the remark "In Europe we look upon America as an industrial country—excellent for electric railroads but not for art." (Fry's angry retort was to say that "although we had excelled in making electric telegraphs to carry ideas without persons, it was not a necessary consequence that we built railroads to carry persons without ideas."[6]) The American pianist Louis Moreau Gottschalk had a similar experience: "Zimmerman, director of the piano classes at the Paris Conservatoire . . . without hearing me refused to receive me because 'l'Amérique n'était qu'un pays de machines à vapeur.' "[7] Cowed by such attitudes, American musicians of the cultivated tradition were not about to celebrate their electric telegraphs or their steam engines, their reapers or railroads. (Vernacular-tradition composers, of popular songs for instance, did, however, celebrate them, as they did American steamboats and streetcars, balloons, baseball, and the Brooklyn Bridge.)

With the European music of Romanticism their main model, and with German music held up as the ideal, Americans welcomed German musicians. They came in large numbers. Gottschalk heard a volunteer military band in Williamsport in 1863: "Is it necessary," he wrote in his journal, "to say that it is composed of Germans (all the musicians in the United States are Germans)?" A year earlier he had only half facetiously noted, "It is remarkable that almost all the Russians in America are counts, just as almost all the musicians who abound in the United States are nephews of Spohr and Mendelssohn." The figure of the German music teacher came to be a familiar one in American towns; Gottschalk, Paris-trained and something of a Germanophobe (but with a perceptive eye and a sharp pen), wickedly described one:

I was introduced [in St. Louis in 1862] to an old German musician with

---

[5] Quoted from the *Edinburgh Review* by J. B. McMaster, *History of the People of the United States*, Vol. I (New York: D. Appleton, 1883), p. 82.

[6] *The Musical World and New York Musical Times*, V/13 (March 26, 1853), 196; quoted in *Dwight's Journal of Music*, II/26 (April 2, 1853), 202. I owe this reference to R. Allen Lott, "Pianos American Style III," *ISAM Newsletter*, XV/1 (November 1985), 12.

[7] Jeanne Behrend, ed., *Notes of a Pianist* (New York: Alfred A. Knopf, 1964), p. 52.

uncombed hair, bushy beard, in constitution like a bear, in disposition the amenity of a boar at bay to a pack of hounds. I know this type; it is found everywhere.[8]

It was inevitable that as the cultivated tradition of American music developed momentum in the nineteenth century, under the sway of European music and musicians here at home, young American musicians affluent enough to do so would go to the source, to Europe, for training. Not surprisingly, when they went, it was to Germany.

Some aspects of Romanticism, working in combination with a new domination of the economics of music by the middle class, confirmed the dichotomy between cultivated and vernacular traditions in American music. Romantic art-music put a premium on the individuality of the composer and on an apparent subjectivity of artistic expression. One result was a broadening of the vocabulary of art-music, for to the degree that a composer used a vocabulary different from others' he could be viewed as unique, as one who was expressing his innermost thoughts as only he felt and knew them, a sort of extraordinary culture hero. (In that male-dominated age, there was hardly any possibility of *heroines*.) Romanticism encouraged the virtuoso composer. But if individuality and novelty were most highly prized assets of the composer, they also collided with the fundamentally conservative tastes of the mass public, which had become the principal patron of music. The agents of the new patronage were the public concert and the public opera, which had replaced the aristocratic soirée musicale and the cathedral service as the principal forums for musical performance. Public concerts depended for their existence on the approbation of a large, heterogeneous audience. Such an audience, with collective ears less finely tuned, less carefully cultivated than those of the earlier aristocratic patrons of music, tended to resist complexity and innovation in the musical language—just what the Romantic-era composer was striving for. The composer was trapped between the conflicting demands of Romantic individualism and the mass audience. Precisely to the degree that the composer spoke in a uniquely personal language, his or her communication with the public—which liked what it knew and knew what it liked—was attenuated. Inevitably, a fissure appeared between the taste of the composer of art-music and that of the ostensible patron, the public. Inevitably, the fissure widened as the nineteenth century wore on. Ultimately, the fissure now a chasm, the public concert would virtually exclude the contemporary composer; the public concert hall and the public opera house would virtually become musical museums. The composer was forced to find other sources of patronage, or at least other

---

[8] This, and the previous two quotations, from *Notes of a Pianist*; in order, pp. 127, 102, 63.

sources of income, to be able to go on composing; as one historian has put it:

> Even as the 19th century approached its end, composing art music had yet to be established as a profession in the U.S. [Such figures as John Knowles Paine, Horatio Parker, and Edward MacDowell], although hired by their universities chiefly for their achievements as composers, earned their livings as pedagogues. The careers of other 19th-century composers of art music confirm the pattern. Anthony Philip Heinrich once described his livelihood as "teaching little misses on the pianoforte, for small quarter money, often unpaid"; William Henry Fry followed a journalist's trade; Louis Moreau Gottschalk toured as a virtuoso pianist; George Frederick Bristow was an orchestral violinist, a church organist, a conductor, and a teacher of private lessons and public school music. Remembered now as composers, all four composed only as a sideline, at that a mostly nonremunerative one.[9]

If the virtuoso composer's lot was a problematic one, the virtuoso performer's was not. Not only were performers a critical success for their unique gifts, which made them appear inspired Romantic individualists par excellence; they were a popular success as well. Technical brilliance is confused with musical profundity in direct ratio to the naiveté of the listener, and the mass-public concert audience of the Romantic era tended to be naive. American concert audiences welcomed the virtuoso, equated virtuosity with artistry, mistook virtuosity for talent. European virtuosos appeared regularly in America. Robert Schumann commented,

> The [European] public has lately begun to weary of virtuosos, and . . . we have too. The virtuosos themselves seem to feel this, if we may judge from a recently awakened fancy among them for emigrating to America; and many of their enemies secretly hope they will remain over there; for, taken all in all, modern virtuosity has benefited art very little.[10]

To America came the Norwegian violinist Ole Bull, who was here for lengthy stays (1843–45, 1852–57), annual winter tours (1867–73), and other visits; the "Swedish nightingale" Jenny Lind, who was brought here in 1850 by the notorious impresario P. T. Barnum and stayed for two years; the German soprano Henriette Sontag, who toured the United States between 1852 and 1854, before going to Mexico; and the virtuoso pianists Leopold de Meyer (U.S. tours 1845–47), Henri Herz (Western hemisphere tours 1846–51),

---

[9] Richard Crawford, "Patronage [in American Music]" (unpublished essay kindly provided by Professor Crawford).

[10] *Gesammelte Schriften über Musik und Musiker*, 5th ed. (Leipzig, 1914), Vol. II, p. 134, trans. Paul Rosenfeld, *Robert Schumann on Music and Musicians* (New York: Pantheon Books Inc., 1946), p. 81.

and Liszt's rival Sigismond Thalberg (U.S. tours 1856–58).[11] (The British virtuoso pianist Richard Hoffman, a pupil of De Meyer, immigrated in 1847, toured with Jenny Lind, and remained in this country; see p. 83.)

One result of the adulation of virtuosos was an emphasis on the performer of music rather than on the composer or even the music itself, that is, on the means rather than the end. Did it matter *what* virtuosos like Paganini or Liszt or Jenny Lind performed, as long as they performed? Symbolic of this view of the musical experience (and still common today) was the listing in announcements of a forthcoming concert not of the music to be heard but only of its performer. In earlier eras, when the virtuoso was primarily an improviser, virtually composing the music while performing it, such an attitude was hardly peculiar and posed no threat to progressive trends in the musical vocabulary. But in the Romantic era, when the art of improvisation was dying under the effect of the composer-as-culture-hero idea, and when at the same time the conservatism of the mass audience meant resistance to innovation, this attitude tended to freeze the concert repertory and to block any change in the musical vocabulary. In this sense the nineteenth-century virtuoso became the real musical hero while only lip service was paid to the living composer, whose heroism often had to await posthumous recognition after the slowly changing taste of the concert public, finally catching up with the composer's vocabulary, allowed a change in the "standard" performance repertory.

The virtuoso conductor, a new kind of virtuoso, was born during the Romantic era. He was no longer merely *primus inter pares*, a musical chronometer keeping time for a group of co-equal instrumentalists, but a kind of super-performer playing a super-instrument, the romantically expansive symphony orchestra. America welcomed increasingly this kind of virtuoso, as was reflected in a number of visiting orchestras and the development of American orchestras themselves, with a parade of European conductors to lead them, further emphasizing the faint exoticism, the "foreignness" from an American standpoint, of the cultivated tradition.

The premium put on virtuosity tended to create higher performance standards in general, thus to increase professionalism in music of the cultivated tradition. This was mirrored in the establishment of America's first musical conservatories. Perhaps more significant in terms of musical attitudes were the increasingly common attempts through private music lessons to

---

[11] Jenny Lind's American sojourn is thoroughly chronicled, with many suggestive illustrations and illuminating quotations from reviews, in W. Porter Ware and Thaddeus C. Lockard, Jr., *P. T. Barnum Presents Jenny Lind: The American Tour of the Swedish Nightingale* (Baton Rouge: Louisiana State University Press, 1980). Similarly, a valuable account of the American years of the three piano virtuosos is R. Allen Lott, "The American Concert Tours of Leopold de Meyer, Henri Herz, and Sigismond Thalberg," Ph.D. dissertation, City University of New York, 1986; besides thoroughly documenting the itineraries of the pianists, Lott discusses issues common to all three, such as audiences, repertory, the role of the impresario, and finances.

train amateurs to professional levels of accomplishment, often with futile
and musically disenchanting results, and always with an affirmation of the
distinction between cultivated and vernacular music traditions. A later but
similar educative aim, one hoping to train people to "professional" levels of
musical understanding, lay behind the phenomenon of "music appreciation"
lectures; the music in question, whose appreciation had to be cultivated,
was of course exclusively cultivated-tradition music.

If the rise of the middle class altered the system of musical patronage
and accelerated a musical professionalism, it also tended to create a vast
new army of amateur performers of art-music, persons with the leisure time
to spend on music making and the aspiration to do so, but with only modest
talent or artistic judgment. Reflective of this aspect of middle-class musical
culture was the rapid growth of the sheet-music publishing industry, which
in America had reached impressive proportions even by the last decade of
the eighteenth century and continued to expand throughout the nineteenth.
The main output of the publishers was naturally music simple enough to be
sold in quantity to amateur musicians across the land, music that in one
sense of the word would be "popular." At first this published popular music
was indistinguishable from the music to be heard on concert programs. This
is true, for example, of late eighteenth-century American sheet music, which
more often than not made an advertising pitch for its desirability by actually
citing its use in concert or opera: Alexander Reinagle's opera air *Rosa* (1800),
". . . sung with great applause by Mrs. Merry in the comedy of *The Secret*,"
or Benjamin Carr's *Federal Overture* (1794) ". . . as performed at the the-
atres in Philadelphia and New York." But here, too, a fissure appeared—
between the taste and capability of the amateur performer and the music of
the professional concert and opera performers. As the latter became ever
more professionalized and as virtuosity tended to increase, concert music
outstripped amateur ability, and the "popular" music of the music sheets
came to be a different thing from the "classical" music of the concerts.

Some of this sheet music was music of the vernacular tradition. But
much of it (songs and piano pieces for the most part) had an aura of pretentious
gentility about it; it derived from and lay within the cultivated tradition
rather than the vernacular, although its accessibility to both performer and
listener kept it near the latter. As composed by innumerable musical poe-
tasters, it actually represented a subdivision of the cultivated tradition that
might well be termed "household" music—a term that in fact was used in
the period, as in the title of a collection of the 1850s: *Household Melodies,
a Selection of Popular Songs, Duets, Trios & Quartettes, Arranged to Household Words*, issued first by W. C. Peters & Sons of Cincinnati and then by
other publishers and distributors in St. Louis, Nashville, Cleveland, Pittsburgh, and Louisville. The term "household music" seems appropriate, for
it suggests an analogy with the other household artifacts of the period like

silverware, ceramics, glass, furniture, rugs, and draperies, which although utilitarian were never acquired solely for their utility but with an eye to their attractiveness and their reflection of fashionable cultivated taste. The early twentieth century would call such music "semi-classical" or "light classical," thus perfectly describing its ambiguous status.

By that time, the two main traditions of American music, cultivated and vernacular, came to be less independent. Some cultivated-tradition music showed the influence of vernacular music; some music based on vernacular traditions showed increased sophistication, artistry, and complexity (e.g., the theater songs of Jerome Kern); and some composers moved back and forth easily between musical genres associated with one or the other tradition (for instance, Victor Herbert between concertos and light opera, John Philip Sousa between band marches and operetta, and George Gershwin between musical-comedy scores and orchestral works). By the mid-twentieth century, although distinctions could be made among such categories as pop music, rock, country music, jazz, the musical, opera, concert music, sacred music, and still others, interpenetrations among them were so complex and commonplace that to discuss them in terms of a dualistic musical culture of vernacular and cultivated traditions seems simplistic and invalid.

In the following three chapters, we shall consider that period in American music when the vernacular and cultivated traditions diverged and remained more or less separate: from about 1820 until about 1920. It will be most convenient to deal first, in Chapter Four, with the cultivated tradition (including the genteel household music) up to the Civil War; next, in Chapter Five, with vernacular-tradition music during the whole period; and then, in Chapter Six, with cultivated-tradition music from the Civil War through World War I.

FOUR

THE CULTIVATED TRADITION, 1820–1865

American music of the cultivated tradition between about 1820 and the end of the Civil War can perhaps best be approached through a discussion of its main genres: church music, song, piano music, orchestral music, and opera.

CHURCH MUSIC

As we have seen (pp. 21–22), the First New England School of composers of psalm settings, hymns, anthems, and patriotic pieces, of fuging tunes and other sacred-secular works in a characteristic, indigenous style, came under criticism toward the turn of the nineteenth century. As early as 1791, when Samuel Holyoke published at Boston his collection titled *Harmonia Americana,* he specifically called attention to his omission of "fuging pieces," claiming in the Preface that "the principal reason why few were inserted was the trifling effect produced by that sort of music; for the parts, falling in, one after another, each conveying a different idea, confound the sense, and render the performance a mere jargon of words." But this argument, an old one against vocal counterpoint, was only part of the reason for the new disfavor in which the Yankee composers found themselves. More significant was the developing taste for "the sublime and beautiful compositions of the great Masters of Music," to recall Andrew Law's phrase—that is, the masters of continental Europe.

Symptomatic of the shift in taste are the collections of church music published by Thomas Hastings (1784–1872), whom we have met (p. 57) as a "decided admirer of German musick" and who was a major figure in nineteenth-century cultivated church music. In 1815 Hastings brought out his first compilation, *Musica Sacra: A Collection of Psalm Tunes, Hymns, and Set Pieces*. Along with original tunes and works by other Americans, he included adaptations from the following Europeans: Giardini (to whose melody the hymn "Come Thou, almighty King" is sung even today in Protestant American churches), Purcell, William Croft, Handel (*Messiah*), Burney, and Madan. The English bias is clear; Hastings had not yet submitted to "the science, genius, the taste [of] German musick." He turned to it increasingly, however, for tunes to include in later hymn collections. By 1849 he could even name one hymn book *The Mendelssohn Collection*. To its main body he added as a sort of appendix a group of older hymns and psalm settings, a concession, apparently, to those who still wanted to sing the old New England favorites. Among them we find Timothy Swan's *China* (see p. 18), but in a completely bowdlerized version. Hastings's condescending footnote reads, "Extensively sung in former times, at funerals. The original harmony was, of course, inadmissible."

Hastings's own output as a hymnodist was considerable: he is said to have written some 600 hymn texts and composed 1000 hymn tunes. Among the best known are "Gently, Lord, O gently lead us," "How calm and beautiful the morn," "Return, O wand'rer to thy home," and most popular of all, "Rock of ages," which appeared as a setting for A. M. Toplady's text in *Spiritual Songs for Social Worship* (1832), a collection compiled jointly by Hastings and the other dominant figure in the cultivated tradition's church music, Lowell Mason.

Mason (1792–1872) has been conceded by even so reluctant an admirer as Gilbert Chase (see *AM*, Chap. 8) to have had "the strongest, the widest, and the most lasting impress on the musical culture" of any nineteenth-century American musician. His first musical success came with sponsorship by the weighty Handel and Haydn Society of Boston, which aimed not only ". . . to introduce into more general practice the works of Handel, Haydn and other eminent composers" but also to support the publication of approved church music. Upon the recommendation of its esteemed organist, George K. Jackson (see p. 39), the society accepted for publication a hymn collection assembled by Mason, who was working at the time as a bank clerk in Savannah, and in 1822 there appeared the first of many editions of *The Boston Handel and Haydn Society Collection of Church Music* (reprinted as *EAM 15*).

Mason's parents and grandfather were all musical, and by the time he had left his native Massachusetts for Savannah he was proficient on several instruments. In Savannah he was taught by a German-born musician, Frederick Abel, who probably contributed much to his esteem for "scientific" music as opposed to the less suave and polished American sacred style. The 1822 *Boston Collection* was based on William Gardiner's English anthology, *Sacred Melodies from Haydn, Mozart, Beethoven and other composers . . . appropriated for the use of the British Church* (1812–15). Besides the Viennese classicists, Mason tapped other European sources, including German chorales; Gregorian chants; and works of Handel, Gluck, Nägeli, and Pleyel.[1]

The Boston Handel and Haydn Society Collection was an immediate and continuing success: twenty-two editions were published between 1822 and 1858. Mason returned to Massachusetts in 1827, to become president of the Handel and Haydn Society until 1832; the next year, together with George James Webb (1803–87) and some other Boston musicians, he founded the Boston Academy of Music; its purpose was to instruct children in music on principles based on the inductive methods of the Swiss educator Johann Pestalozzi. Mason continued to compose, compile, and adapt hymns: later successful collections of his included *The Choir; or Union Collection of Church Music* (1832); *The Boston Academy's Collection of Church Music* (1835); *The Modern Psalmist* (1839); and *Carmina Sacra: or Boston Collection of Church Music* (1841), among others. With the income from these major publications and from his original 1822 collection, Mason's fortune was assured; along with it went extraordinary fame and influence.

The musical style of Mason's hymns, based on European Classic-era music, is one of genteel correctness, neat and tidy in harmony and form, mild in rhythmic vitality and melodic thrust. The airs are now in the tenor voice in the old manner, now in the treble; not infrequently, they are oddly awkward, perhaps because Mason's musical thought as a whole was dominated by considerations of harmony, and as a result even the air is sometimes made to accommodate the harmony rather than fulfilling its own directional impulse. Some of Mason's best-known hymns, like *A Missionary Hymn* ("From Greenland's icy mountains"), *Bethany* ("Nearer, my God, to Thee"), and *Olivet* ("My faith looks up to thee"), share this trait. The texture of all of them is in general unrelievedly homophonic; the "fuging" style of earlier American psalmody is consistently avoided—as are, of course, its folkish harmony and casual counterpoint; in their place are a full triadic vocabulary,

---

[1] See Henry L. Mason, *Hymn-Tunes of Lowell Mason: A Bibliography* (Cambridge, Eng.: The University Press, 1944).

functional harmony with occasional seventh chords, and even secondary dominants. The influence on American congregational songs of Mason's hymns, along with the similar ones of Hastings, was immense; as one scholar put it (beginning with a quoted fragment from Mason's *Address on Church Music* of 1827),

> The "simple, easy, and solemn" pieces found in the collections of Hastings and Mason . . . established a style of Protestant hymnody that has remained virtually unchanged for a century and a half. [Their hymns] are still sung today, in their original harmonization, without arousing the slightest feeling that they are in any way different from other pieces in modern hymnals.[2]

Mason was not only a composer of some 1200 original hymn tunes (though we shall perhaps never know the exact number since he published many without attribution) and adapter of almost 500 melodies from other composers; he was also a dedicated teacher: to him must go credit for getting music admitted into the public-school curriculum of Boston, and indirectly into public-school programs over the entire country. The beginning was the Boston Academy, which provided free extracurricular music classes for schoolchildren. In 1838, after years of propagandizing by Mason, the public schools of Boston began to include musical instruction as a part of the regular curriculum, with Mason appointed as superintendent of music for the city system. It was a historic moment in the history of American music and musical attitudes; for better or worse, Mason's ideals and tastes, and those of a huge circle of musicians and educators associated with him, could now be directed where they would have the greatest impact: among the children.

It may be appropriate here to pause and consider the unique place in American culture that has been held by music education, which since Mason's day has been considered an essential part of the school curriculum. In fact, from the time of Tufts and Walter early in the eighteenth century to the present, musical indoctrination has been considered a matter of importance by Americans. This attitude is uniquely American: as Allen Britton put it in a thoughtful essay, music education has been "an American specialty."[3] Significantly, Americans have viewed musical education as important not just for itself but as a means to a higher goal. In the singing-school era, the end was a greater perfection in religious observance; since Mason's time, it has been a kind of aesthetic and moral improvement. Throughout our history, these goals have been sought through education in "better music"—

---

[2] Charles Hamm, *Music in the New World* (New York: W. W. Norton, 1983), p. 166. Indeed, a number of Mason's hymns are regularly included in "modern hymnals." A performance of "Nearer, My God, to Thee," recorded in 1920 by the baritone Oscar Seagle with an unidentified vocal quartet, is heard on *NW* 224:s2/7.

[3] "Music Education: An American Specialty," *One Hundred Years of Music in America*, ed. Paul Henry Lang (New York: G. Schirmer, Inc., 1961), pp. 211–29. A later, more comprehensive historical survey by Britton is his "Musical Education in the United States of America," *Bulletin of Historical Research in Music Education*, III/2 (July 1982), 91–102.

better, that is, than the vernacular music of the period in question. In Tufts's
and Walter's day, the "better music" was that on the written page, and their
main aim was simply to teach students how to read music. In the early
nineteenth century, the "better music" for the reformers among the singing-
school masters was almost any music other than "those wild fugues" of the
Yankee tunesmiths. For Mason and his circle, and indeed for many music
educators up to the present, the "better music" was the music of Europe's
Classic era. At the same time, because of that lag between the musical
thought of the composer and the musical understanding that we explored
in Chapter Three, education in the elaborately artistic music of Europe was
considered unrealistic. Thus, just as folk and vernacular music was rejected
by school music teachers, so was the very best of "classical" music. Instead,
a bland and bloodless, if correct and irreproachable, music of second- and
lower-rate composers was taught. A lasting result was, as Britton remarks,
that music education has always operated "at a certain distance from the
well-springs of American musical life, both popular and artistic. . . . The
term 'polite' is perhaps as good as any other to characterize much of the
music utilized in schools from the time of Lowell Mason to the present day."
Thus we see a paradox in American educational philosophy: on the one hand,
a unique acceptance of music's importance in the education of every American and, on the other, a narrowly restricted *kind* of music that Americans
are to be "educated" in—a music that has little to do with either the American past or present or with either the rough-hewn virility of folk music or
the craftsmanly elegance of art-music. The effect on many Americans has
been one of disenchantment with music, both as listeners and participators,
in the years after schooling: not only has formal music education, limited
only to the blander and "politer" kind of music, tended to dull the impulse
to lusty, unself-conscious participation in music making for the fun of it; it
has also provided very little understanding, let alone high standards for
performance, of any highly artistic music. A great many Americans, since
the mid-nineteenth century, have come to adulthood without much enthusiasm for *any* kind of music—at least, until the 1960s and later, when the
folk-song revival and the supplanting of the piano by the guitar as the principal "household-music" instrument reawakened American youth (at least)
to the pleasures of informal music making.

SONG

The Anglo-American tradition of the genteel air was maintained during the entire nineteenth century. Songs were the staples of the mid-nineteenth-
century concert repertory; hardly any concert of exclusively instrumental
music was to be heard, and the majority of public concerts were essentially

song recitals. Up to the Civil War, at least, the songs of the public concerts were also heard in the parlor, the very center of middle-class polite society; there, beside horsechair-stuffed chairs and sofas and polite, instructive family magazines, could be found—ever more commonly as the century wore on— a square or an upright piano or a reed organ. There, in the home, their cultural life dominated by the new breed of middle-class woman, nineteenth-century Americans gathered to hear a favorite daughter or bride sing the latest concert-household songs.

If eighteenth-century American songs only occasionally borrowed the sentimental tone and the high-flown language of Thomson's *Seasons* and Goldsmith's *Deserted Village*, nineteenth-century songs went the whole way, reflecting the tastes of an age that reveled in Scott's poems and Gothic romances, after a turn-of-the-century preparation by way of Richardson's *Pamela* and Susanna Rowson's *Charlotte Temple: A Tale of Truth*. Almost entirely vanished were the sturdy unforced optimism of Reinagle's *America, Commerce, and Freedom* or the lightly mocking bow to conventional love of Hopkinson's *My Gen'rous Heart Disdains the Slave of Love to Be*. In their place were set texts of the most extreme sentimentality, often descending to bathos or ascending to manic ecstasy.

Especially important in the background of nineteenth-century American song were the collections of *Irish Melodies* of the poet-musician Thomas Moore (1779–1852)—ten volumes published between 1808 and 1834 in London, each pirated almost immediately by American publishers (in those days without an effective international copyright law). Moore added new texts of his own invention to traditional Irish melodies, also polishing the latter and providing them with up-to-date harmonizations, to create some of the most enduringly popular songs in the English language. Among the most universally known are *Believe me if all those enduring young charms* (to the tune "My lodging is on the cold ground), *'Tis the last rose of summer* (to the tune "The Groves of Blarney"), and *The harp that once through Tara's halls* (to the tune "Gramachree"). The dominant theme of Moore's poems is nostalgia for a past better than the dismal present. In one form or another, that theme was to predominate also in American song through the Civil War, and as Charles Hamm has demonstrated persuasively, the wide diffusion of Moore's Irish songs in the period had much to do with this development.[4]

Models for American songs of the period were provided partly by English singers who barnstormed through the eastern half of the country in the 1830s and 1840s. The most successful and influential of these was Henry Russell (1812–1900; in America from the mid-1830s to the early 1840s). he

[4] See Hamm, *Yesterdays* (New York: W. W. Norton, 1979), Chap. 3 ("'Erin, the Tear and the Smile in Thine Eyes'; or, Thomas Moore's *Irish Melodies* in America").

left the organ bench of the First Presbyterian Church in Rochester, New York, to make a name for himself as a baritone soloist and songwriter. Mining the vein of nostalgia that ran so deep in mid-nineteenth-century America— especially a sub-vein that prized old age for its evocation of "the good old days"—Russell concentrated on "old" songs (*The Old Bell, The Brave Old Oak, The Old Sexton, The Old Clock, The Old Farm Gate*, and many others), for a total he claimed to be over 800 (but a more likely figure is about 250, some 75 of which were written in the United States). Among the most renowned were *Woodman, Spare That Tree* (". . . Touch not a single bough,/ In youth it shelter'd me,/And I'll protect it now") and *The Old Arm Chair*. *The Old Arm Chair*, published in 1840 at the peak of Russell's popularity, illustrates in every detail the genre of the household song. The text is embarrassingly maudlin: the poet gazes on the armchair "with quivering breath and throbbing brow"; religion and filial love are identified ("I almost worshipp'd her when she smiled,/And turn'd from her bible to bless her child"); the chair itself is an object of sentimental veneration ("I love it, I love it, and cannot tear/My soul from a mother's Old Arm Chair"). The cover page, with a lithograph showing Mother and the chair, is characteristic: nineteenth-century song sheets aimed to be visually seductive as well as vocally attrac-/ tive. The music is quite simple, the melodic style essentially declamatory, in easy $\frac{4}{4}$ rhythms, with an occasional touch of affective chromateism and a climactic, shuddering diminished-seventh chord. The form is strophic. The most frequent harmonic progression is the gentle I-IV-I, often made even softer by a tonic pedalpoint. One of Russell's songwriting successors was John Hill Hewitt (1801–90), composer of some three hundred songs, among them the Civil War ballad *All Quiet Along the Potomac Tonight* (1861; NW 202:s1/2). He claimed that because of Russell's limited vocal range *The Old Arm Chair* has "but five notes in its melodic construction." This is untrue, but it *is* restricted to one octave and virtually sings itself, with a predictable curve of line and falling sequences. Most characteristic of the melodic method are the many sighing, drooping appoggiaturas, which strive to confirm the text's tone of deep emotion and which relate to the Italian opera aria style (that of Rossini—with whom Russell may have studied—Bellini, and Donizetti) that is important in the background of this and others of Russell's songs (even such a song of the prairie—". . . the broad prairie,/Where man, like the wind, rolls impulsive and free . . ."—as *A Life in the West*, recorded on NW 251:s1/3). One paradox of the song, typical of the genre, is that despite its lachrymose subject it is cast in the major rather than the minor mode.

   The Old Arm Chair may not be either the best or the worst song of the period, but it is typical of Russell's songs, which were extraordinarily influential in virtually establishing "popular song" in America, and it epitomizes perfectly the concert-household song repertory. Far more extreme examples of bathos could be cited, and by composers highly thought of:

perhaps the nadir was reached by W. B. Bradbury (1816–68)—primarily a hymn composer, associate of Thomas Hastings, and a sort of New York City counterpart of Lowell Mason—in *The Lament of the Blind Orphan Girl* (1847). In this song, the doubly afflicted heroine is made to voice her lament in incongruously skipping rhythms and a modest coloratura (derived in part, certainly, from the Italian opera arias that Bradbury would have heard in New York in the 1840s). It is a remarkable lesson in how to turn sentiment into sentimentality (Example 4-1).

    The Lament of the Blind Orphan Girl was published "as sung with distinguished Applause, by Abby Hutchinson." Abby was the female member of the most celebrated American "singing family" for several decades from 1840 on: the Hutchinsons. They were one of a number of American troupes formed in imitation of European family groups, like the Rainer family from the Tyrolean Alps, which toured the United States during the 1840s and after. The Hutchinsons specialized not only in laments—*Oh! I'm in Sadness, Last Year's Flowers, Give That Wreath to Me, The Guardian of the Grave*—but also in "Alpine" songs. Precisely at the time (1846) the Donner party battled to get to California across the mountain walls of the Rockies, Americans in the East were hearing about

> The mountain top! the mountain top!
>   Oh! that's the place for me;
> I love to mount each craggy steep
>   With shout of joyful glee!

EXAMPLE 4-1. W. Bradbury, *The Lament of the Blind Orphan Girl* (New York: Atwill, 1847), measures 25–30, 73–84.

And on an Albany program in 1842 the Hutchinsons sang *The Snowstorm*, its concluding verses a classic of American melodrama:

> And colder still the wind did blow,
> And darker hours of night came on,
> And deeper grew the drifts of snow,
> Her limbs were chilled, her strength was gone.
> "Oh God!" she cried in accents wild,
> "If I must perish, save my child!"

The Hutchinsons became influential advocates of social reform, espousing such radical causes as anti-slavery, temperance, women's rights, and universal suffrage. Besides original songs by one or another family member—such as John Hutchinson's suffrage song *The Fatherhood of God and the Brotherhood of Man* (NW 267:s2/2)—they often used well-known tunes (the abolitionist song *Get Off the Track* is to be sung to *Old Dan Tucker*; the all-purpose pride-in-America song *Uncle Sam's Farm*, recorded on NW 267:s1/3, to a minstrel-show tune by E. P. Christy), which only increased their popularity. They sang both solo songs and part-songs; for the latter they developed a kind of sweet-sounding, "natural" (i.e., non-operatic and ostensibly uncultivated) close harmony and informal delivery that were to become standard in American popular music for generations to come.[5]

[5] See Dale Cockrell, "The Hutchinson Family, 1841–45; or, The Origins of Some Yankee Doodles," ISAM *Newsletter*, XII/1 (November 1982), 12–15.

It is against this background, of the nostalgic sentimentality of *The Old Arm Chair*, the crocodile tears of *The Blind Orphan Girl*, the hysterical unreality of *The Mountain Top*, that one must view the household songs of Stephen Collins Foster, a few of which so sublime or mitigate the conventions of the genre, and so transcend the songs of his contemporaries, that Foster must be adjudged America's first great songwriter.

Born in 1826 on the Fourth of July, fifty years to the day after the Declaration of Independence, near the still small but booming commercial and industrial town of Pittsburgh, Foster had a typical middle-class upbringing in a family of comfortable means to which household music was no stranger (his older sister played the piano, and his father fiddled a bit). Drawn to music from early childhood (his father commented when Foster was sixteen that "his leisure hours are all devoted to musick, for which he possesses a strange talent"), he nevertheless got scant encouragement. His brother later claimed that Foster "studied deeply, and burned much midnight oil over the works of the masters, especially Mozart, Beethoven, and Weber. They were his delight, and he struggled for years and sounded the profoundest depths of musical science."[6] But Foster's music itself leaves no room for illusions about the extent of his training: there is ineptitude and amateurishness on virtually every page. On the other hand, he had an obvious and undeniable natural gift for melody and clearly a remarkable ability to absorb and synthesize the various musical styles popular in the America of his youth—styles rooted in England, Ireland, Italy, and the United States itself.

Foster's debut as a songwriter was with *Open Thy Lattice, Love* (1844). Text and music are both remarkably restrained for the period, and we seem to be back in the very early nineteenth century, with a typically cool if amorous air set to music that reflects Foster's Anglo-Irish descent (Example 4-2). Within the next twenty years, until his death in New York in 1864, Foster was to publish about 150 such household songs. Most are love songs, but the sweetheart is usually unattainable, either dead or distant,

EXAMPLE 4-2. S. Foster, *Open Thy Lattice, Love* (Philadelphia: Willig, 1844), measures 5–8.

[6] Morrison Foster, *My Brother Stephen* (1896, privately printed; repr. Indianapolis: Foster Hall, 1932), p. 32.

and the poet (usually Foster himself) can dwell with her only in a dream of love. Nostalgic yearning for the irretrievably lost is the keynote, but the poet finds the mournful dream delicious. "I dream of Jeanie with the light brown hair," sang Foster in 1854—but Jeanie is gone:

> Many were the wild notes her merry voice would pour,
> Many were the blithe birds that warbled them o'er.

and we see her only through a gentle haze of nostalgia, "floating like a vapor on the soft summer air." Gentle tenderness, or temperate gentility, characterizes the music as well as the texts of Foster's best household songs. *Gentle Annie* (1856) and *Gentle Lena Clare* (1862) are stereotypes, but both heroines are depicted in memorable melodies (Example 4-3). In one of the

EXAMPLE 4-3.(a) S. Foster, *Gentle Annie* (New York: Firth, Pond & Co., 1856), measures 5–12 (piano part omitted). (b) S. Foster, *Gentle Lena Clare* (New York: S. C. Gordon, 1862), measures 9–16 (piano part omitted).

most thoroughly "composed" loved songs, *Come Where My Love Lies Dreaming* (1855), it is the sweetheart who is dreaming, hence asleep, hence for the moment unattainable. *Come Where My Love Lies Dreaming* is set, atypically for a household song, for vocal quartet, with the soprano part set in relief against three lower voices and given an arching line that derives from the Italian opera to be heard in New York, where Foster had lived for most of 1854 (Example 4-4). The last love song written by Foster is one of the best, musically: *Beautiful Dreamer*, copyrighted shortly after his death (1864).

As in the love songs, nostalgia suffuses an extraordinary proportion of the other household songs of Foster. Perhaps from Moore's *Irish Melodies* and from Henry Russell, whom he had heard sing in Pittsburgh, comes

EXAMPLE 4-4. S. Foster, *Come Where My Love Lies Dreaming*. *Quartette* (New York: Firth, Pond & Co., 1855), measures 13–16.

Foster's favorite adjective "old," meaning usually "of the past," not just "aged": *Old Memories* (1853), *When Old Friends Were Here* (1864), *Farewell, Old Cottage* (1851), *My Old Kentucky Home, Good Night* (1853). Beloved ones lost through death are mourned in *Bring My Brother Back to Me* (1863), *Our Willie Dear is Dying* (1861), and *Little Belle Blair* (1861). In *Ah! May the Red Rose Live Alway* (1850), one of Foster's richest works harmonically, the poet asks "Why should the beautiful die?" (Example 4-5).

EXAMPLE 4-5. Foster, *Ah! May the Red Rose Live Alway* (Baltimore: F. D. Benteen, 1850), measures 9–16.

There are, of course, some happy ones among Foster's household songs. *Fairy Belle* (1859); *If You've Only Got a Moustache* (1864), an Irish reel with coy advice to bachelors; and *There's a Good Time Coming* (1846) are a few. But for the most part a sense of loss and nostalgia for the lost are pervasive. An apostrophe to the family hound, *Old Dog Tray* (1853), leads Foster to mourn a "once happy day":

> The morn of life is past
> And evening comes at last;
> It brings me a dream of a once happy day,
> Of merry forms I've seen
> Upon the village green. . . .

Some historians have seen more than simple sentimentality in the insistent nostalgia of the American mid-nineteenth century, so typified by Foster. The "once happy day," they say, was an unspoiled early America, fresh for clearing and settling, since, as Lewis Mumford put it, "ruin and change lay in the wake of the pioneer, as he went westering." A sense of uneasiness, of dislocation, of transition and change must have permeated post-pioneer life. Mumford reminds us of the fascination the legend of Rip Van Winkle held for the period:

> The old landmarks have gone; the old faces have disappeared; all the outward aspects of life have changed. At the bottom, however, Rip himself has not changed; for he has been drunk and lost in a dream, and . . . he remains, mentally, a boy.[7]

Foster, too, perhaps remained mentally a boy; he did musically, for there is no essential stylistic difference between early works and the late ones among his household songs. (There is, however, between his household songs and his minstrel-show songs, as we shall see.) But with his natural talent as melodist, despite his artlessness, Foster spoke for pre-Civil War America; not for the frontier or for the seaboard cities, perhaps, but for that broadening span in between, settled but unsettled, no longer a frontier to be pierced and conquered but an America to be made into something else, and perhaps frighteningly so.

Foster's last years coincided with the Civil War, which evoked, even more than most wars, a wave of songs for American composers. Hamm has written insightfully (in *Music in the New World*) about how, although the war between the states spawned no great painting, sculpture, poetry, or fiction (or large-scale art-music compositions), it did inspire an enormous burst of accomplishment in photography, journalism, and song. Foster contributed a few songs to the Northern cause—*We are Coming, Father Abraham, 300,000 More*, a poem set by several composers, among them Luther O. Emerson (*NW* 202:s1/3); *We've a Million in the Field;* and others—but they

---

[7] Both quotations from *The Golden Day*, 2nd ed. (Boston: Beacon Press, 1957), pp. 32–33.

are of no particular distinction. Two other composers seem to have caught in a few of their songs the militant spirit of the Civil War far better than did Foster: George Frederick Root (1820–95) and Henry Clay Work (1832–84). Work, an otherwise undistinguished composer incapable of sustained effort, produced in *Marching Through Georgia* (1865) a jaunty valedictory to the war, following on Sherman's unopposed march through Georgia to the sea. Root, after an early association in Boston with Lowell Mason, moved to New York in 1844 and then in the late 1850s to Chicago, where in the 1860s he was music editor for the important music-publishing firm of his brother, Root and Cady. Of his 200-odd songs, almost 30 are Civil War songs, among them *The Battle Cry of Freedom* (1862), *Just Before the Battle, Mother* (1862), and *Tramp! Tramp! Tramp!* (1864). An amusing and revealing footnote to Root's career: having decided to try for some of the popular household-song market occupied by Foster but taking a patronizing attitude toward it, Root sought a pseudonym; in view of the adulation of German musicians at the time, a German translation of his own name was his choice: G. Friedrich Wurzel.

Another kind of song, the glee, was also popular during the period and, like the solo song, was sung both in concerts and at home. A part-song for three or four unaccompanied male voices, the glee (from the Anglo-Saxon *gliw* or *gléo:* "entertainment, music") had been enormously popular in eighteenth-century England. Unpretentious, set to friendly doggerel, glees were a mainstay of the Hutchinsons' repertory and were written by most of the composers we have mentioned (thought not by Foster) for household use and for musical societies, usually made up of amateur musicians, such as the Harvard Glee Club (founded 1828). Many of these were male-only organizations: male chorus singing in America, which preserved the tradition of the glee long after it had waned in England, was stimulated by the influence of the German *Männerchor*; a German singing society of this name was organized at Philadelphia in 1835, and similar groups were formed elsewhere, particularly in the Midwest, where many German immigrants had settled.

Solo songs and part-songs were combined in the secular cantata, which was often cast in dramatic form and sometimes even staged—a sort of homespun genre that to some degree, at least, satisfied the need for musical drama met in European culture by opera. The first such cantatas seem to have been composed by George Root for classes of young women at various educational institutions in New York where he was employed. His earliest was *The Flower Queen, or The Coronation of the Rose* (1851–52), set to a text by his former pupil, the blind poet and author of thousands of hymn texts, Fanny Crosby (1820–1915); perhaps his best-conceived and best-composed cantata—certainly the most popular—was *The Haymakers* of 1857 (Part 2 recorded on *NW* 234; the entire work printed in *RRAM* IX-

X), for which Root provided rather elaborate and instructive directions for staging.

PIANOS AND PIANO MUSIC

If any single instrument can be called the Romantic-era instrument par excellence, it is the pianoforte. Indeed, its invention in early eighteenth-century Florence by Bartolomeo Cristofori, its gradual replacement of the harpsichord during that century, its triumphant hegemony among keyboard instruments during the nineteenth, and the decline in its importance during the twentieth reflect a whole cycle in Western musical history.[8] Unlike the harpsichord and organ, and more resoundingly than the clavichord, the piano responds directly to the player's touch: not only can it play *piano* and *forte* but also it can play all the dynamic levels above, below, and between. Not only is it appropriate for intimate music making at home but also, as enlarged and extended in range during the nineteenth century, it can rival an orchestra in power. Not only can it simulate the sustained, affective melodic curve of a single voice but also it can produce dense polyphonic textures. In a period like the Romantic era, which viewed tonal flux as a musical mirror of life itself, whose centers of music were the small parlor and the large concert hall, and whose favored musical fabric was a blend of cantabile melody and rich harmony, the piano was the ideal instrument. If the organ was still viewed as the imperious king of instruments, the piano was a responsive and versatile queen.

Manufacture and sale of pianos in America boomed in the nineteenth century. It has been estimated that whereas in 1829 some 2500 instruments were built, or one for every 4800 persons in the nation, in 1851 more than 9000 were produced and sold. By 1860 the figures had risen again, to 21,000 pianos manufactured, one for every 1500 Americans, with sales across the country of 30 pianos every working day.[9] If we take into account the longevity of a sturdy pianoforte and its low depreciation and degeneration rates, even the last figures must be low as a reflection of the number of people who had access to a playable piano on the eve of the Civil War.

---

[8] And in social history as well, as has been shown with brilliance and wit by Arthur Loesser in *Men, Women and Pianos: A Social History*. (New York: Simon and Schuster, 1954)

[9] Ibid., pp. 469, 492, 511. The social necessity of a piano in a proper parlor is graphically shown in the design for an ideal *American Woman's Home* (New York, 1869) suggested by Catherine Beecher and Harriet Beecher Stowe. On their first-floor ground plan, they indicated only two pieces of furniture, both in the drawing room: one is a sofa, the other a piano. The design is reproduced in John A. Kouwenhoven, *Made in America* (New York: Doubleday & Co., Inc., 1949), p. 77.

American piano builders (many of them immigrants, of course) were among the best in the world, making significant improvements in the instrument during the period. In 1825 the Massachusetts builder Alpheus Babcock (1785–1842) obtained a patent for a one-piece cast-iron frame, which, well adapted to the extremes of American temperature (and later to American central heating), became the foundation of all later piano development. From the 1820s to the 1850s the standards of piano manufacture were established by the firm headed by Jonas Chickering (1797–1853) of Boston. Like other American manufacturers, he concentrated on the heavy, horizontal, four-footed "square" (actually rectangular) piano that was most popular in America during the nineteenth century, but he and his sons made wing-shaped "grands" as well, and very grand they were: the virtuoso pianist Gottschalk commented in his journal in June 1863 on "two mastodons, which [Thomas] Chickering made expressly for me. . . . The tails of these monster pianos measure three feet in width. Their length is ten feet; they have seven and a half octaves." Piano builders were among the German immigrants of the 1830s and later. Among them were William Knabe, who settled in Baltimore in 1837, and most celebrated of all, Henry Steinway (*recte* Heinrich Steinweg, 1797–1871), who fled the revolutions of 1848, settled in New York in 1850, and with his sons established his own firm in 1853. American's own nineteenth-century dynasty of musicians, the Masons, figured in piano manufacturing through Lowell Mason's son Henry, a co-founder of the Mason & Hamlin Company in 1854. Initially the company built melodeons, one American term for small reed organs (also called cottage organs, parlor organs, or cabinet organs), which, because of their small size and price and their popularity mainly in rural America, Loesser has brightly called "the American piano's little country cousin."

The Romantic fondness for the piano, its versatility and its value both as cultural symbol and source of entertainment, resulted in an extraordinary output of piano music from American publishers. Most of it was frankly utilitarian, intended for household use as pleasant diversion and without pretensions to high artistic value, though with overt claims to cultivated gentility. Hundreds of dilettante composers appeared in print as writers of airy trifles; almost anyone, it seems, could gain publication in that era of a seller's market for parlor piano music. The nonentities are legion and need not detain us. One among them might be cited, however, partly because his music so completely typifies the kinds of piano music of the period and partly because of his fantastic prolificacy: Charles Grobe.

We know very little about Grobe; having served his purpose as composer of parlor pieces, he was promptly forgotten, all the more quickly since he seems not to have been a performer of any caliber. He is said to have been born about 1817 in Weimar and to have come to the United States about 1839. He was appointed music teacher in Wesleyan Female College

(Wilmington) in 1840, and according to John W. Moore (1807–89), America's first musical lexicographer, "in 1842 his pianoforte publications became known, which are very numerous."[10] Moore was putting it mildly: Grobe's production of piano music (apparently the only genre that he worked in) surpasses that of any other known composer. His first publication (1841) was a march on themes from Bellini's *I Capuleti e i Montecchi*. By 1845 he was only up to Op. 45 with the *United States Grand Waltz* ("dedicated as a Tribute of Respect to the Ladies of the U.S."; recorded on *NW* 257:s1/3), but then he began to hit his stride. By 1847, with *The Battle of Buena Vista* ("a descriptive Fantasie for the Piano"), he was up to Op. 101; six years later, he had trebled his output: the *Gothamite Quick Step* of 1853 is Op. 352. Another half-dozen years, and Grobe's extensive and thorough *New Method for the Piano-Forte* (Philadelphia, 1859) came out as Op. 1100. Almost in the same breath was issued an *Italian Medley*, Op. 1102, on opera airs by Rossini, Donizetti, Verdi, and others. The mid-century fad for the jog-trot rhythm of the polka was reflected in Grobe's *Tommy Polka* of 1860, Op. 1211, and the Civil War naturally inspired in him an "American Medley," *Music of the Union* (Boston, 1861). More than 600 more opus numbers were yet to come, ending finally in 1870 with *Sweet Spirit, Hear My Prayer*, Op. 1998!

Programmatic and patriotic pieces, marches and dances, medleys of popular tunes and opera airs, and above all variation sets were the order of the day, pianistically speaking. When Grobe published in 1854 his *Buds and Blossoms: 60 Sacred Melodies with Brilliant Variations for the Piano* (among the melodies were Mason's *Missionary Hymn*, *Adeste Fideles*, Haydn's "The Heavens are Telling," an air from Rossini's *Stabat Mater*, another from "Mozart's 12th Mass"), the publisher obligingly printed on the back cover a catalogue of representative compositions by Grobe (Figure 4-1). One could almost write the history of early nineteenth-century America from the 215 titles listed. For our purposes, it is interesting to note that the 68 sets of variations outnumber any other type of piece; next come 52 waltzes, 28 duets (mostly dances: waltzes, polkas, and schottisches), 25 marches and quicksteps, 18 "gallops," 11 polkas, and a few each of "piano songs" and "rondos, etc."

The popularity of piano variations reveals several things about the era. One was its love of the imaginative and inventive: to the ordinary consumer-musician, what could be more delightfully titillating than to hear, through a shower of fanciful passagework, the hidden outlines of a familiar tune? What more suggestive of a composer's invention—tested, as it is in variation sets, against the given material of a theme? Another, closely related,

---

[10] *Appendix to Encyclopaedia of Music* (Boston: Oliver Ditson Company, 1875), article "Grobe." Moore's *Complete Encyclopaedia of Music* (Boston, 1854) was the first comprehensive American music encyclopedia.

CATALOGUE
OF THE

COMPOSITIONS OF CHARLES GROBE,

Published by LEE & WALKER, (Successors to George Willig,) 188 Chestnut St., Philadelphia.

WALTZES.

A Home that I Love	12½
Alpine Rose	12½
L'Amarante	12½
Amusement de Salon	12½
Barcarole	12½
Charity	12½
Chateau en Espagne	12½
Cologne Water	12½
La Confance	12½
Court Ball	12½
L'Etoile du Matin	12½
Fillmore	25
Home of my Heart	12½
Snow Flake	12½
The Lone Star	12½
The Meteor	12½
Guadalquiver	12½
Hand in Hand	12½
Kate	12½
Ladies' Smile	12½
Mazeppa, (Grand)	25
Mnemosyne, (Valse Brillante)	12½
Monterey	12½
Night and Morning	12½
O Summer Night	12½
Queen of my Soul	12½
Ole Bull's Dream	12½
Orsini, (from Lucretia Borgia)	12½
Pet, ('Call me pet names')	12½
Potpourri, (from the Bohemian Girl)	12½
Ray of Hope	12½
Rose Blanche	12½
Sans Souci	12½
Souvenir de Belleville	12½
Souvenir de Cape May	12½
Spring Flower	12½
'Tis Midnight Hour	12½
Ruby	12½
Don Pasquale	12½
Come to the Old Oak Tree	12½
By the Margin, etc	12½
Snails	12½
The Sky Lark	12½
The Magician	12½
Annie Laurie	12½
Couleur de Rose	12½
Thou art gone from my gaze	12½
True Love	12½
El Cabalera	12½
Metamores	12½
United States Grand Waltz	25
Sophie Waltz, (by Strauss)	12½

GALLOPS.

Banisher of Sadness	12½
Fausta	12½
Flying Cloud	12½
Homage aux Belles du Philadelphia	12½
Hortensia	12½
Ice Cream	12½
Les plus beau de mes jours, etc	12½
Lucy Neal	12½
Maritana	12½
Pine Apple	12½
Ray of Joy	12½
Sentinel	12½
Strawberry	12½
Unassuming	12½
Ever be Happy	12½
Comet's Flight	12½
Short and Sweet	12½
Orlando	12½

DANCES, etc.

Mirror Dance	25
Les Nymphes	25

MARCHES AND QUICKSTEPS.

Adieu et Retour	12½
Brewer of Preston Grand March	12½
Capuletti i Montecchi	25
Captain Walker's Quickstep	12½
Clay Club Quickstep	12½
General Taylor's Grand March	12½
Les Amazones	12½
Lucrezia Borgia	12½
Old Rough and Ready Quickstep	12½
Philadelphia Gals' Quickstep	12½
Alpine Horn	25
Cuba	12½
March from Lucia	12½
Festal Quickstep	12½
Spider and the Fly	12½
Virginia Rosebud Quickstep	12½
Mr. and Mrs. Jones's Quickstep	12½
March from " Il Crociato"	12½
Cuckoo Quickstep	12½
Swiss March	12½
Sixty Miles an Hour Quickstep	12½
Avant Courier Quickstep	12½
Going Ahead Quickstep	12½
Alpine March	12½
Gothamite Quickstep	25

DUETS FOR TWO PERFORMERS.

Flow gently, sweet Afton	12½
Venetian Gallop	12½
Louisville Gallop	12½
Elfin Waltz	12½
La Belle di Sud	12½
Baden-Baden Polka	12½
Affection Waltz	12½
Grand March from the Bohemian Girl	12½
Flower of America	12½
Hohnsteck Polka	25
Mollie's Dream Waltz	25
Morning Star Waltz	25
Evening Star Waltz	25
National Schottisch	25
Redowa Waltz	25
Sounds from Home	25
Henriette Polka	25
Souvenir of Germany, (Schottisch)	25
Emerald Waltz	25
Gipsy March	25
Pet Waltz	25
Jenny Lind Polka	12½
Gertrude's Dream Waltz	12½
'Tis Midnight Hour, (Waltz)	12½
Les Vents, Nos. 1, 2, 3, 4,) each	12½
London Polka Quadrilles	50
March Triumphale	25
Le Retour des Heroes	25

POLKAS.

Fidelia	12½
Lucilla	12½
La Mode	12½
My Heart and Lute	12½
Saratoga	12½
Rosa Alberton	12½
Bona Fide	12½
Ne Plus Ultra	25
The White Violet	25
Fitzgerald's Gift Polka	25
Leap Year Polka	25

PIANO SONGS.

The heart, the heart, oh, let it be	12½
Kindred Hearts	25
Look how the Stars like jewels glisten	25
The Sabbath Bells	25

VARIATIONS.

L'Amitie, (La Fille du Regiment)	38
Amusement des Amateurs	50
Bachelor Polka	50
Les Bords du Hudson	50
Charity	25
Evening Song to the Virgin	38
Les Charmes de l'Amitie	38
Chasse d'Amour	50
Clochette Polka	62½
Dearest Mae	25
I dream of my Fatherland	25
The False Friend	38
Flow gently, sweet Afton	38
O Susanna	25
Oh! would I were a Boy again	38
Ravel Polka	50
Old Uncle Ned	25
Mary Blane	25
Rosa Lee	25
Virginia Rose Bud	25
Gipsy's Wild Chant	50
Hope and the Rose	50
Monterey	25
Les Ideals	50
Song of the Regiment	38
Salut a Philadelphie	38
Les Amoureux	25
Serenade March	25
Les Troubadours	62½
La Solitude	38
What's a' the Steer Kimmer	25
Come, ye Disconsolate	38
From Greenland's Icy Mountains	38
Jerusalem, my Happy Home	38
Henrietta Polka	50
A Life on the Ocean Wave	50
Salut a Baltimore	38
La Liberte	50
Child of the Regiment	38
Song of the Drum	38
Rataplan	38
By the Sad Sea Waves	38
Love Not	25
Les Fleurs du Plaisir	50
Columbia the Gem of the Ocean	38
Jenny Lind Polka	50
Vesper Hymn	38
I would not live alway	38
Strike the Cymbal	38
Peace, troubled Soul	38
Far, far, o'er Hill and Dell	38
Fading, still Fading	38
Messenger Bird	38
Widow of Nain	38
Adeste Fideles	38
There is nothing true but Heaven	38
Sicilian Hymn	38
Pleyel's German Hymn	38
Pilgrim Fathers	38
Prayer from Moses	38
Prayer from Zampa	38
Prayer from Tancredi	38
Watchman, tell us of the Night	38
Faith .... 38 Hope	38
Washington's March	38
Maretzek's Rondo Finale	50
Yes, I Remember, (answer to Ben Bolt)	38
Wings of a Dove	38

RONDOS, etc.

Bellone, (Polonaise a la Militaire)	38
Diane, (Rondeau de Chasse)	25
El Sinsonte de Camagne	25
La Tendresse, (Rondoletto)	12½
The Talisman, (Rondo Militaire)	50
Love's Influence, (Rondo)	25
Potpourri en forme de Rondeau	25

☞ **Just Published, 1st and 2d Nos. of GROBE'S WORLD OF MUSIC,** an unsurpassable Collection of Music, consisting of 100 of the most charming Melodies ever offered to the Musical World.

☞ **LEE & WALKER'S** Publications may be had of the principal Music Dealers in N. York, Boston, Baltimore, N. Orleans, Cincinnati, St. Louis, Louisville, Charleston, Savannah, Pittsburg, Detroit, Chicago, and other Cities of the U. States and Canada.

FIGURE 4-1. A list of piano works (incomplete) by Charles Grobe, from the back cover of his *Wings of a Dove* (1854).

was its love of the improvisatory in performance. The concert pianist at that time was still expected as a matter of course to improvise, sometimes on familiar tunes, often on themes called out to him by the audience. Almost by definition, such improvisations took the form of variations; and if not of variations, then of a "fantasy," less formally strict than variations but no less a matter of creating new shapes out of old. In a survey of New York piano concerts between 1849 and 1865, one researcher found that one out of every

three works presented was a fantasy on popular themes.[11] Variations and
fantasies were also the simplest and most foolproof substructure for virtuoso
scaffolding, since neither form nor thematic content was problematic and all
attention could be paid by both performer and listener to the treatment of
the musical material. It is against this background that some comments made
by Gottschalk toward the end of his career about the improved taste of
American audiences must be read. He noted in his journal for December
8, 1864, that "at the time of my first return from Europe [1853] I was
constantly deploring the want of public interest for pieces purely sentimental;
the public listened with indifference; in order to arouse it, it became necessary to astound it; grand movements, tours de force, and noise had alone
the privilege in piano music." Now, however, audiences were willing to
listen to "pieces purely sentimental"—pieces that, in Gottschalk's terms,
had real musical content and "feeling," not just spectacular fantasies and
pyrotechnical variations.

If Grobe can represent for us the legion of minor composers of piano
music for the household market, a few others of the period before the Civil
War emerge as composers with higher aspirations and more distinct musical
personalities. Most notable are Anthony Philip Heinrich, Richard Hoffman,
William Mason, and Gottschalk.

Heinrich was born in Bohemia in 1781, emigrated to America about
1810, and died in New York in 1861. He was this country's first—and without
a doubt its most wildly enthusiastic—Romantic in music. Intoxicated with
the natural grandeur of the New World, fascinated with the history of his
adopted country, enchanted with the American Indian as "noble savage,"
and above all eager to be called an "American Musician," he poured out
hundreds of pieces of the most extravagantly bizarre Romantic program-
matism. Most of these were on American subjects, although his musical
speech remained essentially that of central Europe.

Heinrich came first to Philadelphia, where he was a merchant and
served as volunteer director of music at the Southwark Theatre. Beset by
financial reverses, in the fall of 1817 he decided to try his lot elsewhere and
traveled via Pittsburgh to Lexington, Kentucky—still virtually a wilderness
village. He began composing music at about that time; to a pathetic plea for
funds written late in his life (1856) he added this postscript:

> P.S. The Composer did not commence writing music until verging upon the
> fortieth year of his age, when dwelling by chance in the then solitary wilds
> and primeval forests of Kentucky. It was from a mere accident that music ever
> became his profession. . . .[12]

---

[11] Andrew C. Minor, "Piano Concerts in New York City 1849–1865" (unpublished
Master's thesis, University of Michigan, 1947), p. 475.

[12] Heinrich, manuscript scrapbook, Library of Congress (Music Division), p. 836.

Once embarked on composition, however, Heinrich poured out songs; piano works; marches and dances; choral music; and orchestral overtures, fantasies, concertos, and symphonies. His "opera prima," published at Philadelphia in 1820, was titled *The Dawning of Music in Kentucky, or The Pleasures of Harmony in the Solitudes of Nature*, a huge collection described by the composer as including "*Songs and Airs for the Voice and Pianoforte, Waltzes, Cotillions, Minuets, Polonaises, Marches, Variations* with some pieces of a national character adapted for the Piano Forte and also calculated for the lovers of the Violin" (Preface reprinted in *ACS*, pp. 42–43; also in *EAM* 10, a facsimile reprint of *The Dawning of Music in Kentucky* and of Heinrich's Op. 2, *The Western Minstrel*). Heinrich might also have noted that he included a minuet version of *Hail! Columbia* and a waltz version of *Yankee Doodle*; that the "military waltz" *Avance et Retraite* is to be played from beginning to end, then backward to the beginning again (note the title); that *A Chromatic Ramble, of the Peregrine Harmonist* is a tour de force of harmonic complexity, a piece that literally must be seen to be believed; and that the collection is crowned with a fantastic quintet for piano and strings, *The Yankee Doodleiad*, based on trumpet calls, *Hail! Columbia*, and *Yankee Doodle* again (with fourteen variations, interrupted in the middle by an interlude on *The President's March* labeled "Huzza for Washington!").

Heinrich's was an expansive and mercurial muse: he himself characterized his music as being "full of strange ideal somersets and capricios." (The pontifical J. S. Dwight of Boston said it was "bewildering . . . wild and complicated.")[13] And this is true of most of his piano music; some of it, however, is gentle, sweet, and direct—for example, "The Laurel Waltz" (*NW* 257:s2/2), from *The Ellsler Dances* of 1841.

Richard Hoffman (1831–1909) came to America from his native England as a boy of sixteen, having already studied with a constellation of German pianists (but not with Liszt, as is often claimed). He settled in New York, where besides teaching and composing he played concerts. Competent and agreeable ("a perfect musician, a distinguished and modest man . . . an artist and a *gentleman*," said Gottschalk with unusual generosity), Hoffman wrote a piano music of flowery grace through almost one hundred opus numbers. *La Gazelle* (1858?) was a favorite, with its Lisztian arabesques (Example 4-6) and its fashionable French title evoking the image of Chopin.

William Mason (1829–1908), the third son of Lowell Mason, was a pupil of Liszt during the last of his five years' study in Germany (1849–54). His main role, like that of his father, was more that of tastemaker and teacher than composer; he was also a most competent performer. He concertized

[13] *The Harbinger*, July 4, 1846. Dwight's lengthy review of a sixty-fifth birthday concert for Heinrich, almost a one-man show, is reprinted in full in W. T. Upton, *Anthony Philip Heinrich* (New York: Columbia University Press, 1939), pp. 199–201.

EXAMPLE 4-6. R. Hoffman, *La Gazelle* (Mainz, Ger., and New York: B. Schott's Söhnen, ca. 1858), measures 8–15.

in the northern states from the East Coast to Chicago, offering solo piano recitals without the usual interpolations of song from an "assisting vocalist"; he played music of high caliber, if almost exclusively Germanic, although his recital-closing improvisations might, because of audience demand, have to be based on *Yankee Doodle* counterpointed with *Old Hundred*. He also formed an influential chamber-music group, the Mason-Thomas Quartet (actually a five-member ensemble—a string quartet and Mason as pianist). For thirteen seasons (1855–68) they offered New York City its finest chamber music; the very first concert (November 27, 1855) included the premiere performance of Brahms's Trio in B major, Op. 8, as well as works by Schubert, Wagner, Chopin, and Mendelssohn, among others. Mason was also a renowned piano teacher. His own piano music seems most often proper but bloodless, without even Hoffman's airy Lisztian flair (an exception being the early *Silver Spring*, Op. 6, recorded on NW 257:s2/6, along with the more typically genteel *Pastoral Novelette* of 1895); Liszt, however, politely called Mason's *Amitié pour amitié* (Example 4–7) "a charming little piece," his *Etude de concert*, Op. 9, and *Valse caprice*, Op. 17, "distinguished in style and of good effect."[14] Chopin's *Berceuse*, Op. 57, is certainly the model for

[14] William Mason, *Memories of a Musical Life* (New York: The Century Co., 1902), pp. 88, 294.

EXAMPLE 4-7. W. Mason, *Amitié pour Amitié*, 2nd ed, (Boston: N. Richardson, 1854), measures 1–8.

Mason's *Lullaby* of 1857; the reference to "Three Blind Mice" is surely unconscious and unintended.

Without question the most colorful personality, the most articulate intelligence, the most talented performer, and the most provocative composer among the mid-nineteenth-century pianists was Louis Moreau Gottschalk (1829–69). Born in the racial and ethnic melting pot of New Orleans, Gottschalk's lineage was itself cosmopolitan: his father was a cultivated English Jew educated in Germany; his mother was the daughter of a prosperous baker of French ancestry. Gottschalk grew up in the Vieux Carré quarter, hearing among other kinds of music that of the many Negroes and Latin Americans in the southern trade center. In 1842 he was sent to Paris to study, not returning to America until 1853 as a renowned virtuoso and keyboard composer. From then on, his life was virtually one long concert tour, all over the United States, Canada, the West Indies, Panama, Mexico, and South America, where he died at Rio de Janeiro, only forty years of age.

Even as a youth in Paris, Gottschalk was praised by Chopin and Berlioz, and his playing was spoken of in the same breath with that of Liszt and Thalberg. He became the darling of the Paris salons not only for his virtuosity but also for his early compositions, which were heard as exotic mélanges of Afro-Caribbean rhythms and Creole melodies, with a Chopinesque overlay of virtuoso passagework. According to a review by Berlioz of a concert in 1851, "everybody in Europe now knows [Gottschalk's] *Bamboula, Le Bananier, Le Mancenillier, La Savane,* and twenty other ingenious fantasies in which the nonchalant grace of tropical melody assuages so agree-

ably our restless and insatiable passion for novelty."[15] Back in the Americas
and embarked on a career as traveling virtuoso, Gottschalk became a sort
of living player piano: "I have become stupid with it. I have the appearance
of an automaton under the influence of a voltaic pile. My fingers move on
the keyboard with feverish heat. . . . The sight of a piano sets my hair on
end." He had just finished his last tour of 1862: "I have given eighty-five
concerts in four months and a half. I have traveled fifteen thousand miles
by train. At St. Louis I gave seven concerts in six days; at Chicago, five in
four days. A few more weeks in this way and I would have become an
idiot."[16] In an age of virtuosity, Gottschalk was the virtuoso incarnate. He
has also rightfully been called "our first matinee idol": the young American
music student Amy Fay lamented in Berlin upon hearing of his death, "The
infatuation that I and 999,999 other American girls once felt for him, still
lingers in my breast."[17]

Like Chopin and other pianist-composers of the era, Gottschalk published little of his music except solo piano compositions, of which there are
just over one hundred. He composed in addition some songs, a few orchestral
works, and several operas (their music mostly lost). The pieces mentioned
by Berlioz are among the earliest and most interesting of the piano compositions, "New Orleans" pieces published in France and advertised there
as the work of "Gottschalk de la Louisiane." Based mostly on Negro and
Creole tunes, they tend to begin with marvelously fresh, strong ideas (see
Example 4-8), which before long are overwhelmed by showers of scales,
arpeggios, passagework of all kinds. Youthful, exuberant, and immensely
promising, they are nevertheless overlong and lacking in tonal or formal
interest, as the genuinely gifted fledgling composer gives way to the virtuoso
prodigy. The slightly later *Le Banjo*, Op. 15 (1854 or 1855; a so-called *Banjo
second* was actually composed first), probably has in common with Stephen
Foster's *Camptown Races* (see Example 5-8) a source in American Negro
song, if it was not based on Foster's. Full of ingenious strumming, *Le Banjo*
is one of Gottschalk's best works, although even an enthusiast like pianist
John Kirkpatrick admits that it has a "characteristic redundance and tonal
monotony."[18]

Gottschalk mined other folk and popular song veins as he toured

[15] Quoted in Jeanne Behrend, ed., *Notes of a Pianist* (New York: Alfred A. Knopf,
1964) p. xxii.
[16] Both quotations from *Notes of a Pianist*, p. 102. Gottschalk's journal, written between
1857 and 1868, is a fascinating, kaleidoscopic account of his travels in the West Indies, the
United States, and Latin America.
[17] *Music-Study in Germany* (New York: Macmillan, Inc., 1897), p. 42. It was Irving
Lowens who first equated the idolatry of Gottschalk with that of later stage and screen stars;
see *MMEA*, pp. 223–33.
[18] "Observations on 4 volumes and supplement of the works of Louis Moreau Gottschalk" (typescript; New York Public Library's Music Division).

EXAMPLE 4-8. L. M. Gottschalk, early "New Orleans" pieces. (a) *Bamboula*, Op. 2, measures 1–7. (b) *Le Bananier*, Op. 5, measures 1–8.

through Spain (*La jota aragonesa*, Op. 14), the West Indies (*Souvenir de Porto Rico*, Op. 31; *Souvenir de la Havane*, Op. 39), and South America (*Grande Fantaisie triomphale sur l'hymne national brésilien*, Op. 69). Only occasionally, as in *Souvenir de Porto Rico* ("*Marche des Gibaros*"), does formal control restrain technical exuberance; however, in that piece of 1857–58, based on a native Christmas song (Example 4-9), Gottschalk achieves a

EXAMPLE 4-9. Puerto Rican *aguinaldo*, beginning, and L. M. Gottschalk, *Souvenir de Porto Rico* (Mainz, Ger.: B. Schott's Söhnen, 1859), measures 17–20.

minor masterpiece with the arching dynamic curve, waxing and waning, of a "patrol" piece and the strong syncopations of Afro-Caribbean dance music (Example 4-10). Perhaps Gottschalk's greatest *pastiche* on folk and popular

EXAMPLE 4-10. Gottschalk, *Souvenir de Porto Rico*, climax (measures 189–193).

source materials, and certainly the noisiest, was *l'Union*, Op. 48 (1852–62), a grand "paraphrase de concert sur les airs nationaux" (*Yankee Doodle, The Star-Spangled Banner, Hail! Columbia*, and some trumpet calls) completed at the height of the Civil War and received in Philadelphia, according to the composer's journal, with "unheard-of enthusiasm . . . recalls, encores, hurrahs, etc.!"

Another side of Gottschalk's art was that of the "purely sentimental" piece, as he called it, the genre piece of meditative and "poetic" reflection. Among the most carefully worked of these are *Ricordati*, "méditation," Op. 26, a Chopinesque nocturne; *The Last Hope*, "méditation religieuse," Op. 16 (1854), Gottschalk's monument to pious sentimentality, his most notoriously successful tear-jerker, but withal a shrewdly contrived series of daringly chromatic introductions to an indestructible arc of songful melody; *Berceuse*, Op. 47 (ca. 1861), based on a French folk song, *Fais dodo, mon bébé*; and *Suis-moi*, Op. 45 (ca. 1861). *The Dying Poet* (1863?), one of "some contraband pieces that are to be published under the aegis of a borrowed paternity" (as Gottschalk archly described his pseudonym "Seven Octaves"), and *Morte!!* (1868?), which had, said Gottschalk, "un succès de larmes," were famous pieces in the vein of *The Last Hope*.

Gottschalk noted in his journal one night in 1865 that his had been a life of "playing the piano, of having composed two or three hundred pieces, of having given seven or eight thousand concerts, of having given to the poor one hundred or one hundred and fifty thousand dollars, [and] of having been knighted twice." The remark may have been one of Romantic hyperbole, but so were Gottschalk's personality and his music.

ORCHESTRAS

The Romantics loved the orchestra. Convinced that instrumental music in general was the purest, most sublime music, they conceived of the orchestra as a kind of super-instrument. And seeking an ever-broader coloristic and expressive spectrum, they enlarged it from a smallish ensemble of one or two dozen players into a giant symphonic machine of more than a hundred. If during the era the organ was king of instruments, the piano the queen, the orchestra was emperor.

One of the most characteristic trends in American music since the mid-nineteenth century has been the proliferation of independent symphony orchestras. Whereas in Europe such orchestras have hardly existed apart from opera houses (although a few, typically state-subsidized, are now virtually independent), here the symphony orchestra has tended to develop as an independent entity, reflecting our penchant for concerts rather than opera. The American notion of a "permanent" orchestra, and one supported by public subscriptions and box-office receipts, has been a by-product of the rise of public concerts and a mass audience that I discussed in Chapter Three. Two decades before the Civil War, the first "permanent" orchestra still in existence today, the New York Philharmonic, was founded. In 1984, the American Symphony Orchestra League counted 162 American orchestras in the largest categories: 30 "major" orchestras (with annual operating budgets over $3,250,000), 37 "regional" ($900,000 to $3,250,000), and 95 "metropolitan" ($240,000 to $900,000); and this was only the tip of the iceberg, for in the same year the league recorded 1410 other orchestras in lesser categories (urban, community, college, and youth), and still others probably existed.[19]

The beginnings of this astonishing development go back to the early nineteenth century, when Gottlieb Graupner, who had been one of the musicians in Salomon's London orchestra during the famous visit of Haydn in 1791–92, organized a group of Boston instrumentalists into a "Philo-Harmonic Society" to meet informally and play through symphonies of Haydn and others. Notices of rehearsals appeared regularly in the semi-weekly Boston newspapers from October 4, 1809, and the society soon began playing for the public. John Rowe Parker, editor of the first American music periodical, *The Euterpeiad, or Musical Intelligencer* (1820–23), signalized the historic importance of Graupner's instrumental organization (and the other society Graupner helped to found) when he wrote, "Until the formation of the Philo-Harmonic for instrumental, and the institution of the Haydn and Handel Societies, for vocal performances, regular concerts have never succeeded in this metropolis" (*Euterpeiad*, April 8, 1820). They did not succeed well enough, apparently, for the Philo-Harmonic Society of Boston gave its last concert late in 1824.

Meanwhile, in Philadephia a Musical Fund Society was organized in 1820 by Benjamin Carr and others; it was active as a choral-orchestral orga-

---

[19] The figures derive from the illuminating article "Orchestras," by Howard Shanet, in *TNGDAM*.

nization to 1857, and more sporadically to the present. In the nearby Moravian center of Bethlehem a Philharmonic Society was founded, also in 1820, which flourished until about 1839. And in 1842 a group of musicians led by Ureli Corelli Hill (1802–75), Henry Christian Timm (1811–92), and William Scharfenberg (1819–95) founded the New York Philharmonic Society; its first concert included Beethoven's Fifth Symphony, Weber's *Oberon* overture, another overture (by the Bohemian-German composer Kalliwoda), a piano quintet by Hummel, and various vocal solos and duets. Numbering about fifty-five players, give or take the few who found it impossible to give up other jobs to play in the three concerts of the first season (four in each season thereafter through 1858), the New York Philharmonic initially had no single conductor; six of the musicians shared the duties. From the 500-seat hall of the Apollo Rooms on Broadway below Canal Street, the orchestra graduated to Niblo's Theatre (Broadway and Prince Street), then in 1856 further uptown to the elegant Academy of Music at 14th Street and Irving Place.

That our first permament orchestra should have been established in New York City reflected an important social development: New York's sky-rocket rise, stimulated especially by the opening of the Erie Canal in 1825, to supremacy as the nation's first port, largest city, and principal commercial center. As such it became also the nation's center of those performing arts that rested on a foundation of mass-audience support. New York's pre-eminence as a musical performance center already by the mid-nineteenth century is confirmed by the fact that not until 1881 would the second permanent American symphony orchestra, the Boston Symphony, be established.

Three other orchestras heard in pre-Civil War America should be cited briefly here for their catalytic influence on American music. One was the Germania Musical Society, a group of twenty-five young musicians who left Berlin in May 1848, heading for the United States "in order to further in the hearts of this politically free people the love of the fine art of music through performance of the greatest German composers."[20] The Germanians' first concerts in New York led to others elsewhere, and the well-trained, well-balanced ensemble was heard, before its dissolution in 1854 (all its members by then American citizens), in more than nine hundred concerts in many American and Canadian cities from Richmond to Minneapolis and from Boston to St. Louis (where one young woman, hearing Beethoven's Second Symphony for the first time, remarked, "Well, ain't that funny music!"). American attitudes as to the "standard repertory" of orchestral music were strongly shaped by this group's concentration on Germanic works from Haydn to Wagner.

[20] H. F. Albrecht, *Skizzen aus dem Leben der Musik-Gesellschaft Germania* (Philadelphia, 1869), trans. H. Earle Johnson, "The Germania Musical Society," *MQ*, XXXIX (1953), 75.

Another, briefer symphonic visitor was the orchestra brought from London to New York for one year by the French conductor Louis Antoine Jullien (1812–60). "A splendid, bold, and dazzlingly successful humbug," wrote the New York *Courier and Enquirer*. To his twenty-seven piece orchestra Jullien added more than sixty local musicians (among them two young violinists named George Bristow and Theodore Thomas, of whom more shortly); on August 29, 1853, after a strenuous advertising campaign, he initiated a series of "Monster Concerts for the Masses" at Castle Garden. The *Courier and Enquirer* had to admit that "the discipline of his orchestra is marvelous." The *New York Clipper* was not so charitable; that lively precursor of *Variety* and *Billboard*, which proclaimed itself "A Weekly Sporting Paper, devoted to the Ring, the Turf, Yachting, Pedestrianism, Cricket, Rowing Matches, Theatricals, Music, and the various sports of the Old World and the New," took up the cudgel against "these 'highfalutin' gimcracks" in its issue of September 3:

> There were not quite 3,000 persons in the building, and perhaps not quite 2,500 who paid for their tickets [at 50¢ each]. . . . It is now more difficult to humbug us than it was a few years since. . . . With encouragement, America can produce musical wonders as well as reaping machines; an American Forrest [Edwin Forrest (1806–72), American actor] as well as American Clippers. . . . Several European celebrities have lately returned to their homes, not at all pleased with our reception of them. Stand fast, Americans! encourage those who are with us. . . . Monster concerts for the masses, indeed!

The chauvinist tone is of interest: here spoke the vernacular tradition of American culture, weary of the European monopoly over American cultivated taste. In its next issue (September 10) the *Clipper* chuckled over the "but middling success" of Jullien's nightly concerts, and on September 17, headlining "A Failure in New York" for Jullien, it urged its readers to "encourage our own musicians, and endeavor to do away with the puffing system adopted by foreign professionals." Jullien's concerts had not in fact failed, but he got the message: he began to include some works by American-born composers on his programs, among them Bristow and William Fry. It was the first recognition that American composers of symphonic music had had.

A notable graduate of Jullien's orchestra and of nine years' playing experience with the New York Philharmonic (1854–63) was Theodore Thomas (1835–1905). His potential as a director was recognized when he was a violinist in the group organized by William Mason in 1855 for chamber-music evenings: Mason conceded in his *Memories* that Thomas's "was the dominating influence, felt and acknowledged by us all." After some tentative beginnings in 1862 and 1863, Thomas initiated a long and brilliant career as conductor of his own orchestra late in 1864. An astute impresario and a canny program builder, Thomas knew how to create and hold an audience with programs that might be called crescent-shaped, with the heaviest fare in the center; thus he might flank orchestral movements by Beethoven, Schubert, Mendelssohn, even the radical Wagner, with simpler music: the waltzes of Strauss, the Bach-Gounod *Ave Maria*, and other crowd-pleasers. It was an original format, which gave up the old reliance on maintaining interest by a potpourri of instrumental and vocal works, and one destined to become a stereotype. Characteristic is the following program[21] from one of Thomas's Summer Night Concerts in New York's Central Park Garden (August 7, 1868):

Coronation March	Johann Strauss
Overture to *Die Heimkehre aus der Fremde*	Mendelssohn
Waltz from *Masaniello*	Auber

Intermission

Overture to *Tannhäuser*	Wagner
2nd movement, Symphony No. 8	Beethoven
3rd movement (Scherzo), Symphony No. 7 (C major)	Schubert

Intermission

Grand March for the Schiller Centenary	Meyerbeer
Overture to *Mignon*	Thomas
Ave Maria	Bach-Gounod
Waltz, "Die Sphärenklänge"	Johann Strauss
Turkish March [arranged from Piano Sonato, K. 311?]	Mozart

Between 1869 and 1878 the Thomas Orchestra made regular, lengthy tours through the East and the Middle West as far as Chicago, with a roster of about fifty players.[22] Both in New York and throughout the country, its influence on standards of performance and on ideas of a standard orchestral repertory was immense. The modern symphonic ideal, according to which dozens of players submit through careful rehearsal to the rigorous, not to say autocratic, direction of a conductor in the interests of polished perfection, was Thomas's ideal. His ideas on repertory were inevitably governed by an

---

[21] Adapted from Rose Fay Thomas, *Memoirs of Theodore Thomas* (New York: Moffett, Yard and Company, 1911), p. 49. Later programs of Thomas's orchestra had fewer "light" works and included complete symphonies; some were one-man exhibitions of works by a single composer.

[22] When it played the opening concert of Harvard's Sanders Theatre, November 21, 1876, the makeup of the orchestra was eight first violins, eight second violins, four violas, four cellos, and four basses, plus woodwinds and brasses in pairs, according to *Dwight's Journal of Music*, XXXVI (March 3, 1877), p. 398. Presumably there was a percussionist as well.

Austro-Germanic bias; nevertheless, he occasionally played music by American composers. They were very few, however; Thomas had high standards and, as he put it, "I do not believe in playing inferior works merely because they are American" (*Memoirs*, p. 67).

Thomas became conductor of the New York Philharmonic in 1877, resigned for an abortive year as first head of the Cincinnati College of Music, resumed the Philharmonic directorship in 1880, then moved permanently to Chicago in 1891 to become conductor of the newly established Chicago Symphony Orchestra. For the last half of the nineteenth century he was the acknowledged master of the symphony orchestra, the first American virtuoso conductor.

ORCHESTRAL MUSIC

What about American orchestral music, as opposed to American orchestras, in the period up to the Civil War?

With only a few orchestras in the land and with orchestral music, as distinct from music for solo instruments or small chamber groups, identified mainly with European composers and conductors, it is not surprising that American composers produced comparatively little symphonic music. Nevertheless, a few composers stand out as our first symphonists.

"The Beethoven of America" is what Parker's *Euterpeiad* called Anthony Philip Heinrich in its issue of April 13, 1822. We have met Heinrich previously (see pp. 82-83) as a composer of bizarre and extravagant virtuoso piano music, songs, and chamber works. He also had orchestral aspirations (and was to fulfill them); in fact his first historically noteworthy act, upon arrival in Kentucky in the autumn of 1817, was to organize a benefit concert—the beneficiary was Heinrich himself—in which he not only played the violin and the piano but also directed the "full band" in a "Simfonia con Minuetto" by Beethoven—perhaps the First Symphony, not one of the bigger, later ones, but certainly an extraordinary kind of work to present in the pioneer town of Lexington, Kentucky, in November 1817.

The major part of Heinrich's orchestral music consists of descriptive symphonies in several elaborately titled movements, or one-movement programmatic fantasies divided into contrasting sections. Their subjects are those of a hyper-enthusiastic, Romantic newcomer to America: Indian lore (*Pushmataha, a Venerable Chief of a Western Tribe of Indians*, 1831; *Manitou Mysteries; or The Voice of the Great Spirit. Gran sinfonia misteriosa indiana*, before 1845); American history (*The Treaty of William Penn with the Indians. Concerto grosso. An American national dramatic divertissement, for a full orchestra, comprising successively 6 different characteristic* movements, united in one . . ., 1834, revised 1847; *Der Felsen von Plymouth; oder, Die Landung der Pilger Väter in Neu-England*); the American land-scape (*The War of the Elements and the Thundering of Niagara. Capriccio grande for a full orchestra*, before 1845); hero-worship (*Schiller. Grande sinfonia dramatica*, in five movements composed at various times between 1820 and 1857; *The Tomb of Genius: To the Memory of Mendelssohn-Bartholdy. Sinfonia sacra, for grande orchestra*, after 1847 and before 1857; *To the Spirit of Beethoven*, in fourteen "tableaux," before 1845); and finally, patriotic encomiums (*The Jubilee. A Grand national song of triumph*, for orchestra and chorus, 1840). Heinrich's friendship with the great ornithol-ogist and painter John James Audubon led to two programmatic symphonies, *The Columbiad; or, Migration of American Wild Passenger Pigeons* (1837) and *The Ornithological Combat of Kings; or, The Condor of the Andes and the Eagle of the Cordilleras* (1847, rev. 1856). Heinrich considered the latter (recorded on *NW* 208:sl) his finest work; "A grand symphony. Extracted and arranged for a full orchestra, with some deviations, from a descriptive con-certo grosso vocale of the same title and subject," the twenty-five-minute piece is in four movements—"The Conflict of the Condor in the Air," "The Repose of the Condor," "The Combat of the Condor on Land," and "Victory of the Condor."

The style of these extraordinary orchestral outbursts is indeed one of "strange . . . somersets and capriccios" (to borrow Heinrich's own charac-terization of his music), mingling simple dance tunes (especially folkish Ländler types) and elaborately chromatic melodies; crystal-clear Classic-era harmo-nies and wildly modulating passages; basically homophonic, diatonic textures and a profusion of decorative chromatic counterpoints (most often solo wood-wind voices over a background of strings); predictable, periodic phrase forms and surprising extensions (or instead of the latter, the opposite: unexpected grand pauses of dead silence). For a latecomer to composition, Heinrich had a remarkable ear for orchestral color and an expansive imagination that led him to write for unusual instruments as well as the conventional orchestral core. The third ("The Adagio") of the four movements of the symphonically scaled *Manitou Mysteries* includes extensive and effective use of pizzicato; the first movement of *The Ornithological Combat of Kings* (the scoring of which occasionally reaches as many as thirty-seven different parts) reveals imaginative use of triangle and the third movement freshly conceived writing for percussion and for solo woodwinds. Among the instruments called for in the very large orchestra of *The Indian War Council* is a "harmonicon" or "glasschord," the mechanized set of musical glasses that had been improved or perhaps even invented by Benjamin Franklin. *Pushmataha* is a fourteen-minute fantasy for thirty-three different orchestral voices including piccolo, basset horn, serpent, contrabassoon, three kinds of drums, triangle, cymbals, and tambourine as well as the normal full orchestra. For reasons unclear (but possibly relating to the first public Independence Day celebration at which S. F. Smith's *America* was sung to the tune: July 4, 1831), this paean to a mighty Indian chief culminates with a majestic and characteristically chromaticized quotation of *God Save the King* (Example 4-11).[23]

EXAMPLE 4-11. A. Heinrich, *Pushmataha* (1831), measures 460–65 (reduced from the Library of Congress copy of the orchestral score).

It might be expected that the intense musical life of the German-speaking communities in Pennsylvania would have inspired some orchestral music, but the Moravians seem for the most part to have been content with European scores, and thus far we know of no orchestral productions of the other sects. One of the earliest known American orchestral works is a Symphony in D, in two tiny movements, by William C. Peters (1805–86), composed

[23] Wilbur R. Maust offers another conjecture in his interesting essay "The American Indian in the Orchestral Music of Anthony Philip Heinrich," in *Music East and West: Essays in Honor of Walter Kaufmann*, ed. Thomas Noblitt (New York: Pendragon Press, 1981), pp. 309–25: "The . . . introduction of this tune may be due to the facts that Pushmataha was an ardent supporter of the U.S. and that he was honored at his funeral 'with a great procession and booming guns'." (The quotation is from the entry on Pushmataha by Katherine E. Crane in the *Dictionary of American Biography*.)

in 1831 for the Harmony Society of Economy, beyond Pittsburgh in western Pennsylvania and hardly more than a frontier settlement in 1831. Charles Hommann (ca. 1800–after 1862) won a prize in 1835 from the Musical Fund Society of Philadelphia for an overture and contributed a four-movement symphony in E♭ and an overture in C to the Philharmonic Society of Bethlehem.

George F. Bristow (1825–98) and William H. Fry (1813–64) were the best-known mid-century composers of orchestral music in New York. Bristow was the better trained, a professional violinist and conductor who composed several symphonies in a polished Mendelssohnian style, among them the fine Third Symphony in F♯ minor, Op. 26 (performed by the New York Philharmonic under Carl Bergmann in 1859), and a more lengthy Fourth Symphony ("Arcadian"), Op. 49 (1874), which includes perhaps the first use of an American Indian melody in a work of art-music. The opera *Rip Van Winkle* (1855) and cantatas *The Great Republic* (1879) and *Niagara* (1898) have strong overtures. Fry, famous as a noisy champion of American composers amid the deluge of Europeans just before the Civil War, composed four symphonies, *Santa Claus, The Breaking Heart, Childe Harold,* and *A Day in the Country,* all performed by Jullien's orchestra in 1853–54 and all provided with interminable programs which explain, but do not make coherent, the naive tone-painting and narrative forms of the works. An *Overture to "Macbeth"* (1862) reminiscent of Auber is well scored and never dull.

The Romantic tendency to gigantism, exemplified by Jullien's "monster concerts," is suggested also by two in which Gottschalk was involved in Cuba and Rio de Janeiro. For a concert at Havana early in 1860 Gottschalk composed several works, among them the *Marcha Triunful y Final de Opera,* long thought lost. His orchestra, he reported in his journal, numbered 650, plus 87 choristers, 15 solo singers, 50 drums, and 80 trumpets—"that is to say, nearly nine hundred persons bellowing and blowing to see who could scream the loudest." And at Rio in 1869, for a concert which included the Andante of his symphony *La Nuit des tropiques* (1858–59), Gottschalk dreamed of "eight hundred performers and eighty drums to lead."[24] He got about 650, made up from bands of the Brazilian National Guard, the Imperial Navy, the Army, and the War Arsenal, and from three orchestras assembled for the occasion (November 11, 1869). *La Nuit des tropiques,* which may or may not be complete with the Andante and Finale movement that are extant, is a colorful work in the French tradition of Berlioz; John Kirkpatrick's "Observations . . ." cite its "poetic atmosphere" and "surprising expansion" of line.[25] The brilliant, brassy Finale, which calls for separate sections of

[24] Octavia Hensel, *Life and Letters of Louis Moreau Gottschalk* (Boston: Oliver Ditson Company, 1870), p. 174.
[25] The complicated history of the "Night in the Tropics" is well told by Richard Jackson in his notes for NW 208 (side 2 of which offers the work in a two-piano transcription).

cornets, trumpets, trombones, and euphoniums, with each section divided, is overwhelming. Another symphony by Gottschalk is the one-movement Symphony No. 2, "A Montevideo" of 1865–68 (the score of which, like those of the other Gottschalk works just cited, is in the New York Public Library).

OPERA

Of all the kinds of art-music of the American cultivated tradition between 1820 and the Civil War, the least significant, and probably the least widely heard, was opera. The ballad opera of the eighteenth century, or at least plays with music, continued in unbroken tradition through the period. Their function, however, changed with the introduction of other kinds of music and musical theater, which tended to keep the musical play a vernacular entertainment without any growing pretensions to becoming "fine art." By the 1860s the ballad opera as such was virtually nonexistent, except in transformations like *The Black Crook* of 1866 (an extravagant mixture of Frenchy ballet and Germanic melodrama, to an American variation on the plot of Weber's *Der Freischütz*) or parodies like those of the minstrel shows at Buckley's Ethiopian Opera House in New York. European operas gained a foothold in America during the period, however, and the first "grand operas" by American composers were produced.

By far the most lively, as well as the earliest, operatic center was New Orleans, where a cultivated French contingent of the cosmopolitan population had maintained support for French opera from 1796, when the theater on St. Peter Street produced Grétry's *Sylvain*. In the 1805–6 season alone, the St. Peter Theatre produced sixteen different operas by nine composers, among them Monsigny, Grétry, Dalayrac, Boieldieu, Méhul, and Paisiello—and all these for a town of only twelve thousand people. With the establishment of a permanent opera company at the Orleans Theater, New Orleans was unrivalled as operatic center of America. Northern cities— Boston, Philadelphia, Baltimore—heard their first grand opera when the New Orleans company toured during the seven summers from 1827 to 1833; and New York admitted that the southern troupe was "fully equal to that we imported from foreigners," referring to Manuel García's Italian-opera company, which had given New York its first foreign-language opera in 1825.[26]

García's, the first of a number of traveling companies to play in New York, was to stay a year. Its repertory favored Rossini: *Il Barbiere di Siviglia* was the first production, followed by *Cenerentola, Semiramide, Tancredi,*

---

[26] The quotation, from the New York *American* as cited in the New Orleans *L'Argus* of August 24, 1827, is given in Henry Kmen, *Music in New Orleans* (Baton Rouge: Louisiana State University Press, 1966), p. 125.

Il Turco in Italia, and Mozart's *Don Giovanni*. Later troupes discovered a substantial opera audience in New York, especially for Italian works—not only by Mozart and Rossini but even more especially by Bellini, Donizetti, and early Verdi. This vogue culminated in the construction and opening of the Astor Place Opera House in 1847 and, in 1854, the Academy of Music (with 4600 seats the largest theater in the United States). Opening night at the Astor Place featured Verdi's *Ernani;* at the Academy of Music, Bellini's *Norma*. German opera gained a foothold only after the wave of German immigration after 1848; in the 1862–63 season, however, New Yorkers heard some sixty-five performances of German operas, the favorites being Weber's *Der Freischütz*, Beethoven's *Fidelio*, and Mozart's *Magic Flute* and *The Abduction from the Seraglio*.

As with orchestral music in New York, the American names to reckon with in opera of the period are those of Fry and Bristow. Fry's early life was spent in Philadelphia, and it was at the Chestnut Street Theatre on June 4, 1845, that his *Leonora*, a full-scale three-act work on a libretto derived by Fry's brother from Bulwer-Lytton's *The Lady of Lyons* (1838), was first heard. Presented in what must have been an unusually lavish production for the time, at the hands of the English company of Arthur Seguin with an orchestra of sixty and a chorus of eighty, *Leonora* had a successful run of sixteen performances. Its fashionably Romantic plot and Belliniesque music must have made it seem very up to date. Fry composed three other operas, only one of which, *Notre Dame de Paris*, was produced.

Fry was perhaps less gifted as a composer than as a journalist. As such he was a belligerent and articulate champion of the rights of American composers to be heard in America. Ironically, however, it was not Fry but his friend Bristow who turned to American subjects: his *Rip Van Winkle* (1855) was successful; his *Columbus* was never finished. The former is less derivative from Italian opera than is Fry's *Leonora* and reveals Bristow's solid grounding in German instrumental music of his time, although the gap between his fluid, chromatic harmony and his square-cut phrase structure is seldom successfully bridged.

BIBLIOGRAPHICAL NOTES

Robert Stevenson's *Protestant Church Music in America* (New York: W. W. Norton, 1966) is a well-documented basic source on the material in this chapter. Arthur Rich's *Lowell Mason* (Chapel Hill: University of North Carolina Press, 1946) has been largely superseded by Carol Ann Pemberton's dissertation-based *Lowell Mason: His Life and Work* (Ann Arbor: UMI Research Press, 1985). Mason's own *Musical Letters from Abroad* (1853) have been reprinted (New York: Da Capo Press, 1967). The first edition of Mason's *Boston Handel and Haydn Society Collection of Church Music* is reprinted as *EAM* 15.

Richard Crawford writes provocatively about musical education in "Musical Learning in Nineteenth-Century America," *American Music*, I/1 (Spring 1983), 1–11.

We still lack a comprehensive survey of American song, though Charles Hamm's *Yesterdays* covers much of the early nineteenth-century repertory (when the lines between popular and art-song were blurred), and Nicholas Tawa's *Sweet Songs for Gentle Americans: The Parlor Song in America, 1790–1860* (Bowling Green, OH: Bowling Green Popular Press, 1980) is a broad study of that repertory. W. T. Upton's *Art-Song in America* (Boston: Oliver Ditson Company, 1930; supplement, 1938) has been superseded, at least for the pre-Civil War period, by Grace D. Yerbury's *Song in America, from Early Times to about 1850* (Metuchen, NJ: Scarecrow Press, 1971). Hamm's liner notes for *An Evening with Henry Russell* (Nonesuch H-71338, 1977) are illuminating. J. T. Howard's *Stephen Foster, America's Troubadour* (New York: Thomas Y. Crowell Company, 1934; rev. eds. 1953, 1962) remains the standard biography; William W. Austin's *Susanna, Jeanie, and The Old Folks at Home* (New York: Macmillan, Inc., 1975) analyzes Foster's songs closely and also inquires most perceptively into the reasons for their extraordinary durability in American culture. Twenty-two of Foster's household songs are reprinted in *EAM* 12; other valuable anthologies, similarly facsimile-reprint editions, are Richard Jackson's compilation *Popular Songs of Nineteenth-Century America* (New York: Dover Publications, 1976) and Richard Crawford's *The Civil War Songbook. Complete Original Sheet Music for 37 Songs* (New York: Dover Publications, 1977).

George Frederick Root's *Story of My Musical Life: An Autobiography* (1891) has been reprinted by Da Capo Press (New York, 1970). The publishing firm of Root & Cady has been authoritatively chronicled by Dena Epstein in *Music Publishing in Chicago Before 1871: The Firm of Root & Cady, 1858–1871* (Detroit: Information Coordinators, 1969). A volume of songs by Henry Clay Work has been reprinted as *EAM* 19.

The chapters on the United States in Loesser's *Men, Women and Pianos* make fascinating reading. Both Richard Hoffman and William Mason wrote their memoirs, characteristically devoting the most space to their European years; see Hoffman, *Some Musical Recollections of Fifty Years* (New York: Charles Scribner's Sons, 1910), and Mason, *Memories of a Musical Life* (New York: Century Co., 1902). Jeanne Behrend's edition of Gottschalk's *Notes of a Pianist* (New York: Alfred A. Knopf, Inc., 1964) is excellent. John G. Doyle's *Louis Moreau Gottschalk 1829–1869: A Bibliographical Study and Catalog of Works* (Detroit: Information Coordinators, 1983) is definitive but not easy to use; see my review in *Fontes artis musicae*, XXX/3 (July-September 1983), 168–70. All Gottschalk's works for piano, reprinted in facsimile from early editions, are included in a five-volume set, *The Piano Works of Louis Moreau Gottschalk* (New York: Arno Press and The New York Times, 1969); Robert Offergeld contributes a substantial critical-biographical introductory essay.

Jullien's flamboyant life is chronicled by Adam Carse in *The Life of Jullien*

(Cambridge, Eng.: W. Heffer & Sons, 1951). *Theodore Thomas: A Musical Autobiography*, ed. George P. Upton (Chicago: A. C. McClurg, 1905), has been reprinted by Da Capo Press (New York, 1964), with an introduction by Leon Stein and some valuable appendices. Philip Hart's *Orpheus in the New World: The Symphony Orchestra as an American Cultural Institution* (New York: W. W. Norton, 1972) is fascinating; Howard Shanet zeroes in on a single orchestra in *Philharmonic: A History of New York's Orchestra* (New York: Doubleday & Co., Inc., 1975).

The basic (so far the only) biography of Heinrich is that of W. T. Upton (New York: Columbia University Press, 1939). Upton is also the biographer of *William Henry Fry, American Journalist and Composer-Critic* (New York: Thomas Y. Crowell Company, 1954).

For opera in New Orleans to 1841, see H. A. Kmen's *Music in New Orleans* (Baton Rouge: Louisiana State University Press, 1966); in New York, Julius Mattfeld's *A Hundred Years of Grand Opera in New York* (New York: New York Public Library, 1927).

FIVE

THE VERNACULAR TRADITION, 1820–1920

Having considered the development of the cultivated tradition through the Civil War, let us go back to the early nineteenth century to consider vernacular-tradition music, carrying forward the discussion to the end of World War I and treating religious music, especially that of the revivals and camp meetings; the music of the popular lyric theater, especially the minstrel show; dance music; marches and other band music; and ragtime, at first a music of limited use among American midwestern blacks but by the turn of the twentieth century a music of national popularity.

SPIRITUAL FOLK SONGS, REVIVAL AND GOSPEL HYMNODY, AND BLACK SPIRITUALS

We have noted in the foregoing chapter the rejection of the music of the First New England School in the very area that had spawned it. Under the influence of the composers of "scientific" church music led by Lowell Mason and Thomas Hastings, the fuging tunes, anthems, and set-pieces of the Yankee tunesmiths were gradually eliminated from the churches as well as the singing-schools, not only of New England but of the Middle Atlantic states as well. The imaginative shape-note notation of Smith and Little's *Easy Instructor* and its imitators was equally rejected in the North as being no more than "dunce notes" (Hastings's epithet). By 1853, as we have seen (p. 55), a Boston historian of American church music believed that shape-note tunebooks and their music, "if used at all, have been crowded to the far west, mostly out of sight and hearing."[1]

He was wrong. Shape-notes and the music of the New Englanders were still within "sight and hearing" of many Americans. They had indeed been crowded out of the northern and eastern cities, but they were flourishing in the Upland South and the Deep South, as well as in the "far west" (by which Gould probably meant any land west of the Appalachians). Spurned by the urban arbiters of cultivated taste in music, the tunesmiths' pieces had become essentially a rural music in the sparsely settled South and toward the frontier. There they were to join with several other kinds of religious song to form the basis of a vernacular music tradition that is still alive today. These other kinds of song are our immediate concern: the spiritual folk songs and the revival hymns of the camp meetings, gospel hymns of the "City Revival" of the 1870s and later, and spirituals of American blacks.

The beginnings of the migration to the South of the shape-note tunebooks are reflected in several Pennsylvania publications of the first two decades of the nineteenth century. For the English-speaking population appeared such imitations of *The Easy Instructor* as the 1807 edition of *Philadelphia Harmony, Ecclesia Harmonia* (1807), and *The Musical Instructor* (1808). German-speaking Pennsylvanians first learned shape-note singing from Joseph Doll's *Der leichte Unterricht* of 1810 (its title a literal translation of *The Easy Instructor's*) and Johannes Rothbaust's *Die Franklin Harmonie* (1821). The latter two were published by a Harrisburg printer, John Wyeth (1770–1858), who also issued English-language tunebooks, among them *Repository of Sacred Music* (1810) and *Repository of Sacred Music, Part Second* (1813). The *Part Second* proved to be "the first really influential anthology of what the late George Pullen Jackson dubbed spiritual folksong."[2]

Spiritual folk songs are just what the term implies: religious songs set to folk melodies, whether secular song melodies, patriotic airs, or popular

---

[1] Nathaniel Gould, *Church Music in America* (Boston: A. N. Johnson, 1853), p. 55. It might be noted, however, that some exceptional compilations of earlier psalmody were published as interesting "antique" music: *The Stoughton Collection* (Boston, 1829) was followed by such collections as *The Billings and Holden Collection* (Boston, 1836) and Simeon Cheney's *The American Singing Book* (Boston, 1879; reprinted as *EAM* 17).

[2] *MMEA*, p. 134. The reference is to the pioneer studies of Jackson in a series of books from 1933 on, and specifically to his *Spiritual Folk-Songs of Early America*.

dance tunes. Three types of spiritual folk songs may be distinguished: religious ballads, folk hymns, and revival spiritual songs. Wyeth's collection of religious songs in two, three, and four voice parts included both ballads and hymns, besides many tunes from earlier New England collections (Billings, Jenks, Law, Chapin) and thirteen by Elkanah Dare (1782–1826), who seems to have been Wyeth's musical adviser. *Heavenly Union*, for example, is a ballad in some ten strophes, which begins with the balladeer's typical invitation to listen to a story:

> Come, saints and sinners, hear me tell
> The wonders of Emmanuel,
> Who saved me from a burning hell,
> And brought my soul with him to dwell,
>   And gave me heav'nly union.

The tale goes on in a characteristically folkish, colloquial way:

> When Christ the Saviour from on high
> Beheld my soul in ruins lie,
> He look'd on me with pitying eye,
> And said to me as he pass'd by,
>   "With God you have no union."

The folk hymns are briefer, non-narrative pieces; many are new settings to anonymous tunes of old favorite texts by Watts or Wesley. *Hallelujah* (Example 5-1 [a]) is one of three settings of the popular text of Robert Robinson, eighteenth-century English hymnodist, "Come thou fount of ev'ry blessing"; the tune, which was to be resecularized to the text "Tell Aunt Rhody," appears in print for the first time in Wyeth's *Repository* as an anonymous and presumably well-known folk tune; a later, gospel-hymn version shows how decades of popular usage reshaped the tune into the form known best today (Example 5-1 [b]).

As one can hear in *Hallelujah*, with early nineteenth-century folk hymnody we are back again in the musical world of the Yankee tunesmiths: the parallel fifths of measures 2–3 and 4; the implied modal harmony; the "gapped" melody, which makes the tune seem fundamentally pentatonic; the simple, sturdy rhythm. These old-style characteristics are maintained, indeed emphasized, in Wyeth's shape-note hymn collection, which was to be the model for later tunebooks in the developing tradition of southern spiritual folk songs.

"Spiritual folk song" suggests the better-known term "spiritual." And in fact songs like *Hallelujah* have been termed "white spirituals" by historians beginning with Jackson, who coined the terms for his *White Spirituals in the Southern Uplands* (1933). The complex relationships between such white

EXAMPLE 5-1. (a) *Hallelujah, Repository of Sacred Music, Part Second,* 2nd ed. (Harrisburg, PA): J. Wyeth, 1820), p. 112. (b) *Come, Thou Fount,* attributed to John Wyeth in *Gospel Hymns. Nos. 1 to 6 Complete* (New York: Biglow & Main Co., 1894), No. 633 (soprano part only).

spirituals and the spirituals of blacks are not yet wholly clear, though it seems certain that the Negro spirituals, which were hardly ever discussed in print (nor their melodies transcribed) before the Reconstruction period after the Civil War, arose out of the evangelical songs of the great revivals in the American South and West in the period after 1800.[3] These began with the Great Revival of 1800 in Kentucky, which set off a wave of emotional religious revivalism, led by the aggressive Methodists, Presbyterians, and Baptists, that soon swept across Georgia, the Carolinas, Pennsylvania, Tennessee, and Ohio. The instrument of the revivals was the camp meeting of worshippers who brought tents, bedding, and food for the four- or five-day (and night) marathons of preaching, praying, and singing. Attendance could run in the thousands: at Cane Ridge, Kentucky, in 1801, more than thirty ministers preached to a crowd estimated variously to be between 10,000 and 20,000. With meetings of such size, a new kind of religious song inevitably appeared—the revival hymn—simpler even than the traditional hymns and having the text repetitions or verse-and-refrain structure found in many folk cultures. This kind of song was often termed a "spiritual song," as in the title of John C. Totten's pocket-sized book of hymn texts, *A Collection of the Most Admired Hymns and Spiritual Songs, with the choruses affixed, as usually sung at camp-meetings* (New York, 1809). At least one critic of camp-meeting revivalism believed that the repetitive choral refrains of the new type of hymn derived from the practice of blacks: John F. Watson, in a tract of 1819 bemoaning what he called *Methodist Error*, spoke of one

> . . . most exceptionable error, which has the tolerance at least of the rulers of our camp meetings. In the *blacks'* quarter [of the camp ground], the coloured people get together, and sing for hours together, short scraps of disjoined affirmations, pledges, or prayers, lengthened out with repetition choruses. These are all sung in the merry chorus-manner of the southern harvest-field, or husking-frolic method, of the slave blacks.

Watson lamented that "the example has already visibly affected the religious manners of some whites":

> From this cause, I have known in some camp meetings, from 50 to 60 people crowd into one tent, after the public devotions had closed, and there continue the whole night, singing tune after tune . . . scarce one of which were in our hymnbooks. Some of these from their nature, (having very long repetition choruses and short scraps of [text] matter) are actually composed as sung, and are indeed almost endless.[4]

---

[3] See Bruno Nettl and Gerard Béhague, *Folk and Traditional Music of the Western Continents*, 2nd ed. (Englewood Cliffs, NJ: Prentice-Hall, Inc., 1973) pp. 182–85. The claims and counterclaims of various scholars regarding the origins of American spirituals are well summarized in section II(2)—"African and European Sources"—of the article "Spirituals" in *TNGDAM*; Dena Epstein's "A White Origin for the Black Spiritual? An Invalid Theory and How It Grew," *American Music*, I/2 (1983), 53–59, is persuasive.

[4] Quoted in Don Yoder, *Pennsylvania Spirituals* (Lancaster: Pennsylvania Folklife Society, 1961), pp. 27–28.

"Short scraps" of verse, interspersed with "repetition choruses," sung in a "merry chorus-manner," often "actually composed as sung"—this is as good a definition as any of the typical revival hymn. It first appeared in print in pocket songsters, without the music but often with a separate section of "choruses" that could be added to or interpolated in the song leader's chanting of the verses. Wyeth's *Repository . . . Part Second* contained no such revival hymns, but the later Southern tunebooks, which otherwise borrowed so much from Wyeth (Yankee fuging tunes and other pieces, religious ballads, and folk hymns), added revival hymns as well. The most successful such tunebooks—all with shape-note notation—were Ananias Davisson's *Kentucky Harmony* (1816) and its *Supplement* (1820); Allen Carden's *Missouri Harmony* (1820); the *Columbian Harmony* (1825) of William Moore from Wilson County, Tennessee; William Caldwell's *Union Harmony* (Maryville, Tennessee, 1837); John Jackson's *Knoxville Harmony* (1838). Especially notable, because so popular, are *The Southern Harmony* of William Walker and *The Sacred Harp* of B. F. White and E. J. King.

"Singin' Billy" Walker (1809–75) of Spartanburg, South Carolina, published *The Southern Harmony* in 1835. In the Preface to his *Christian Harmony* (1866; repr. *ACS*, pp. 67–69), he claimed to have sold 600,000 copies of the earlier work, and he is known to have added proudly to his signature the initials A.S.H. ("author *Southern Harmony*"). The Index to the 1854 edition, the last and largest, names 334 pieces, including many new tunes "suitable for revival occasions." Walker's name is attached to forty of the compositions; in his Preface to the first edition, he explains that in addition to having "composed several tunes wholly," he also "composed the [accompanying] parts to a great many good airs (which I could not find in any publication, nor in manuscript), and assigned my name as the author." Thus was a popular tune turned into a spiritual folk song. One such tune was *Auld lang syne*, which appears with the title *Plenary* as a setting of Watts's hymn "Hark! from the tombs a doleful sound." Another, attributed in *The Southern Harmony* to a David Walker, is *The Hebrew Children*, an infectious hexatonic tune that is known also as a Negro spiritual ("Wonder where is good ole Daniel?"), an Ozark Mountains play-party song ("Where, O where is pretty little Susie?"), and, of later vintage, a college song ("Where, O where are the pea-green freshmen?").[5] The thrice-asked question of each stanza, "Where are the Hebrew children?" (. . . the twelve apostles? . . . the holy Christians? etc.), is answered by the refrain, "Safe in the promised land," in a characteristic form of the verse-with-refrain revival hymn.

[5] Walker's *The Hebrew Children* is in *MinA*, No. 97, along with the first stanza of the Negro version, apparently taken from R. Nathaniel Dett, *Religious Folk-Songs of the Negro as Sung at Hampton Institute* (Hampton, VA: Hampton Institute Press, 1927), p. 73. The play-party version is in Vance Randolph, ed., *Ozark Folk Songs*, 4 vols. (Columbia, MO: State Historical Society, 1946–50), III, 364. The college version is part of my own experience.

Typical of the compilers of southern shape-note tunebooks, Walker drew tunes that pleased him from no matter what source, transforming them into the rugged, sonorous shape-note style by the addition of two or three surrounding parts. Thus, not only do we find in *The Southern Harmony* borrowmgs from the eighteenth-century Yankee composers, newly composed pieces by Walker and others, but also even Lowell Mason's *Missionary Hymn* and the patriotic song *Hail! Columbia*. The Scottish folk song *Braes o' Balquhidder* is made over into *Lone Pilgrim*, and both *Thorny Desert* and *Something New* sound like folk-hymn variants of Scotch-Irish reels.

Even more lastingly popular than *The Southern Harmony* was *The Sacred Harp* (1844) of Benjamin Franklin White (1800–79) and his lesser-known co-compiler E. J. King (d. 1844). This shape-note tunebook went through many editions; J. S. James's of 1911, affirmatively retitled *The Original Sacred Harp*, was edited by the Alabama singing-school master S. M. Denson (1854–1936), who added alto parts to those of the 600-odd tunes that were set in only three parts (about half of them). Denson's own revision of 1936 was still being published, in a fourth edition, as late as 1971. The twentieth-century *Sacred Harp* preserves the "dispersed harmony" (wide spacing of the upper voices, as opposed to the "close harmony" of other religious song), the four-shape notation (*fa* △, *sol* ○, *la* □, *mi* ◇), and the traditional introduction on "The Rudiments of Music." Even the basic "Old Time" style is fairly well preserved. Example 5-2 shows the beginning of the moving folk hymn *Wondrous Love* in the three-part setting common to both *The Southern Harmony* (in the second edition of which [1840] it first appeared in print) and the first edition of *The Sacred Harp*, with Denson's alto part added in cue-sized notes. Occasionally the "modern" full triad sound is created by Denson's adding a third to the original's open fifth.

I spoke previously of this music as belonging to a "vernacular music tradition that is still alive today." Indeed it is, in the rural South and southern Midwest, where hundreds of "singings" from shape-note tunebooks take place every year. One such singing is well represented on NW 205, recorded in 1959 at a weekend meeting of the Alabama Sacred Harp Convention in Fyffe, Alabama. Folk hymns like *Wondrous Love* are included, as are others attributed to the shape-note tunebook compilers, such as William Walker's *Hallelujah*, White's *The Morning Trumpet* (of which a black variant—or perhaps the black *original*—is known, with the chorus "You may bury me in the East,/You may bury me in the West,/But I'll hear that trumpet sound in the morning!"), and James and Denson's *Traveling On*; so too are pieces from the First New England School, such as the fuging tunes *Sherburne* (by Daniel Read), *Northfield* (by Jeremiah Ingalls), and *David's Lamentation* (by William Billings). Traditionally, shape-note singers seat themselves in a hollow square, sopranos on one side, tenors on another, and so on. For each hymn, generally, an elder or well-recognized singer rises to call for a piece

EXAMPLE 5-2. The folk hymn *Wondrous Love*, measures 1–8. Soprano, tenor, and bass parts from W. Walker, *The Southern Harmony* (New Haven, CT, 1835), 1854 ed., p. 252. Alto part composed by S. M. Denson for "Denson Revision" (1936) of *The Sacred Harp* (Philadelphia, 1844); *Sacred Harp* version is whole tone lower in original.

*Although early printed sources consistently give this note as E♭, shape-note singers sing it, just as consistently, as E♮ (thus making the entire last phrase unroll in parallel fifths).

(by number in the tunebook); set its pitch; and conduct it in a rather solemn, simple, strong, straight-armed way. Almost always, a hymn is first sung through just to the "fasola" syllables, then repeated to the text. And always men and women alike sing the treble and the tenor parts (and sometimes the alto), to make for a greatly enriched sonority. The rhythm is powerful, and usually some singers stomp as they sing; they also tend to breathe before the "downbeat," regardless of the text's punctuation. Participation is a matter of infectious enthusiasm and warmth—also of fellowship and spiritual exaltation. One imagines that the singing-schools of an earlier time must have been very much like this.

One of the best-known American spiritual folk songs, *Wayfaring Stranger*, appeared in print for the first time in the 1844 *Sacred Harp*. Its poignant text and mournful pentatonic tune tend to disguise the revival-hymn refrain of the final couplet (Example 5-3a; *NW* 294:s2/5 is an affecting

EXAMPLE 5-3. Two revival hymns from *The Sacred Harp* (1844). (a) *Wayfaring Stranger* (p. 457 of Denson Revision; tenor part only). (b) *The Old Ship of Zion* (p. 79 of Denson Revision; tenor part only).

(a)

> I am a poor way-far-ing stranger, While jour-ne'ing thru this world of woe,
> Yet, there's no sick-ness, toil nor dan-ger, In that bright land to which I go.

> I'm go-ing there to see my fath-er, I'm go-ing there no more to roam; I'm on-ly

> go - ing o- ver Jor-dan, I'm on- ly go - ing o- ver home. [home.]

(b)

> What__ ship is__ this__ that will take us all home, O __
> And__ safe - ly__ land__ us on Ca - naan's bright shore? O __

> glo - ry Hal - le - lu - jah, 'Tis the old ship of Zi - on, hal - le -
> glo - ry Hal - le - lu - jah.

> lu, hal - le - lu, 'Tis the old ship of Zi - on, hal - le - lu - jah.

unaccompanied performance by a fine Ozark singer). More characteristic of the lusty vigor of most revival songs is *The Old Ship of Zion*, a tune known in several variants including Negro ones, that of *The Sacred Harp* identified by William Hauser in his tunebook *The Olive Leaf* (see overleaf) as a "North Carolina Version" (Example 5-3 [b]).

Besides the tunebooks previously cited, which used the four-shape notation of Little and Smith's *Easy Instructor* based on a *fa, sol, la, mi* solmization system, others appeared in a seven-shape notation that reflected the pressures of the "scientific" school of musical thought to adopt the European *do, re, me, fa, sol, si* (or *ti*) system. The first of these was *The Christian Minstrel* (Philadelphia, 1846), compiled by Jesse Aikin (1808–1900). Aikin, who showed his respect for Lowell Mason by including eighteen of Mason's hymns in the work, used the same four shapes as *The Easy Instructor* and *The Sacred Harp* but added three others of his own invention. (Other seven-shape tunebook compilers, imagining that Aikin had patented his new shapes, invented yet others; hence the occasional application of the name "patent notes" to shape-notation.) Another seven-shape book, destined to be almost as long-lived as *The Sacred Harp*, was the eastern Tennessee tunebook *The Harp of Columbia* (Knoxville, 1848); present-day singers from this book call themselves "Old Harp Singers" as opposed to the "Sacred Harp Singers." One of the last shape-note tunebooks in the traditional style of spiritual folk song, and one that used Aikin's seven shapes, was *The Olive Leaf* (1878), printed at Wadley, Georgia, by William Hauser (1812–80). But this book also reveals the impact of a new style in American vernacular hymnody, that of the gospel hymn.

The gospel hymn, like the earlier revival hymn, was the product of a revival movement. However, unlike the earlier nineteenth-century revival hymn, which arose mainly in the back country and on the frontier, the gospel hymn of the last half of the century was urban. Its musical background was the correct, bland style of Mason and Hastings, but its harmony tended to be more chromatically engorged, its texts more sentimentally swollen. From the earlier revival hymnodists, the gospel-hymn writers, equally intent on engaging large masses in cathartic songfests, took the idea of repeated refrain-choruses. As Stevenson puts it, "the verse-and-refrain pattern of the revival song joins with Sweet Adeline harmonies to make the gospel song"; Edwin Pierce remarks perceptively on the influence of German secular *Volkslieder* (as they might have become known in the American initiations of the *Männerchöre*).[6]

William B. Bradbury, whom we have met as the composer of *The Lament of the Blind Orphan Girl* (see p. 71), foreshadowed the gospel-song style in his *Woodworth* of 1849 (best known as sung to the text beginning "Just as I am, without one plea"; NW 224:s2/9 is a performance recorded in 1959 by a choir organized for an "Australian Crusade" of the evangelist Billy Graham). However, the biggest names among gospel-hymn composers (and the "show-biz" connotation of that terminology is not inappropriate considering the polished publicity and commercial enterprise of the urban revivals) were those of Philip P. Bliss (1838–76); Ira D. Sankey (1840–1908); and a somewhat lesser light, Rev. Robert Lowry (1826–99). Lowry's *Beautiful River* ("Shall we gather at the river?") appeared in *The Olive Leaf*; its skipping rhythms entranced generations of Americans and were incorporated in instrumental works by Charles Ives ("Children's Day at the Camp Meeting" violin sonata) and Virgil Thomson (*Variations on Sunday School Tunes*). Sankey, fresh from a two-year revival tour of Great Britain (1873–75) as organist and song-leader for the spellbinding evangelist Dwight L. Moody and immersed in Moody's revival meetings at the Brooklyn Rink across the East River from New York City, for which he directed a choir of 250 in addition to playing the organ for his own singing, still found time to see into

---

[6] Robert Stevenson, *Protestant Church Music in America* (New York: W. W. Norton, 1966), p. 90n; Edwin H. Pierce, "Gospel Hymns," *MQ*, XXVI (1940), 355–64.

print a conflation of Bliss's *Gospel Songs* (1874) and an earlier collection of his own, under the title *Gospel Hymns and Sacred Songs* (Cincinnati, 1875). It was enlarged the very next year, and after Bliss's death Sankey and other collaborators continued to issue enlargements through a sixth cumulative volume, *Gospel Hymns. Nos. 1 to 6 Complete* (1894; reprinted 1973 as *EAM 5*).

     The gospel hymns of Bliss and Sankey have been denigrated as a "slough of sentimental music-hall sloppiness . . . flabby and futile," as a British observer has put it. But the same historian, shifting critical gears, views them rightly in the context of an American urban vernacular tradition when he admits that "at its best this music is honestly flamboyant and redolent of the buoyancy of the civilization that created New York and Pittsburgh and Chicago."[7] Bliss's *Pull for the Shore* may have a text as metaphorically exaggerated as a seventeenth-century Italian opera aria and as artfully homespun as the doggerel of Rod McKuen, but its chorus is an almost irresistible march, perfectly suited to its soul-stirring evangelistic purposes (Example 5-4).

EXAMPLE 5-4. P. Bliss, *Pull for the Shore*, No. 51 of *Gospel Hymns. Nos. 1 to 6 Complete* (New York: Biglow & Main Co., 1894), Chorus only.

     [7] Erik Routley, *The Music of Christian Hymnody* (London: Independent Press, 1957), p. 166.

The universality of some gospel-hymn tunes and text phrases is undeniable. The tune everyone has sung as "How dry I am!" can be found as No. 543 in the 1894 *Gospel Hymns*, beginning "O happy day that fixed my choice/On Thee, my Saviour and my God." Bliss's *Hallelujah, 'tis Done* (No. 2 of the 1883 compilation) became the irreverent parody, "Hallelujah, I'm a bum." Snatches of gospel-hymn texts have become commonplaces in the American vernacular: "Sweet by-and-by" (No. 110, 1894 collection; *NW* 220:s1/1), "Arise and shine" (No. 103), "Throw out the life-line" (No. 441), "Hold the fort" (No. 11), "The old, old story" (No. 28), "Where is my wand'ring boy tonight?" (No. 631), and many others.

The same post-Civil War period that saw the rise of urban gospel hymnody saw the dissemination of black spirituals and their rise in the national consciousness as a music of popular appeal and familiarity. The publication in 1867 of the first collection of songs of black Americans—*Slave Songs of the United States*, gathered and compiled by William Allen, Charles Ware, and Lucy McKim Garrison—was a symbolic step in this development. More important practically was the formation at the newly founded Fisk University in Nashville, Tennessee, of a group of black student musicians, who as the Fisk Jubilee Singers toured the United States regularly, beginning in 1872, and Europe in the mid-1870s; with heartfelt—and polished—performances of spirituals in four-part harmony (besides other types of song), they introduced this music to audiences far and wide. Their success sparked the formation of other groups of "jubilee" singers and the publication of a considerable number of slave-song anthologies.

BLACKFACE MINSTRELSY

Early in 1854, when Jullien's orchestra was in New York offering "monster concerts for the masses," when the St. Charles Theatre in the Bowery had been presenting German opera for several months, when an Italian opera company producing Donizetti and Bellini was struggling to survive, and when Fry and Bristow were complaining of the New York Philharmonic's neglect of American composers, *Putnam's Monthly* for February called attention to another kind of musical entertainment:

> The only places of Amusement where the entertainments are indigenous are the African Opera Houses, where native American vocalists, with blackened faces, sing national songs, and utter none but native witticisms. These native theatricals . . . are among the best frequented and most profitable places of amusement in New York. While even [the] attempt to establish an Italian Opera here, though originating with the wealthiest and best educated classes,

has resulted in bankruptcy, the Ethiopian Opera has flourished like a green bay tree.

This report pinpoints nicely the high point of a kind of American vernacular lyric theater, eschewed perhaps by the "wealthiest and best educated classes" but flourishing among the others. A few months earlier the *Musical World* (October 8, 1853) had noted that "Ethiopian Minstrelsy is on the increase. We now have, in New York, six companies of Minstrels in full blast." The "native theatrical" of blackface minstrelsy was in full flower.

The American minstrel show had crystallized as a form of public entertainment in the early 1840s. Like many other facets of early nineteenth-century American culture, it had British antecedents. In the 1700s it was not uncommon for British dramas to include black characters and so-called "Negro songs," usually of a patronizing and sentimental character. Some British comedians blackened their faces and impersonated blacks; one of these, Charles Mathews, came to America in 1822. Unfamiliar with American blacks, he was fascinated by them, especially their dialect and their humor. In New York, at the blacks' own theater, he noted their performance of *Hamlet* and transcribed the song *Opossum up a Gum Tree*. In Philadelphia he heard a black revivalist preacher and tried to reproduce on paper the sermon's dialect. He collected "scraps of songs and malaprops."[8] With such first-hand experience as a basis, Mathews's skits, mock lectures, and dialect songs were important in the background of an American style of stage impersonation of blacks, on which some twenty years later the minstrel show was to be based.

Other northern comedians exploited the fad for sketches of blacks in the 1820s and 1830s, and two stereotypes tended to crystallize, perhaps first in the work of George Washington Dixon (1808–61), who created such songs as *Coal Black Rose* and *Long Tailed Blue*. Like the other two early American comic heroes—the shrewd, taciturn Yankee peddler and the lusty, bragging backwoodsman—the two Negro stereotypes were oversimplified exaggerations of real life. One was the plantation hand, a tatterdemalion of low estate but high spirits; the other was the urban dandy with affectedly modish ways and a fashionable "long-tailed blue" dress coat. Jim Crow or Gumbo Chaff, Zip Coon or Dandy Jim—these were the archetypes as sketched by early American blackface comedians like Dixon and Thomas Dartmouth ("Daddy") Rice (1808–60), who created the internationally famous stage character of Jim Crow, legendarily based on a black stable groom in Louisville, where Rice was playing in 1828.

Bit by bit such comedians, with faces blackened by burnt cork, enlarged

---

[8] *Memoirs of Charles Mathews, Comedian, by Mrs. Mathews* (London, 1839), III, 391.

their repertory of skits, songs, and dances; organized themselves into small troupes; and began to develop the format for a whole program. One important milestone was the formation of a minstrel band of instruments associated with blacks (fiddle, bones, banjo, and tambourine) by four star comedians in New York—Dan Emmett, Frank Brower, Billy Whitlock, and Dick Pelham. The *New York Herald* announced the premiere performance of the group, set for February 6, 1843, as one of the major attractions of the Bowery Circus:

> First Night of the novel, grotesque, original, and surprisingly melodious Ethiopian band, entitled the *Virginia Minstrels*, being an exclusively musical entertainment combining the banjo, violin, bone castanets, and tambourine, and entirely exempt from the vulgarities and other objectionable features which have hitherto characterized negro extravaganzas.

Successful in New York, the four Virginia Minstrels enlarged their act into a full evening's entertainment of songs, dances, and a parody "lecture on locomotives" and opened with it at the Masonic Temple in Boston on March 7; they called it an "Ethiopian Concert." It was the first real minstrel show.

Following the success of the Virginia Minstrels, other troupes were formed, and the ones already in existence enlarged their shows; soon Christy's Minstrels, Bryant's Minstrels, The Sable Harmonists, The Kentucky Rattlers, The Ethiopian Serenaders, and dozens of others were traveling across the country. Dialect solo songs; satirical stump speeches and dialogues; burlesques; instrumental numbers and dances, either solo or group; and "walk-arounds" (small-scale vernacular *Gesamtkunstwerke* combining solo song, choral song, and dancing to instrumental "symphonies") became the staples of the minstrel shows, as the craze for them rose to a peak in the 1850s. Through them all, at this period, ran a strain of mild caricature of the black, who was portrayed both as jokester and butt of jokes, as comedian and (less often) tragedian. Even if by today's standards the stereotypes and the heavy dialect of the early blackface minstrels are offensive, they did present the black as a comic hero—if, however, one to be laughed at as well as with.[9] The minstrel shows had their villains, but they were of other kinds. Standing up for American popular culture, the minstrels lashed out in stinging parodies and burlesques at the arty and pretentious, the foreign and imported. In the 1850s the "Tyrolean business," mocking the vogue of singing families like the Hutchinsons and the Rainer family, was often to be heard, with such titles as "Tyrolean Solo, displaying a flexibility and volume

---

[9] See Constance Rourke, *American Humor* (New York: Harcourt, Brace & Co., 1931), Chap. III; also her *Roots of American Culture* (New York: Harcourt, Brace & Co., 1942), pp. 262–74. See also the excellent notes by Robert B. Winans for NW 338 (*The Early Minstrel Show*), which contains by far the most authentic reconstructions of minstrel-show music on recordings.

of voice astonishing and inimitable" and "We Come from the Hills, burlesque
à la Rainer family." Italian opera was a favorite target: *Lucia di Lammermoor*
was burlesqued as "Lucy Did Lam a Moor." The *New York Clipper* of January
21, 1854, crowed over the Christy Minstrels' satire on Jullien's monster
concerts. The virtuosity of visiting violinist Ole Bull and of the fabled Paganini was deprecated by the minstrels, who claimed that

> Loud de banjo talked away,
> An' beat Ole Bull from de Norway;
> We'll take de shine from Paganini,
> We're de boys from ole Virginny.

This was an echo of "Daddy" Rice's *Jim Crow*, who had boasted about 1828
that

> I'm a rorer on de fiddle,
> And down in ole Virginny
> Dey say I play de skientific
> Like massa Pagganninny.

Sometimes the minstrels portrayed the black as the same kind of swaggering
superman as the frontiersman heroes:

> My mama was a wolf
> My daddy was a tiger,
> I am what you call
> De Ole Virginny Nigger:
> Half fire, half smoke,
> A little touch of thunder,
> I am what you call
> De eighth wonder.

And sometimes, in transparent disguise, he was shown as a clever outsmarter
of authority:

> A bullfrog dressed in soger's close
> Went in de field to shoot some crows,
> De crows smell powder an' fly away,
> De bullfrog mighty mad dat day.

The music of the minstrel shows was a mélange of well-known popular
songs (even some of the sentimental household type), of adaptations from
other sources (even of British and Italian opera airs), of dance tunes and
dialect songs. These last were the mainstays of the shows and had the most
remarkable music.

The typical minstrel band of the 1840s was that established by the Virginia Minstrels: banjo, tambourine, bone castanets, and violin, with perhaps also an accordion, a triangle, or a second banjo. All these except the accordion were instruments associated with southern blacks, particularly the banjo, which in fact had African origins. A British minister and lexicographer who had spent many years in Maryland and Virginia wrote,

> . . . The favourite and almost only instrument in use among the slaves there was a *bandore*; or, as they pronounced the word, *banjer*. Its body was a large hollow gourd, with a long handle attached to it, strung with catgut, and played on with the fingers.[10]

In the minstrel shows, a singer often accompanied himself on the banjo, tapping his foot in a steady metronomic beat and varying his sung melody on the instrument. Thus *The Boatmen's Dance*, claimed by Dan Emmett as his own song but known at least in part on the Ohio River in the 1820s and 1830s, might have been played as shown in Example 5-5 (b). The variation style of short, even running notes is not new: we have met it in the dance music, under English influence, of the late eighteenth and early nineteenth centuries (see Example 2-7).

EXAMPLE 5-5. (a) D. Emmett, *De Boatmen's Dance* (Boston: C. H. Keith, 1843), measures 13–16 (air only). (b) *The Boatman's Dance*, Frank B. Converse, *Frank B. Converse's Banjo Instructor* (New York, 1865), measures 1–4. After *Dan Emmett and the Rise of Early Negro Minstrelsy*, by Hans Nathan. Copyright 1962 by the University of Oklahoma Press.

Much more novel, indeed so fresh as to be a source for the indigenous American rhythms of ragtime and early jazz, are the banjo "jigs" of the minstrel-show dances. Hans Nathan, who first called attention to these remarkable tunes, describes them thus:

> The motion . . . is animated by many irregular stresses: hectic offbeat accentuations projected against the relentless, metrical background of the accompanying

[10] Jonathan Boucher, *Boucher's Glossary of Archaic and Provincial Words* . . . (London: Black, Young and Young, 1832), p. BAN; quoted in Dena J. Epstein, "African Music in British and French America," *MQ*, LIX (1973), 61–91. See also Epstein, "Slave Music," *Notes*, XX (1963), 201.

taps [of the feet], which change $\frac{2}{4}$ into $\frac{6}{8}$. A large number of accentuations result from sudden, brief rests on one of the four beats in the measure.[11]

A fine example is Emmett's *Pea-Patch Jig,* one of forty-eight banjo tunes in an early manuscript compiled by Emmett; surprisingly, it also appeared in print in *Kendall's Clarinet Instruction Book* (Boston, 1845). The combinations of triplets and duplets and of even and uneven rhythms in running passages, the repeated notes, and above all the frequent accentuated rests on strong beats contribute to the propulsive, "swinging" character of the music (Example 5-6; the jig is recorded on *NW* 338:s2/5).

EXAMPLE 5-6. D. Emmett, *Pea-Patch Jig,* first (= closing) strain only. From *Dan Emmett and the Rise of Early Negro Minstrelsy,* by Hans Nathan. Copyright 1962 by the University of Oklahoma Press.

[Sounds an octave lower]

Evidence suggests that although the ultimate source of this style lay in British, especially Scottish and Irish, folk-dance music, the concentration of offbeat accents and other rhythmic shifts derived from the manner in which such music was played by American blacks, who then provided the direct models for northern minstrel-show banjoists. As the clarinet instruction book mentioned previously shows, the banjo-jig idiom was imitated on other instruments: it crops up not only in Kendall's clarinet book but in violin, fife, and flute manuals as well, and the piano music of early ragtime is clearly indebted to it.

Something of the same buoyant, swingy, chattering spirit informs the dialect songs and the music for walk-arounds of the minstrel shows. The two outstanding composers were Daniel Decatur Emmett (1815–1904) and Stephen Foster. Emmett was the more versatile: banjoist, fiddler, singer, and comedian; author of lyrics, stump speeches, plays for the minstrel stage, and instruction manuals for both fife and drum. He also composed in addition to banjo tunes many songs for the minstrel shows; about seventy were published. By far the most famous is *Dixie* (*NW* 202:s1/1), originally presented by Bryant's Minstrels on April 4, 1859, and announced on the playbill as "Mr. Dan Emmett's new and original song and dance, *Dixie's Land,* intro-

[11] Nathan, *Dan Emmett,* p. 195.

ducing the whole troupe in the festival dance." Nathan's description cannot be improved upon:

> The tune is characterized by a heavy, nonchalant, inelegant strut. . . . If music, lyrics, and dance style are taken as an entity, there emerges a special kind of humor that mixes grotesqueness with lustiness and down-to-earth contentment—comparable, to overstate the case, to a blend of Brueghel and Mickey Mouse. . . . "Dixie" indeed is no polite genteel tune. It has a considerable measure of toughness. . . .[12]

Like others of Emmett's walk-arounds, *Dixie* derived from various sources: its "song" and "chorus" melodies can be related to English and Scottish dance tunes as well as to *Gumbo Chaff*, a minstrel song of the 1830s; its closing instrumental "dance" was published in Emmett's *Fife Instructor* with the title "Albany Beef" and is a jig of Irish-Scottish ancestry. Nevertheless, like the best of Emmett's other songs and walk-arounds, *Dixie* integrates these raw materials in a new synthesis. Its rhythmic jolts, related to the banjo-jig syncopations, and its ridiculous homespun humor, common to the minstrel show but originating on the American frontier, make for "a very characteristically national music," as the songs of American minstrelsy were described in a Scottish encyclopedia of 1864.

Essentially, although it appeared on the minstrel-show stages of northern cities, the early minstrel song's earthiness, lustiness, lack of sentimentality, and sinewy vigor came from the world of the frontiersman and the boatman, when the frontier was just over the next range of hills and when rivers and canals were the highways of America. This connection with "primitive" America was certainly one reason why the genteel society of the cities—"the wealthiest and best educated classes," to recall the phrase of *Putnam's Monthly*—looked down their collective noses at the minstrel show and its music. And this is why the other outstanding composer of minstrel-show song, Stephen Foster, had to justify with a fine but defensive show of resolution his decision to move wholeheartedly into the field of minstrel-song composition. In a letter of 1852 to E. P. Christy, leader of Christy's Minstrels, Foster declared, "I have concluded . . . to pursue the Ethiopian business without fear or shame and . . . to establish my name as the best Ethiopian songwriter."[13] By 1852 Foster was a well-known songwriter, both of household songs and of minstrel-show songs. His comment to Christy shows, however, the lingering doubts he must have had about the propriety and gentility of identifying himself unreservedly with the latter. (He had an economic reason, however, for overcoming those doubts, for his biggest hit, *Old Folks at Home*, had

---

[12] Ibid., pp. 247–48, 250.
[13] The entire text of this interesting letter is printed, along with three other letters to Christy, in *ACS*, pp. 54–57.

been published under Christy's name as composer; Foster rationalized in the same letter to Christy that "I cannot write at all unless I write for public approbation and get credit for what I write.")

Foster's first songs for the minstrels, four published between 1847 and 1848, were already in the full-fledged indigenous style of the minstrel music of the earlier 1840s. The banjo twang on the afterbeats in the accompaniment to *Lou'siana Belle* and the strumming, rattling rhythm of *Away Down South* (Example 5-7) made those songs immediate successes, and *Uncle Ned* as well. But of the four early songs it was *Oh! Susanna* that was to prove indestructibly vital. *Oh! Susanna* was probably derived in part from the earlier, anonymous *Gwine 'long Down* (1844), just as Foster's later *Nelly Bly* (1849) seems to have come from *Clare de Kitchen* (late 1830s) and his *Camptown Races* (1850) from *Picayune Butler* (1847). But like Emmett's *Dixie, Oh! Susanna* was a transcendent synthesis of varied elements, not only

EXAMPLE 5-7. S. Foster, early minstrel songs. (a) *Lou'siana Belle* (Louisville & Cincinnati: Peters, 1847), measures 9–12. (b) *Away Down South* (Louisville & Cincinnati: Peters, 1848), measures 9–16.

because of the fine swinging movement of its solo verses and the solid stomp of its five-part chorus (with a potent rhythmic jolt on the last two syllables of "Oh! Su-*san-na*") but also because of the deadpan nonsense humor of its text.

> It rained all night the day I left,
> The weather it was dry,
> The sun so hot I frose to death,
> Susanna don't you cry.

Between the summers of 1849 and 1850 Foster published nine songs for the minstrel shows, as compared with five for the parlor. Among them were *Nelly Bly*, with its "dulcem melody" rocking along in a heavy-footed two-step rhythm, and *Camptown Races*, with its perfect matching of text and music and its irresistible verve (Example 5-8). Its chorus bears a striking

EXAMPLE 5-8. S. Foster, *Camptown Races* (Baltimore: Benteen, 1850), measures 8–15.

resemblance to that of *Lord, Remember Me*, first printed in the significant collection of black songs, *Slave Songs of the United States* (1867)—which suggests the interesting probability of some black songs' being indebted to the ubiquitously popular songs of Foster (a much more likely route of influence than the opposite, despite common misconceptions about Foster's debt to black music sources). Also a product of this period was *Nelly Was a Lady*, its text unusually sympathetic and sweet:

> Nelly was a lady—
> Last night she died;
> Toll de bell for Lubly Nell,
> My dark Virginny bride.

In the summer of 1851 appeared the song that would be most completely identified with Foster's name, despite its publication under Christy's: *Old Folks at Home*. Wilfrid Mellers was the first to point out[14] that with this song Foster introduced into the minstrel-show context the same nostalgia that pervades his household songs:

> All up and down the whole creation,
> Sadly I roam,
> Still longing for the old plantation,
> And for de old folks at home.
>
> . . .
>
> One little hut among de bushes,
> One dat I love,
> Still sadly to my mem'ry rushes,
> No matter where I rove.

The same note is heard in the other, later "best-loved" Foster songs issued as "plantation melodies": *My Old Kentucky Home, Good Night* (1853), and *Old Black Joe* (1860). Interestingly, as if conscious of having blurred the distinction between household and minstrel songs, Foster published these two without any black dialect spellings.

The reaction of the cultivated-tradition establishment to the fantastic popularity of *Old Folks at Home* was predictable. In its issue of October 2, 1852, *Dwight's Journal of Music* reported with perplexed incredulity on the universal appeal of the song:

> *Old Folks at Home* . . . is on everybody's tongue, and consequently in everybody's mouth. Pianos and guitars groan with it, night and day; sentimental young ladies sing it; sentimental young gentlemen warble it in midnight serenades; volatile young "bucks" hum it in the midst of their business and pleasures; boatmen roar it out . . . all the bands play it.

More than a year later (November 19, 1853) *Dwight's* was forced to an all-out attack—the cultivated against the vernacular tradition:

> We wish to say that such tunes . . . become catching, idle habits, and are not popular in the sense of musically inspiring, but that such and such a melody *breaks out* every now and then, like a morbid irritation of the skin.

---

[14] *Music in a New Found Land* (New York: Alfred A. Knopf, Inc., 1965), p. 249.

We can see now that Dwight's criticism was silly—like downgrading daisies because they are not orchids. It was also futile: Negro minstrelsy and its "morbid irritations" were on the rise in the 1850s. The genre was to continue through the 1860s as the most vital kind of "native theatrical," with some thirty established non-touring companies and many other traveling companies. From the 1870s on, however, the character of the minstrel show began to change: it tended to become more and more of a variety show, foreshadowing vaudeville and burlesque; its integrity was diluted by the introduction of non-black characters and sketches; its format was inflated in a trend to gigantism reflected in the names of such troupes as Haverly's Mastodons, Cleveland's Colossals, and Leavitt's Giganteans. One irony of the minstrel show's declining years was the appearance on the minstrel stage of actual blacks, sometimes even in blackface makeup. (Ironic, yes, but also a significant step toward broader acceptance of blacks as professionals in the American theatrical world.) One such performer, and one of the few notable composers of the later period of minstrelsy, was James A. Bland (1854–1911), who began his theatrical career as a singer and banjoist with the Original Black Diamonds of Boston and became a star in Haverly's Genuine Colored Minstrels. (He later paid homage to his old partners in Haverly's troupe in the song *De Golden Wedding*, recorded on NW 265:s1/7.) Bland probably did not write the 600 or 700 songs often claimed for him (only 40 were deposited for copyright), but he did produce some exceptionally popular ones, including *Carry Me Back to Old Virginny* (1878), *Oh, Dem Golden Slippers* (1879), and *In the Evening by the Moonlight* (1880). Another successful black composer of songs for the minstrel shows, though not as celebrated a performer, was Gussie Lord Davis (1863–99), whose *In the Baggage Coach Ahead* (1896) was an early hit of the dawning Tin Pan Alley age of the sheet-music industry, selling more than a million copies in a short time.

DANCES AND DANCE MUSIC

American social dances underwent major changes in the 1820–1920 period, largely as a result of the shifting patterns of immigration, which brought new dances—and appropriate music for them—from central and eastern Europe; by the end of the era, dance styles originating with American blacks had also had a considerable impact.

The English country dances and their French derivative, cotillions, which I discussed earlier (see pp. 42–46) as the most popular dances of the Federal era, continued in popularity well into the Jacksonian era. "Longways" dancing, however, in which men and women lined up in two rows opposite each other, tended to give way to dancing in "squares," each square being made up of four couples. Whereas early in the century dancers memorized the various patterns of such dances, in the 1840s it became increasingly common to have a "caller" prompt the participants. Moreover, in the urban centers other dances wrested popularity from the older dances, which thus became identified with rural areas and with country folk, and also with improvised music based on traditional tunes. (As such, these "square dances" and their music are preserved to the present day, not only as normal vernacular expressions in rural areas but also as pleasant nostalgic diversions for urbanites and suburbanites.)

Not many publications of cotillions postdate the 1818–19 issues by the Philadelphia publisher George Willig of eight "setts"—each with a dozen different dance patterns (and music for them)—by the leading dance bandleader in Philadelphia, the black cornetist, violinist, and composer Frank Johnson (1792–1844); publishers were more ready to issue the more fashionable offshoot of cotillions—quadrilles. Thus by the mid-1850s, when Stephen Foster published a collection of instrumental solos, duets, trios, and quartets for chamber ensemble (*The Social Orchestra*, 1854), he included no cotillions but, among the quartets, two sets of quadrilles, *Old Folks Quadrilles* and *Village Festival*.

The cotillion developed in two different directions. Out of it came not only the very highly structured quadrille, with its many patterns and great length, but also the "german"—similarly lengthy but not systematically patterned. Both these dances submitted to the influence of the newer "round" dances, for individual couples, emphasizing turning movements. Of these the waltz had been the first to gain popularity: as we have seen, it was introduced to America in the late eighteenth century, but it really became popular only in the 1820s and 1830s—and it remained popular throughout the entire century, and beyond, in a variety of forms (all, however, based on the idea of a couple dancing, in an embrace, to music in $\frac{3}{4}$ time). From the 1830s on the galop, a fast $\frac{2}{4}$ couples' dance (often used as the finale of a quadrille) was popular; a later, slightly slower version of the galop, the two-step, superseded the waltz in the 1890s as the most popular round dance of all; it was danced to a march-like music in $\frac{2}{4}$ or $\frac{4}{4}$. (John Philip Sousa's march *The Washington Post* of 1889 was identified with the two-step, and in England the two-step is still referred as a "Washington Post.").

In the mid-1840s the polka was introduced in America, one of the first dances to reflect the immigration of significant numbers of central Europeans; slightly later came the similar but slower schottische (not really "Scottish" but Germanic, though perhaps influenced by the steps and heel-taps of the Scots reel). From the same area of Europe came several dances related to the waltz but considered as "fancy dances"—the mazurka, the *redowá*, and the *varsovienne*.

The dance styles of American blacks had hardly any direct influence on white Americans until well after emancipation. The way was prepared, however, by imitations of black dancing in the northern blackface minstrel shows, which emphasized loose-limbed, pseudo-spontaneous duple-meter dances and, in the walk-arounds, prancing, strutting, turning, and bowing movements that were to characterize the later cakewalk. When all-black minstrel troupes came into existence after the Civil War, "essence" dances and soft-shoe numbers came with them, as did the cakewalk. The latter became a staple also in vaudeville and burlesque, as well as in the black musicals of the 1890s, such as *Clorindy, or the Origin of the Cakewalk* (1898) by Will Marion Cook (1869–1944) and the collaborative shows of the comedians Bert Williams and George Walker (among them *A Lucky Coon*, 1899; *Sons of Ham*, 1900; and *In Dahomey*, 1902). One characteristic common to all the dances of black origin was their basis in duple-meter music, which could serve, of course, for other dances as well, as is suggested by the subtitle (in the sheet-music version) of the best-known cakewalk song, Kerry Mills's *At a Georgia Camp Meeting* of 1897: "a characteristic march which can be used effectively as a two-step, polka, or cakewalk."

BANDS AND BAND MUSIC

The vernacular tradition's equivalent to the symphony orchestra was the wind band. By the early twentieth century hardly an American hamlet was without its village band; hardly a public occasion passed without the sound of the brasses, woodwinds, drums, and cymbals of a band; hardly anyone in the Western world was ignorant of at least one American band composer, John Philip Sousa.

The American band developed out of the pre-Revolution British Army regimental bands. Early American bands were often attached to units of the local militia; as well as playing for parades and drills, they sometimes gave concerts. Two early bands whose rosters were exclusively filled with militiamen were the Massachusetts Band, organized in 1783, and the U.S. Marine Band (1798). In 1800 the Marine Band was made up of two oboes, two clarinets, two horns, a bassoon, and a drum; thus its constitution differed from that of a chamber orchestra only in its lack of stringed instruments. With the invention in Germany about 1815 of valves for cornets, trumpets, and horns, these instruments (admirably suited to the band's outdoor requirements of portability and plenty of sound) gained a new flexibility, hence new popularity. As the bands added brasses to their complements, the woodwinds were first forced out entirely (as, for instance, from New York's City Brass Band, reorganized in 1834 by Thomas Dodworth as an exclusively brass-instrument ensemble) only to be reintroduced, about the middle of the century, in even greater numbers to balance the noisier brass.

Band concerts up to the Civil War, like other concerts, were pot-
pourris inevitably alternating solos by "guest vocal performers" with pieces
by the band. Each item was carefully numbered in the printed programs of
the day, hence the colloquial use of "number" for a musical composition.
The staples of the mid-century band repertory were quicksteps and other
marches; dances, especially the popular waltz and polka, with usually a fast
$\frac{2}{4}$ galop in conclusion; an occasional overture; and almost always a solo for
keyed bugle or the novel valve cornet to amaze the audience with the newly
won agility of the brass instruments. The high-brass soloists were the stars,
and often the conductors, of American bands; one of the most celebrated
early ones was Edward ("Ned") Kendall (1808–61), who formed the Boston
Brass Band in 1835 and was noted for his performances of such virtuoso
display pieces as John Holloway's *Wood Up Quick Step* (1835). Example
5-9 shows the third strain of *Wood Up* as published in 1839, in an unusual
arrangement by Holloway himself which reproduces Kendall's agile embel-
lishments; the music is printed, as was common in the period, in keyboard
short score rather than full score, for since there was no standard instrumentation for bands, each band usually made its own arrangements. There
were important exceptions, both in score publications—as in *Keith's Collection of Instrumental Music* (Boston, 1844)—and publications of parts—
as in G. W. E. Friedrich's 1854 compilation of twenty-four pieces, *Brass
Band Journal*, with parts for a twelve-piece band composed of two Eb soprano
saxhorns (or cornets); two Bb alto saxhorns (or cornets); one Eb trumpet; two

EXAMPLE 5-9. J. Holloway, *Wood Up. A Quick Step* (Boston: Oliver Ditson, 1839),
measures 25–32 (3rd strain).

E♭ tenor saxhorns; one baritone horn; two bass horns; and two drums, one "small" and the other "bass.")

Besides Kendall, prominent among the mid-century bandleaders were several members of the Dodworth family, connected with a band of that name based in New York and renowned from the mid-1830s through the 1870s. Even more celebrated, eventually, were several bands directed by Patrick S. Gilmore (1829–92), who had come from his native Ireland to the United States in 1849, already a cornet virtuoso as a lad of nineteen. After directing several bands in the Boston area, Gilmore resigned from the leadership of the Salem Brass Band in 1858 to establish his own band, a professional concert-giving, dance-playing, and public-occasion-enhancing ensemble of thirty-two members know as Gilmore's Grand Boston Band. During the Civil War, Gilmore was for a time in New Orleans, where he organized the first of the gargantuan concerts he became noted for. Like Berlioz, Gottschalk, Jullien, and others, Gilmore dreamed of a monster concert to end monster concerts. Back in Boston after the war, he began organizing such an affair on an unheard-of scale, a National Peace Jubilee to be held in 1869 and to surpass by far the chorus of 5000 and band of 500 (plus supplementary drum and bugle corps) he had mustered in New Orleans. Support for the idea was not easy to come by: Dwight, the Handel and Haydn Society, and other Boston nabobs were shocked at the Barnumesque plan. However, Gilmore cleverly gained the backing of first one, then both of the rival directors of the newly established (1867) Boston and New England Conservatories; launched a careful publicity campaign; found building funds for a three-and-a-half-acre Coliseum to house the festival; issued periodic rehearsal orders like a battlefield general to some 100 choral organizations totaling 10,296 singers; inveigled the great Ole Bull into being concertmaster of 525 orchestra players; commandeered a band of 486 wind and percussion players; and on June 15, 1869, as scheduled, the Jubilee was on. It lasted five days, with a grand opening concert, a second day's "symphony and oratorio" concert, a fourth's "classical" concert, and a final "Children's Day." The third day's concert was called "People's Day"; it featured three overtures, several national and religious songs, a trumpet solo, and two marches. The *pièce de résistance* was the "Anvil Chorus" from Verdi's *Il Trovatore* for the entire massed ensemble plus electrically operated city bells and a dozen cannon, with "the Anvil part performed by One Hundred Members of the Boston Fire Department."

Pleased with the popular (and financial) success of the National Peace Jubilee, Gilmore aimed to outdo it. Termination of the Franco-Prussian War gave him an excuse to try, and in 1872, in a new Coliseum holding an audience of 50,000, he staged a World's Peace Jubilee. A chorus of 20,000 (some from points as remote from Boston as Milwaukee, St. Louis, Iowa City, and San Francisco) and an instrumental assemblage of almost 2000 proved, not surprisingly, unmanageable; the second Jubilee was a monumental failure, although somehow all ten days' concerts were presented.[15] Gilmore attempted no more musical gigantism; nevertheless, having associated himself in 1873 with the 22nd Regiment of New York, he enlarged its band to sixty-six players. For almost two decades this new Gilmore Band was the foremost professional band in the country; Gilmore took it on successful and influential tours (to the West Coast in 1876, to Europe in 1878, then across the United States every fall and spring in the 1880s), and it kept growing in size until eventually its roster numbered one hundred.

Gilmore died in 1892, on tour and playing at the St. Louis Exposition. His band settled on a new leader a year later, an Irish-born cellist and composer named Victor Herbert (1859–1924); Herbert was to remain director of the 22nd Regiment Band for seven years. Meanwhile, another bandmaster was rising to prominence: John Philip Sousa (1854–1932).

As a bandmaster, Sousa became internationally renowned. Appointed in 1880 leader of the Marine Band, he made it into a balanced ensemble, which by 1891 included forty-nine players (twenty-six reeds, twenty brass, three percussion). Sousa organized his own band in 1892 and with it toured the United States, Canada, Europe, and in 1910–11, the world. He hired the most spectacular virtuosos as soloists—such as the cornetists Bohumir Kryl, Alessandro Liberati, and Herbert L. Clarke; the clarinetist Herman Bellstedt; the trombonist Arthur Pryor; and the sopranos Estelle Liebling and Marjorie Moody—and increased the size of his band, until in the 1920s it averaged seventy players, with about forty reed, twenty-five brass, and five percussion instruments. It became, quite simply, the most celebrated band in history. Long-lived, Sousa is the first musician we have encountered in this study to have lived into the radio-and-recording era and to have helped enlarge the popular audience through the new technology of the twentieth century (although, ironically, he had various members of the Sousa Band—notably Pryor, until 1903, when he left Sousa to form his own band— conduct for recordings since he felt that "canned music"—a term he coined— was a menace to musical culture, on several counts).

As the last sentence implies, Sousa had larger concerns than just those of directing a commercial band. He was an active fighter for composers' rights, an important advocate of copyright reform, and one of the founders in 1914 of the American Society of Composers, Authors and Publishers (ASCAP). This, the first performing-rights organization in the United States, licenses to commercial users the rights to perform copyrighted musical compositions; collects royalties on such performances; and distributes the royalties to composers, lyricists, and publishers.

---

[15] A historical footnote: concluding the fifth day's program, with the audience requested to sing the last two verses, was the venerable hymn *Coronation* (1793) by the eighteenth-century singing master Oliver Holden.

As a composer, Sousa essayed many kinds of popular music, notably songs and operettas; the well-known march *El Capitan* was fashioned from two of the songs in an operetta (1896) of that title. But it was as a composer of wind-band marches that Sousa triumphed. He lived at a time when the march was especially popular: not only was it the foundation of the repertory of military and parade bands and of the ubiquitous village bands; it also provided the music for many ballroom dances (e.g., the two-step of the 1890s), songs, and hymns. The marches of Sousa were so keenly attuned to his time's temper, so finely honed, such perfect exemplars that Sousa understandably came to be known as "The March King."

The typical Sousa march is a fairly brief work in, of course, duple meter—an even-pulsed $\frac{2}{4}$ or $\frac{2}{2}$ or a galloping $\frac{6}{8}$—with a number of 16- or 32-measure strains preceded by a 4- or 8-measure introduction. Within this conventional framework Sousa was able to achieve remarkable flexibility and variety, particularly in the harmony, which is by no means predictable and is often surprisingly wide-ranging, given the narrow confines of the march form. Sousa's most famous march, *The Stars and Stripes Forever* (1897), is constructed like this: introduction (4 measures); first (16) and second (16) strains, each repeated; Trio (32); "break" (24), unstable, dramatic, and suspensive, leading to a repetition of the Trio, louder and with new piccolo counter-melody; repetition of the "break," leading again to the Trio, with yet another counter-melody in trombones added (see Example 5-10). Typ-

EXAMPLE 5-10. J. P. Sousa, *The Stars and Stripes Forever* (1897), after a photostat of the autograph manuscript, Music Division, New York Public Library. (a) Introduction and first-strain theme. (b) Second-strain theme. (c) Trio theme. (d) "Break," beginning.

ically, although the march begins in E♭, the Trio is in A♭ and the piece ends in the key a fifth lower than its beginning.

Sousa composed about 140 marches between *The Revival* of 1876 (which appropriately uses for its Trio theme the gospel hymn *In the Sweet By-and-By*) and *The Kansas Wildcats* of 1931. About half are in the skittish ⁶⁄₈ meter, including some of the best known: *Semper Fidelis* (1888), *Washington Post* (1889), and *The Liberty Bell* (1893). *El Capitan* combines ⁶⁄₈ and ²⁄₄, as do several others taken from operettas. Richard Franko Goldman (1910–80), like his father Edwin Franko Goldman (1878–1956) a prominent bandmaster, urged more performances of "such magnificent examples as *The Fairest of the Fair* (1908), *Hands Across the Sea* (1899), *The Invincible Eagle* (1901), *The Gallant Seventh* (1922)."[16] Like the earlier favorites, these live up to Sousa's own ideal of a band march: "It must be as free from padding as a marble statue. Every line must be carved with unerring skill. Once padded, it ceases to be a march." Having thus spoken as an artist, Sousa spoke also for the free-and-easy eclecticism of the vernacular tradition:

> The composer must, to be sure, follow accepted harmonization; but that is not enough. He must be gifted with the ability to pick and choose here and there, to throw off the domination of any one tendency. If he is a so-called purist in music, that tendency will rule his marches and will limit their appeal.[17]

Sousa saw himself as a highly skilled and tasteful purveyor of entertainment: true to the vernacular tradition, he was not concerned with elevating his audience but with pleasing it. He unconsciously but sharply distinguished between the thought of the cultivated and vernacular traditions in a reflection made after spending an afternoon with Theodore Thomas:

[16] "John Philip Sousa," *Hi Fi/Stereo Review*, XIX/1 (July 1967), 35–47; reprinted in R. F. Goldman, *Essays and Reviews 1948–1968*, ed. Dorothy Klotzman (ISAMm 13 [1980]).
[17] *Marching Along* (Boston: Hale, Cushman and Flint, 1928), p. 359.

Thomas had a highly organized symphony orchestra . . . I a highly organized
wind band. . . . Each of us was reaching an end, but through different methods.
He gave Wagner, Liszt, and Tchaikowsky, in the belief that he was educating
his public; I gave Wagner, Liszt, and Tchaikowsky with the hope that I was
entertaining my public.[18]

Mechanical Instruments

A note on mechanical instruments is appropriate here. American
technology of the nineteenth century led to a wide variety of them, the so-
called nickelodeons of public places and the player pianos of American living
rooms. The former, cheaper in the long run for barrooms, poolrooms, brothels, restaurants, and ballrooms than live musicians, came in all shapes, sizes,
and degrees of complexity. The Automatic Harp of the Rudolph Wurlitzer
Co. was advertised as "especially desirable where a piano cannot be used,
on account of its being too loud." The Violano-Virtuoso of the Mills Novelty
Co. was a coin-operated, mechanically played violin with piano accompaniment. The Banjorchestra, when fed a nickel, would produce music from an
automatic banjo, with support from piano, triangle, drums, tambourine, and
castanets. Orchestrions, basically mechanical pipe organs with extras, ranged
in size and cost up to the two Wurlitzer behemoths, the Paganini Violin
Orchestra and the Pian-Orchestra. The Seeburg Company's catalogue described
the "KT Special" orchestrion as "piano, xylophone, mandolin attachment,
bass drum, snare drums, tympani, cymbal, triangle, castanets, tambourines,
Chinese block," all encased in a head-high glass-fronted cabinet of rich birds-
eye maple.

Mechanically operated player pianos or "pianolas" (the name reflecting the great success of the Aeolian Company's Pianola model, invented in
1895) were the domestic counterpart. Activated by foot pedals or electricity,
bellows-operated, and fed with perforated music rolls, player pianos were
fabulously popular from the 1890s through the 1920s, when radio, phonorecordings, and ultimately the Great Depression spelled their demise. A
later connoisseur and collector, Lewis Graham, claimed that "between 1895
and 1912 there were more player pianos in the United States than bath-
tubs,"[19] and according to U.S. Department of Commerce statistics, some
205,556 of the 347,589 pianos sold in 1923 were player pianos (it was the
peak year of their manufacture).

---

[18] Ibid., p. 132. A number of Sousa's lesser-known marches, with others by his contemporaries, are recorded on *NW* 226; *NW* 282 (*The Sousa and Pryor Bands*) reissues only
original recordings, 1901–26, and is thus a most valuable document.

[19] *New York Times*, November 3, 1966.

RAGTIME

In 1899 the novelist and musical enthusiast Rupert Hughes (1872–1956) commented,

> . . . If Negro music has its "Go down, Moses" . . . so it had also its hilarious banjo-plucking and its characteristic dances. It is the latter mood that is having a strong renascence and is sweeping the country like a plague of clog-hopping locusts.[20]

Hughes was speaking of the craze for ragtime, which indeed swept the country in the 1890s through the media of piano players, player pianos, dance bands, and commercial sheet music (both songs and piano pieces). In the diluted form of the cakewalk march, it was played by Sousa's and other concert bands here and in Europe, where according to a publisher's blurb "the native bands have taken up this peculiar style of distinctly American music, even going so far as to play the *Marseillaise* in rag time."

Many threads of earlier American music came together to form the fabric of the ragtime of the 1890s. Earliest, perhaps, was an emphatic use of syncopation by American blacks, partly derived from African drumming, partly from Afro-Caribbean dance rhythms. Among the few reports we have on secular slave music, several mention the practice of "patting Juba." Reading between the lines of these brief comments, one gets the impression that the practice involved intricate rhythmic patterns played off against a regular beat—syncopation, in short, but of a consistent, insistent kind. Thus, a correspondent of Edgar Allan Poe, likening irregularities in poetic meters to "clapping Juba," described the latter for Poe in a letter of 1835:

> There is no attempt to keep time to *all* the notes, but then it comes so pat & so distinct that the cadence is never lost. . . . Such irregularities are like rests and grace notes. They must be so managed as neither to hasten or retard the beat. The time of the bar must be the same, no matter how many notes are in it.[21]

One source couples the Negro dance-name "Juba" with the English dance-name "jig" and speaks of "patting" as an intricate rhythmic accompaniment to such a "jig"; another, a Mississippi planter discussing in 1851 how to

---

[20] "A Eulogy of Rag-Time," *Musical Record* (Boston), No. 447 (April 1, 1899), pp. 157–59.

[21] *The Complete Works of Edgar Allan Poe*, ed. James A. Harrison (New York: Thomas Y. Crowell Company, 1902), Vol. 17, p. 22.

manage a plantation, tells of his slaves' Saturday night dance music: "Charley's fiddle is always accompanied with Ithurod on the triangle and Sam to 'pat.' "[22] A particular *kind* of syncopated rhythm, conceivably one essence of "patting Juba," shows up in two disparate sources of the late 1850s. Gottschalk's *Souvenir de Porto Rico* of 1857 (see Example 4-10) opposes a typical $\frac{2}{4}$ *danza* bass rhythm of the Caribbean to a strongly syncopated upper part, emphasizing ♫♩ and ♫♫ patterns. In 1859, James Hungerford, of Maryland, published an autobiographical novel, *The Old Plantation*, and in it reproduced a "corn song" one of his slaves had sung on an outing in 1832. Prominent in an otherwise regularly accented $\frac{4}{4}$ meter are the syncopes ♫♩ and, one level higher, ♩♩ ♪. Even before the 1850s, however, such patterns were well known and were identified with blacks: they are commonplaces in the songs of the minstrel shows of the 1840s (see Example 5-8; also the choruses of *Oh! Susanna* and *Dixie*), particularly the walk-arounds, the dancing for which, in later minstrelsy, was the cakewalk, with its prancing kick-steps, bows back and forward, and salutes to the spectators. These particular mild syncopes became in fact the hallmarks of the cakewalk two-steps played by the northern bands of the 1890s. Compare, for example, the excerpts in Example 5-11 from the "corn song" transcribed in 1859 by Hungerford and from the "Cake Walk-Two Step" *Bunch o' Blackberries* of 1899, as played by Sousa's band.

EXAMPLE 5-11. Negro slave song and cakewalk rhythms. (a) *Roun' de Corn, Sally!* as transcribed in James Hungerford, *The Old Plantation, and What I Gathered There in an Autumn Month* (New York: Harper & Brothers, 1859) p. 191 (excerpts). (b) Abe Holzmann, *Bunch o' Blackberries* (New York: Feist & Frankenthaler, 1899), Trio (treble melody only), measures 1–8.

Ragtime included the simple syncopations just cited, plus others. Perhaps the earliest American music to suggest the intricate and fanciful rhythms of ragtime is that of the banjo dances of the early minstrel shows (see pp. 116–17). Again, we can relate at least one aspect of these—accentuated rests—to "patting Juba." The poet and musician Sidney Lanier

---

[22] Both comments quoted in Epstein, "Slave Music," 383.

(1842–81) observed that

> . . . every one who has noticed a Southern Negro's "patting" will have been apt to hear an effect . . . produced by omitting the stroke, of foot or of hand, which the hearer expects to fall on the accented note at the first of the bar, thus:

Allegro vivace

♩♪♪♪♪│⁊ ♪♪♪│⁊ ♩ │♩̂ ⁊ │

and similar forms.[23]

The minstrel-show banjo tunes were generally called *jigs*. So was early ragtime: until about 1897, when the terms *rag* and *ragtime* gained currency, a pianist or a band that played in the ragtime style was called a *jig pianist* or a *jig band*. (Here we see the origin of the malodorous equation of the term *jig* with *black*). Thus, in its rhythmic aspects, ragtime derived from the banjo dance-tune style, which may itself be related to "patting Juba."

Ragtime typically involves two layers of rhythmic activity: a regularly accented, even bass and a strongly cross-accented treble. Against the bass, which normally stomps along with a heavy two-beat (♩ ♩) or prances in the band-like oom-pah oom-pah rhythm of ♫ ♫ , the treble is "ragg'd" by throwing accents onto other, sub-beats. Melodic phrasing of even sixteenths can do it: ♬♬ or, more common, ♬♬ (the relationship of the first pattern to the *danza's* ♪.♫ is worth noting). Variants of these, throwing an accent on the fourth sixteenth (the bass would come down on the fifth), are common in the early printed rags: ♬♩, ♬♫, ♬♫ and ♬♬ all begin the same way. The phrase may run along evenly but bump into an offbeat accent—♬♬, ♬♫—or be drily articulated: ♫⁊⁊♫ . Accentuating the eighth sixteenth in a measure, usually by anticipating the first note of the next and holding it over the barline, is also common (♫♬│♩) especially in patterns borrowing the cakewalk motif (♬♬│♩ or ♬♬♬│♩). In Scott Joplin's *Stoptime Rag* (1910) the old banjo-tune technique of accentuated rests is expanded: the composer instructs that ". . . the pianist should stamp the heel of one foot heavily upon the floor, whenever the word 'stomp' appears in the music," which it does on *rests* appearing on normally accented beats.

This brief discussion of ragtime rhythms has been based only on

[23] *The Science of English Verse* (New York: Charles Scribner's Sons, 1880), p. 189.

printed rags. First-hand experience of the playing of old-timers among ragtime pianists—like Willie "the Lion" Smith (1897–1973) or Eubie Blake (1883–1983)—suggests that, as with most dance music of any era, printed ragtime tends to be a simplified form of the music as performed.

The formal design and the basic meter and tempo of ragtime, as it was first published in the 1890s, came from Euro-American dances (quadrilles, polkas, schottisches) and especially post-Civil War marches, with their several strains, each repeated and one or two dipping into the subdominant key, and their heavy two-beat meter. Joplin's celebrated *Maple Leaf Rag* (1899), the best-known early piano rag to be published, is in $\frac{2}{4}$, marked "Tempo di Marcia"; Joplin elsewhere indicated "Slow March Tempo" and even cautioned performers, "Notice! Don't play this piece fast. It is never right to play 'Ragtime' fast." *Maple Leaf Rag*, from the formal standpoint, might almost be a Sousa march: first strain (16 measures, repeated); second strain (16, repeated); first strain again; "Trio," so named and consisting of a third strain (16, repeated) in the subdominant and a fourth strain (16, repeated) back in the tonic.

The earliest appearance of the word *rag* in connection with a musical work was in the sheet music of Ernest Hogan's song *All Coons Look Alike to Me* (1896), which has an optional syncopated accompaniment cited as a "Negro Rag." And indeed, although later ragtime revivals (in the 1950s and especially the 1970s) tended to concentrate on instrumental rags, ragtime was originally as much a vocal music as instrumental, its principal vehicle being the so-called *coon song* (*coon* being an old term used by American whites, usually mockingly or disparagingly, to refer to blacks). As with the music of the earlier minstrel shows, coon songs were initially written and performed by whites, on the newly popular vaudeville stage; one celebrated "coon shouter" was May Irwin, perhaps best known for her delivery of Charles E. Trevathan's *Bully Song* (1896; recorded on NW 221:s1/8). Some blacks, however, were leading composers of the genre, notably Bob Cole (1863–1911) in collaboration with the Johnson brothers (James Weldon Johnson [1871–1938] and J. Rosamund Johnson [1873–1954]); the most successful of their many joint songs was the winsome *Under the Bamboo Tree* (1902), the beginning of which is given as Example 5-12.

The first published instrumental rag so titled, *The Mississippi Rag* (January 1897), was composed by a white bandmaster in Chicago, William Krell. The man soon to be acknowledged as "The King of Ragtime," however, was the black pianist and composer Scott Joplin (1868–1917). Joplin grew up in Texarkana, Texas, and began his career as an itinerant pianist, playing in honky-tonks and brothels. He went to Chicago briefly in 1893 to try his luck in the entertainment halls that had sprung up around the World's Columbian Exposition of that year; by 1896, after more restless wandering (he never really settled down), he was in Sedalia, Missouri. There his first

EXAMPLE 5-12. Bob Cole, James Weldon Johnson, and J. Rosamund Johnson, *Under the Bamboo Tree* (New York: Jos. W. Stern. & Co., 1902), measures 1–10 of Chorus.

published piano rag, *Original Rags*, came out in March 1899; later the same year appeared *Maple Leaf Rag*, named for a saloon and dance hall in Sedalia. The piece was eventually a resounding success and became the most famous of all piano rags. By the time of his death Joplin had published more than thirty original rags and other piano pieces, songs, and arrangements as well. He had even larger aims: in 1899 in Sedalia he staged a ballet called *The Ragtime Dance*, and in 1903 in St. Louis an opera, *The Guest of Honor* (unpublished and now apparently lost); in 1911 he published another opera, *Treemonisha*. The artistic success of these larger works is debatable, but that of Joplin's piano rags is not; they can only be described as elegant, varied, often subtle, and as sharply incised as a cameo. They are the precise American equivalent, in terms of a native style of dance music, of minuets by Mozart, mazurkas by Chopin, or waltzes by Brahms. They can be both lovely and powerful, infectious and moving—depending, of course, on the skill and stylishness of the pianist, for they are not easy music technically and they demand a clean but "swinging" performance. Joplin wrote poignantly of the genre in a brief manual of ragtime exercises that he published in 1908:

> That all publications masquerading under the name of ragtime are not the genuine article will be better known when these exercises are studied. That real ragtime of the higher class is rather difficult to play is a painful truth which most pianists have discovered. Syncopations are no indication of light and trashy music. . . .[24]

The earliest published piano rags were a mature kind of music that had merely lacked crystallization in print. They were also a music of metrical precision for all their cross-accents and rhythmic jolts, music for marching or dancing, music that could adequately and accurately be reproduced on the popular player pianos of the time—which they were, and the wide dissemination of the piano roll undoubtedly stimulated ragtime's acceptance and popularity. Ragtime on player-piano rolls is thus the very earliest American music we can actually hear in contemporaneous performances.

One such performance is Joplin's of his own *Weeping Willow* (1903), recorded for Connorized player-piano roll No. 10277 (transferred to tape in 1956 and reissued on Riverside RLP–12–110). Like most early rags, the form of *Weeping Willow* is built on four different strains plus introduction, played in order Intro–1–2–1–3–4; in Joplin's recorded performance the repetition of each strain finds the treble thrown up an octave to provide new color (Example 5-13). In some later rags, for example, the harmonically adventuresome *Euphonic Sounds* (1909), Joplin turned to a clear-cut rondo form, whereas in the darkly colored, dense-textured *Magnetic Rag* (1914) the form is a rounded Intro–1–2–3–4–1–Coda. Other ragtime composer-performers modified still other aspects. The New Orleans pianist Ferdinand "Jelly Roll" Morton (1885–1941) exemplified the Crescent City's style of fairly slow rags, with swingier rhythms than the St. Louis manner of Joplin and with melodic "walking" basses, as in Morton's *King Porter Stomp* (1906). Elements of Negro blues (see p. 208), both formal structure and "blue notes," crept into rags from the time of W. C. Handy's *Memphis Blues* (1912), actually subtitled "A Southern Rag," which preceded by two years the publication of Handy's most celebrated and universally known blues, *St. Louis*

---

[24] *The School of Ragtime*, reprinted in *The Collected Works of Scott Joplin*, ed. Vera Brodsky Lawrence (New York: The New York Public Library, 1971), Vol I, p. 283. Some of the comments in this paragraph are adapted from my review (in *Stereo Review*, XXVI/4 [April 1971], 84) of Joshua Rifkin's recording of *Scott Joplin: Piano Rags* (Nonesuch H-71248), which, more than any other single thing, spurred a ragtime revival in the early 1970s.

EXAMPLE 5-13. S. Joplin, *Weeping Willow* (St. Louis, MO: Val A. Reis Music Co., 1903). (a) First strain, beginning. (b) Second strain, beginning. (c) Third strain, beginning. (d) Fourth strain, beginning.

Blues. The New York "stride" piano style, exemplified by the music of James P. Johnson (1894–1955), marked the turn from ragtime to jazz: in works like *Carolina Shout* (ca. 1917), *Caprice Rag* (1917), and *Harlem Strut* (1921), Johnson's striding left hand emphasizes the offbeats and transforms the older two-beat meter into a jazzy four, while his right-hand style dissolves the classic ragtime syncopes into long-breathed runs of even eighths (not quite even, in actual performance) and triplets (Example 5-14). Another master stride pianist, and one who in fact studied with Johnson, was Thomas "Fats" Waller (1904–43); many of his recordings leave ragtime far behind stylistically, but others, such as the dazzlingly virtuoso *Handful of Keys* of 1929, are clearly in the ragtime tradition.

This shift in style, however, marked the end—temporarily, at least— of the short, happy public career of ragtime and the beginning of the era of blues, at least in the public consciousness of Americans.

EXAMPLE 5-14. *Caprice Rag*, measures 5–8, by James P. Johnson. Copyright © 1963 by Mills Music, Inc. Used by permission.

BIBLIOGRAPHICAL NOTES

George Pullen Jackson's books on the shape-note tradition, beginning with the seminal *White Spirituals in the Southern Uplands* (Chapel Hill: University of North Carolina Press, 1933), are necessarily the foundation for any further study; Buell E. Cobb's *Sacred Harp: A Tradition and Its Music* (Athens: University of Georgia Press, 1978) is also valuable. Wallace White writes engagingly about the annual "Big Singing" in Benton, Kentucky—a gathering of people from far and wide to sing shape-note hymns from Walker's *Southern Harmony*—in *The New Yorker*, January 19, 1987, pp. 78–85. The music of the white gospel tradition is considered by James C. Downey in "The Music of American Revivalism" (Ph.D. dissertation, Tulane University, 1968).

Dena J. Epstein's valuable research, over at least two decades, on black music before the Civil War is brought together in the masterly *Sinful Tunes and Spirituals: Black Folk Music to the Civil War* (Urbana: University of Illinois Press, 1977); a later study by her is especially relevant to this chapter: "Black Spirituals: Their Emergence Into Public Knowledge," *Black Music Research Newsletter*, VIII/2 (Spring 1986), 5–9. The epochal anthology by William Allen, Charles Ware, and Lucy McKim Garrison, *Slave Songs of the United States* (New York: A. Simpson & Co., 1867), has been reprinted twice: by Peter Smith in 1951 and by Books for Libraries Press in 1971. John Lovell's *Black Song: The Forge and the Flame* (New York: Macmillan, Inc., 1972; repr. New York: Paragon House Publishers, 1986) is a thoroughgoing survey. Irene V. Jackson has made a helpful bibliographical contribution with *Afro-American Religious Music: A Bibliography and a Catalogue of Gospel Music* (Westport, CT: Greenwood Press, 1979).

Carl Wittke's *Tambo and Bones* (Durham, NC: Duke University Press, 1930) is complemented by Robert C. Toll's *Blacking Up: The Minstrel Show in Nineteenth-Century America* (New York: Oxford University Press, 1974), but both are weak on the music of the minstrel shows; Hans Nathan's study of *Dan Emmett and the Rise of Early Negro Minstrelsy* (Norman: University of Oklahoma Press, 1962) is richer in that regard. Especially notable are two essays by Robert B Winans: "The Folk, the Stage, and the Five-String Banjo in the Nineteenth Century," *Journal of American Folklore*, LXXXIX (1976), 407–37; and "Early Minstrel Show Music, 1843–1852," in *Musical Theatre in America: Papers and Proceedings of the Conference . . .*, pp. ed. Glenn Loney (Westport, CT: Greenwood Press, 1984), 71–97. Henry Sampson's *Blacks in Blackface: A Source Book on Early Black Musical Shows* (Metuchen, NJ: Scarecrow Press, 1980) is a good guide.

Pauline Norton's major article "Dance" in *TNGDAM* and Thornton Hagert's lengthy liner notes for *NW* 293 (*Come and Trip It: Instrumental Dance Music, 1780's–1920's*) are both illuminating. See also the following essays in *Chronicles of the American Dance*, ed. Paul Magriel (New York: Henry Holt, 1948): Lillian Moore, "John Durang—The First American Dancer" (pp. 15–37); Marian Hannah Winter, "Juba and American Minstrelsy" (pp. 39–63); George Freedley, "The Black Crook and the White Fawn" (pp. 65–79); and Rosetta O'Neill, "The Dodworth Family and Ballroom Dancing in New York" (pp. 81–100).

The periodical *Journal of Band Research* (1964/65–00) is a good source on American bands and band music; for the period dealt with in this chapter, Frank J. Cipolla's "Annotated Guide for the Study and Performance of Nineteenth Century Band Music in the United States" (XIV/1 [Fall 1978], 22–40) is helpful. Jon Newsom's "The American Brass Band Movement," *Quarterly Journal of the Library of Congress*, XXXVI/2 (Spring 1979), 114–39, is especially well illustrated and well documented. Sousa has been admirably served in several books by Paul Bierley, including *John Philip Sousa, American Phenomenon* (New York: Appleton-Century-Crofts, 1973) and *The Works of John Philip Sousa* (Columbus, OH: Integrity Press, 1984), and in the collection edited by Jon Newsom, *Perspectives on John Philip Sousa* (Washington, DC: Library of Congress, 1983).

Mechanical instruments have been chronicled in Harvey N. Roehl's *Player-Piano Treasury* (Vestal, NY: The Vestal Press, 1963) and Q. David Bowers's *Put Another Nickel In* (Vestal, NY: The Vestal Press, 1966).

Edward A. Berlin's *Ragtime: A Cultural and Musical History* (Berkeley: University of California Press, 1980) is the most authoritative account, superseding the still admirable pioneering study by Rudi Blesh and Harriet Janis, *They All Played Ragtime*, the fourth edition of which (New York: Oak Publications, 1971) includes as a bonus the music of sixteen complete piano rags. *Ragtime: Its History, Composers, and Music*, ed. John Hasse (New York: Schirmer Books, 1985), is an uneven but useful grab-bag of an anthology, with especially helpful biblio-discographic appendices. Joplin's music is reprinted from early editions in Vera Brodsky Lawrence, ed., *The Collected Works of Scott Joplin*, with an introduction by Rudi Blesh (New York: New York Public Library, 1971); a revised edition justifying the new title *The Complete Works of Scott Joplin*, with an added preface by Carman Moore, was issued in 1981.

SIX

THE CULTIVATED TRADITION, 1865–1920

American music of the cultivated tradition from the end of the Civil War to the end of World War I was largely dominated by the attitudes, the ideals, and the modes of expression of nineteenth-century Europe, particularly Austria and Germany. Virtually all our leading composers were initiated into music by Americans who had emigrated from Europe; they were trained professionally during sojourns in Europe; and when they came back their music was played by ensembles, choruses, and orchestras led either by Europeans or European-trained conductors. Some of their music was even published first in Europe, by Breitkopf & Härtel in Leipzig or by the Leipzig branch of the Boston firm of Arthur P. Schmidt (1846–1921), who in grateful return for an American career (he was German-born) made it a point of conscience to publish American music. In Chapter Three we examined the sources of this Germanophilia; in Chapter Four we saw evidences of its rising tide up to the Civil War; in the present chapter we see its highwater mark. However, toward the turn of the twentieth century the work of a few composers reflected other currents: a new interest in American folklore, in developments in French and Russian music, and in topical subject matter related to the American scene. By the end of the period one remarkable individualist, Charles Ives, had completed most of a body of work which, drawing on both the cultivated and vernacular traditions, offered the possibility of a new synthesis.

INSTITUTIONAL FOUNDATIONS

It was during the 1860–1920 period that the institutional foundations of the cultivated tradition were firmly consolidated. Music conservatories were founded, among them some still considered pre-eminent: in 1857 the Peabody Conservatory in Baltimore (at which, however, instruction was delayed by the Civil War and other problems and began only in 1868); in 1865 the Oberlin Conservatory in Ohio; in 1867 the New England Conservatory in Boston as well as the Cincinnati Conservatory and the Chicago Academy of Music (later renamed the Chicago Musical College); in New York City, the New York College of Music in 1878, the National Conservatory in 1885, the Institute of Musical Art in 1905 (merged in 1926 with another conservatory to become the Juilliard School of Music), and the Mannes College of Music in 1916; in 1919 the Community Music Center in San Francisco.

Thanks to Lowell Mason's efforts of the 1830s, music was a part of school curricula across the land. After the Civil War it entered the colleges and universities as well: Vassar College, the University of Pennsylvania, and Harvard University established music professorships in the 1870s, and they were followed soon by Yale University and others. The Music Teachers National Association was founded in 1876, and the Music Educators National Conference in 1907 (under the name of Music Supervisors National Conference).

The first American copyright act, that of 1790, had not mentioned musical compositions (though some collections of music categorized as "books" were protected), but a revision of 1831 did; a third revision in 1909 provided performing-rights protection for musical works presented "for profit" but left unmentioned the important technological developments of player-piano rolls and sound recordings. Composers, lyricists, and music publishers alike were benefited by the establishment in 1914 of the first performing-rights organization, ASCAP (the American Society of Composers, Authors and Publishers). Performing musicians had organized sporadically in protective associations ever since the founding of the Musical Fund Society of Philadelphia in 1820; by the end of the nineteenth century the AFM (American Federation of Musicians) was the principal musicians' union (with a membership by 1913 of 64,000 in 636 locals.)

With monies provided not by government but by groups of private citizens spearheaded by individual philanthropists, major concert halls were built: Philadelphia's Academy of Music (1857), Cincinnati's Music Hall (1878), the Auditorium in Chicago (1889); Carnegie Hall in New York (1891); Boston's Symphony Hall (1900). The Metropolitan Opera House in New York was inaugurated in 1882 (razed 1966).

During the entire period New York City was the performance center of the cultivated tradition. But the ideological center was undoubtedly Boston, where John Sullivan Dwight (1813–93) reigned through his *Journal of Music* (1852–81) as chief spokesperson for the tradition. A Harvardian who had trained for the ministry, Dwight began his career as the first really significant and broadly influential American music critic and arbiter of taste with a series of more than one hundred articles in *The Harbinger*, journal of the Transcendentalist community at Brook Farm from 1845 to 1849. *Dwight's Journal*, which ran through 1051 issues in its nearly thirty years of publication, was the most substantial and long-lived music periodical America had known (although by no means the first), despite a comparatively small subscription list. It included critical reviews; analyses; reports on concert life in both Europe and the United States; essays on music history and theory; and translations from German and French music treatises, biographies, and journals. Throughout its existence, it was informed with Dwight's unshakably high-minded belief in music—fine-art music, at least—as the language of feeling and of natural religion, whose purpose was "to hallow pleasure, and to naturalize religion" (as he expressed it in an address to the Harvard Musical Association as early as 1841). In announcing his *Journal*, Dwight promised that "it will insist much on the claims of 'Classical' music . . . because the *enduring* needs always to be held up in contrast with the ephemeral."[1] The *Journal* did so insist, with Dwight of course determining what was to be considered "the enduring."

Among the contributors to *Dwight's Journal* who might appropriately be mentioned in this summary of the "institutional foundations" of the cultivated tradition were America's first musicologist and the first historian of America's music: Alexander Wheelock Thayer (1817–97), whose *Ludwig van Beethovens Leben* (1866–79, completed posthumously by Deiters and Riemann; English versions published in 1921 and 1964) is still valuable, and the Alsatian-born Frédéric Louis Ritter (1834–91), whose *Music in America* (New York, 1883) was the first attempt at a comprehensive survey. Ritter relieved himself, however, of any responsibility to treat the vernacular or folk traditions by saying flatly, as he began a last chapter on "The Cultivation of Popular Music," that "the people's song . . . is not to be found among the American people"!

If Dwight and contributors to his journal like Thayer and Ritter were the literary voices of the art-music of the age, a group of New England

---

[1] Quoted in George Willis Cooke, *John Sullivan Dwight* (Boston: Small, Maynard & Co., 1898), p. 147.

composers was the musical voice. I shall call them the Second New England School, grouping them together by virtue of their common inheritance, attitudes, and general style much as I grouped the late eighteenth-century composers of the First New England School.

THE SECOND NEW ENGLAND SCHOOL

Oldest of the group, and teacher of many of its younger members, was John Knowles Paine (1839–1906). His first musical studies were with Hermann Kotzschmar, who had come to America in 1848 with the Saxonia Band, an ensemble like the Germanians, and had settled in Paine's home town of Portland, Maine. Aiming to become a church organist, Paine went to Germany in 1858 and stayed nearly four years, studying with the Berlin organist Karl August Haupt (as did almost forty younger Americans) and others, and acquiring some reputation as a performer. Back in America in 1861, he got a post as organist in a Boston church. The next year he was appointed instructor at Harvard, to teach a non-credit music course and serve as university organist. By the mid-1870s the university was convinced of the validity of a music curriculum, and the 1875–76 academic year began with Paine as Harvard's first professor of music.[2] He was to remain at Harvard for thirty years, until his retirement in 1905. As Kenneth Roberts has written appreciatively and perceptively (in the entry on Paine in *TNGDAM*),

> He made Cambridge a center of musical America [and] pioneered not only in the setting up of a collegiate department of music, but in being a "composer-in-residence," in contrast to the nature of appointments in contemporary European universities.

Paine's work as a composer ranged from piano and organ pieces and chamber music to incidental music for plays, overtures, symphonic poems, and two symphonies; from songs, hymns, and choral cantatas to an oratorio, a Mass, and a grand opera. Most of it cannot be faulted in workmanship, none of it in seriousness of purpose: Paine took very seriously music's mission to "hallow pleasure," and if his music seems somewhat over-aspiring to profundity, hardly daring to relax or smile, this should be ascribed not to incompetence but to his aesthetic attitude and to the difficulty of attempting to emulate the masterworks of Europe's mature cultivated tradition from a base in a still-New World.

---

[2] Not the first in the country, as is often claimed: Ritter, at Vassar, preceded Paine in holding a professorial chair in music, as did Hugh A. Clarke at the University of Pennsylvania.

Stylistically, most of Paine's music falls within the orbit of the Viennese Classicists and the early German Romantics; he also held J. S. Bach in high esteem, was one of the first American organists to perform Bach's works regularly, and developed considerable contrapuntal craft. Mendelssohn is the strongest influence on choral works like the *Centennial Hymn* (1876; on a text by Whittier), the cantata *Realm of Fancy* (1882; after Keats), and the oratorio *St. Peter* (1872). Earlier than these works is the extraordinary Mass in D (first performed in Berlin in 1867, with Paine conducting— extraordinary not only as a work of "grandeur and haunting beauty" (as Gunther Schuller, who exhumed the work in 1972 and conducts it on *NW* 262/263, describes it) but also as the first major concert composition by an American to be performed in Europe, not to mention its being extremely unusual as a setting of the Roman Catholic Mass text by a young Protestant American composer (whose inspiration for writing it, except perhaps in emulation of Beethoven's *Missa solemnis*, remains mysterious). Beethoven's earlier symphonies, especially the Fifth, are the major models for Paine's First Symphony (1875; premiered in Boston by the Theodore Thomas Orchestra); Schumann's four, for Paine's Second ("In the Spring"; 1879).

Paine spoke in 1872 in favor of "adherence to the historical forms, as developed by Bach, Händel, Mozart, and Beethoven" as a "healthy reaction" to the "extremely involved and complicated technics of music, like Wagner, Liszt, and their adherents."[3] However, his own style eventually reflected the music of the latter group. An orchestral prelude, part of Paine's choral and instrumental incidental music for Sophocles's *Oedipus Tyrannus*, Op. 35 (1881), is quite Lisztian in its design and its thematic transformations (Example 6-1). And Paine admitted that in his opera *Azara* (1900; libretto by Paine on the medieval legend of Aucassin and Nicolette) he had "followed throughout the connected orchestral rhythmical flow, and truth of dramatic

EXAMPLE 6-1. Thematic transformations in J. Paine, *Oedipus Tyrannus*, Op. 35 (Boston: Arthur P. Schmidt, 1881), Prelude, measures 26–29, 54–57, 78–80.

[3] Speech at Boston University; quoted in M. A. DeWolfe Howe, "John Knowles Paine," *MQ*, XXV (1939), 257-67.

expression characteristic of Wagner."[4] Nevertheless, Paine's basic musical attitude was conservative; on one of the very few occasions when he permitted himself to turn to a bit of light Americana for source material, he used it as the subject of a fugue remarkably dry, considering the theme (that of the one-liner about baseball, "Over the fence is out, boys!"), given as Example 6-2; the entire little piece is recorded on *NW* 206:s1/3.

EXAMPLE 6-2. J. Paine, "Fuga Giocosa," *3 Piano Pieces*, Op. 41 (Boston: Arthur P. Schmidt, 1884), No. 3, measures 1–2.

After Paine as unofficial members of the Second New England School came a group of composers about a generation younger: Arthur Foote (1853–1937), George Chadwick (1854–1931), Arthur Whiting (1861–1936), Horatio Parker (1863–1919), Amy Cheney Beach (1867–1944), and Daniel Gregory Mason (1873–1953). Of these, Chadwick and Parker emerge as the most gifted, or at least the strongest, musical personalities.

Chadwick is notable among the group for his sympathy—reflected, however, unevenly in his works—for the American vernacular tradition's music; for his achievement in approaching a natural declamation in the setting of English texts; and for an earthy humor (occasionally joined to a social consciousness) not common to his rather aristocratic, more isolated peers. A prolific composer, productive from his student days in Leipzig (*Rip Van Winkle* overture, 1879) until the 1920s, he was the most versatile of the New Englanders. His Symphony No. 2 (1885) includes melodies prophetic of the "Negro" themes of Dvořák's much-discussed "New World"

---

[4] Letter to Henry T. Finck, May 27, 1900; quoted in Kenneth C. Roberts, Jr., "John Knowles Paine" (Master's thesis, University of Michigan, 1962), pp. 2-3.

Symphony, and a folk-like pentatonicism crops up here and there in works of varied character, as in the opening measures of a Sinfonietta in D (1904) or the "Jubilee" movement of his best-known orchestral work, the *Symphonic Sketches* of 1895–1904 (Example 6-3). Such "American" references are sometimes well assimilated; often, however, they are lodged in a lushly harmonized and orchestrated matrix that contradicts their very nature.

EXAMPLE 6-3. Folk-like themes of Chadwick. (a) Symphony No. 2 (Boston: Arthur P. Schmidt, 1888), 2nd movement, measures 5–8 and rehearsal-letter "M" (accompaniment omitted from both). (b) Sinfonietta in D (New York: G. Schirmer, Inc., 1906), 1st movement, measures 4–13 (violin part only). Quoted by permission. (c) *Symphonic Sketches* (New York: G. Schirmer, Inc., 1907), "Jubilee," measures 58–61 (string parts omitted). Quoted by permission.

One specialist in Chadwick's music has emphasized that the later works, from about 1907 to 1920, reveal "a gradual discard of the German conservatory style [and] a more mature musical language, combining pentatonic melody, subdominant-modal harmony and syncopated rhythmic elements."[5] The "syncopation" is generally limited to the short-long pattern common to English two-syllable words (cf. *witching* and *éxile* in Example

[5] Victor Yellin, "The Life and Operatic Works of George Whitefield Chadwick" (Ph.D. dissertation, Harvard University, 1957), p. 291.

6-5; *slúmber* and the related *lamentátion* in Example 6-6) but even so, Chadwick's use of such natural speech rhythms, long a commonplace in songs of the vernacular tradition, sets him apart from Paine, Parker, and others of the Second New England School, who tend to set English as if it were German or Latin. Chadwick transfers this rhythmic motif to instrumental music as well, as in the "Scherzino" of the Sinfonietta (Example 6-4).

EXAMPLE 6-4. G. Chadwick, Sinfonietta in D (New York: G. Schirmer, Inc., 1906), "Scherzino," measures 21–28. Quoted by permission.

A song like "Adversity," one of more than a hundred by Chadwick, is in the slow waltz tempo often heard in late nineteenth-century American ballrooms and even approaches popular song style, transcending it, however, in a sensitive darkening of the harmony at the last line (Example 6-5).

Chadwick's stage works, seven operas and operettas, range in mood and manner from the playful pasticcio *Tabasco* (1894), a "burlesque opera" (really an operetta) containing galops, marches (one of them recorded on NW 266:s2/2), hymn tunes, waltzes, jigs, and a "plantation ballad," to the sobriety, drenched in a Saint-Saëns-like lyricism and laced with Wagnerian leitmotifs, of *Judith* (1901; see Example 6-6). Perhaps least deserving of its neglect is *The Padrone* (1912–13; refused by the Metropolitan Opera Company and not yet performed). It is a lone example of American turn-of-the-century *verismo*, its subject the exploitation of Italian immigrants in Boston by their dockside guarantors and landlords, the *padroni*.

Chadwick, like Paine, became literally an academician, joining the faculty of the New England Conservatory in 1882 and serving as its director from 1897 until 1930. So, too, did Horatio Parker, who became professor at Yale University in 1894, after a musical apprenticeship under Chadwick and,

EXAMPLE 6-5. G. Chadwick, "Adversity," *Six Songs for Mezzo-Soprano or Baritone* (New York: G. Schirmer, Inc., 1902), No. 3, measures 1–11, 28–38. Quoted by permission.

EXAMPLE 6-6. G. Chadwick, *Judith* (New York: G. Schirmer, Inc., 1901), Act I, scene 5 ("The Vision of Judith"), measures 54–62. Quoted by permission.

from 1882 to 1885, Josef Rheinberger in Munich. Parker's most illustrious student said of him: "I had and have ['great' crossed out] respect and admiration for Parker and most of his music. It was seldom trivial." Charles Ives then went on to pinpoint Parker's strengths and weaknesses:

> His choral works have dignity and depth that many contemporaries, especially in religious and choral compositions, do not have. Parker had ideals that carried him higher than the popular, but he was governed by the "German rule." . . . Parker was a bright man, a good technician, but perfectly willing to be limited by what Rheinberger had taught him.[6]

The major part of Parker's creative output was music for chorus, on medieval or religious subjects, all serious in tone. They range from a cappella Latin motets (*Adstant Angelorum Chori*, 1899; on a text by Thomas à Kempis) through occasional pieces (*Hymnos Andron*, ode on a Greek text for the bicentennial of Yale, 1901; *The Spirit of Beauty*, ode for the dedication of the Albright Art Gallery in Buffalo, 1905) to epitomes of the Victorian cantata (*The Dream King and His Love*, 1891) and oratorio for soloists, chorus(es), and orchestra (*The Legend of St. Christopher* [1897] and *Hora Novissima* [1892]). The last-named is accounted Parker's masterpiece: an hour-long choral cantata in eleven big movements, it is a setting of a portion (describing the glories of Heaven) of a twelfth-century Latin poem. The spacious work is all the more impressive for its disguise of the rigid tercets of the poem ("Hora novissima/tempora pessima/sunt, vigilemus") through long, leisurely, wide-ranging harmonic sequences, extensive fugues on expansive subjects, and masterly handling of the choral-orchestral medium. In one aria (No. 3, "Spe modo vivitur") $\frac{4}{4}$ and $\frac{3}{4}$ measures in alternation—something of a novelty for the time—hide the metrical rigidity of the verses. Though its solo movements suggest Italo-French influence, the main atmosphere of *Hora Novissima*, like other choral works of Parker, is that of a German-American hymnic grandeur, rich in sound and powerfully stable in rhythm; this may be suggested by the several fugue subjects given in Example 6-7 or the organ fugue in C minor, Op. 36, No. 3, recorded on *NW* 280:s2/2.

At least two others of the Second New England School deserve comment here as able, craftsmanlike composers (who, incidentally, after decades of neglect began to enjoy a modest revival in the 1970s). Arthur Foote was unusual among the group in being trained exclusively in the United States: he studied with the influential Boston musician B. J. Lang (1837–1909) and with Paine at Harvard (where he was awarded in 1875 the first American M.A. degree in music). Though an organist (like most of his Bostonian colleagues), he wrote a polished, Brahmsian chamber music, and his most

[6] Quoted in Henry Cowell and Sidney Cowell, *Charles Ives and His Music* (New York: Oxford University Press, 1955; rev. ed. 1969), pp. 33–34.

EXAMPLE 6-7. Fugue subjects by Horatio Parker. (a) *Hora Novissima* (London & New York: Novello, Ewer and Co., 1893): (1) No. 4, measures 27–31; (2) No. 10, measures 1–5; (3) No. 11, measures 41–44. (b) *Adstant Angelorum Chori* (New York: G. Schirmer, Inc., 1899), measures 88–92. (c) *The Legend of St. Christopher* (London & New York: Novello, Ewer and Co., 1898), p. 134 (Act III, scene 2).

highly acclaimed compositions are for strings: the Suite in E for string orchestra (1907) and *A Night Piece* for flute and strings (a 1922 revision of a *Nocturne* for flute and string quartet). Amy Marcy Cheney conformed to the convention of her time and referred to herself as Mrs. H. H. A. Beach after her marriage to a socially prominent Boston physician; she did not conform to convention, however, in remaining, as a woman, merely a dilettante in music: both as a pianist and composer, she worked at truly professional levels and was unarguably the foremost American woman composer of her time. Her output is dominated by piano works but also includes a number of beguiling chamber compositions (notably a Quintet for Piano and Strings published in 1909), an impressive symphony (the "Gaelic," of 1894), and a piano concerto (each of the last two works the first of its kind by an American woman). Beach's songs number about 120; they were regularly performed by international recitalists (such as the celebrated soprano Emma Eames or the German-born Johanna Gadski, whose performance of *The Year's at the Spring*, from the very successful set of *Three Browning Songs*, Op. 44, of 1900, is on *NW* 247:s1/2).

Yet another New Englander, though not a member of the circle of Bostonians we have been considering, achieved considerable renown in the late nineteenth century—the Connecticut-born Dudley Buck (1839–1909), who worked in Hartford, Chicago, and Boston as an organist and choir director but finally settled in Brooklyn. Buck's expansive choral works impressed audiences at Patrick Gilmore's World's Peace Jubilee of 1872 (*Festival Hymn*), the Third Triennial Festival of Boston's Handel and Haydn Society in 1874 (*The Forty-Sixth Psalm*), and the U.S. Centennial Celebration in Philadelphia in 1876 (*The Centennial Meditation of Columbia*). Buck also seems to have been the first American to compose a full-scale organ sonata—the Grand Sonata in E♭ of 1866, its last movement a climactic fugue and fantasy based on the tune of *Hail! Columbia* (*NW* 280:s1/1–4).

The composers of the Second New England School have been called "the Boston academics" (by Rupert Hughes, writing in 1900) and "the Boston classicists" (by Benjamin Lambord in 1915; more recently by Gilbert Chase in *AM*). But not all of them were academicians; nor, if the term "academic" is one of disparagement, were they all or always hidebound. And none of them was a "classicist" except in the sense that Brahms was a classicist: they belong to that wing of romanticism that maintained a belief in the viability of the abstract instrumental forms. Like Brahms, and like Beethoven, Schubert, Schumann, and Mendelssohn before him, they wrote symphonies, sonatas, and chamber music; like Brahms, and like Handel, Bach, Mozart, and Beethoven before him, they wrote fugues and contrapuntal choruses. To the late nineteenth century such composers as Paine, Chadwick, Parker, Foote, Beach, and Buck might have seemed "classicists"; our perspective should let us rather see them in context as a group of Romantics of a particular persuasion.

EDWARD MACDOWELL

To another wing of Romanticism belonged Edward MacDowell (1860–1908). Not for him the abstract traditional forms of symphony and string quartet nor the semi-abstract forms of orchestral overture or choral cantata. In the tradition of the "New German School" of Liszt and Wagner, MacDowell saw himself as a "tone-poet," trusting in the evocative power of richly colored harmony (especially when the response was directed by a suggestive programmatic title) and narrative, ongoing forms rather than the problem-solving constructivism of imitative counterpoint or the balanced logic of sonata-form. MacDowell believed that Bach was "one of the world's mightiest tone-poets [who] accomplished his mission, not by means of the contrapuntal fashion of his age, but in spite of it," and for him Mozart's instrumental sonatas were "entirely unworthy of the author of *The Magic Flute*."[7] In a climate of aesthetic opinion like that of the later nineteenth century, these attitudes must have seemed truly progressive, truly Romantic, untinged by a "classicistic" bent. Not surprisingly MacDowell was viewed, about the turn of the twentieth century, as America's foremost modern composer by those who shared his aesthetic—which is to say, all but a few.

Of Scotch-Irish descent, MacDowell was born in New York. In 1876 he was enrolled in the Paris Conservatory, but, dissatisfied, he moved to Frankfurt in 1878 for two more years of study as a pianist and composer; a powerful influence on him there was the conservatory's director, the composer Joachim Raff. Except for one trip to America to get married, MacDowell remained in Germany teaching, composing, and playing piano concerts until 1888, some twelve years after leaving the United States. He then lived in Boston until 1896, when he accepted an appointment as the first professor of music at Columbia University. In 1904, after some unfortunately public wrangling with the university administration, MacDowell resigned. Mental illness, exacerbated by a horse-cab accident, prevent his composing any more; he declined more or less steadily until his death.

MacDowell's works were all composed between about 1880 (First Modern Suite for piano; First Piano Concerto) and 1902 (*Summer Wind* for women's chorus; *New England Idyls* for piano). They consist mainly of some sixteen collections of "character-pieces" for piano, plus four suggestively titled sonatas and two concertos; forty-two songs for solo voice and more than twenty for chorus; four symphonic poems; and two orchestral suites. All the favorite themes and images of romanticism are explored: landscapes and seascapes (*Woodland Sketches*; *New England Idyls*; *Sea Pieces*), medieval romances (the symphonic poem *Lancelot and Elaine*; Piano Sonata No. 2 ["Eroica"] on the Arthurian legend), exoticism (Second ["Indian"] Suite for orchestra; *Les Orientales* for piano), and reminiscences of childhood ("From Uncle Remus," *Woodland Sketches*; "Of Br'er Rabbit," *Fireside Tales*). Shakespeare inspired the symphonic poem in two parts, *Hamlet and Ophelia*; Romantic poets are interpreted pianistically in *Six Idyls after Goethe* and *Six Poems after Heine*. In the latter collections MacDowell printed the poems at the head of the music; in many others, he wrote verses of his own to stand as the "program" of individual pieces.

Considering the brevity of the composer's creative life (comparable

---

[7] MacDowell, *Critical and Historical Essays* (Boston: Arthur P. Schmidt, 1912), pp. 265, 194.

to Foster's or Gottschalk's), a lack of stylistic development should not surprise us. More surprising, in view of MacDowell's extraordinary reputation about 1900 (the Columbia University trustees who hired MacDowell announced that he was "the greatest musical genius America has produced"), is the fact that having begun boldly as a composer of piano concertos of truly Lisztian sweep and breadth, he then tended to produce ever smaller, more rarefied works. After the Second Suite (1891–95) he wrote no more orchestral music. He never attempted opera. Of the later works, only the Third ("Norse") and Fourth ("Keltic") piano sonatas approach large-scale forms, described by MacDowell as " 'bardic' rhapsodies" on their subjects. MacDowell ended up as a composer of concise, evocative genre pieces, surprisingly terse even when their subject matter is grandiose ("To the Sea," "From a German Forest"); basically very economical and clean of line, even fragile sometimes ("To a Wild Rose," "To a Water Lily," both from *Woodland Sketches*); and very precisely fashioned and clearly projected.

MacDowell was himself a competent concert pianist, and some of his most successful piano music demands a virtuoso technique, as in the "Scherzo" of the Second Piano Concerto and various études among the Twelve Virtuoso Studies (recorded on *NW* 206:s2), notably "March Wind." More of it, however, is relatively easy to play and reveals MacDowell to be a late nineteenth-century composer of "household music." He has also in common with that earlier American music a considerable nostalgia: Mellers has remarked trenchantly that MacDowell's best pieces "are a boy's view of the American past, looked back to from a premature middle age,"[8] as in the song collection *From an Old Garden*, "From an Indian Lodge" and "A Deserted Farm" in *Woodland Sketches*, and "From a Log Cabin" and "From Puritan Days" in *New England Idyls*.

The composer's vocabulary, which has often been likened to that of Edvard Grieg (whom MacDowell admired and to whom he dedicated the Third and Fourth piano sonatas), shares with Grieg's a remarkable integrity, homogeneity, and identifiability. The most characteristic features of MacDowell's style are its Wagnerian chromatic harmony, full of enharmonic modulations, appoggiatura dissonances, and inversions of triads, seventh chords, and ninth chords; its texture, which tends to be thick and fat and, although ranging freely over the entire keyboard, seems to emphasize the lower registers; and its ebb and flow of rhythmic activity and dynamic contour, both in a state of constant flux. Example 6-8, from a piece reported by MacDowell's first biographer to be one of the composer's own favorites,[9]

---

[8] Wilfrid Mellers, *Music in a New Found Land* (New York: Alfred A. Knopf, 1966), p. 27.

[9] Lawrence Gilman, *Edward MacDowell, A Study* (New York: John Lane Co., 1908), pp. 70–71. Gilman's study has been reprinted with an introduction by Margery L. Morgan (New York: Da Capo Press, 1969).

EXAMPLE 6-8. E. MacDowell, "In Mid-Ocean," *Sea Pieces*, Op. 55 (Boston, Leipzig, New York: Arthur P. Schmidt, 1899), No. 8, measures 1–8.

shows most of these hallmarks of his style. In another vein, however, are many works that derive, no matter how indirectly, from dance meters, including Mendelssohnian scherzos. These are lighter in texture, "snappy" in rhythmic shape (often literally so: MacDowell's Scots background was strong and "Scotch snap" iambs appear regularly), and less chromatic in harmony, though never wholly diatonic. The "Uncle Remus" pieces of *Woodland Sketches* and *Fireside Tales*; the fifth of the Goethe *Idyls*; the third of the Heine *Poems*; "Humoreske" and "March" in the Four Pieces, Op. 24, are of this type, as are the "Love Song" and "In War-Time" movements of the "Indian" Suite for orchestra. So, too, is "To a Wild Rose" (MacDowell's best-known single work), although it is often mistaken for a "poetic" and sentimental piece, played with rubato not even hinted at in the score and at a tempo considerably slower than that indicated by the composer. Faintly reminiscent of Schumann's "Traümerei" in its design, it moves "with simple tenderness" to a single strategically placed climax and a lone, conclusive iamb (Example 6-9).

EXAMPLE 6-9. E. MacDowell, "To a Wild Rose," *Woodland Sketches* (1896), Op. 51 (Boston, Leipzig, New York: Arthur P. Schmidt, 1899), No. 1, measures 43–51 (conclusion).

OTHER CURRENTS

Inevitably, a reaction against the predominantly Germanic cast of post-Civil War fine-art music took place. It took two forms: some composers sought to refresh American music with an infusion of folkloristic elements; others turned enthusiastically to the new modes of expression emanating from Russia and France or to even more exotic sources.

Folklorism was hardly unknown to the European Romantics. A fascination with "primitive" peasant culture or with traditional anonymous folk forms was one manifestation of the Romantics' infatuation with the untrammeled expression of childhood, the "folk" being viewed as national or regional or even racial children. Ultimately Americans came to share this aspect of Romantic thought. The problem for composers was: what was American musical folklore? A few men had given tentative hints of *their* answer to the question: MacDowell, Chadwick, even old Father Heinrich. Others now followed the hint: all too simplistically, they looked to the most "primitive" kinds of music in the nation, the music of American Indians and blacks. That there might be other "folkish" music in their past and under their very noses, that the vernacular tradition of popular music might provide a usable stock of invigorating source materials, seems not to have occurred to most of these composers. But then, did not Frédéric Ritter claim that America had no "people's song"? Had not the great composer Antonin Dvořák (at the time in New York as director of the National Conservatory) suggested, in articles in both the *New York Herald* (December 15, 1893, one day before the premiere performance of his symphony "From the New World") and *Harper's New Monthly Magazine* (February 1895), that "inspiration for truly national [American] music might be derived from the negro melodies or Indian chants"?

Besides their (perhaps unconscious) Romantic interest in "folk" materials, some American composers of the late nineteenth century saw them as a nationalistic instrument as well, as had some Europeans earlier, the "Russian Five," for example. For to the degree that a nation's composers could borrow from indigenous musical sources they were assured a certain national identity; their music would be different from that of other regions or nations.

In late nineteenth-century America, and indeed through the first three decades of the twentieth, this aspect of folklorism exerted a strong pull on many composers, who yearned to free themselves from a European musical yoke, hoping to be somehow recognizably "American."

Aggressive steps in this direction were first taken by the Middle Westerner Arthur Farwell (1872–1952). He turned to Indian music in a number of arrangements, such as *Impressions of the Wa-Wan Ceremony of the Omahas* (1905) and *Three Indian Songs* (1908; recorded on NW 213:s1/1), and also original works based on Indian melodies, such as his *Navajo War Dance* for piano (1905)—much later (1937) arranged for unaccompanied chorus (both versions recorded on NW 213:s2/1–2—or his String Quartet "The Hako" (1922). Perhaps even more significant was his enthusiastic championing of new currents in American music through publication by the Wa-Wan Press, which he established in 1901. Looking about him, Farwell saw a "quantity of compositions . . . and my own work, all blocked as to publication." He determined to "combine my work with that of these others— we were all in the same boat—and launch a progressive movement for American music, including a definite acceptance of Dvořák's challenge to go after our folk music."[10] When the Wa-Wan Press was sold to the firm of G. Schirmer in 1912, it had published works by thirty-seven composers. Among them were a number with folkloristic interests, especially in Indian and Negro music.

Matching Farwell's preoccupation with Indian music was the interest in black music of Henry F. B. Gilbert (1868–1928), composer of *Comedy Overture on Negro Themes* (ca. 1906) and *The Dance in Place Congo* (ca. 1908; revised 1916), which is recorded on NW 228:s1/1. Other composers published by Wa-Wan Press who had less self-consciously "Americanist" aims were men like Arthur Shepherd (1880–1958) and Edward Burlingame Hill (1872–1960). Hill, who had been a pupil of both Paine and Chadwick, was one of the first Americans to feel the lure of the new French music of the 1890s, reflecting it in his own works and passing on a taste for it to such of his students at Harvard as Walter Piston and Virgil Thomson. In fact, Boston, long the ideological center of American music's Germanophilia, was at last beginning to rebel, beginning to see in the moré or less individual styles of Saint-Saëns, D'Indy, Fauré, Debussy, and Ravel a refreshing change. *The Musical Record* of December 1890 quoted approvingly from the *Boston Home Journal*:

A plea for more French music and less German is demanded. . . . We grope about in German mists . . . and say it is purer and healthier than clear air and

---

[10] Quoted in Edward Waters, "'The Wa-Wan Press: An Adventure in Musical Idealism," *A Birthday Offering to Carl Engel*, ed. Gustave Reese (New York: G. Schirmer, Inc., 1943), pp. 214–33. *Wa-Wan* is an Omaha word identified with a ceremony of peace, fellowship, and song.

a blue sky. We pay American money for the privilege of submitting to German dictation.

Another composer trained at Harvard, John Alden Carpenter (1876–1951), shared Hill's partiality toward French music and showed it in works like the song cycle *Gitanjali* of 1913 (two songs from which are recorded on NW 247:s2/4–5), the orchestral suite *Adventures in a Perambulator* (1914), and a Concertino for piano and orchestra (1915).

Charles Martin Loeffler (1861–1935) was a composer so hospitable to French poetry and the *raffinement* of the modern French musical style of the turn of the century that he has often been called a French-American. Actually, although perhaps born in Alsace, he came of German stock, and his formative years were spent successively in Russia, Berlin, and Paris. Trained as a violinist, he came to New York in 1881 but was snatched off to Boston by Major Henry Lee Higginson, patron of the Boston Symphony Orchestra. He sat at the first desk of the orchestra's violin section until 1903, when he resigned to devote himself to composition. An exquisite craftsman, almost obsessively revising his scores again and again, Loeffler published comparatively little; the music he did allow into print is of high polish and a kind of *fin-de-siècle* fastidiousness. Among his orchestral works, *A Pagan Poem* (1906) has proved durable. Many works combine voices and instruments; of these, perhaps the most perfectly realized is a setting of St. Francis of Assisi's *Canticum Fratris Solis* for soprano and chamber ensemble, commissioned for the first concert sponsored by the Elizabeth Sprague Coolidge Foundation at the Library of Congress (October 28, 1925). Typifying Loeffler's interest in unusual instruments and instrumentation are *La mort de Tintagiles* (1897; recorded on NW 332:s1), for full orchestra with solo viola d'amore, and two delicate chamber Rhapsodies for oboe, viola, and piano (1901); the latter are derived from a pair of songs, which like a number of others by Loeffler, add a string instrument (viola or violin) to the conventional piano accompaniment.

Another composer who was susceptible not only to the new French music but also to Russian, particularly that of Scriabin, was Charles T. Griffes (1884–1921). After four years in Germany (1903–07), his early works were, not surprisingly, Teutonic; among them are some strong songs of 1909, to poems by Heine, Lenau, Eichendorff, and others. But Griffes must have considered these works as preliminary to his real beginnings; he later commented, "When I began to write I wrote in the vein of Debussy and Stravinsky; those particular wide-intervalled disonances are the natural medium of the composer who writes today's music."[11] In a number of songs of 1912 to poems by Oscar Wilde, including *Symphony in Yellow* and *La Fuite de la*

---

[11] Quoted in Edward Maisel, *Charles T. Griffes* (New York: Alfred A. Knopf, Inc., 1943; repr. with additions 1984), p. 112.

lune, Debussyesque harmony predominates, with however a rather firm, chiseled melodic line close to Ravel's (Example 6-10). Related in style are the *Roman Sketches* for piano (1915–16), which include the best known of Griffes's works, *The White Peacock* (later to be orchestrated delicately by the composer).

EXAMPLE 6-10. C. Griffes, *Symphony in Yellow*, Op. 3, No. 2 (New York: G. Schirmer, Inc., 1915), measures 1–8. Quoted by permission.

An interest in Oriental music shows up in *The Pleasure Dome of Kubla Khan* (piano version 1912; revised and orchestrated 1917). Oriental flavor is pervasive in a group of songs on pentatonic and hexatonic scales, *Five Poems of Ancient China and Japan*; and for a ballet titled *Sho-Jo* (1917) Griffes composed a unique score on Japanese themes, with orchestration "as Japanese as possible: thin and delicate, and the muted string *points d'orgue* serve as neutral-tinted background, like the empty spaces in a Japanese print. The whole thematic material is given to the flute, clarinet, and oboe— akin to the Japanese reed instruments: the harp suggests the koto."[12] *Sho-jo* was never published, nor was another unique dance-drama of the previous year, *The Kairn of Koridwen*, scored for an eight-piece ensemble of flute, two clarinets, two horns, harp, celesta, and piano. These works, related to Schoenberg's *Pierrot Lunaire* (1912) and Stravinsky's *Histoire du soldat* (1918) in their novel chamber-music instrumentation, must have been considered too exotic to be publishable.

[12] Ibid., p. 206

In his penultimate year, Griffes renounced the delicate shades of the French style and the Orient ("I don't want the reputation of an Orientalist and nothing more") and produced several works of power, even ferocity, that suggested he was approaching a mature synthesis of the several styles in which he had successively immersed himself. The Piano Sonata (Example 6-11), a *Notturno* for orchestra (different from the *Nocturne* transcribed from the Piano Sonata's slow section), the *Poem* for flute and orchestra, and a group of *Three Poems* to texts by Fiona MacLeod (including the shattering song *The Lament of Ian the Proud*) reveal Griffes as an American composer on the brink of greatness. The promise of these works was not to be realized, however: Griffes died at the age of thirty-five after a creative career of fewer than fifteen years.

EXAMPLE 6-11. C. Griffes, Piano Sonata (New York: G. Schirmer, Inc., 1921), concluding measures. Quoted by permission.

BIBLIOGRAPHICAL NOTES

The following entries in *TNGDAM* are helpful on the "institutional foundations" of cultivated-tradition music, 1865–1920: "Education in Music"; "Copyright"; "American Society of Composers, Authors and Publishers"; and "Unions, musicians'." *Dwight's Journal* has been issued in a reprint edition (New York: Arno Press, 1968); its predecessors and successors are discussed and exhaustively listed in the entry "Periodicals" in *TNGDAM*.

No extensive studies have been made of the Second New England School as a whole. Various dissertations (on Dwight, *Dwight's Journal*, Paine, Chadwick, Parker, Foote, and Beach) have been completed. Gunther Schuller's extensive, appreciative record notes for *NW* 262/263 (Paine's Mass in D) are valuable, as are Herbert A. Kenny's notes for *NW* 268 (violin sonatas by Amy Beach and Arthur Foote), emphasizing the Boston context. Wilma Reid Cipolla has published a useful catalogue of the works of Foote (Detroit: Information Coordinators, 1980). Adrienne Fried Block's essays on Beach—the introduction to a reprint edition of Beach's Piano Quintet (New York: Da Capo Press, 1979) and the entry on Beach in *TNGDAM*—are authoritative. *EAM* includes reprints of the scores of Paine's First Symphony (*EAM* 1) and his complete piano music (*EAM* 27); Chadwick's Second Symphony (*EAM* 4), *Judith* (*EAM* 3), and songs to poems by Arlo Blake (*EAM* 16); Parker's *Hora Novissima* (*EAM* 2); and Foote's string-orchestra music and the Piano Quintet (*EAM* 24 and 26).

MacDowell's *Critical and Historical Essays* (Boston: Arthur P. Schmidt, 1912; repr. New York: Da Capo Press, 1968) reveal his attitudes clearly. Lawrence Gilman's study of 1908 (see footnote 9) remains the most extensive survey; Francis Brancaleone has studied the character pieces for piano in "The Short Piano Works of Edward MacDowell" (Ph.D. dissertation, City University of New York, 1982). Four collections of piano pieces and five sets of the later songs are reprinted in *EAM* (vols. 8 and 7 respectively).

The entire output of Farwell's Wa-Wan Press has been reprinted in facsimile, with a fine introductory essay by Gilbert Chase (New York: Arno Press, 1970). Ellen Knight's writings on Loeffler (see her article in *TNGDAM* and the bibliography appended to it) represent the latest research; she is also the editor of a collection of his songs with chamber accompaniment, in preparation as a volume of *RRAM*

A generous representation of works by Griffes is recorded on *NW* 273; the record notes are by Donna K. Anderson, who is also the compiler of the definitive catalogue of Griffes's works (Detroit: Information Coordinators, 1977). Songs by him are recorded on *NW* 305, his complete piano works on *NW* 310–11.

SEVEN
CHARLES IVES

The most extraordinary and significant American composer of the late nineteenth and early twentieth centuries was Charles Edward Ives (1874–1954). Because of heart attacks (the first on October 1, 1918) and other serious illness, Ives composed very little after about 1921; ironically, it was only after he had stopped intensive composing and had "cleaned house," as he put it, by printing (at his own expense) the Second ("Concord") Piano Sonata (1920), some *Essays Before a Sonata* (1920), and a volume of *114 Songs* (1922) that his music began to be generally known at all. Acceptance was slow even then: not until the 1940s were many works by Ives performed. After World War II, however, the number of performances, publications, and phonorecordings grew steadily, as did Ives's influence on other composers' thought. By the mid-1970s there were few who would have differed with the first sentence of this paragraph: Ives had become a kind of national hero musically, especially among the youth of the nation; the first American society dedicated to an American composer was the Charles Ives Society (activated in 1973); and the first international conference organized around an American composer was the Charles Ives Centennial Festival-Conference (1974), co-sponsored by Brooklyn College's Institute for Studies in American Music and Yale University's School of Music.

IVES'S LIFE AND CREATIVE CAREER

Ives grew up in Danbury, Connecticut. In later years he emphasized the importance of his father in shaping his musical thinking. George Ives (1845–94) was in some ways a typical late nineteenth-century provincial American musician: leader of the Connecticut Heavy Artillery First Brigade Band during the siege of Richmond, he returned after the Civil War to Danbury, where he played the piano for dances and the organ for church services, gave music lessons, organized the Danbury Band, and was in general a musical jack-of-all-trades. He knew academic music theory, was a practical music arranger, and composed a little. Where he differed from other such "town" musicians was in his passionate curiosity about sound, his experimental attitude, and his open-mindedness; all these were to be reflected concretely in his son's music and musical thought. From the age of five, Charles Ives was taught by his father: "Bach and the best of the classical music, and the study of harmony and counterpoint etc., and musical history [and] the use of the ears . . . and the mind to think for themselves and be more independent—in other words, not to be too dependent upon customs and habits."[1] Ives was thus trained in music of the cultivated tradition; he was exposed, through his father's multifarious musical occupations, to both cultivated and vernacular traditions; and he was encouraged toward an open-minded independence of musical thought that could encompass both traditions.

Ives's formal music study was completed at Yale (1894–98) under Horatio Parker, for whom he had a qualified respect (see p. 149) and from whom he got a rigorous training in advanced harmony and counterpoint and stern coaching and criticism of "free" composition in the larger forms of the Classic-Romantic European tradition. Upon graduation, already aware that his music was "impractical" and sharing his father's view that "a man could

---

[1] *Charles E. Ives: Memos*, ed. and with many appendices by John Kirkpatrick (New York: W. W. Norton, 1972), p. 115. My quotations of statements by Ives come mainly from three sources: Ives's *Memos*, written in the early 1930s "to answer questions from people curious about his music" (as Kirkpatrick puts it); Charles Ives, *Essays Before a Sonata and Other Writings*, ed. Howard Boatwright (New York: W. W. Norton, 1970); and John Kirkpatrick, *A Temporary Mimeographed Catalogue of the Music Manuscripts and Related Materials of Charles Edward Ives 1874–1954* (New Haven, CT: School of Music Library, Yale University, 1960). These will be referred to as *Memos*, *Essays*, and *Kirkpatrick*.

keep his music-interest stronger, cleaner, bigger, and freer, if he didn't try to make a living out of it" (*Memos*, p. 131), Ives decided on a business career in life insurance. He pursued it with great success from 1898 until his retirement in 1930. For a time (1898–1902) he was also a practicing musician as organist and choirmaster at the First Presbyterian Church in Bloomfield, New Jersey, then at Central Presbyterian Church in Manhattan; but from 1902 on he limited himself to business and to composing—furiously, at white heat—during evenings, weekends, and vacations. The *boyhood* period in Danbury (1874–94) and the period of *apprenticeship* in college and the first four years in New York (1894–1902) were succeeded by a period of *innovation and synthesis* (1902–08); this was followed by "nine years [which] saw the conception and creation of the greatest and best-known works of Ives's *maturity* (1908–17)," the declining productivity of the period of his *last works* (1918–26), and an autumnal period of *tinkering*—"tinkering with the music he had already produced, in some cases making substantial changes and finishing or restoring incomplete or partially lost pieces, but producing no new compositions" (1927–54).[2]

In all but the first and (most of) the last of these six periods, Ives lived a double life—to which some have attributed his debilitating illnesses—as (public) businessman and (private) composer. He claimed never to regret it; in a well-known statement, he said,

> . . . The fabric of existence weaves itself whole. You cannot set art off in the corner and hope for it to have vitality, reality and substance. There can be nothing *"exclusive"* about a substantial art. It comes directly out of the heart of experience of life and thinking about life and living life. My work in music helped my business and my work in business helped my music."[3]

The demands on his time of business, the non-acceptance of his music, and the lack of direct involvement with the professional music world freed, or forced, the mature Ives to develop his own aesthetic. It was a unique one, and we must understand it if we are to view his music in proper perspective.

IVES'S MUSICAL THOUGHT

Ives prized what he called "substance" rather than "manner" in both music and its performance. "Manner" for Ives approached what others might

---

[2] The periodization of Ives's life given here, and the quotations, are from J. Peter Burkholder, *Charles Ives: The Ideas Behind the Music* (New Haven, CT: Yale University Press, 1985), pp. 43–44.

[3] Quoted first in Henry Bellamann, "Charles Ives: the Man and his Music," *MQ*, XIX (1933), 45–58.

call "technique," on the part of either composer or performer. "Substance
. . . is practically indescribable," admitted Ives, but it "suggests the body
of a conviction which has its birth in the spiritual consciousness, whose youth
is nourished in the moral consciousness, and whose maturity as a result of
all this growth is then represented in a mental image." (*Essays,* p. 75)
Common notions of beauty have nothing to do with it; it "has something to
do with character. . . . The substance of a tune comes from somewhere near
the soul, and the manner comes from—God knows where." (*Essays,* p. 77)
On this philosophical ground Ives based some startling concrete ideas. If
substance has nothing to do with beauty or manner, then the very sound of
music may be insignificant compared to the spirit in which it is produced.
The roots of this idea are apparent in an anecdote about Ives's father:

> Once a nice young man . . . said to Father, "How can you stand it to hear old
> John Bell (the best stone-mason in town) sing?" (as he used to at Camp Meet-
> ings)[.] Father said, "He is a supreme musician." The young man . . . was
> horrified—"Why, he sings off the key, the wrong notes and everything . . .
> and he bellows out and hits notes no one else does—it's awful!" Father said,
> ". . . Look into his face and hear the music of the ages. Don't pay too much
> attention to the sounds—for if you do, you may miss the music." (*Memos,* p.
> 132)

"The music," the *real* music, resided in the humanity of its producer, in
the spirit of its performer. This is why Ives could cry out passionately, "My
God! What has sound got to do with music!" (*Essays,* p. 84) This is why, in
recalling revivalist camp meetings, he could speak with affection of the
aberrations in the hymn-singing and of ". . . the great waves of sound . . .
when things like *Beulah Land, Woodworth, Nearer My God to Thee, The
Shining Shore, Nettleton, In the Sweet Bye and Bye* and the like were sung
by thousands of 'let out' souls. . . . If they threw the poet or the composer
around a bit, so much the better for the poetry and the music. There was
power and exaltation in these great conclaves of sound from humanity."
(*Memos,* pp. 132–33) This is why he could even drive the argument to its
logical conclusion and say, "That music must be heard is not essential—
what it *sounds* like may not be what it *is*." (*Essays,* p. 84) And this in turn
helps to explain a puzzling statement in the "Postface" to *114 Songs*: "Some
of the songs in this book . . . cannot be sung,—and if they could perhaps
might prefer, if they had a say, to remain as they are,—that is, 'in the leaf.'
. . . A song has a few rights the same as other ordinary citizens."
     Ives's music often shares the variety, the apparent disorder, the co-
existence of seemingly unrelated things of life itself; characteristic is a planar,
heterophonic polyphony occasionally so dense that the ear simply cannot
distinguish the separate strands. Ives analogized between such co-existent

but independent ideas in his music and a game of tennis doubles—"Having
four nice different men playing tennis together doesn't always destroy personality" (*Memos*, p. 50)—or the participants in the unstructured discussion
and argument of a New England town meeting. In a sketch for the Second
String Quartet, whose movements are titled "Discussions," "Arguments,"
and "The Call of the Mountains," Ives described the work as a "S[tring]
Q[uartet] for 4 men—who converse, argue (in re 'Politics'), fight, shake
hands[,] shut up—then walk up the mountain side to view the firmament."
He seemed to view musical texture sometimes as a microcosm in which the
co-existence of disparate elements does not threaten order any more than,
say, in a forest the co-existence of different trees, rocks, mosses, flowers,
animals, and insects threatens order; "order," in this instance, is an irrelevant
concept, or one too narrowly conceived. Traditional devices for "ordering"
musical form (repetitions, periodic phrase structure, classical tonality, and
the like), although not always lacking in Ives's music, are not by any means
always present. Ives could scoff at such devices, questioning for instance
"how far repetition is an essential part of clarity and coherence. . . . If nature
is not enthusiastic about explanation, why should Tschaikowsky be?" (*Essays*,
p. 99) Ives admired quite another order-principle, which he expressed most
clearly in his essay on Emerson:

> His underlying plan of work seems based on the large unity of a series of
> particular aspects of a subject rather than on the continuity of its expressions.
> As thoughts surge to his mind, he fills the heavens with them, crowds them
> in, if necessary, but seldom arranges them along the ground first. (*Essays*, p.
> 22)

This is a fair description of the tumultuous congeries of materials, and their
apparent lack of continuity, in many of Ives's works.

The subject matter of Ives's music was equally life itself, or "a series
of particular aspects" of it. The pages of his manuscripts are studded with
verbal comments that particularize the diary-like outpourings of his musical
mind. One of the most illuminating examples is found in a manuscript copy
of the first movement of the First Piano Sonata:

> What is it all about—Dan S. asks. Mostly about the outdoor life in
> Conn[ecticut] villages in the '80s and '90s—impressions, remembrances, &
> reflections, of country farmers in Conn. farmland.
> On page 14 back, Fred's Daddy got so excited that he shouted when
> Fred hit a home run & the school won the baseball game. But Aunt Sarah was
> always humming *Where Is My Wandering Boy*, after Fred an' John left for a
> job in Bridgeport. There was usually a sadness—but not at the Barn Dances,
> with their jigs, foot jumping, & reels, mostly on winter nights.

> In the summer times, the hymns were sung outdoors. Folks sang (as *Old Black Joe)*—and the Bethel Band (quickstep street marches)—& the people like[d to say] things as they wanted to say, and to do things as they wanted to, in their own way—and many old times . . . there were feelings, and of spiritual fervency! (*Memos*, p. 75)

Thus viewing some of his music as reminiscences, or re-creations in sound, of life experiences, many of which included actual music or were easily associable with specific kinds of music, Ives constantly used pre-existent music in his works: most often it is not just baldly "quoted" but instead is the very basis of the musical fabric, the pre-existent material giving rise to reshapings, reformulations, reorderings that transform and transmogrify it into a new, genuinely Ivesian music. Traditional American hymn tunes, marches, patriotic songs, and bits of ragtime are the most commonly referred to, but material from other composers also appears, from Handel, Haydn, Beethoven, and Tchaikowsky to Foster, Mason, Bradbury, and Sankey. Such borrowings had nothing to do with nationalism, folklorism, or mere "local color"; they bespoke rather an acceptance of the validity, even divinity, of all things under God that Ives had known, felt strongly, and believed to have vitality and "substance." Without naming names, but perhaps referring to Farwell, Ives wrote that the composer born in America and "so interested in 'negro melodies' that he writes a symphony over them [cannot, if he] has not been interested in the 'cause of the Freedmen'," produce something with substance, only with "color." Yet, "if a man finds that the cadences of an Apache war-dance come nearest to his soul," he can use them "fervently, transcendentally, inevitably, furiously, in his symphonies, in his operas, in his whistlings on the way to work [and] his music will be true to itself and incidentally American." (*Essays*, pp. 79–80)[4]

Just as no kind of musical source material was excluded from the Ives grab-bag, no kind of performance was either. Ives found the mix-ups and mistakes, the wrong notes and off-key playing of amateur musicians, just as "substantial" and thus in his view as "musical" as polished perfection, perhaps more so. Some of his music was planned to include such "mistakes": in a score-sketch for "The Fourth of July," third of his set called *Holidays*, Ives twice warned his copyist, "Mr. Price: Please don't try to make things nice! All the wrong notes are *right*. Just copy as I have—I want it that way. . . . Mr. Price: Band stuff—they didn't always play right & together & it was as good either way." (*Kirkpatrick*, p. 11) Ives wanted performances of his music to have a sense of involvement in action, of spontaneity and vitality. When

---

[4] Ives's use of pre-existent music has been widely discussed, most thoroughly and perceptively by J. Peter Burkholder in "The Evolution of Charles Ives's Music: Aesthetics, Quotation, Technique" (Ph.D. dissertation, University of Chicago, 1983); part of his argument there was published as " 'Quotation' and Emulation: Charles Ives's Use of His Models," *MQ*, LXXI (1985), 1–26.

Three Places in New England was first played in New York (1931) and conductor Nicolas Slonimsky apologized for a ragged performance, Ives reassured him, "Just like a town meeting—every man for himself. Wonderful how it came out!"[5] In some of his scores, Ives offers choices to the performer: a passage in the Second Sonata for violin and piano may be repeated "2 or 3 times decr[escendo] and rit[ardando] gradually," and a cadenza in the *Scherzo: Over the Pavements* is "to play or not to play! if played, to be played as not a nice one—but evenly, precise & unmusical as possible!"

"Nice" meant to Ives something weak, lily-livered, conventional, effetely genteel. Among his manuscripts is a *Take-off* on the Andante of Haydn's "Surprise" Symphony, marked "nice little easy sugar plum sounds," and under some harmonically knotty measures of his *Browning Overture* Ives wrote, "Browning was too big a man to rest in one nice little key . . . he walked on the mountains not down a nice proper little aisle." Ives felt that people's ears and minds could encompass much more than they thought possible. He equated harmonic complexity with strength; remembering Thanksgiving as a holiday celebrating the early American colonists, he noted on one of the sketches for the "Thanksgiving" movement of *Holidays* that "our forefathers were stronger men than can be represented by 'triads' only—these are too easy sounding." (*Kirkpatrick*, p. 13)

Persons of a "nice" conformist gentility were epitomized by Ives with the name "Rollo," borrowed from a mid-nineteenth-century series of children's books about a boy insufferably priggish, proper, and perfect. To "Rollo," Ives addressed many sarcastic marginal comments in his manuscripts: in the Second String Quartet, "too hard to play—so it just can't be good music—Rollo"; in the *Browning Overture*, "R. B[rowning]'s mental workmanship is as sound logical & strong as easier plans [that] Rollo likes."

The other side of that ideological coin was Ives's own willingness to try anything musically, his rejection of dogmatic and exclusive musical concepts, and the embodiment of his theoretical speculations not in verbal tracts but in musical works. In the one essay that comes closer to being a rounded theoretical statement than anything else he wrote—"Some 'Quarter-tone' Impressions" (1925; reprinted in *Essays*)—Ives's open-mindedness is trenchantly expressed in two sentences: "Why tonality as such should be thrown out for good, I can't see. Why it should be always present, I can't see." (*Essays*, p. 117)

In sum, Ives believed in substance over manner, in spirit over technique; he believed in music as a re-creation in sound of life itself; he felt that passionate, honest self-expression, by composer and/or performer—no matter how unusually organized—would create a "unity" far more significant than traditional order-principles; he accepted as source material any sort of

[5] Henry Cowell and Sidney Cowell, *Charles Ives and His Music* (New York: Oxford University Press, 1955; rev. ed. 1969), p. 106.

musical idea, his own or others', cultivated or vernacular, he identified difficulty with strength; he abhorred the "nice," the easy-sounding, and the genteel; and he was willing to try anything. He had a streak of Transcendentalism in him—maybe more than a streak—but Burkholder has argued persuasively that Transcendentalist thought was not a constant, let alone a lifelong persuasion, with Ives (contrary to almost every earlier writer on him); rather, that it crystallized briefly only toward the end of his creative life, as is reflected in the "Concord" Sonata and the book of *Essays Before a Sonata* of 1920—which, after all, were *about* a group of Transcendentalist thinkers and writers.[6]

IVES'S MUSIC

Ives was a fairly prolific composer, especially considering that his creative life was not particularly long (from 1886 to 1926) and that during most of it (from 1898 on) he had a full-time job apart from music. Kirkpatrick's *Temporary Catalogue*, as revised in the works-list of his entry on Ives in *TNGDAM*, is the most accurate listing of Ives's compositions; they may be summarized in five categories:

1. *Orchestral music*
   a. Large orchestra: four numbered symphonies; the four-movement *Holidays*; two three-movement sets (Ives's preferred term for a coherently balanced group of instrumental pieces), the first one best known by its subtitle, *Three Places in New England*; the twenty-minute-long *Robert Browning Overture*; and incomplete works including *Universe Symphony* for multiple orchestras.

   b. Small orchestra (chamber orchestra or "theater" orchestra): youthful "popular entertainment" pieces like *Holiday Quickstep*, "Country Band" *March*, and *Overture and March "1776"*; "songs with or without voices" like *The Pond*, *The Rainbow*, and the last movement of the *Set for Theatre or Chamber Orchestra*; the pair of "contemplations" *The Unanswered Question* and *Central Park in the Dark*; and the scherzo with the cadenza "to play or not to play," *Over the Pavements* plus other, slighter works.

2. *Chamber music*
   About fifteen complete compositions, including four violin-and-piano sonatas; two string quartets; a trio for violin, cello, and piano; and other sets and single movements (the best known being *From the Steeples and the Mountains*, for trumpet, trombone, and four sets of eight bells each, and *Hallowe'en*, for string quartet, piano, and optional drum).

---

[6] Burkholder, *Ives: The Ideas Behind the Music*, especially Chap. 3, "Ives and Transcendentalism: A Second Look."

3. *Keyboard music*

About forty works, mostly for piano (although two well-known ones are for organ: *Adeste Fidelis* [sic] *in an Organ Prelude* and *Variations on "America"*). Of the two major piano sonatas, the second ("Concord, Mass., 1840–1860") is probably Ives's most famous work; a third sonata, briefer but very original in shape, is called *Three-Page Sonata*. Besides a series of single-movement experimental "studies," there are two unusual larger late works: *Varied Air and Variations* and, for two pianos tuned a quarter-tone apart, *Three Quarter-Tone Pieces*.

4. *Choral music*

a. Sacred works, notably a series of short anthems and psalm settings (from the early *Psalm 67* to the late *Psalm 90*), the quasi-sacred set of three *Harvest Home Chorales*, and the sprawling concert cantata *The Celestial Country*; many other choral compositions for church use are lost.

b. Glees and other part-songs, only a few of which, from the Yale years, survive (such as *A Song of Mory's* and *The Bells of Yale*).

c. Other secular works for unison chorus and varied instrumental ensembles, the best known of which are *He Is There!*, *Lincoln the Great Commoner*, and *Majority or The Masses*.

5. *Solo songs*

Composed throughout Ives's career, from *Slow March* (ca. 1887) to *Sunrise* (1926; Ives's last newly composed work; recorded on NW 300:s1/5); they total about half again as many as Ives included in *114 Songs*.

The extraordinary diversity of Ives's music is well seen in his songs. Some sense of the bewilderment with which other composers greeted the book of *114 Songs* is conveyed in Aaron Copland's breathless summary:

> Almost every kind of song imaginable can be found—delicate lyrics, dramatic poems, sentimental ballads, German, French, and Italian songs, war songs, songs of religious sentiment, street songs, humorous songs, hymn tunes, folk tunes, encore songs; songs adapted from orchestral scores, piano works, and violin sonatas; intimate songs, cowboy songs, and mass songs. Songs of every character and description, songs bristling with dissonances, tone clusters, and "elbow chords" next to songs of the most elementary harmonic simplicity.[7]

Clearly, one cannot hope to describe such an oeuvre easily. A close look at one or two songs can, however, suggest some aspects of them, and of Ives's mature music in general.

Two Little Flowers (1921) is superficially simple, sweet, uncomplicated. The text, written by Ives and his wife, tells of "two little flowers"

---

[7] "One Hundred and Fourteen Songs," *MM*, XI (January–February 1934), 59–64.

seen in the backyard on sunny days; other blossoms may be beautiful, but "fairest, rarest of them all are Edith and Susanna" (young Edith Ives and her playmate). The atmosphere of both text and setting is that of the nineteenth-century sentimental household song, and the melody moves predictably in smooth contours of pitch and rhythm (Example 7-1 [a]). Suddenly, however, three tiny rhythmic jolts occur, at "one in green," "passing fair," and "ever rare"; they point up, in a subtle way, the syntactical divisions of the verses, and they prepare for the wholly original melodic climax with its downward vaulting of an octave and a third (unless the singer can't make it; and Ives offers a simpler alternative) and its suspensive pause on "all," gratefully low in the singer's range (Example 7-1 [b]). The accompaniment has its subtleties, too; initially sounding like a commonplace arpeggiated vamp, it turns out to revolve in groups of seven (not eight) eighth notes, and rather than outlining a conventional triadic harmony it is quintal, spanning the interval D-E. This whole-tone interval is the basis for the harmonic events through two-thirds of the song, as each of these notes moves outward in whole-tone motion: D-E, C-F♯, A♯-G♯. Aproaching the end, Ives shifts to a V-of-ii, V-of-V, I$_4^6$ pattern, full of harmonic energy (measures 23–24) but returns to the whole-tone idea at the climax: superimposed on the surprising, dark chord at the word "all" is an even more surprising C-E third high in the piano, as if the B♭-D interval were going to move upward to the E-G of the next measure (through C-E and D-F♯) but couldn't wait. The song ends with chords that sound like ii-V-I, but each contains the critical whole-tone interval: E-D, A-B, D-E.

Even this brief analysis makes the music seem more complicated than it sounds: the total effect of the song is that of simplicity and "familiarity," yet the commonplace is everywhere avoided and we recognize a work in which the familiar is transcended.

EXAMPLE 7-1. C. Ives, *Two Little Flowers* (1921). Copyright 1935 Merion Music, Inc.; used by permission. (a) Measures 1–10. (b) Measures 23–27.

Less traditional by far in melody, harmony, and rhythm is *Cradle Song* (1919), given in its entirety as Example 7-2, although within its tiny nine-measure span it speaks just as evocatively and directly as *Two Little Flowers*. Each of the three phrases of the vocal line comes to rest on G♯, establishing that note as one tonal center, although the scale basis of the melody might suggest F♯. The accompaniment is less certain about its tonality, finally settling on A (but G♯ appears here, too, linking voice with accompaniment). No systematic harmony is present, except an *avoidance* of simple triads: there are Debussyesque bichords (measures 1, 9), added-sixth chords (1, 2, 9), Wagner's "*Tristan* chord" with complications (5), and other simultaneities inexplicable as single sonorities without taking into account linear aspects (e.g., the F♯ of measure 4, part of a treble line moving C♯-E-F♯-G♯). Harmonically, the song seems to "float" in a void, an effect consonant with the text. The rhythm of the piece confirms this effect, as it sways gently between ²₄ and ⁶₈, the ²₄♩ = ⁶₈♩ prescription precluding any sense of regular meter at all and allowing the rhythm to float, unmoored to a metric anchor. In measure 8, voice and accompaniment are really in different meters, the voice part ending on a disguised ²₄ measure, the accompaniment continuing in its broad ⁶₈.

EXAMPLE 7-2. C. Ives, *Cradle Song* (1919). Copyright 1935 Merion Music, Inc.; used by permission.

sleep · ing en · cum · bers.___
leaf · lets are fly · ing.___
love___ flow for ev · er.___

For 1st and 2nd Verses

l.h. *r.h.*

For 3rd Verse

Notes: End song on ⌒; This chord may be repeated very quietly at the end of verse sung last.
*It will be observed that a ♩ of the $\frac{2}{4}$ measure is a ♩ of the $\frac{6}{8}$ and not a ♩.

One of the lengthiest and most powerful songs, *General William Booth Enters into Heaven* (1914), on portions of a poem by Vachel Lindsay, exemplifies Ives's use of "imitative dissonance" and of musical quotation. The hectic, militant atmosphere of the text, which celebrates the fanatic revivalism of the first commanding general of the Salvation Army, leads Ives to begin the song with a typical marching band's drumbeat: the whack of the snare drums and the thud of the bass drum, lagging a bit behind, are projected in dissonant clusters (Example 7-3 [a]). Where Lindsay's poem quotes parenthetically (from a Salvation Army hymn, "Are you washed in the blood of the Lamb?"), so does Ives, though he uses the revival hymn tune *Cleansing Fountain* ("There is a fountain filled with blood"). His equivalent to parenthesizing it is to present it in a key far removed from the tonal sphere of the context. This melody, redolent of American gospel hymnody in general, is developed in all kinds of ways in the course of the song; other melodies quoted are the introduction to James A. Bland's minstrel-show song *Golden Slippers* (responding to the text's mention of a banjo; measures 52–55, piano part) and trumpet calls (at the mention of trumpets, measures 69–72, and of marching, measures 103–5). One of the most moving passages of the song (Example 7-3 [b]) finds the singer circling "round and round" on a three-note figure, the pianist's right hand circling similarly but in a two-note cycle, while in the middle of the accompaniment, strangely askew, the melody of *Cleansing Fountain* winds its tranquil way. *General William Booth* ends with a haunting, parenthetically off-key statement of *Cleansing Fountain* set to hymn-book harmony; then the drumbeats, lower pitched as if in the distance, fade—"as a band marching away," wrote Ives in the manuscript.

Other notable songs of Ives, which I can cite only briefly here, are *Charlie Rutlage* (1920 or 1921), a cowboy ballad in which Ives turns to unpitched rhythmic declamation for the climactic measures; *The Circus Band*

EXAMPLE 7-3. C. Ives, *General William Booth Enters Into Heaven* (1914). Copyright 1935 Merion Music, Inc.; used by permission. (a) Measures 1–10. (b) Measures 82–91.

(1894), with much prancing band music; *Serenity* (1919), to a tranquil poem by Whittier in which a virtually monotonous chant-like vocal line is spun out against an other-wordly, "floating" harmonic oscillation; *Walking* (1902), in which the diffuse, cloudy overtones of church bells are captured subtly, and also the propulsive syncopations of ragtime. In *Majority* (originally for chorus and orchestra, 1915; arranged for voice and piano, 1921), with its perfervid Whitmanesque text, there is an equation between "the Masses" of the poem and massive chords (as many as fifteen notes) built in clusters of massed seconds; these must be played either with the forearm or a board or with the help of a second pianist. *Soliloquy* (1907) is subtitled "a study in 7ths and other things" and systematically explores non-traditional harmonies and retrograde motion.

A number of the *114 Songs* were originally choral works, but the bulk of Ives's choral music was for the church: some forty sacred choruses remain. Best known among these is a setting of *Psalm 67* (1894?), based on a bitonal plan with the men's voices in the sphere of G minor, the women's in C major. Most awesome is an eleven-minute setting of *Psalm 90* (1894; lost but reconstructed, or recomposed, in 1924) for choir, organ, and bells, underscored throughout by a low C in the organ. A number of the choral works seem to be compositional études; they reveal the experimental vein of Ives's thought, akin to Milhaud's studies in bichords and Bartók's in scales and intervals. Among these are *Psalm 24* (1894?), which is based on mirror-image counterpoint and systematic interval expansion (Example 7-4 [a]) and the *Processional "Let There Be Light"* (1901), whose harmonies are based on consistently changing structural intervals; I have shown the plan of the chords of its core passage in Example 7-4 (b) (P = perfect; A = augmented; M = major; m = minor).

Among the secular choral works are *Harvest Home Chorales* (1898, 1901) for chorus, brass ensemble, and organ—"a kind of outdoor music," according to Ives, in which the tangled yet harmonious co-existence of "the trees, rocks, and men of the mountains in days before machinery" is expressed through radically independent counterpoint among the three sound components.[8] *Lincoln the Great Commoner* (1912), for (mostly unison) chorus, orchestra, and piano, exceeds even the *Chorales* in density of texture and heterophonic polyphony; quotations from *The Battle Hymn of the Republic, Hail! Columbia, The Red, White & Blue* ("O Columbia, the gem of the ocean"), *The Star-Spangled Banner, America,* and *The Battle Cry of Freedom* appear in almost cinematic collage, and more than once the voices split into a tumult of shouted tone-clusters, a kind of "choral noise" of overwhelming power.

EXAMPLE 7-4. Compositional études" of Ives. (a) *Psalm 24* (1894?), measures 1–6 (after the manuscript). (b) *Processional "Let There Be Light"* (1901), harmonic plan of measures 9–18 (after the manuscript).

[8] The passages quoted are from an Ives letter published in Gertrude Norman and Miriam Lubell Shrifte, eds., *Letters of Composers* (New York: Alfred A. Knopf, Inc., 1946), pp. 345–46.

The shorter instrumental works of Ives, like the songs, are remarkable for their diversity and individuality: each seems to create its own expressive world; taken together, they cover an immense range of affective ends, achieved by an equally broad spectrum of technical means.

Among the shorter piano pieces are various Studies (1907–9?), part of an incomplete series of twenty-seven (after Chopin's 27 Etudes?), including *Some South-Paw Pitching*, a showpiece for the left hand under right-hand variants of Foster's *Massa's in de cold cold ground*; *The Anti-Abolitionist Riots in the 1830's and 1840's*; and 22 (i.e., twenty-second in the series). Interesting for its relationship to Schoenberg's twelve-tone row technique (of which Ives knew nothing) is the theme of the *Varied Air and Variations* (1923?): likened by Ives to "the old stone wall around the orchard," it is made up of four interlocked, row-like chromatic series—for Ives the musical embodiment of the New England fence where none of the stones is exactly the same size or shape. The *Three-Page Sonata* (1905), actually a substantial eight-minute work, compresses the traditional four-movement form into a dramatic first section, lyric slow section, and last section alternating clangorous march motifs and jerky ragtime rhythms.

Free from the necessity to accommodate his music to conventional performance media, Ives wrote works for an astonishing variety of small instrumental ensembles, from two pianos tuned a quarter tone apart (*Three Pieces*, 1923–24) to the combination of brass and bells of *From the Steeples and the Mountains* (1901–2?). Many of the chamber works derived from, or were rebuilt into, other pieces. Among those originally conceived for small orchestra ("theater" orchestra) are two well-known works of 1906 often performed separately but considered by Ives as a pair—*The Unanswered Question* and *Central Park in the Dark in "The Good Old Summertime"*; the first "A Contemplation of a Serious Matter," the second "A Contemplation of Nothing Serious." *The Unanswered Question*, for trumpet, four flutes, and strings, has an elaborate metaphysial program explaining the three sound components: the strings represent "the silence of the druids," the trumpet asks "the perennial question of existence," and the flutes—"Fighting Answerers"—attempt to find a satisfactory response. But no explanation is needed for the delicate balance in which the three components are suspended: the strings move slowly and placidly in spacious, diatonic harmony from beginning to end; the trumpet periodically sounds a disturbingly repetitive, atonal phrase from another musical world; and the flutes, increasingly raucous and agitated, provide a dynamic arc for the whole structure; few works by Ives so immediately and movingly bring us in touch with his faith

---

[9] The "atonal" trumpet phrase was not always thus: when Ives wrote the work in 1906, it was comparatively tonal, but when he "tinkered" with it before its publication by Peer-Southern (1953), he altered it, making it more dissonant and atonal (as he did in revising many other early works). The revised critical edition (1985) of *The Unanswered Question* includes both the original and the "atonalized" trumpet parts.

in the harmonious co-existence of disparate elements.[9] *Central Park in the Dark* is for a totally different ensemble (piccolo, flute, oboe, clarinet, bassoon, trumpet, trombone, percussion, two pianos, and strings) but similarly juxtaposes quiet sounds (this time atonal) with what Ives called "off tunes and sounds" (diatonic and based on popular-song and ragtime sources).

Ives was capable of musical contemplation not only of cosmically serious matters but also of earthily comic ones. *Hallowe'en* (1906), for string quartet and piano with drum *ad libitum*, is a cacophonic spoof combining the humorous surprise of April Fools' Day jokes with the crude pranks of Halloween. The first violin plays in the key of C, the second in B, the viola in D♭, the cello in D; the piano is atonal. Seldom do accents coincide. Only eighteen measures long, the piece may be repeated three or four times, omitting or altering various parts each time until the last, when, with a drum adding to the general din, the tempo is to be "as fast as possible without disabling any player or instrument." (What is hardly apparent, as the work rushes by in a blur, is the rigorous contrapuntal texture of the string parts— "canonic," says Ives, "not only in tones, but in phrases, accents, and duration or spaces." [*Memos*, p. 91]) The *Scherzo: Over the Pavements*, which includes

EXAMPLE 7-5. C. Ives, *Scherzo: Over the Pavements* (1906–13), measures 59–61. Copyright 1954 by Peer International Corporation. Used by permission.

the cadenza "to play or not to play," is for piccolo, clarinet, bassoon, trumpet, three trombones, cymbal, drum, and piano. It grew out of a work called *Rube Trying to Walk 2 to 3!!*, which suggests its emphasis on rhythmic counterpoint; this reaches a knotty climax (Example 7-5) in the second section of the A B C cadenza C′ B′ A′ form. Ives has the last laugh on the struggling performers in a comic ending, which sees them all together in an oom-pah, oom-pah vamp on a simple C-major triad—a mocking concession to "Rollo."

Ives combined several groups of chamber pieces into "sets." One such set, a three-movement group of which the second is lost, he called *Tone Roads* (1911–15). No. 3, for woodwinds, brass, strings, piano, and chimes, is interesting for its repetitions of sections at varied tempos; its use of quarter-tone inflections; and the "tone road" of the chimes (in all but one section of the work), which approximates a twelve-tone row and is treated at the beginning like a medieval *color*, its pitch pattern repeated in a varied rhythmic pattern (Example 7-6).

In more conventional media, and somewhat more conventional forms, are the sonatas for piano and for violin and piano and the symphonies.

Besides the *Three-Page Sonata*, Ives composed two numbered piano sonatas and began a third, now lost. The Second Sonata ("Concord, Mass., 1840–1860") is a giant four-movement cycle reflecting Ives's admiration for

EXAMPLE 7-6. C. Ives, *Tone Roads*, No. 3 (chimes part only), measures 1–12. After a photostat of the manuscript in the Library of Congress.

some of the American literary giants of the mid-nineteenth century. Howard Boatwright has written in his edition of the *Essays Before a Sonata*, which Ives had printed in conjunction with the music:

> For some composers, one work, more than any other, may become a channel through which the streams of philosophical concept, musical technique, and style flow in singular unity. For Charles Ives, the Concord Sonata was such a work. It reflects programmatically, and also in deeper, less obvious ways, the influence of the Concord Transcendentalists; it is representative of Ives' highest achievements in richness of harmony and freedom of rhythm. (*Essays*, p. xiii)

Ives himself spoke of the work (*Essays*, p. xxv) more diffidently, saying it was " a group of four pieces, called a sonata for want of a more exact name, as the form, perhaps substance, does not justify it." He described the four movements as "impressionistic pictures of Emerson and Thoreau, a sketch of the Alcotts, and a *scherzo* supposed to reflect a lighter quality which is often found in the fantastic side of Hawthorne." Emerson, for Ives, conjures up a musical portrait of power and density; the first movement, although based on a sonata-form idea, reminds one of Ives's view of Emerson's own "plan of work" (see p. 165). The scherzo on Hawthorne rushes by in a blur except for one quiet, slow passage colored by two-octave-wide cluster-chords vibrating sympathetically high in the treble and another in which Simeon Marsh's hymn *Martyn* appears in a hushed, halting, hymn-book harmony. The Alcotts evoke a gentle variant of *Martyn* (which relates also to the opening motif of Beethoven's Fifth Symphony which appears throughout the "Concord" Sonata) and several of "old Scotch airs," one of *them* related (coincidentally?) to the minstrel-show song *Stop That Knocking at My Door* (1843) of A. F. Winnemore. The final movement, "Thoreau," is deceptively calm in spirit; it builds to a single climax, then unwinds in a long denouement synthesizing materials from earlier movements and closing with a hauntingly tentative final gesture. Said Ives of the "Concord" Sonata:

> Every time I play it or turn to it, [it] seems unfinished. . . . Some of the passages now played haven't been written out . . . and I don't know as I ever

shall write them out, as it may take away the daily pleasure of playing this music and seeing it grow and feeling that it is not finished. (I may always have the pleasure of not finishing it) . . . (*Memos*, pp. 79–80)

Besides a "Pre-First" Violin Sonata and a "Pre-pre First" Sonata lost or destroyed (the terminology is Kirkpatrick's), Ives wrote four sonatas for violin and piano between 1902 and 1916. More than any similar group of Ives's works, the four sonatas seem all of a piece, citizens of the same musical world. All are in three movements; all end with hymn-tune finales; all are characteristically "easy" pieces (by Ives's standards), lacking the tangled thickets of the texture of, say, the first movement of the "Concord" Sonata. Sonatas Nos. 1 and 3 are abstract; Sonata No. 2 offers portraits of "Autumn" and a square dance ("In the Barn") plus a nostalgic view of the mounting intensity of a camp meeting ("The Revival"). Sonata No. 4, entirely based on hymn tunes, is called "Children's Day at the Camp Meeting." "The Revival" movement of Sonata No. 2 is an ingeniously worked piece, a sort of freely unfolding stream of variations on the old hymn tune *Nettleton* (or *Hallelujah*; see p. 104). The ingenuity and integrity with which Ives "recomposed" such borrowed material can be suggested by comparing a passage from "The Revival" (Example 7-7 [a]) with the opening of the third movement of String Quartet No. 1 (Example 7-7 [b]). In the former, Ives sets the tune as a bitonal canon at the tritone over cloudy pedal points on the tonic and dominant of the respective keys; in the latter, he invents a new ending and sets the tune to a cross between Schubertian and barbershop harmony.

EXAMPLE 7-7. Two uses of *Nettleton* by Ives. (a) Sonata No. 2 for violin and piano (New York: G. Schirmer, Inc., 1951), third movement, measures 22–23. (b) String Quartet No. 1, third movement, measures 1–4. © Copyright 1961 and 1963 by Peer International Corporation. Used by permission.

The First String Quartet (1896) is an assemblage from earlier organ pieces: its last three movements were originally a Prelude, Offertory, and Postlude composed for New Haven's Center Church (where Ives was organist during his years at Yale); the first movement derives from a fugue—on Lowell Mason's *Missionary Hymn* (see p. 66), soon combined with Oliver Holden's *Coronation* (see p. 127)—that Ives had written for a class of Parker. (Ives later adapted it to form the slow movement of the Fourth Symphony.) The Second String Quartet (1907–13) has been mentioned (p. 000); it is a thoroughly mature and "tough" work, one of the most striking examples of Ives's involving the performers in "discussions" and "arguments." The third movement finds the arguments resolved and the participants "viewing the firmament," to material based on the hymn tunes *Nettleton* and *Bethany* (Mason's "Nearer, my God, to thee") and the change-ringing melody of *Westminster Chimes.*

As in the violin sonatas, Ives seems in his symphonies to have been mindful of traditional broad, formal procedures. Following the early First Symphony (1898) in four movements came a Second (1902) in five. Its last movement is the most "Ivesian," with its pileups of tune quotations (*Camptown Races*, another more lyric melody reminiscent of *Old Black Joe*, country-fiddle-style counterpoints, *The Red, White & Blue*, and *Reveille*); Ives made it all the more "Ivesian" in a late (and dubiously tasteful) change of the very last chord from a tonic F-major triad to a raucous eleven-note squawk. The earlier movements seem somewhat labored in their conventionality, particularly the self-proclaiming "developments" of material in the style of European symphonists from Beethoven to Brahms and Dvořák. The Third Symphony (1904), slighter but more individual, is characterized by its subtitle, "The Camp Meeting"; it is a broad, hymnic three-movement work of which both first and last movements betray their origins as organ pieces.

Between the Third Symphony and the completion of the Fourth, Ives wrote three other works of symphonic proportions. The work originally entitled *A Symphony: New England Holidays* (1904–13) is a gathering of four separate orchestral movements into a kind of American "Four Seasons": "Washington's Birthday," "Decoration Day," "The Fourth of July," and "Thanksgiving." *Three Places in New England* (1908–14)—the First Orchestral Set— is a three-movement work. Its first movement, "The 'St. Gaudens' in Boston Common," is a brooding piece, with some of Ives's most subtle, highly developed use of older melodies. Inspired by the monument by Augustus Saint-Gaudens commemorating Colonel Robert Shaw and the regiment of blacks he led during the Civil War, Ives based his music on Foster's *Old Black Joe*, Root's *Battle Cry of Freedom*, and Work's *Marching Through Georgia.* Example 7-8 shows one moment when Ives finds a common denominator (*a* in the example) between the phrase "I'm coming" of Foster's song and "[Hur]rah! hurrah!" in Work's, combines that material with the chorus

("The Union forever, Hurrah boys, Hurrah!") of *The Battle Cry of Freedom* (*b*), fashions an ostinato bass (c_1) from a pentatonic motive (c_2) common to the two Civil War songs, and underscores the whole with a traditional military band's drum cadence (*d*). The second movement of *Three Places*, "Putnam's Camp," combines the gay, brassy music of a late nineteenth-century Fourth of July picnic at a Revolutionary War campsite (complete with the village brass band) and a child's fantasizing about the apparition of figures from the Revolution; the middle section finds the march beat of Example 7-8 (*d*) going along at two different speeds in the proportion $\circ = \downarrow$. in a famous example of polytempo. The movement is full of hilarious gaiety and ends in a fine Independence Day burst of pyrotechnical pandemonium and a rather besotted blast of *The Star-Spangled Banner*. *Three Places* concludes in murmuring tranquility, with an autumnal evocation of hymn singing heard across a New England river: "The Housatonic at Stockbridge." A Second Orchestral Set (1912–15) is also in three movements: "An Elegy to Our Forefathers," "The Rockstrewn Hills Join in the People's Outdoor Meeting," and "From Hanover Square North, at the End of a Tragic Day, the Voice of the People Again Arose." The last movement, largely built around the gospel hymn *Sweet Bye-and-Bye*, builds to perhaps the most spine-tingling climax in all Ives's work. A Third Orchestral Set and the *Universe Symphony* (see *Memos*, pp. 106–8) were left unfinished.

EXAMPLE 7-8. C. Ives, *Three Places in New England*, first movement ("The 'St. Gaudens' in Boston Common"), measures 66–69. Quoted by permission of Mercury Music Corporation.

Ives labored off and on between 1909 and 1916 at his Fourth Symphony, one of the most grandly conceived works in the history of American music. Scored for a huge orchestra and chorus plus a "distant choir" of strings and harps and a special "battery unit" of percussion, it had to wait until

April 26, 1965, for its premiere performance (under Leopold Stokowski, assisted by two other conductors). Two movements had been performed in 1927, and program notes for that performance were written by Henry Bellamann, obviously from information supplied by his friend Ives:

> This symphony . . . consists of four movements,—a prelude, a majestic fugue, a third movement in comedy vein, and a finale of transcendent spiritual content. [The order of the second and third movements was later reversed.] The aesthetic program of the work is . . . the searching questions of What? and Why? which the spirit of man asks of life. This is particularly the sense of the prelude. The three succeeding movements are the diverse answers in which existence replies. . . . The fugue . . . is an expression of the reaction of life into formalism and ritualism. The succeeding movement [i.e., the movement ultimately made the second] . . . is a comedy in the sense that Hawthorne's Celestial Railroad is a comedy.[10]

Ives added to Bellamann's notes a word on the last movement: ". . . an apothesis of the preceding content, in terms that have something to do with the reality of existence and its religious experience."[11]

The four movements of the Fourth Symphony resolve into two pairs. The Prelude, with its choral inquiry ("Watchman, tell us of the night/What the signs of promise are"), leads to the "comedy" movement, in which nostalgic song passages are constantly interrupted by strident marches, rags, square-dance tunes, and patriotic ditties—not just separately but sometimes all at once. The fugue, stately, hymnic, suffused with 16- and 32-foot organ pedal color, serves as preparation for the last movement, which is even more complex in texture than the second, but a tapestry of murmurs rather than shouts. It begins mysteriously, like a distant march, with a complex percussion pattern that never ceases; is wholly independent of the rest of the movement's music; and, lingering after the orchestra (with wordless voices) dissolves, fades off in the distance as the symphony ends. For all its growing, then ebbing, complexity, the movement breathes a spirit of utter tranquility. Ives wrote no more profoundly conceived and perfectly realized music than this.

Seen against the nineteenth-century background of an American musical culture sharply divided between cultivated and vernacular traditions, Ives's historical position is a unique one. Alone among his contemporaries, he embraced both traditions without reservation: his works emphatically declared that in its vernacular tradition American music had an artistically usable past; they also embodied the highest aspirations of the cultivated

---

[10] Quoted in John Kirkpatrick's extensive preface to the published score (New York: Associated Music Publishers, 1965), p. viii. Kirkpatrick includes a detailed account of the background of the symphony and identification of its many musical quotations.
[11] Ibid.

tradition. Moreover, Ives's open-mindedness and freshness of musical imagination were to be a continuing challenge to American composers after 1920.
Ives is seen by many as the fountainhead of a new tradition in American
music, a basically experimental, pathfinding one. In a few sentences that
are rather Ivesian in their bluntness and humor, Virgil Thomson, com-
menting on "the composer who lives by non-musical work," has remarked,

> [He] makes up his music out of whole cloth at home. He invents his own
> aesthetic. When his work turns out to be not unplayable technically, it often
> gives a useful kick in the pants to the professional tradition. The music of . . .
> Charles Ives did that very vigorously indeed.[12]

BIBLIOGRAPHICAL NOTES

The basic documentary works on Ives are cited in footnote 1. Other important
book-length studies include the first critical biography of the composer, still
valuable, by Henry Cowell and Sidney Cowell, *Charles Ives and His Music*
(New York: Oxford University Press, 1955; rev. ed. 1969); Vivan Perlis's compilation of reminiscences, *Charles Ives Remembered: An Oral History* (New
Haven, CT: Yale University Press, 1974); Frank R. Rossiter's exceptionally
well-documented *Charles Ives and His America* (New York: Liveright, 1975);
and *An Ives Celebration: Papers and Panels of the [1974] Charles Ives Centennial Festival-Conference*, ed. H. Wiley Hitchcock and Vivian Perlis (Urbana:
University of Illinois Press, 1977). The most notable dissertations have been,
I think, Clayton Henderson's "Quotation as a Style Element in the Music of
Charles Ives" (Washington University, 1969), David Eiseman's "Charles Ives
and the European Symphonic Tradition: A Historical Reappraisal" (University
of Illinois, 1972), Laurence Wallach's 'The New England Education of Charles
Ives" (Columbia University, 1973), Nachum Schoffman's "The Songs of Charles
Ives" (Hebrew University of Jerusalem, 1977), and J. Peter Burkholder's "The
Evolution of Charles Ives's Music: Aesthetics, Quotation, Technique" (University of Chicago, 1983). Part of the last named has been published as the
very valuable, revisionist *Charles Ives: The Ideas Behind the Music* (New
Haven, CT: Yale University Press, 1985), and one or two other volumes based
on it are also to be published by Yale.

My *Ives*, the first book on an American in the Oxford Studies of Composers
series (London: Oxford University Press, 1977), was slightly revised and pub-

---

[12] *The State of Music*, 2nd rev. ed. (New York: Random House [Vintage Books], 1962),
p. 85. In his *American Music Since 1910* (New York: Holt, Rinehart and Winston, 1971), pp.
22–30, Thomson discusses what he calls "The Ives Case" rather less charitably than this
quotation would suggest.

lished with the more helpful title *Ives: A Survey of the Music* (ISAMm 19 [1983]). Other especially valuable analytic studies are (in chronological order of publication) Robert P. Morgan's "Rewriting Music History: Second Thoughts on Ives and Varèse," *Musical Newsletter*, III/1 (January 1973), 3–12, and III/2 (April 1973), 15–23; William Brooks's "Unity and Diversity in [the first movement of] Charles Ives's Fourth Symphony," *Yearbook for Inter-American Musical Research*, X (1974), 5–49; Judith Tick's "Ragtime and the Music of Charles Ives," *Current Musicology*, No. 18 (1974), 105–13; Stuart Feder's psychoanalytic "Decoration Day: A Boyhood Memory of Charles Ives," *MQ*, LXVI (1980), 234–61; Rita H. Mead's "Cowell, Ives, and New Music," *MQ*, LXVI (1980), 538–59; Arthur Maisels Schenkerian "*The Fourth of July* by Charles Ives: Mixed Harmonic Criteria in a Twentieth-Century Classic," *Theory and Practice*, VI/1 (August 1981), 3–32; Nachum Schoffman's "Serialism in the Works of Charles Ives," *Tempo: A Quarterly Review of Modern Music*, No. 138 (September 1981), 21–32; and composer Larry Austin's discussion of his realization (from the sketches) of a portion of *Universe Symphony*, "Charles Ives's Life Pulse Prelude for Percussion Orchestra," *Percussive Notes*, XXIII/6 (September 1985), 58–84.

Other writings of particular interest include Elliott Carter's swings back and forth between admiration and deprecation of Ives in no fewer than ten articles beginning in 1939; these are reprinted in *The Writings of Elliott Carter*, eds. Else Stone and Kurt Stone (Bloomington: Indiana University Press, 1977); Lou Harrison's "On Quotation," *MM*, XXIII/4 (Summer 1946), 166–69; David Wooldridge's provocative, quirky, and not altogether trustworthy *From the Steeples and Mountains: A Study of Charles Ives* (New York: Alfred A. Knopf, Inc., 1974), reviewed by John Kirkpatrick in *High Fidelity/Musical America*, XXIV/9 (September 1974), MA33–MA36, and argued over between Wooldridge and Kirkpatrick in the same magazine, XXIV/12 (December 1974), MA18–MA20; Davd Eiseman's "George Ives as Theorist: Some Unpublished Documents," *PNM*, XIV/1 (Fall-Winter 1975), 139–47; and Vivian Perlis's listing of the holdings of Ivesiana (complementing Kirkpatrick's *Temporary Catalogue*) at Yale: *Charles Ives Papers* (New Haven, CT: Yale University Music Library, 1983).

part three

Between The World Wars (1920—1945)

EIGHT
THE 1920s

REACTIONS TO THE CLASSIC-ROMANTIC TRADITION

The period surrounding World War I, roughly from about 1910 to the mid-1920s, was a critical one for Western music in general and for American music as part of the larger scene. Many young European composers felt that the main Classic-Romantic tradition had reached a crisis point and that new means had to be found to renovate it. Various reactions to the tradition, more or less violent, became apparent during this period, which was one of the most turbulent aesthetically and stylistically in the history of Western music. Paris, especially, was a cauldron of ferment; but so was Vienna, for so long a center of the tradition. Composers of other nationalities shared the same sense of crisis as well, partly out of a nationalistic urge for musical independence from central European domination.

In some works, barbs of satire and ridicule were aimed at the presumed hyperexpressivity and bombast of the tradition. Thus Claude Debussy slyly, quoted Wagner's *Tristan und Isolde* in "Gollywog's Cakewalk," the most offhand piece in his *Children's Corner* suite (1906–8), with a tongue-in-cheek instruction to the pianist to play "avec une grande émotion." Erik Satie became virtually a professional musical satirist. The young Darius Milhaud reacted against the inordinate length and grandiloquence of the post-Romantic symphony and opera forms with three-minute symphonies (1917) and *opéras minutes* (1927).

Another kind of reaction was that of an outright rejection of the tradition and an attempt to revolutionize musical expression, especially in media related to the machine age: this was the aim of the Futurist group at first centered in Italy, then in Paris, where concerts of noise instruments— hissers, exploders, cracklers, buzzers, screamers, and the like—were given.

Older, established composers like Ralph Vaughan Williams, Richard Strauss, Gabriel Fauré, and Jean Sibelius, not sharing the sense of crisis of their younger colleagues, more or less unconsciously extended the tradition. But the group of composers in Vienna around Arnold Schoenberg sought *consciously* to extend it beyond past limits, particularly its element of chromaticism. Considering Classic-Romantic tonality a procrustean bed ill fitted to the increasingly chromatic vocabulary of melody and harmony, they wrote an ultra-chromatic music that avoided traditional tonality and approached a free atonality. In another sort of evolutionary extension of the tradition, the Czech composer Alois Hába began working with microtones, intervals smaller than the traditional chromatic semitones of the twelve-note tempered scale.

Finally, an immense number of works of the period suggest attempts to revitalize and enlarge the tradition by exotic and atavistic borrowings from musical cultures distant in space, spirit, or time. Thus the primitivistic manner of Igor Stravinsky's *Le Sacre du printemps* (1913) and *Les Noces* (1917–23); the delving into the heart of folk music of Béla Bartók; and the popularesque manner based on urban café music of Milhaud's *Le Boeuf sur le toit* (1920), Arthur Honegger's Concertino for piano and orchestra (1925), and Francis Poulenc's Sonata for piano duet (1918). Related in impulse to these works, which looked to primitive, folk, and popular music for a fresh note, were others that looked back, beyond the Romantic era, to the Classical, Baroque, and even earlier periods in Western music for inspiration: Sergei Prokofiev's "Classical" Symphony (1916–17); Stravinsky's *Pulcinella* (1920) and Octet for wind instruments (1923); Schoenberg's chamber *Serenade*, Op. 24 (1923), and neo-Classic Suite for piano, Op. 25 (1924); Maurice Ravel's *Le Tombeau de Couperin* (1914–17); Ottorino Respighi's *Antiche arie e danze* (1916–31) and *Concerto gregoriano* (1922).

In sum, the atmosphere of European music just before and after World War I was charged with various currents and cross-currents of progressivism: "New Music" marched under a variety of banners. This atmosphere was characteristic also of the United States, slightly later, between the end of World War I and the economic collapse of 1929. An era of unprecedented prosperity in the United States, the 1920s were notable in American music as years when progressive currents could flourish, and did; years when youthful composers could afford to spurn the achievements of the generation that preceded them, and did.

The older generation, composers in their forties and fifties in the decade after World War I, continued to write in an essentially nineteenth-century manner, to get performances and continued respect. Chadwick, Hill, Frederick Converse (1871–1940), Rubin Goldmark (1872–1936), and Daniel Gregory Mason (1873–1953) carried forward the traditionalism, the solid craft if not notable inventiveness, of the Second New England School. Converse, who studied with Paine and Chadwick and returned to Boston after completing his training in Munich with Rheinberger, saw his opera *The Pipe of Desire* produced by the Metropolitan Opera in 1910, the first by an American to be performed there; his symphonic poem *The Mystic Trumpeter* (1904) has maintained its early reputation (nominally, if not in many performances) as his best work. Goldmark came to be best known as a teacher from his position as head of the composition department of the Juilliard School. Mason, grandson of Lowell Mason, achieved a considerable success with his overture *Chanticleer* (1926) but wielded more influence as a writer on music for the general public—not necessarily a positive influence since he was both an arch-conservative and a rather unpleasantly anti-Semitic one in an era when Jewish patrons, performers, and composers, of both concert and popular music, were becoming increasingly significant.

Some slightly younger composers were gaining reputations as the inheritors of the American cultivated-tradition ideal of a music of serious import and large-scale edification—"Americans who work along more or less conservative lines and make no attempt to write anything departing from general types of European music."[1] Among those who were to maintain some prominence during and after the decade of the 1920s was Howard Hanson (1896–1981), a composer of big rhetorical works like the choral cantata *The Lament for Beowulf* (1925), the Second ("Romantic") Symphony (1930), and the opera *Merry Mount* (1933; after Hawthorne; one *scena* for baritone solo recorded on *NW* 241:s1/6). Hanson was also immensely influential as the director of the Eastman School of Music in Rochester, New York, from 1924 to 1964 and as an officer of many national music organizations. Others in this group were Leo Sowerby (1895–1968), an organist-

---

[1] Henry Cowell, in an introductory chapter dated January 1933 for *American Composers on American Music* (1933; 2nd ed. New York: Frederick Ungar Publishing Co., 1962), p. 9. It is interesting to compare Cowell's "grouping of composers according to accomplishments and ideals" with that of Aaron Copland written a few years earlier: "America's Young Men of Promise," *MM*, III/3 (March–April 1926), 13–20.

composer who provided much viable music for his instrument, and Randall Thompson (1899–1984), who became strongly identified with works for chorus—notably the witty, satirical settings of texts from H. L. Mencken's *American Mercury* entitled *Americana* (1932; recorded on *NW* 219:s1/1–5), the cantata *The Peacable Kingdom* (1936), and a very widely performed unaccompanied *Alleluia* (1940).

A few other composers leavened their academic heritage with sprinklings of folk- or popular-music idioms. Charles Wakefield Cadman (1881–1946), interested in the lore of native Americans, published in 1909 a set of *Four American Indian Songs*; one of them, *From the Land of the Sky-Blue Water*, achieved great popularity. His opera *Shanewis, or the Robin Woman*, based on the life of an Indian woman with whom he had given lecture-recitals, was enough of a success at the Metropolitan in 1918 that the company produced the work again the next year; it was the first American opera to be so honored. John Powell (1882–1963) delved in Anglo-American and black-American folk song; Emerson Whithorne (1884–1958) and Henry Eichheim (1870–1942), in oriental music. Eichheim made no fewer than five trips to the Far East; his *Oriental Impressions* (1918–22), in piano, chamber, and orchestral versions, was widely performed during the 1920s, and later compositions by him were among the first by an American to actually include Asian instruments in their scoring—e.g., *Java* (1929) and *Bali* (1933). John Alden Carpenter's ballet scores *Krazy Kat* (a "jazz pantomime" of 1921; recorded on *NW* 228:s1/1) and *Skyscrapers* (1923–24) were indebted to some rhythmic aspects of American dance music. The strains of the pseudo-jazz of white America's ballrooms and dance halls were useful for Louis Gruenberg (1884–1964) in a number of works that were highly thought of during the period, among them *The Daniel Jazz* (1924) for tenor and chamber ensemble, *Jazz-Suite* (1925) for orchestra, *Jazzettes* (ca. 1925) for violin and piano, and *Jazzberries* (1925?) for piano solo. Gruenberg's best dramatic work in this vein was the opera *The Emperor Jones*, produced at the Metropolitan in 1933. (The aria *Standin' in the Need of Prayer*, sung by Lawrence Tibbett, who created the title role, is recorded on *NW* 241:s1/5.)

More notable than these, however, more characteristic of the era of the "Roaring '20's," were younger composers grappling with the new ideas, the new materials, the new approaches to organizing sound that had been proposed by the European leaders of "New Music" (Stravinsky; Schoenberg; the sassy young French composers; the Futurists) and by the new American "urban folk music" of jazz. As Aaron Copland, along with George Gershwin the most prominent young composer of the decade, wrote, "Contemporary music as an organized movement in the U.S.A. was born at the end of the First World War."[2]

---

[2] *Our New Music* (New York: McGraw-Hill Book Company, 1941), p. 137.

NADIA BOULANGER; AARON COPLAND

Copland (b. 1900) was one of a large group of American composers to become the student, in Fontainebleau and Paris, of the remarkable musician and teacher Nadia Boulanger (1887–1979). Boulanger's unique combination of exacting severity and liberating encouragement (the latter given in exquisitely precise proportion to the pupil's efforts) was to be a magnet for several generations of young Americans; in the 1920s, as one of her pupils of that decade has commented, "What endeared [Boulanger] most to Americans was her conviction that American music was about to 'take off,' just as Russian music had done eighty years before."[3] She was capable of training young composers without dictating one exclusive style: the measure of her phenomenal gifts as a teacher was the variety of personal styles developed in her *atelier*. Nevertheless, the example of Stravinsky was most often set before her students, and certainly Copland's work in the 1920s reveals the impact of Stravinsky more than of any other composer. It also reveals a preoccupation with "Americanism"—with a national identity. The models of Farwell and Gilbert, who had turned to black and Indian materials, seemed irrelevant, perhaps especially to Copland, a Brooklyn-born Jew; that of Ives was as yet unknown. Besides, as Copland recalled later,

> Our concern was not with the quotable hymn or spiritual: we wanted to find a music that would speak of universal things in a vernacular of American speech rhythms. We wanted to write music on a level that left popular music far behind—music with a largeness of utterance wholly representative of the country that Whitman had envisaged.[4]

In a few works written after his return from three years (1921–24) in Paris under Boulanger, Copland seemed to have imagined that the jazzy rhythms and blue notes of contemporary dance music would provide sources for the music he sought to write. The first of these works was *Music for the Theatre* (1925), a twenty-minute suite for small orchestra in five symmetrically ordered movements with a "motto" theme appearing in each (Example 8-1). The scale of the work, its chamber medium, its orderly structure, and its crisp unsentimental tone all reflect the precise anti-romanticism of Copland's French experience. Its crackling sonorities, bichordal harmonies, and jerky motoric rhythms suggest Stravinsky and the younger French composers. Its declamatory "motto" (Example 8-1 [a]), on the other hand, has been related (by fellow composer Arthur Berger) to Copland's Jewish backgrounds;

---

[3] Virgil Thomson, *Virgil Thomson* (New York: Alfred A. Knopf, Inc., 1966), p. 54.

[4] *Music and Imagination: the Charles Eliot Norton Lectures*, 1951–1952 (New York: Mentor Books, 1959), p. 111.

and the rhythmic and pitch inflections especially of the second ("Dance") and fourth ("Burlesque") movements relate to dance music of the 1920s like the charleston (Example 8-1 [c]). Rather similar in manner but larger in conception is a Concerto for piano and orchestra of 1926–27. In later works of the 1920s Copland gave up the limited expressive range of dance music and turned to a more abstract, less self-consciously "American" manner— but one equally hard, lean, and rhythmically knotty—in a *Dance Symphony* (1929; three movements adapted from the earlier ballet *Grohg*); a trio, *Vitebsk* (1929); a *Symphonic Ode* (1927–29); and a set of *Piano Variations* (1930).

EXAMPLE 8-1. A. Copland, *Music for the Theatre* (1925). (a) "Motto," first movement, measures 2–5 (trumpet part only). (b) First movement, measures 14–17. (c) Second movement, measures 1–7 (bassoon part only). Copyright 1932 by Cos Cob Press Inc. Renewed 1960 by Aaron Copland. Reprinted by permission of Boosey & Hawkes, Inc. Sole licensees.

For many, the *Piano Variations* mark the summit of Copland's achievement. Based on a theme that has a certain hard-edged grandeur (Example 8-2 [a]), the work, from the outset, treats the piano anti-romantically as a basically percussive instrument, with hammers (which of course it is). The continuous set of twenty close-knit, mainly clangorous variations culminates in an overwhelmingly resonant coda. Certain variations suggest that Copland had by this time absorbed the principle of Schoenberg's tone-row technique, perhaps unconsciously, into his own lucid, often brittle, and generally rhythm-dominated style (Example 8-2 [b]). The *Variations* seem to mark a synthesis by Copland of his American background, his French training, and a range of expression and means of tonal organization related to the Viennese School; they come very close to achieving Copland's ideal in the 1920s of a music that would "speak of universal things . . . with a largeness of utterance wholly representative of the country." (Copland's own performances of the *Piano Variations*, as recorded in 1945, and his *Four Piano Blues*, begun in the 1920s, are heard on *NW* 277:s2/1 and 3.)

Many other young composers hied themselves to Boulanger's studio in the 1920s: Virgil Thomson, Roy Harris, Walter Piston, Elliott Carter, Robert Russell Bennett, Marc Blitzstein, and others. These, however, did not gain the early prominence of Copland; their works belong more to the story of American music after the 1920s, and I shall refer to them in later chapters.

EXAMPLE 8-2. A. Copland, *Piano Variations* (1930). (a) Theme, measures 1–11. (b) Variation 2, measures 21–24. Copyright 1932 by Aaron Copland, Renewed 1959. Reprinted by permission of Aaron Copland, Copyright Owner, and Boosey & Hawkes, Inc., Sole Publishers and Licensees.

EDGARD VARÈSE

The "organized movement" in contemporary music in the 1920s spoken of by Copland was reflected in the many groups founded to give concerts of new music, like the series produced between 1928 and 1931 by Copland and Roger Sessions; in the contributions of some major conductors who performed new works, notably Serge Koussevitzky (1874–1951), conductor of the Boston Symphony Orchestra from 1924 to 1949, and Leopold Stokowski (1882–1977), conductor of the Philadelphia Orchestra from 1912 to 1938; and in the formation of composers' groups, especially the League of Composers (which sponsored the important journal *Modern Music*, 1924–46), the International Composers' Guild (1921–27), and the Pan American Association of Composers (1928–34).[5]

Founder of both the Guild and the P.A.A.C., and in the vanguard of American music in the 1920s (and again in the 1950s), was the Paris-born composer Edgard Varèse (1883–1965), who came permanently to New York City late in 1915. In the 1920s Varèse founded no school of composers, but with his first American work, purposely and meaningfully titled *Amériques* (1918–22), he offered a challenge to musical tradition that was reiterated with each of his important compositions of the 1920s (*Offrandes, Hyperprism, Octandre, Intégrales, Arcana*) and the celebrated all-percussion piece *Ionisation* (1930–31). Perhaps because of the last-named work and the high proportion of percussion instruments he called for in others, Varèse's name has sometimes been linked with the Futurists and their *bruitisme*. Actually, Varèse stood alone: he was uninterested in a revolutionary "noise music" or a "machine music" as such; he believed, however, in the legitimacy of *any* sound as a vehicle for musical expression, and (as he put it in a lecture at Princeton University, September 4, 1959) he became "a sort of diabolic Parsifal looking not for a Holy Grail but for a bomb that would blow wide open the musical world and let in sound—all sounds, [including those] at that time, and sometimes even today, called 'noise.' " As early as 1917 he was writing of a "dream of instruments obedient to my thought, and which

---

[5] On the Copland-Sessions concerts, see Carol J. Oja, "The Copland-Sessions Concerts and Their Reception in the Contemporary Press," *MQ*, LXV (1979), 212–29. On the League of Composers, and especially its journal *Modern Music*, see Minna Lederman, *The Life and Death of a Small Magazine (Modern Music, 1924–1946)* (ISAMm 18 [1983]). On the International Composers' Guild, see R. Allen Lott, " 'New Music for New Ears': The International Composers' Guild," *Journal of the American Musicological Society*, XXXVI (1982), 266–86. On the Pan American Association of Composers, see Deane L. Root, "The Pan American Association of Composers (1928–1934)," *Yearbook for Inter-American Musical Research*, VIII (1972), 49–70. All three articles cited here give complete lists of the music performed in the concerts sponsored by the organizations they discuss; Wayne D. Shirley has compiled a valuable index to *Modern Music* (New York: AMS Press, 1976).

with their contribution of a blossoming of unsuspected timbres will . . . bend to the demands of my inner rhythm."[6] That dream was to be realized, but only in the electronic era of the 1950s; in the 1920s Varèse had to content himself with conventional instruments—assembled, however, in unusual groupings and supplemented with a large number of so-called percussion instruments, some not so conventional. Important among the latter were sirens, whose arching curves of sound embodied and projected one of Varèse's most important concepts: that of music as a spatial art, as "moving bodies of sound in space." Not only are sirens employed in *Amériques* but in *Hyperprism* (1922) and *Ionisation* as well. Their use, and that of an inexhaustible variety of drums, cymbals, gongs, tam-tams, bells, chimes, woodblocks and castanets, slapsticks and rattles, chains and anvils, bespoke Varèse's definition of music simply as "organized sound" limited in no way to traditional notions of "musical tone" as against "noise."

Varèse's music of the 1920s is marked especially by an emphasis on sheer sonority, often achieved by multiple repetitions of notes or aggregates of them, by writing at the extremes of an instrument's range, and by spacing of "chords" in unconventional ways or dispersing their notes through a huge registral spectrum. Stridency of sound is characteristic: the performance-indication "hurlant" (yelling, howling, roaring) is not uncommon. Traditional formations of harmonies do not typically appear, yet neither is the music organized by anything like Schoenberg's chromatic tone-rows. Individual sounds, pulsating with a life of varied intensities and changing timbres, are important, as at the opening of *Hyperprism*, where a C♯ introduced by a trombone is variously mutated, first by different attacks and approaches; then by coloration in horn; then by dynamic, timbral, and articulative shifts among three horns (Example 8-3 [a]). That single note and the D-C♯ interval formed when the bass trombone enters are examples of what Varèse called "sound-masses":

> There is an idea, the basis of an internal structure, expanded and split into different shapes or groups of sound, constantly changing in shape, direction, and speed, attracted and repulsed by various forces. The form of the work is the consequence of this interaction. (Princeton lecture)

Varèse likened such "an idea, the basis of an internal structure," to a crystal, which although restricted in internal form can appear in limitless external forms. In *Hyperprism* the most important such "crystal" would seem to be the major seventh interval (or its inversion, a semitone): this interval appears in innumerable aggregates. The sonority of measures 12–13, for instance, is a "splitting" of the C♯ sound (measure 11) into a four-note aggregate

---

[6] My translation from *391*, No. 5 (New York, June 1917).

EXAMPLE 8-3. E. Varèse, *Hyperprism* (1922). (a) Measures 1–6 (percussion parts omitted). (b) Measures 11–13 (percussion parts omitted). © 1924 by Edgard Varèse & assigned to Colfranc Music Publishing Corp., New York. By permission of the Publisher.

composed of two pairs of sevenths: flute C and clarinet D♭, and trumpet C♯ and trombone C (Example 8-3 [b]). These sevenths relate back, of course, to the first interval heard in the work, the D-C♯ of measure 5 (see Example 8-3 [a]); and the final sonority of the entire piece is a nine-note aggregate made up of the following transpositions of that interval: C-B, B♭-A, G-F♯, E-E♭, F♯-F. (To be noted, especially in view of some procedures in *Intégrales*, is that the initial D-C♯ is specifically omitted at the close).

"Thematic" material in a traditional sense is not characteristic of Varèse's music: "sound-masses," whether based on pitch, timbre, or rhythm replace it. These are then varied, developed, interlocked, or superimposed somewhat the way themes might be. Ironically, in view of the furor that attended its early hearings, *Ionisation* contains a very important idea (presented by the *tambour militaire* in measures 8–13) that approximates the periodic organization of a "theme," with its mid-point signaled by an isolated *sforzando* bang (Example 8-4). To follow this idea through the entire work, in which there is no melody or harmony in the traditional sense, only rhythms and an extraordinary variety of timbres produced by thirteen players on about forty instruments, is a fruitful approach to Varèse's concept of musical crystals, the variety of external forms they may assume, and their "attraction and repulsion" by various forces. Another idea in *Ionisation* interesting to trace through its various manifestations is the cloudy metallic sonority of gong, high tam-tam, and low tam-tam first announced in measure 1.

EXAMPLE 8-4. E. Varèse, *Ionisation* (1930–31), measures 8–13 (*tambour militaire* part only). © 1934 by Edgard Varèse & assigned to Colfranc Music Publishing Corp., New York. By permission of the Publisher.

Both *Hyperprism* and *Ionisation* lead to massive single climaxes near their conclusion, *Hyperprism* on an *hurlant* sonority at top volume (measures 72–75), *Ionisation* on an all-metal crash (measure 65). *Intégrales*, a larger work of 1924 for woodwinds, brass, and percussion, is organized in three broad sections, each with characteristic sound-mass material; it too climaxes toward its close (measures 153–54).[7]

HENRY COWELL AND HIS NEW MUSIC

Another composer who embodied the progressivism of American music of the 1920s in his own music, in his energetic and generous support of new trends, and in his writings was Henry Cowell (1897–1965). Cowell was a Californian, a fact of significance in its suggestion of the end of the American frontier and the broadening of America's musical base to encompass the entire continent—also in its reminder that though American composers had traditionally looked eastward across the Atlantic to European cultural models, they could also look westward across the Pacific to the Orient. In a long career as aesthetic gadfly of American music, Cowell sought to find a context in *world* music for that of America, interesting himself in traditional and folk music of the entire world's peoples.

[7] An authoritative approach to analyses of two works is made by Varese's former pupil Chou Wen-chung in the section on *Intégrales* in "Varèse: A Sketch of the Man and His Music," *MQ*, LII (1966), 151–70, and "*Ionisation*: The Function of Timbre in its Formal and Temporal Organization," in *The New Worlds of Edgard Varèse*, ed. Sherman Van Solkema (ISAMm 11 [1979]), pp. 26–74. Leo Kraft discusses the famous solo flute piece of 1936, *Density 21.5*, in his analytic guidebook *Gradus* (New York: W. W. Norton, 1976), Book II, Part 1, pp. 143–44.

In the 1920s Cowell became notorious for novel uses of the pianoforte, including "tone-clusters"; for extensions of the rhythmic range of music; and for many other explorations into *New Musical Resources*, as the title of his 1919 book (published 1930) put it. His fertile musical imagination first addressed itself to the piano and its untapped reservoir of sound possibilities: while still in his teens, Cowell amazed San Francisco music-club audiences with pieces like *The Tides of Manaunaun* (1917?), which superimposes folkish melodic material over deep oceanic roars produced by playing the lowest notes of the piano with the flat of the left hand or with the forearm. *Advertisement* (1917) finds fistfuls of tone-clusters cascading frantically from top to bottom of the keyboard, in a satiric evocation of the repetitious raucousness of advertisers. Besides his use of tone-clusters of massed seconds on the keyboard, Cowell achieved other new sonorities by playing directly on the piano strings. In *The Banshee* (1925) the lower bass strings (which are wrapped in metal coils) are stroked along their length; this produces sounds four octaves above the keyboard tones, with a curious and even terrifying wailing effect. In *Sinister Resonance* (1930) Cowell applied to the piano strings various techniques—of stopping, muting at the bridge, and producing harmonics—that had previously been used only on such stringed instruments as violins. (Several of these piano works are recorded on *NW* 203:s1/1–3).

Cowell also made music with textures fashioned of melodic strands in extremely independent rhythms: the piano piece *Fabric* (1920), for instance, begins with a three-voice texture in which the relationship of beats between the voices in the first measure is as 8 to 6 to 5, in the second measure 9 to 7 to 5, etc. Believing that human limitations precluded the realization of the full range of polyrhythms he envisioned, Cowell developed (in cooperation with the musical-instrument inventor Leon Theremin) the rhythmicon, an instrument capable of producing very complex combinations of beat patterns; it was combined with orchestra in a work of 1931 entitled *Rhythmicana* (retitled later *Concerto for Rhythmicon and Orchestra*), which had to wait, however, until 1971 for its premiere, in a version in which the rhythmicon part was realized with the help of a computer since the original machine no longer functioned. Other works reflecting Cowell's originality of thought and his preoccupation—one among many—with expanded rhythmic usage include the "rhythm-harmony" quartets, Quartet Romantic (1917) for two flutes, violin, and viola (recorded on *NW* 285:s1/1) and Quartet Euphometric (1919) for string quartet (recorded on *NW* 218:s2/1). In these works rhythmic structure is inextricably linked with harmonic structure (e.g., two notes creating a perfect fifth harmonically, hence in the vibration ratio 3:2, are rhythmically related to that harmony by Cowell as three pulses sounding together with two in the same period of time); both quartets are virtually atonal, being written in the "dissonant counterpoint" that Cowell liked in this period. A later work of similar though less rigid rhythmic complexity, with a sort of "wheels-within-wheels" quality like that of intricate clockwork, is *Ostinato pianissimo* (1934), for eight percussion players. Cowell went on, over a long creative career ended only by his death in 1965, to become the most prolific American composer since Charles Grobe—and an infinitely more versatile and free-thinking one.

Cowell was a fighter for others' new music as well as his own. In 1927 he founded a quarterly publication of innovative scores, *New Music*. In an introductory note to Volume I, Number 1, he commented on the dilemma of progressive composers, even in an era of "modernism":

. . . There are very few opportunities at present for the modern American composer to publish his works, as publishers cannot afford to risk losing money in such publications, with the result that many of the finest works ever written in America remain unpublished. When modern works are published in America, few copies are sold. The work is therefore not distributed, and the composer gains no financial profit. . . .

As editor of *New Music* until 1936, Cowell bravely and selflessly sought to change that situation. The first issue (October 1927) consisted of a piece for small orchestra, *Men and Mountains*, by Carl Ruggles (1876–1971), an older New England composer rather like Charles Ives in his disdain for popular success, his alternation of composing and non-musical activity (painting, in Ruggles's case), and his forging of a unique personal style. By no means a prolific composer (his complete music was recorded on two long-playing records, in CBS Masterworks album M2-34591), Ruggles produced a handful of tough, dense-textured contrapuntal works of an uncompromising integrity and a very high incidence of secundal dissonance. (On his studio wall hung the motto "Dissonant chords should have talismanic ecstasy.") Ruggles's major composition is the sixteen-minute symphonic work *Sun-Treader*, begun in 1926 and completed in 1931; other important ones are *Angels*, originally (1920–21) for six trumpets; *Portals* (1925) for thirteen strings; *Evocations* for piano (1937/43), revised later for orchestra; and *Organum* for full orchestra (1944–47).

Cowell helped many other composers, too, by publishing their works in *New Music*. Ives was one: the unprecedentedly complex score of his Fourth Symphony's second movement was published in 1929, the *Set for Theatre or Chamber Orchestra* in 1932, and collections of *34 Songs* and *19 Songs* a bit later. (Ives was the principal—but anonymous—financial supporter of Cowell's publishing and recording ventures.) Other composers who seemed poised on the leading edge of musical practice during the later 1920s and who were helped by Cowell included George Antheil (1900–59), Wallingford Riegger (1885–1961), John J. Becker (1886–1961), Colin McPhee

(1900–1964), Adolph Weiss (1891–1971), and Ruth Crawford (1901–53; known also by her married name of Seeger).

Antheil, who liked to think of himself as a "bad boy of music" (as he titled his autobiography of 1945), had a patchy career that climaxed early with the extraordinary score (for a film never made) *Ballet mécanique*, initially written for sixteen player pianos and elaborate percussion but first performed publicly in Paris in 1926 in a reduced version for one amplified player piano, two ordinary pianos, three xylophones, electric bells, airplane propellers, siren, and percussion.

Reigger's was initially a hard-luck story: his progressive early scores—the finest of which are *Study in Sonority* (1927), for ten violins or any multiple thereof, and *Dichotomy* (1931–32) for chamber orchestra—earned him respect from his peers but boos and hisses from audiences; only much later, after World War II, was he to gain critical respect and a modicum of success as a composer of concert music (as well as music for dance, which dancers from the 1930s on had greatly admired).

Becker, too, remained largely unappreciated, especially after he turned stylistically to a dissonant modernist manner with the *Symphonia brevis* of 1929 and wrote such avant-garde pieces as the all-percussion work *The Abongo* (subtitled "A Primitive Dance"; 1933; recorded on *NW* 285:s2/1); he later was claimed, perhaps over-generously, as one of an "American Five" (by analogy with the group of five Russian nationalists of the nineteenth century), including also Ives, Ruggles, Cowell, and Riegger.

McPhee eventually came to be known as an ethnomusicologist *avant la lettre*, living in Bali from 1931 to 1938 and writing affectionately about it in *A House in Bali* (1946), penetratingly about its music in *Music in Bali* (1966). Cowell saw in him a promising composer and published his neo-Classic *Concerto for Piano, with Wind Octette Accompaniment* (1928) in *New Music*; he was to laud (in *MQ* XXXIV [1948], 412) McPhee's orchestral masterpiece—the glittering, gamelan-inspired symphony *Tabuh-Tabuhan* (1936)—as "an important landmark" in its exploration and integration of musical materials from more than a single culture.

Weiss was the first American to study with Schoenberg (in Berlin, in 1926), the first to adopt Schoenberg's newly developed method of "composition with twelve tones related only to each other," and the first to teach twelve-tone techniques to other Americans. (John Cage was one of his pupils.)

Crawford's early promise—climaxing in such works as *Four Diaphonic Suites* for differing chamber combinations (1930); *Three Songs* to texts by Carl Sandburg (1930–32; recorded on *NW* 285:s2/2); and especially a unique, uncommonly advanced String Quartet (1931)—was never really realized: after her marriage to Charles Seeger, her creative activity was deflected primarily into transcribing and arranging folk songs, especially for children. (She was a gifted and dedicated teacher.)

POPULAR MUSIC AND MUSICAL COMEDY

The 1920s also saw major developments in popular music. Some of the most important were technological: the establishment of commercial, public radio stations and the development of the electrical recording process (with disc recordings as its product), the public address system, and the sound track for film. All used the microphone and the sound amplifier, with significant impact on the nature of orchestration and popular vocal style, hence on the ideas of performers, arrangers, and even songwriters. All tended to broaden the audience for popular music—in a sense to nationalize it—but at the same time to make it a more passive audience, an audience of listeners rather than participants. This tended to heighten the importance of professionalism and sophistication among both performers and arrangers; it also tended to increase commercialism in the transmission (the "distribution") of popular music to its audience. Thus the era of the American popular-music *industry* was born—an inevitable concomitant of the electronic age's "mass media" (though the term was yet uncoined).

New York City was the power center of the popular-music industry during the 1920s: it had Broadway and Shubert Alley, center of American popular lyric theater (the declining operetta and the developing musical comedy), and it had the so-called Tin Pan Alley, center of the songwriting business and the still-powerful sheet-music publishers. ("So-called" since the term was simply a metaphor for that part of the city most heavily populated by popular-music publishers; the "Alley" moved, first in the 1890s from East 14th Street to West 28th Street; then between the world wars to the Brill Building and others near it, on Broadway at about 50th Street.) The recording studios and the radio networks were also based in New York. But recordings and radio opened up possibilities for a striking new development: they made available, to any who cared to listen, kinds of popular music heard previously only in limited geographical areas or by specific ethnic and social groups—especially the blues, gospel songs, and jazz of black Americans (at whom a subsection of the recording industry aimed so-called "race records") and the traditional music of the southern Appalachians and other rural areas of the South and West ("hillbilly music," as a term coined in this period defined it. The hillbillies' country music was not to affect the mainstream of American popular music until much later, but black-American secular styles began to influence American popular music in general in many ways in the 1920s; the novelist Scott Fitzgerald could even call the era "The Jazz Age"—which, although an exaggeration, reflected the inroads of black-American musical influence on the consciousness of the nation at large.

Out of the popular mania for ragtime at the turn of the century had come an American craze for dancing. By the second decade, the older waltz, two-step, and cakewalk gave way—especially under the influence of the smooth, elegant models of Irene and Vernon Castle, the foremost dance team of the time—to a brisk but modest $\frac{4}{4}$ dance for couples: the foxtrot. With many variants, it was to be the basic step in "ballroom dancing" for decades, relieved occasionally by more exotic ones like the tango, the rumba, and the maxixe. But another dance is even more strongly identified with the 1920s (and especially with the New American Woman of the 1920s, now a legal voter and thought to be emancipated in various other ways over her Victorian mother and grandmother). This was the athletic charleston, which despite its name and its anything but langorous tempo, probably derived

musically from Latin sources: its basic rhythm ($\frac{4}{4}$ ♩. ♩. ⸰ | ♩. ♩. ⸰ |),

like that of the tango, was related to the Spanish *habanera*. (Music for each of the dances mentioned in this paragraph is recorded on NW 293:s2; excellent notes are provided by Thorton Hagert.)

Responding to the new popularity of dancing two by two (and also, as Irving Berlin's song of 1935 put it, "cheek to cheek"), dance bands proliferated in the 1920s. But in retrospect the period seems more notable for an explosion of songs and songwriters than for instrumental music and composers of it (except in jazz). Individual songs were published in great numbers; some were immensely popular, like the ballad (a term connoting, in popular music, not a story-telling song but a slow, often introspective love song) *Star Dust* (1927; published 1929) by Hoagy Carmichael (1899–1981), which originated as a piano piece but was furnished with memorable lyrics by Mitchell Parish (sung—and whistled—by the composer on NW 272:s1/6). But the most successful songs, in every sense, came out of the newly popular form of American lyric theater, the musical comedy (or just "musical"). The combination of a play with interpolated songs and dances was not new: as we have seen, it had been part of the American tradition from the eighteenth century and, after minstrel-show interlude, had regained popularity, in the form of operetta, late in the nineteenth. But the musicals of the 1920s had a different style and feeling from those of operetta: they tended to avoid the sentimentality and the slightly aristocratic tone (which came out of Viennese operetta); they were more brash and brassy, lively and spicy, colloquial and earthy; they incorporated more identifiably American elements of dance and music; and they mirrored faithfully the optimism and hedonism, the motoric energy, and the devil-may-care attitudes of the post-war boom era.

The American musical has been likened to a latter-day ballad opera, but the balance and inter-relationship of its components are vastly different. The ballad opera had been basically a play dotted with occasional songs; the musical, at least that of the 1920s, was essentially a garland of songs and dances strung on a thin plot line, with occasional spectacular "production numbers" planned at strategic points. Least important, perhaps, in a musical comedy of the period was the "comedy"—the drama. The success of a musical depended essentially on three things: the quality of the actor-singers and dancers (and of the director who guided them), the quality of the songs themselves, and a delicate balance between the music and the other components of the whole work. It was the necessity for the latter, perhaps more than anything else, which resulted in the inevitable out-of-town tryouts (i.e., in other places than New York) during which songs were shuffled about, rewritten, replaced, or dropped entirely until, it was hoped, a "hit" was assured. The ad hoc and ad hominem attitudes that went into the making of a musical, whereby it components were all separable from each other, ready to be reassembled into various shapes and orders, meant that never was such a work subject to the single-minded vision or the unique control of one individual; all kinds of "specialists" were involved—producer, director, author, lyricist, composer, arranger, conductor, choreographer, and various associates and assistants (not to mention those performers who would actually project the work across the footlights). This splintering of authority over a musico-dramatic work, even greater than in the mounting of an opera, was and remains one of the greatest problems of musical comedy.[8]

The major songwriters of the 1920s who dominated the field of the musical were Jerome Kern, Irving Berlin, Richard Rodgers, and George Gershwin.

Jerome Kern (1885–1945) began as a composer of songs interpolated in American adaptations of British operettas and musical comedies; his first hit was *How'd You Like to Spoon With Me?*, written to go into the British show of 1905 *The Earl and the Girl* (and recorded on NW 221:s1/7). He turned to a more colloquial, popular American manner at about age thirty; more than one critic of American popular song dates the shift as 1914, with the poignant *They Didn't Believe Me*, written for the New York version of the British show *The Girl From Utah*.[9] Over a long career, with about 1000 songs in over 100 works for the stage to his credit, Kern achieved many hits with a song style that tended to be gentle, lyrical, and virtually untouched by elements of blues or jazz. In fact, many of his songs border on an operetta-like theatricality (*Ol' Man River* and *Bill*, from *Show Boat* of 1927, considered by many Kern's masterpiece) or "artiness" (*Yesterdays* and *Smoke Gets in Your Eyes*, from *Roberta* of 1933; *All the Things You Are*, from *Very Warm for May* of 1939, his last musical). The harmonic scheme of the refrain of *All the Things You Are* (Example 8-5) suggests how rapidly American popular songwriters had developed in sophistication of harmonic thought. In less

---

[8] A fascinating account emphasizing this aspect is Don Dunn, *The Making of No, No, Nanette* (New York: Dell Publishing Co., Inc., 1972), which is a chronicle of the 1970 revival of a 1924 musical with a score by Vincent Youmans.

[9] See Alec Wilder, *American Popular Song: The Great Innovators, 1900–1950* (New York: Oxford University Press, 1972), pp. 32, 34–36, and Charles Hamm, *Yesterdays* (New York: W. W. Norton, 1979), pp. 341ff.

than a half century, a basic vocabulary of little more than tonic, dominant, and subdominant chords, seldom in any but the tonic key, had increased immensely, to include major sevenths as consonances (measures 4, 12), enharmonic changes (23–24), sudden changes of mode (8–9), and altered chords (30); and tonal sensibility had been refined to allow for such uncertain, floating tonality as we hear in this song—until it ends declaratively in A♭, we cannot be certain whether it is in the key of F minor, A♭ major, C major, C minor, E♭ major, G major, or E major.

EXAMPLE 8-5. Basic melodic and harmonic design of Jerome Kern/Oscar Hammerstein II, *All the Things You Are*, "Burthen" (= Chorus) only. Copyright © 1939 T. B. Harms Company. Copyright renewed (c/o The Welk Music Group, Santa Monica, CA 90401). International Copyright secured. All Rights Reserved. Used by Permission.

Irving Berlin (b. 1888) has survived several major shifts in American popular musical taste and until the rock revolution, at least, went on writing songs at an incredible pace, for a total that has been estimated at about 1500, almost 900 of which are still in print. Berlin's first great popular hit was *Alexander's Ragtime Band* (1911), which ironically is lacking in any shred of rag rhythm. In the 1920s he was associated with Flo Ziegfeld, the extraordinary producer of super-spectacular "revues," and wrote songs for a number of the periodic *Ziegfeld Follies* beginning with that of 1919 (which included *A Pretty Girl is Like a Melody*). Later, his knack for pouring essentially old familiar musical wine into slightly different bottles and having it come out seeming fresh and beguiling led to some apparently timeless songs: *Say It with Music* (1921), *Always* (1925), *Blue Skies* (1927), *How Deep Is the Ocean?* (1932), *The Girl that I Marry* and *I Got the Sun in the Morning* (both from the musical *Annie Get Your Gun* of 1946) are a few. In a special class altogether are two other songs by Berlin—*White Christmas* (from the 1942 film *Holiday Inn*), which with its yearning lyrics matched by a surprisingly sensuous chromatic line has become virtually a popular hymn, and *God Bless America* (instantly popularized by singer Kate Smith in 1939 although it had lain unused since 1918), which has become a sort of unofficial national anthem.

A few extremely effective collaborations between musical-comedy songwriters and lyricists arose in the 1920s. Among them was the team of Richard Rodgers (1902–79) and Lorenz Hart (1895–1943), who worked together from 1919 (when Rodgers was only sixteen) until 1940. Most of Rodgers's more than 250 songs were composed for the stage; an unusual number of them became hits. More than either Kern or Berlin, Rodgers picked up from popular dance music rhythmic devices it had in turn derived from jazz; they appear in the opening "verse" and following "chorus" of both *The Blue Room* (from the very successful musical *The Girl Friend*, 1926) and *Thou Swell* (1927; from *A Connecticut Yankee*). Less colloquial, more "arty," are others, like the top hit of 1929 by Rodgers and Hart, *With a Song in My Heart*. Almost all—and this can be said of the overwhelming majority of American popular songs after about 1925 and for the following quarter century—share certain formal characteristics. An opening "verse," apt to be somewhat tentative and suspensive musically, and frequently declamatory in vocal style, is followed by a "chorus" (by which the entire song is generally identified, at least by all but pop-song connoisseurs). The "chorus" is more shapely and memorable from the musical standpoint; it is typically thirty-two measures long, in eight-measure phrases, in an AABA form (or variants of it). The B phrase is called for no good reason whatsoever the "release"—a real misnomer, for it usually wanders afield harmonically and the tensions thus created are not released until the return of the A material. The overall bipartite form (verse, chorus) resembles, and may well have derived from, the recitative/aria form of opera and operetta.[10]

Another brilliant collaboration of the 1920s was that between George Gershwin (1898–1937) and his brother Ira (1896–1983). Together they wrote some of the gayest musical-comedy scores of the decade, especially *Lady, Be Good* (1924), *Oh, Kay!* (1926), and *Funny Face* (1927), all seeming in retrospect to be preparation for the political satire *Of Thee I Sing* (1931), the first musical to weld together so firmly plot, dialogue, and music that it received the Pulitzer Prize for drama. Gershwin's later *Porgy and Bess* (1935), which he characterized as "folk opera—opera for the [popular] theatre, with drama, humor, song, and dance," was a more pretentious but hardly more artistically successful contribution. It relied mainly on some

[10] Hamm's *Yesterdays*, pp. 293–94 and 358–61, includes a valuable discussion of the verse/chorus form and the thirty-two-bar chorus structure of Tin Pan Alley songs.

memorable songs (*Summertime, I Got Plenty o' Nuttin', It Ain't Necessarily So*) which displayed the same special characteristics as Gershwin's earlier show songs: beguiling rhythms (as in *Fascinating Rhythm*, 1924, and *I Got Rhythm*, 1930); unusual form (*Embraceable You*, 1930); a relaxed, jazzy swing (*'s Wonderful*, 1927; *Nice Work if You Can Get It*, 1937); and harmonic materials richer than those of most American popular songs (*The Man I Love*, 1927; *Liza*, 1929; *So Are You!*, 1929). *Porgy and Bess* has had a checkered career, both in the variety of its productions (many cut savagely, others badly cast, still others wavering uncertainly between Broadway-musical and grand-opera approaches) and its critical reception. One even-handed historian concludes,

> Opera critics have objected to arias that sound too much like Broadway songs and to the score's lack of organic symphonic integration. Black critics have found Gershwin's evocations of their music inauthentic. For all of these criticisms, and others, *Porgy and Bess* is full of moments that show Gershwin at his most convincing.[11]

That the boundary between cultivated- and vernacular-tradition American music was becoming blurred once again is suggested not only by the sophistication and artistry, albeit on a small scale, of many of the songs mentioned in the preceding paragraphs, together with their undeniable popular mass appeal, but also by such a phenomenon as Gershwin's moving back and forth from popular to "serious" music, or the critical success of his musical comedy *Of Thee I Sing* alongside the popular success of his full-scale opera *Porgy and Bess*. More than a decade before the latter work, in fact, Gershwin had successfully introduced the idioms of Tin Pan Alley into the concert hall, first with *Rhapsody in Blue* (1924), a concerto-like work for piano and dance band (later orchestrated more fully) that achieved unparalleled popularity. Belatedly, Gershwin conscientiously sought to learn some techniques of "classical" composition—the *Rhapsody* had been scored not by the composer but by Ferde Grofé (1892–1972)—and produced several other concert works, among them a Concerto in F (1925) for piano and orchestra and *An American in Paris* (1928) for orchestra alone. Three Preludes for piano (1926), smaller in scale and better controlled than the orchestral works, are unpretentious but charming trifles, among the very best "household music" of the 1920s.

[11] Richard Crawford, "George Gershwin," *TNGDAM*; see also Crawford's articles "It Ain't Necessarily Soul: Gershwin's 'Porgy and Bess' as Symbol," *Yearbook for Inter-American Musical Research*, VIII (1972), 17–38, and "Gershwin's Reputation: A Note on *Porgy and Bess*," *MQ*, LXV (1979), 257–64. For another sympathetic, and highly original, view, see Ned Rorem, "Living With Gershwin," *Opera News*, XLIX/13 (March 16, 1985), 10ff.

CITY BLUES AND JAZZ

For many people, Americans and others alike, the most significant American music of the 1920s, the most indigenous and unprecedented, was jazz. Jazz had existed long before the 1920s, as had the special vocal styles and forms of blues, but only as a music of blacks and virtually unknown to the larger American community. What had been a music of and for southern blacks began to be diffused, thanks to the earliest phonograph recordings (sporadically from 1917, then in greater numbers from 1923); World War I (which found blacks, jazz performers among them, spread over both North America and Europe);[12] commercial radio stations (from 1920); and the increased mobility of southern blacks, particularly in the direction of northern cities like Chicago, Detroit, and New York. In New York, especially, a massive influx of blacks and their concentration in the Harlem area of upper Manhattan was important in the development of jazz and its diffusion to the white community. Harlem night spots, with blues singers and jazz groups, were active inter-racial entertainment centers. A whole series of "black musicals" appeared "downtown," just off Broadway; important among them were the collaborations of Eubie Blake and Noble Sissle (1889–1975) in such shows as *Shuffle Along* (1921), *The Chocolate Dandies* (1924), and *Shuffle Along of 1933*. The original *Shuffle Along* included the hit songs *Love Will Find a Way* and *I'm Just Wild About Harry* as well as Walter Donaldson's *How Ya' Gonna Keep 'Em Down on the Farm* (these and other songs recorded on *NW* 260).

The surest sign of the impact of jazz on America at large was the appearance in the popular entertainment world of jazz-influenced dance bands like that of Paul Whiteman (1890–1967) and others, and the characterization of the entire decade as "The Jazz Age." (It had been Whiteman who commissioned *Rhapsody in Blue* from Gershwin and premiered it in a famous concert, "An Experiment in Modern Music," presented in New York on February 12, 1924. The polish and versatility of his dance band made it a powerful influence on American popular music of the 1920s.) The end of the decade saw jazz recognized as a national phenomenon, though centered in the black ghettoes of northern cities, notably Kansas City, Chicago, Detroit, and New York (besides, of course, southern centers like New Orleans and

---

[12] One important group was the 369th Infantry ("Hell Fighters") Band, led by Lieutenant James Reese Europe (1881–1919) in France. Before the war, in New York, Europe had directed dance bands (Europe's Society Orchestra) and concert groups like the Clef Club Symphony Orchestra (100 to 150 strong, including as many as 50 mandolins, 30 harp-guitars, 10 banjos, and saxophones, along with other more conventional components of a "symphony" orchestra). (The 369th Infantry Band is heard on *NW* 269:s1/3–4 and *NW* 260:s2/4–6, Europe's Society Orchestra on *NW* 269:s1/1–2.)

Memphis). It saw the faithful emulation of black jazz musicians by whites, not just the diluted strains of "symphonic jazz"; it saw a whole new sub-industry of the phonorecording business ("race records"—jazz and blues recordings initially produced for and distributed to the American black community); it saw the beginnings of world interest in jazz as a new music; and it saw the first major shift in jazz style itself, from the small "combo" of early jazz to the "big band."

Early jazz was a synthesis of the march/dance beat and overlaid syn-copations of ragtime; other kinds of syncopated dance rhythms of Afro-Caribbean origin; a rudimentary but dynamic harmony rooted in the Euro-American traditions of dance music and revival hymnody; and the expressive, flexible vocal style of various branches of American black song, such as the repetitive, chant-like, and usually responsorial worksong, the solitary field holler, the religious spiritual, and (hardly different from the last-named in musical style) the secular blues.

In the formally standardized, instrumentally accompanied form of "city blues" (as opposed to the formally unstandardized and earlier "country blues")[13] the blues was to become one of the two major foundations of 1920s jazz (the other being rags). City blues, as recorded by such classic female blues singers as Mamie Smith (1883–1946), Ma Rainey (1886–1939), Bessie Smith (1894–1937), and Ida Cox (1896–1967), tended to be strophic songs with a text typically based on two-line strophes (but with the first line of each strophe's text repeated, AAB) and a standard succession of harmonies underlying each strophe's melody. Jazz musicians appropriated the *musical* structure of such blues; from then on, the term *blues*, whether sung or not, connoted that structure. Basically, the structure of blues is one of a repeated twelve-measure pattern ("12-bar blues"), which is divided into three four-measure phrases accompanied by a standard basic harmonic progression, as indicated:

$$
\begin{array}{c}
\frac{4}{4} \quad \overline{\begin{array}{cccc} 1 & 2 & 3 & 4 \end{array}} \; \overline{\begin{array}{cccc} 5 & 6 & 7 & 8 \end{array}} \; \overline{\begin{array}{cccc} 9 & 10 & 11 & 12 \end{array}} \\[4pt]
\text{I} \text{———————} \quad \text{IV———I———} \quad \text{V} \;\; \text{(IV)} \;\; \text{I———}
\end{array}
$$

Other lengths than twelve measures are found, and elaborations of the basic harmonies are legion; I have indicated in measure 10 one of the most common in the 1920s; after that time, the general tendency was to add more and more elaborate variants to the scheme of harmonies, preserving, however, the twelve-measure structure and the principle harmonic pillars.

---

[13] Two valuable discussions of the latter are Alan Lomax's notes for *Roots of the Blues* (*NW* 252) and the section on "Origins" of Paul Oliver's entry "Blues" in *TNGDAM*. Helpful on the distinctions between country and city blues is Charles Keil, *Urban Blues* (Chicago: University of Chicago Press, 1966), especially Chap. II and Appendix C.

In vocal blues, the three phrases of song per stanza are superimposed on this basic structure. Each phrase of the singer typically lasts for three measures of the four-measure unit, leaving a "hole" until the beginning of the next unit; this hole is filled, in a way perhaps going back to primordial call-and-response techniques, by some sort of instrumental or hummed or spoken response to the singer's phrase. The whole combination, then, might be suggested this way:

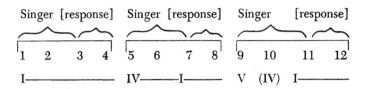

One particularly clear example (available in both a recording and a notated transcription)[14] among many that might be cited is the performance by Jelly Roll Morton of *Mamie's Blues*. In an introduction to the music, spoken as he begins to play, Morton explains that this is "no doubt the first blues [he] ever knew," which (if we can believe his memory) would place it around the turn of the century.

If blues contributed to jazz one of its most common formal structures, it contributed even more importantly to its instrumental style. Early blues *vocal* style was one of great variety and flexibility of intonation, mode of attack, tone color, vibrato, degree of nasality or gutturalism, and regular rhythm or rubato. These freedoms (from the viewpoint of a singer trained in the Euro-American cultivated tradition of art-song or opera) were partly inherent in the folkish lack of "sophistication" of the country blues singers, partly the result of vestiges of the primordial African style concepts of American blacks. Significant for jazz in the vocalism of the blues was the transfer from voice to instrument of this blues style: jazz instrumentalists, unbound by notions of "correct" performance on a trumpet, a trombone, a banjo or guitar, used instruments as substitutes for, or extensions of, the voice, bringing to them the same broad range of expression as that of the blues singer's voice. The various narrowly prescriptive attempts that have been made to categorize the "blue notes" of jazz (usually vastly oversimplified as the flatted third and seventh of the major scale) arise from a preconception, dominated by the cultivated tradition's ideas of the musical scale and of instrumental performance technique, about what is and what is not "basic" or "natural" in musical structure and style.

Rags were the other major source of the repertory of jazz in the 1920s,

[14] *New Orleans Memories Plus Two* (Commodore Records XFL-14942); Alan Lomax, *Mister Jelly Lord*, 2nd ed. (Berkeley: University of California Press, 1973), pp. 269–71.

thanks to the broad popularity of ragtime as a kind of marching and dancing music early in the century. The historic first recordings of jazz, ironically made by the all-white performers of the Original Dixieland Jazz Band (1917–18), included blues and rags in about equal measure, like *Livery Stable Blues* or *Clarinet Marmalade Blues* and *Tiger Rag* or *Sensation Rag*; so did the musically more significant recordings, from the middle 1920s, of the bands of King Oliver (1885–1938), Louis Armstrong (ca. 1898–1971), and Jelly Roll Morton. Among these are the epochal 1923 recordings of Oliver's Creole Jazz Band, including *Dipper Mouth Blues* (reissued on *SCCJ*:s1/6) and *High Society Rag*; the 1925–27 recordings by Armstrong's Hot Five or Hot Seven of *S.O.L. Blues* (reissued on *SCCJ*:s2/6) and *Muskrat Ramble*, the latter a rag composed by the trombonist Kid Ory (1886–1973); and the 1926 recordings by Morton's Red Hot Peppers of *Dead Man Blues* (reissued on *SCCJ*: s1/8) and *Black Bottom Stomp* (*SCCJ*:s2/1).

Jazz instrumentalists brought to the performance of ragtime the same flexible, vocalistic nuances of pitch and rhythm that they brought to the blues; thus, in performance style the two types of early jazz were equivalent. Within the frameworks of blues or ragtime forms, early jazz performances were built on a principle of improvisatory variation; in terms of the broad Euro-American Western tradition, the result was close to the Baroque era's "strophic variations," a chain of varied repetitions of a basic "tune." In jazz, the "tune" was more a matter of the underlying harmonies of an original piece than its melody, and virtually any music could *become* jazz, by adoption of its "tune" as the basis for improvisatorily varied repetitions in jazz style. Most of the early jazz recordings were made by New Orleans musicians, and despite attempts to challenge the legendary primacy of the Crescent City as the sole birthplace of jazz, it remains important as the first major center. The New Orleans jazz bands were typically small groups (combos) made up mainly of clarinet, cornet, trombone, and drums, deriving from the military and civic marching bands of the post-Civil War period. They played outdoors for parades and funerals and, seated in placarded wagons, for advertising; indoors, in brothels, barrelhouses, and dance halls, with perhaps a ragtime piano and a banjo or guitar, for dancing. The ensemble style, as heard typically in the first chorus (stanza) and the last, "ride-out" chorus(es) of a piece, was a roughly contrapuntal music with the powerful cornet projecting the main melodic voice, the clarinet weaving a treble counter-melody, the trombone providing a solid but melodic bass, and the drums and other instruments supplying the basic beat against which raggy syncopations could work. Between first and last choruses, individual musicians would play one or more improvisatory solo choruses in succession.

Example 8-6 shows the improvisatory melodic style of such New Orleans jazz, taken from a later recording (1947) by Louis Armstrong; the example is chosen partly to suggest the absorption by jazz, as the 1920s closed, of a third formal pattern in addition to those of ragtime and blues: that of the thirty-two-measure chorus, in AABA design, of the popular songs of Tin Pan Alley. In Example 8-6, (a) is the original melody of the pop song *Black and Blue* (1929), with its harmonies indicated. The transcription of Armstrong's cornet melody (b) does not attempt to show the nuances of pitch and tone quality in his solo; it does however attempt to show rhythmic nuances, as Armstrong plays slightly earlier (+) or later (−) the notes as indicated in the notated version.

EXAMPLE 8-6. (*What Did I Do to Be So*) *Black & Blue* by Andy Razaf, Thomas Waller, and Harry Brooks. Copyright © 1929 by Mills Music, Inc. Copyright renewed © 1957 by Mills Music, Inc. Used by Permission. (a) As published. (b) As played by Louis Armstrong on the recording *Satchmo at Symphony Hall* (Decca DL 8037); my transcription.

Following the early successes of the original Dixieland Jazz Band, other white musicians took up jazz in the 1920s. Early in the decade a group in Chicago centered on three musicians originally from New Orleans—trumpeter Paul Mares, clarinetist Leon Roppolo, and trombonist George Brunies—was formed as the New Orleans Rhythm Kings; later came Bix Beiderbecke (1903–31), a gifted cornetist, and the Wolverines, as well as a group of Chicago musicians who, playing together from their school days, came to be known as the Austin High School gang. Among them were Bud Freeman (b. 1906) and Frank Teschemacher (1906–32), both players of the saxophone, an instrument that although not commonly used in New Orleans jazz was to become indispensable in later jazz groups. Other instruments assuming new importance in jazz of the late 1920s were the trumpet, replacing the more mellow but less brazen cornet; the guitar, replacing the earlier banjo; and the string bass, replacing the tuba of the brass bands.

Another important development in jazz of the 1920s was the formation of "big bands;" rather than small "combos." Any group larger than, say, a half dozen players needed some kind of musical arrangement, a plan of action, whether sketched out in notation or worked out empirically through rehearsals; it could not rely on the collective improvisation within the spare, linear contrapuntal texture of the small group. Early examples of such "arranged" jazz, which required a real composer or at least a dominant director and organizer, are the 1926 recordings of Jelly Roll Morton and his Red Hot Peppers. Even the earliest recordings by this band (which numbered seven or eight members)—including *Grandpa's Spells* (reissued on SCCJ:s1/7), *Smokehouse Blues*, and *The Pearls*—have been described (by

Gunther Schuller, in his *TNGDAM* article on Morton) as "a triumphant fusion of composition and improvisation," and Morton himself as "the first important jazz composer."

Three other pianists, each with a different orientation from Morton's (which was, of course, that of New Orleans jazz), proved equally skillful and even more progressive leaders of big-band jazz in the 1920s. One was Fletcher Henderson (1897–1952), who was born in Georgia but drifted into jazz only after he moved to New York in 1920 and absorbed the New York style of stride piano playing and other Harlem dance music. Henderson's music director and arranger was Don Redman; he developed an immensely satisfactory and influential technique of scoring, especially for the brass and reed sections of a big band, that gave the music the feeling of freedom, mobility, and relaxation of a small combo (e.g., in the 1926 recording of *The Stampede*, reissued on *SCCJ*:s3/6). He treated each section like a single voice; they alternated with each other in call-and-response fashion, or one backed up the other with repetitive, improvisatory phrases (later called "riffs"); and individual soloists—like Louis Armstrong, who joined Henderson's band in 1924 and was a major influence in turning it into a propulsive "swinging" group—could still improvise freely over cleverly arranged backgrounds. Famous recorded examples of Henderson's early style, featuring Armstrong as soloist, include *Copenhagen* (1924) and *Sugar Foot Stomp* (1925), the latter based on King Oliver's *Dipper Mouth Blues*. The Henderson band went into a decline in the late 1920s, but in the mid-1930s, its best arrangements bought by Benny Goodman for *his* band and nationally popularized, it was to have a triumphant vindication.

Another pianist important in the development of successful big-band style was Bennie Moten (1894–1935), whose six-piece group became the most popular jazz combo in Kansas City in the early 1920s. Reflecting the Southwest origins and popularity of ragtime, Moten's band (as heard on recordings from 1923 on) played very differently from either the New Orleans or New York schools: it emphasized a heavy beat, even eighth-note rhythms, and frequent blues patterns. By 1926 Moten was recording with a ten-piece band and had developed both an earthy, rocking beat (*Kansas City Breakdown*, 1928) and a "pushy" rhythmic drive based on the motoric ostinato cycles of boogie-woogie piano (*New Tulsa Blues*, 1927). Out of this style was to develop the powerful "Kansas City" swing style of the 1930s.

The last of the three progressive big-band pianist-leaders of the 1920s to be cited here—and, quite simply, one of America's greatest composers— is Edward Kennedy "Duke" Ellington (1899–1974). Initially a leader of dance bands in Washington, DC, Ellington moved to New York in 1923 and began working with his band, the Washingtonians, at the Hollywood Club (renamed in 1925 the Kentucky Club); from 1927 on, well into the 1930s, they embellished (and made famous) the Cotton Club in Harlem. Ellington cut his first electrical recordings in 1926, with a twelve-piece band. An important element in roughening and individualizing the otherwise rather sweet, "white" dance-band sound of the group was the plunger-mute technique and raspy "growling" of trumpeter James "Bubber" Miley and trombonist Joe "Tricky Sam" Nanton. Miley's original compositions and his ideas on arranging for the band were also important in the crystallization of the "Ellington sound," which, emphasizing at first so-called "jungle" effects, was documented in the three major early works the band recorded: *East St. Louis Toodle-Oo* (reissued on *SCCJ*:s6/4), *Black and Tan Fantasy*, and *Creole Love Call* (late 1926–late 1927). The last of these broadened even further the group's sonorous palette by employing a wordless voice—that of Adelaide Hall—as an extra instrument (as does *The Mooche* of 1928). Besides his "jungle" pieces, Ellington also explored new jazz sonorities in bluesy "mood" compositions like *Misty Mornin'* and *Awful Sad* (both recorded in 1928), which seem in retrospect to have been precursors of the most famous such composition, *Mood Indigo* (1930; reissued on *NW* 272:s2/1). Ellington also sought restlessly to expand and vary the conventional forms of jazz, which—at least on recordings—had been limited to the brief time span of one side of a 10-inch, 78 rpm disc (about three minutes). This search culminated first with the double-side composition *Creole Rhapsody* (two versions completed by 1931, the first of which, briefer than the second, is reissued on *SCCJ*:s6/6); the stage was set for the even larger and more complex works of later decades.

BIBLIOGRAPHICAL NOTES

A book that communicates vividly the sense of ferment in European music and the other arts in the period 1885–1918 is Roger Shattuck's *The Banquet Years* (1958; rev. ed. New York: Vintage Books, 1968). The most comprehensive survey of early twentieth-century music is William Austin's *Music in the 20th Century* (New York: W. W. Norton, 1966). Eric Salzman's *Twentieth-Century Music: An Introduction*, 3rd ed. (Englewood Cliffs, NJ: Prentice-Hall, Inc., 1988), written from a composer's standpoint, is insightful on matters of musical style and thought; Peter Hansen's *An Introduction to 20th Century Music*, 4th ed. (Boston: Allyn and Bacon, 1978), and Bryan Simms's *Music of the Twentieth Century: Style and Structure* (New York: Schirmer Books, 1986) are also helpful.

Arthur Berger offers a sympathetic study of Copland's pre-World War II music in *Aaron Copland* (1953; repr. Westport, CT: Greenwood Press, 1977). Copland's own account of those years, interlarded with oral-history interview-derived remarks by many of his contemporaries, is in his book (with co-author

Vivian Perlis) *Copland: 1900 Through 1942* (New York: St. Martin's Press, 1984). Nadia Boulanger's complex personality is well caught in Suzanne R. Hoover's "Nadia Boulanger," *The American Scholar*, XLVI/4 (Autumn 1977), 496–502.

Varèse's early years (to 1928) are recounted authoritatively by his wife, Louise, in *Varèse: A Looking-Glass Diary* (New York: W. W. Norton, 1972); see also Fernand Ouellette's *Edgard Varèse* (1966; English trans. New York: Orion Press, 1968; repr. New York: Da Capo Press, 1981). Portions of Varèse's 1939 Princeton lecture are published, as edited and annotated by Chou Wen-chung, in "The Liberation of Sound," *PNM*, V/1 (Fall-Winter 1966), 11–19, and in *Contemporary Composers on Contemporary Music*, eds. Elliott Schwartz and Barney Childs (New York: Holt, Rinehart and Winston, 1967), 201–4.

Although no full-scale biography of Cowell has appeared, Rita Mead's *Henry Cowell's New Music, 1925–1936: The Society, the Music Editions, and the Recordings* (Ann Arbor: UMI Research Press, 1981) is rich in detail and touches on many of the composers published in *New Music*. Martha Manion's *The Writings About Henry Cowell* (ISAMm 16 [1981]) is a very copiously annotated bibliography, with many quotations from critics' reactions to Cowell's progressive music. Andrew Porter discusses the Romantic and Euphometric quartets most lucidly in his *Music of Three More Seasons: 1977–1980* (New York: Alfred A. Knopf, Inc., 1981), pp. 184–88. I have analyzed *Ostinato Pianissimo* in *MQ*, LXX (1984), 23–44.

Charles Hamm's *Yesterdays: Popular Song in America* (New York: W. W. Norton, 1979) and Alex Wilder's *American Popular Song . . . 1900–1950* complement each other nicely. Cecil Smith's *Musical Comedy in America* of 1950 has been updated by Glenn Litton, 2nd ed. (New York: Theatre Arts Books, 1981). Four books by Gerald Bordman (all published by Oxford University Press) add up to a virtually comprehensive account of the American popular lyric theater: *American Musical Theatre: A Chronicle* (1978), *American Operetta: From* H.M.S. Pinafore [1879] *to* Sweeney Todd [1979] (1981), *American Musical Comedy: From* Adonis [1884] *to* Dreamgirls [1981] (1982); and *American Musical Revue: From* The Passing Show [1894] *to* Sugar Babies [1979] (1985). An enthralling and illuminating account of no fewer than thirty-three productions of the Kern/Hammerstein masterpiece *Show Boat*, lavishly illustrated and meticulously documented, is Miles Kreuger's *Show Boat: The Story of a Classic American Musical* (New York: Oxford University Press, 1977).

The best biographical account of George Gershwin is by Edward Jablonski and Lawrence D. Stewart: *The Gershwin Years*, rev. ed. (New York: Doubleday and Co., Inc., 1973). Besides the articles by Richard Crawford cited in footnote 11, his *TNGDAM* article on Gershwin is a valuable discussion, especially of Gershwin as songwriter, as is Leonard Bernstein's deceptively off-hand article "Why Don't You Run Upstairs and Write a Nice Gershwin Tune," reprinted from *The Atlantic Monthly* of April 1955 in his *The Joy of Music* (New York: Simon & Schuster, Inc., 1959). Ira Gershwin's *Lyrics on*

Several Occasions (New York: Alfred A. Knopf, Inc., 1959; repr. with an introduction by Betty Comden and Adolph Green, New York: Viking Press, 1973), more than just a collection of his lyrics, has fascinating commentary on the craft of the lyricist.

Thomas Riis's "Black Musical Theatre in New York, 1890–1915" (Ph. D. dissertation, University of Michigan, 1981) is a path-breaking study. Robert Kimball and William Bolcom treat the lives of two later black-musical leaders in *Reminiscing with Sissle and Blake* (New York: Viking Press, 1973).

Paul Oliver's studies of blues (see the bibliography of his *TNGDAM* article "Blues") are masterly, as is Robert Palmer's *Deep Blues* (New York: Viking Press, 1981).

By far the best book on the stylistic development of jazz, with many transcriptions notated from recordings, is Gunther Schuller's *Early Jazz: Its Roots and Musical Development* (New York: Oxford University Press, 1968); a second volume is forthcoming. James Lincoln Collier's *The Making of Jazz: A Comprehensive History* (Boston: Houghton Mifflin Co., 1978) is a broader survey. The pianistic artistry of Jelly Roll Morton is documented in the extraordinary collection of transcriptions of his recorded performances by James Dapogny, *Ferdinand "Jelly Roll" Morton: The Collected Piano Music* (Washington, DC: Smithsonian Institution Press, 1982). Mark Tucker's definitive study, "The Early Years of Edward Kennedy 'Duke' Ellington" (Ph. D. dissertation, University of Michigan, 1986), is to be published by the University of Illinois Press.

NINE

THE 1930s AND EARLY 1940s

The 1930s in American music were a complete contrast to the 1920s. The optimistic, progressive, strident voices of the 1920s were muted in the decade of the Great Depression. As Virgil Thomson wrote later in his autobiography, "The time was not for novelty." Copland, in a famous statement about the trend to simplicity in his own works of the 1930s, said,

> The old "special" public of the modern music concerts had fallen away, and the conventional concert public continued apathetic or indifferent to anything but the established classics. . . . I felt that it was worth the effort to see if I couldn't say what I had to say in the simplest possible terms.[1]

A characteristic gesture of the concert-music establishment was that of the Philadelphia Orchestra's management in announcing just before the 1932 season opened that "debatable" new music would be avoided on the orchestra's programs. Even the lusty voice of jazz was stilled after the stock market crash of 1929; with a few notable exceptions, it was not widely heard again for about six years, and then it spoke differently from before. This musical

---

[1] Aaron Copland, *Our New Music* (New York: McGraw-Hill Book Company, 1941), p. 229.

atmosphere of conservatism, probably due in largest part to the impact of the Depression, seems not to have been broken until after the end of World War II (1946); thus "the 1930s" as an era in American musical history actually extended to the mid-1940s.

THEMES OF THE PERIOD

Even if the most characteristic atmosphere of the period was one of a broad conservatism, the music of the Depression era revealed several new and distinctive trends. Perhaps the strongest was a historical or regional Americanism. This was certainly related to the political and social thought of the era, its populist and collectivist temperament and its tendency to an American isolationism; the latter was reflected musically in a suspicious attitude toward the "Europe-ness" of the international new-music movement of the 1920s. One might speak of an "American Wave" in music of the 1930s as art historians do of the work of painters like Charles Burchfield, Edward Hopper, Thomas Hart Benton, and Grant Wood.

Closely related to this trend was a new and persistent preoccupation of composers with their relationship to the broad musical community and to society at large. The century's new mass media of communication (radio; phonorecordings; sound films; and, from late in the 1930s, television) had created a vast new potential audience for music, but a different one from the concert audiences of the past; many composers saw these media as a challenge to their ability to communicate on a broad scale. At the same time, conflicting impulses of individualism and integrity beset them; the role of the composer in an industrial society, wishing both to serve and be served by it, was an issue. As one major figure of American music of the 1930s, Roy Harris, put it, "How to serve society as a composer, how to become economically and socially recognized as a worth-contributing citizen, how to establish durable human contacts with individuals or groups is a harassing problem."[2]

One common way in the 1930s to become "economically recognized" was of course through trade-union organization; and in place of the idealistic and music-minded modern-music societies of the 1920s, composers of the 1930s banded together in hard-headed, economics-minded protective associations. In addition to the theretofore virtually monopolistic American Society of Composers, Authors and Publishers (ASCAP), the period saw the formation of the American Composers Alliance (ACA; organized 1937) and

---

[2] "Problems of American Composers," in Henry Cowell, ed., *American Composers on American Music* (1933; 2nd ed. New York: Frederick Ungar Publishing Co., 1962), p. 164; the entire essay repr. *ACS*, pp. 147–60.

Broadcast Music, Inc. (BMI; organized 1939). Performers too became more solidly organized: the American Federation of Musicians (organized 1896) became ever more aggressively protective under its president, James C. Petrillo; the American Guild of Musical Arts (AGMA), organized in 1936, watched over the fortunes of musicians, especially singers, and other artists in opera, oratorio, ballet, and concerts in general. Some aid to both composers and performers during the depths of the Depression was forthcoming from the government via the Federal Music Project of the Works Progress Administration. Created in 1935, by 1938 the project was providing work for about 10,000 persons. Project-supported concerts, music lending libraries, and music education in rural and congested urban areas helped to broaden the American audience; programs of collecting folk and ethnic music stimulated interest in these fields. Composers were not, however, subsidized for free musical composition (as were painters under the Federal Art Project of the WPA); they were assigned other musical tasks of various sorts, and a few were asked to supply music for documentary films.

The major works of Aaron Copland during this 1930–45 period reflect the themes I have cited: a conservative trend, a historical or regional Americanism, and a search for a broader public. Abstract music with the ferocity and astringency of the *Piano Variations* or *Vitebsk*, from the late 1920s, was replaced with gentler, smoother, and generally more accessible works, virtually all of them on regional or topical themes.[3] The orchestral tone-poem *El Salón México* (1936) was based on popular-song material from south of the border. The ballet scores for *Billy the Kid* (1938) and *Rodeo* (1942) evoked the spirit of the far West and included some skillfully recomposed cowboy tunes, whereas *Appalachian Spring* (1944) dealt with early nineteenth-century Pennsylvania rural life, expressed in country-fiddle-style tunes and hymn-like cantilenas and climaxing with some lucid variations on the Shaker song *Simple Gifts*. In a cheerfully utilitarian spirit, Copland wrote works for amateur and school ensembles, like the high school play-opera *The Second Hurricane* (1937) and *An Outdoor Overture* (1938) for orchestra. For the new mass media he composed works like *Music for Radio* (1937; subtitled *A Saga of the Prairie*) and film scores for *The City* (1939), *Of Mice and Men* (1939), *Our Town* (1940), *The Red Pony* (1948), and others. The entry of the United States into World War II evoked several frankly patriotic works from him, among them *Lincoln Portrait* (1942), which mingled Stephen Foster song fragments and folk songs (notably *On Springfield Mountain*) with narrated excerpts from Lincoln's speeches, and *Fanfare for the Common Man* (1942). The latter's wide-intervalled, jagged diatonic theme typified Copland's new melodic manner, one that somehow was inevitably associated

[3] The exceptions that proved the rule were two abstract sonatas, for piano (1934–41) and for violin and piano (1943), and *Statements* (1933–35) for orchestra, in which something of the acid bite of the *Piano Variations* is to be heard.

with the broad plains and rugged mountains of the country, though it came from the pen of an urbane New York City composer (Example 9-1).

EXAMPLE 9-1. A. Copland, *Fanfare for the Common Man* (1942), measures 1–16 (percussion omitted). Copyright 1943 by Aaron Copland. Reprinted by permission of Aaron Copland, Copyright Owner, and Boosey & Hawkes, Inc., Sole Publishers and Licensees.

Most of these works not only were aimed at the broad new American audience but also drew from a wide spectrum of the American experience for subject matter and from the American past for musical materials. Indeed, the American musical past was generally viewed with new interest and re-evaluation during the period. In 1931 appeared the first really comprehensive history of American cultivated-tradition music, *Our American Music*, by John Tasker Howard (1890–1964). By 1946, so much new research had been done that Howard had to revise the book completely. Especially notable was the rediscovery (perhaps it would be more accurate to say the "discovery") of the music of Charles Ives—pianist John Kirkpatrick's premiere performance in 1939 of the "Concord" Sonata was a landmark—and of earlier American music, especially the eighteenth-century New England singing-school music and American folk music in general. These rediscoveries were reflected in the form of innumerable "Hoedowns," "Hayrides," "Square Dances," and the like, in a variety of media. Ross Lee Finney (b. 1906), a Middle Westerner trained under Nadia Boulanger and Alban Berg in Europe, found inspiration in Colonial music for his choral work *Pilgrim Psalms* (1945), which drew on melodies from Ainsworth's psalter, and in Federal-era music for his orchestral *Hymn, Fuguing and Holiday* (1943), which went back to the Yankee tunesmiths, as did the *Prelude to a Hymn Tune (after William Billings)* (1937) of Otto Luening. Henry Cowell began a long series of works for different combinations of instruments but each entitled *Hymn and Fuguing Tune* (1944–64). William Schuman made use of a ubiquitous American children's call (phoneticized by him as "wee-awk-eee") in *American Festival Overture* (1939); his *William Billings Overture* (1943) drew from three sing-ing-school pieces of the early Boston composer.

THOMSON, HARRIS, AND BLITZSTEIN

Three composers who shared a common background of study in the 1920s with Boulanger and who participated in the musical "American Wave" were Virgil Thomson, Roy Harris, and Marc Blitzstein. The first two were interested in America's musical past, Blitzstein in certain aspects of the present. Of Harris and Thomson, both Middle Westerners, Harris was the more aggressively "Americanist," but Thomson's music suggested an equally profound immersion in, and sympathy for, the American musical heritage; and his uses of it, which went back to the late 1920s, antedated other composers'.

Thomson once wrote a quotably succinct autobiographical note:

I was born November 25, 1896 in Kansas City, Missouri, grew up there and went to war from there. That was the other war. Then I was educated some more in Boston and Paris. In composition I was a pupil of Nadia Boulanger. While I was still young I taught music at Harvard and played the organ at King's Chapel, Boston. Then I returned to Paris and lived there for many years, till the Germans came, in fact. Now I live in New York, where I am Music Critic of the *Herald Tribune* [from which he resigned in 1954].[4]

Thomson has called his *Sonata da Chiesa* (1926) for clarinet, trumpet, viola, horn, and trombone in three dissonant, neo-Baroque movements (Chorale, Tango, Fugue) a "bang-up graduation piece" from Boulanger's studio, but the inclusion of the popular dance rhythms of a tango suggests the impact of Satie and the younger French composers, as had the piano works *Two Sentimental Tangos* (1923) and *Synthetic Waltzes* (1925). As early as 1926, however, Thomson, a Protestant and an organist, began to turn to American hymnody. One important result was a *Symphony on a Hymn Tune* (two movements sketched 1926; completed 1928). At about the same time he composed some pointedly irreverent and very funny *Variations on Sunday School Tunes* (1927) for organ, and settings of several texts by Gertrude Stein, who had accepted Thomson as an artistically fastidious, amusing, and courageous fellow expatriate in Paris (the song *Susie Asado*, 1926; the choral piece *Capital Capitals*, 1927). Thomson's Francophilia, his sophisticated,

---

[4] Quoted in Peggy Glanville-Hicks, "Virgil Thomson," *MQ*, XXXV (1949), 210.

pseudo-innocent way with American hymn-book harmony, his respect for language, his wit, and his close relationship with Stein were to result in one of the most extraordinary works of American music: the opera *Four Saints in Three Acts*, first produced by the Friends and Enemies of Modern Music of Hartford, Connecticut, in 1934. Stein's own account of the genesis of the work runs like this:

> Virgil Thomson had asked Gertrude Stein to write an opera for him. Among the saints there were two saints whom she had always liked better than any others, Saint Theresa of Avila and Ignatius Loyola, and she said she would write him an opera about these two saints. She began this and worked very hard at it all that spring [1927] and finally finished Four Saints and gave it to Virgil Thomson to put to music. He did. And it is a completely interesting opera both as to words and music.[5]

Four Saints is a work of fantasy, liveliness, and inexplicable charm. Impossible to interpret literally, equally impossible to dismiss as meaningless, it offers a child-like, surrealistic procession of tableaux about saints (many more than four) doing what we suppose saints do: receiving visitors, posing for earthly reproductions, discussing human problems and saintly ones too, loving Christ, rejoicing. Thomson's setting is similarly child-like: "With meanings already abstracted, or absent, or so multiplied that choice among them was impossible . . . you could make a setting for sound and syntax only, then add, if needed, an accompaniment equally functional," he said;[6] and he composed deceptively simple music, which both supports discreetly and projects impeccably the verses of Stein. The original chamber orchestration of nineteen players is dominated by the sound of an accordion, which gives a pungent reediness to the successions of plain chords that characterize the harmony. The very beginning of the Prologue establishes the tone of affected yet effective simplicity, with a waltz vamp underlying a metrically variable exhortation by the chorus, in crystal-clear octaves, to "prepare for [four?] saints" (Example 9-2). Saint Theresa is introduced with affectionate malice as one who pontificates repetitiously about the obvious ("There are a great many persons and places near together"); Thomson's music leads to a neo-Handelian climax marked "Grandioso (liberamente)." A celebrated Vision of the Holy Ghost ("Pigeons on the grass alas") begets strangely moving music. A Saints' Procession finds Thomson retiring almost completely into the background, allowing Stein's leaden processional ("In wed in dead/in dead wed led/in led wed dead") to plod solemnly across the stage, over sustained chords. Ultimately the work defies description and perhaps analysis; as John Cage has sensitively written, "To enjoy it, one

[5] *The Autobiography of Alice B. Toklas* (New York: Harcourt, Brace & Co., 1933), p. 281.

[6] *Virgil Thomson* (New York: Alfred A. Knopf, Inc., 1966), p. 90.

EXAMPLE 9-2. V. Thomson, *Four Saints in Three Acts* (1934), measures 1–8. Quoted by permission of Beekman Music. Inc.

must leap into that irrational world from which it sprang, the world in which the matter-of-fact and the irrational are one, where mirth and metaphysics marry to beget comedy."[7]

Historically, *Four Saints* more than any other single work offered a model for the new simplicity in American music of the 1930s and suggested how the triadic harmony of the American past could be used with fresh incisiveness: as Thomson commented in his saucy survey of *The State of Music* in 1939, it had music that was "simple, melodic, and harmonious . . . after twenty years of everybody's trying to make music just a little bit louder and more unmitigated and more complex than anybody else's." A similar artful simplicity pervades the later Stein-Thomson collaboration, *The Mother of Us All* (1947), an opera about political life in nineteenth-century America centered on the women's-rights activist Susan B. Anthony. Its music is wholly of Thomson's contrivance, but it has a warmly nostalgic atmosphere; he spoke of the work as

a memory-book of Victorian play-games and passions . . . with its gospel hymns and cocky marches, its sentimental ballads, waltzes, darned-fool ditties and intoned sermons . . . a souvenir of all those sounds and kinds of tunes that were once the music of rural America.[8]

---

[7] Kathleen Hoover and John Cage, *Virgil Thomson: His Life and Music* (New York: T. Yoseloff, 1959), p. 157.

[8] Quoted in the informative liner notes, by Robert Marx, for the recording (NW 288/ 289).

Thomson was the first major American composer of concert music to write for films. But he did not enter the highly specialized and, for a concert-music composer, infinitely frustrating musical wing of the Hollywood indus-try; he wrote instead scores for several government-sponsored documentary films: two directed by Pare Lorentz, *The Plow that Broke the Plains* (1936) and *The River* (1937), and a wartime propaganda film for the Office of War Information, *Tuesday in November* (1945). His best-known film score, for Robert Flaherty's *Louisiana Story* (1948), was similarly composed for a doc-umentary, produced by the Standard Oil Company. In all these, Thomson's sympathy for American folk and vernacular-tradition music was apparent: *The Plow* draws on cowboy songs; *The River* on white spirituals from *South-ern Harmony* and *The Sacred Harp*; *Tuesday in November* on waltzes, hymns, and *Yankee Doodle*; *Louisiana Story* on the Acadian ("Cajun") songs and dances of the bayou country.

Roy Harris (1898-1979) was another of the early pupils of Boulanger (1926-29). A prolific composer, by the early 1940s he had produced a vast number of works in almost all media except opera. From his Op. 1, a Piano Sonata (1928-29), Harris's style seemed firmly and idiosyncratically estab-lished: it was marked by expansive, rolling melodies, often modal but equally often chromatic; bichordal harmony of an immediately recognizable sort; contrapuntal textures and devices of all kinds; and a sense of form that avoided the neo-Classic types popular in the 1930s with many composers, but did include neo-Baroque principles like fugue, ostinato, and passacaglia. Harris displayed his American interests in works like the Symphony No. 4 with chorus (*Folksong Symphony*; 1940); the orchestral piece *When Johnny Comes Marching Home* (1934; subtitled "An American Overture"), which Harris based on a Civil War song and planned precisely in length and form to fit the two sides of a 78-rpm recording; *Gettysburg Address Symphony*, No. 6 (1944); *Railroad Man's Ballad* (1941) for chorus and orchestra; and *American Ballads* (1942) for piano. Many works, however, were musically abstract, like the two that some still consider, almost four decades later, to be his most masterly: the Quintet for Piano and Strings (1936) and the Third Symphony in One Movement (1939). Characteristic of the long-breathed melodic line of Harris is the theme of the second ("lyric") section of the symphony: very chromatic, uncertainly focused on any single tonic note; fluid in tempo, phrase length, meter, and dynamics but even-paced in rhythm, it seems boundless, a grand rhetorical prose-like utterance (Example 9-3 [a]). In sharp contrast is the terse, motive-filled, energetic yet asymmetrical subject of the fugal section of the symphony; not identifiably related to anyone else's music, its internal cross-rhythms and ambiguous meter never-theless stamp it as "Made in the U.S.A." (Example 9-3 [b]). The "pastoral" section of the Third Symphony is justly famous for its "seemingly endless succession of spun-out melodies" (the phrase is Copland's); few seem to have

EXAMPLE 9-3. R. Harris, *Third Symphony in One Movement* (New York: G. Schirmer, Inc., 1939). Quoted by permission. (a) "Lyric" theme (measures 60–97). (b) "Fugue" subject (measures 416–21).

noticed its basis in a bellows-like ostinato figure, expanding and contracting in the bass, or its carefully planned polychordal harmony, gradually increasing in density, resonance, and tension until it bursts into the resolute fugue. The Piano Quintet is less originally shaped; represents the more retrospective, contrapuntal turn of Harris's mind with its three movements, Passacaglia, Cadenza, and (triple) Fugue.

If works like Thomson's *Hymn Tune Symphony* and Harris's *Folksong Symphony* suggested a new rapprochment between concert music and the music of America's older vernacular and folk traditions, many works by Marc Blitzstein (1905–64) for the lyric theater, legitimate theater (incidental music), films, and radio bespoke a similar rapprochement with contemporaneous popular music. In such operas as *The Cradle Will Rock* (1936–37) and *No for an Answer* (1938–40), Blitzstein was strongly influenced by the musicodramatic works of Bertolt Brecht and Kurt Weill (particularly *Die Dreigroschenoper*, which Blitzstein later translated and adapted as *The Threepenny Opera*); his main achievement, one might claim, was to raise the style of the Broadway musical to an exquisitely calculated level of harsh refinement. Both works were morality plays written from a leftist political and social viewpoint; both may be seen as modern ballad operas based on the style of the American pop song and the speech of the American streets; both were deceptively "easy" works; and neither could have been composed by anybody without the thorough training (both with Schoenberg in Berlin and Boulanger in Paris) and high intelligence of Blitzstein. Preferring to call these works "plays with music," Blitzstein cunningly built up substantial scenes with a unique combination of spoken dialogue, precisely rhythmic speech (notated in score), and song; take any of these elements away, and much of the peculiar power of their blend is lost. "Penny Candy," from *No for an Answer*, is a murderous satire on a do-gooder's morbid curiosity about addiction; without its preliminary monologue, spoken over a sparse, dry accompaniment, the song itself seems only silly. Yet even the briefest excerpt of "Honolulu," from *The Cradle Will Rock*, can suggest Blitzstein's subtle transformation of popular song style: the clichés of the vocal line are cancelled out by the freshness of the accompaniment, with its irregular texture underlying the first four phrases; its hint of Hawaiian steel guitars under "-lulu" and "banned"; its offbeat accentuation of the bass under the raucous refrain; and its acrid inversion of a dominant ninth under "isle" (Example 9-4).

Blitzstein was committed to an ideal of moral persuasion in his art. One of the songs in *The Cradle Will Rock* summarizes his scorn for other ideals:

> Art for Art's sake,
> It's smart, for Art's sake,
> To part, for Art's sake,
> With your mind, for Art's sake,
> Be blind, for Art's sake,
> And deaf, for Art's sake,
> And dumb, for Art's sake,
> Until, for Art's sake,
> They kill, for Art's sake,
> All the Art for Art's sake.[9]

EXAMPLE 9-4. M. Blitzstein, "Honolulu," *The Cradle Will Rock* (1937), measures 1–13. Quoted by permission of the Estate of Marc Blitzstein.

[9] Quoted by permission of the Estate of Marc Blitzstein.

That's just the isle for you, And you'll have your work too,

This was a point of view common enough among socially conscious, leftist artists of the 1930s. But periodic revivals of *The Cradle Will Rock* as well as the success of his later (and more elaborate) opera *Regina* (1949) and his powerful adaptation of *The Threepenny Opera* (1952) suggest that it was not so much the message as the music that was significant in Blitzstein's art.

IN THE GROVES OF ACADEME

Reflecting a new approach to the education of professional musicians (and confirming the fact that few composers of concert music could make a living by composing alone), many of the most highly esteemed composers of the period occupied professorial chairs in American colleges and universities.

Roger Sessions (1896–1985) taught at several institutions before settling at Princeton University (1935–44), going to the University of California at Berkeley (1944–53), then returning to Princeton until his retirement in 1965 (after which, however, he taught at the Juilliard School for years). His early studies at Harvard and Yale linked him with the academic tradition of the Second New England School (as did his later long residence, 1926–33, in Europe), but more significant in his development were years of study and association with the Swiss-American composer Ernest Bloch (1880–1959). In the 1930–45 period, Sessions's style was moving from the diatonic neo-Classicism of his First Symphony (1927) and First Piano Sonata (1930), through the more chromatic and expressionistic manner of a Violin Concerto (1935) and a First String Quartet (1936), to the highly chromatic, long-lined, and dense-textured Second Piano Sonata and Second Symphony (both 1946).

Walter Piston (1894–1976) returned in 1926 from studying in Paris with Boulanger to Harvard (where he had trained in the first place) and remained on the faculty there until *his* retirement (in 1960). His music is of an elegant neo-Classic sort, beautifully crafted and mostly limited to abstract, traditional instrumental genres. A perfect example is the Symphony No. 6

(1955), twenty-four minutes long in four movements, composed for the Boston Symphony Orchestra, which Piston, as a Boston-area resident, knew intimately (reissued on *NW* 286:s1). An influential teacher, Piston reinterpreted Boulanger's French scholastic pedagogy in several influential textbooks: *Principles of Harmonic Analysis* (1933), *Harmony* (1941), *Counterpoint* (1947), and *Orchestration* (1955).

Quincy Porter (1897–1966) taught at Vassar and the New England Conservatory, then (1946) returned to Yale, where he had begun as a pupil of Horatio Parker. He was emphatically a composer of chamber music, e.g., nine string quartets, in an international style. Douglas Moore (1893–1969) was at Columbia and well into a career emphasizing operas on American subjects: *The Headless Horseman* (1936) and *The Devil and Daniel Webster* (1938) were to be followed after World War II by the highly successful, musically nostalgic opera *The Ballad of Baby Doe* (1956) and another, *Carry Nation* (1966). William Schuman was at Sarah Lawrence College; Ross Lee Finney, at Smith College. Roy Harris moved from school to school.

The presence on college and university campuses of these and other eminent composers reflected the fact that especially in institutions beyond the eastern seaboard, the professional training of young musicians, formerly limited typically, as in Europe, to music conservatories, was being taken up by academic institutions. The major conservatories in the United States, such as the Juilliard School in New York, Peabody Conservatory in Baltimore, the Curtis Institute in Philadelphia, and the New England Conservatory in Boston, still offered the most thorough professional training. But more and more the colleges and universities, better endowed than the small conservatories, assumed the function of training ground for musicians. This was to have broad ramifications in the post-World War II years in the development of college instrumental ensembles and opera workshops of remarkably high caliber, and the establishment of professional performing groups, soloists, and composers "in residence." But before the war, the picture was dominated by the composer-professors, attempting to maintain their integrity as composers while employed as full-time professors.[10]

To many colleges and universities in the 1930s, furthermore, came refugees from Europe during the Nazi and Fascist regimes. The 1940s opened with such composers in America as Stravinsky, Schoenberg, Hindemith, Bartók, Weill, Krenek, Martinu, Wolpe, and Milhaud, most of whom were soon attached to college-level music departments. Their very presence contributed to a breakdown of the American tendency, during this period, to a musical isolationism, and ultimately to a new role for the United States

---

[10] Sessions offered some sober speculations on the composer as professor in a "Conversation With Roger Sessions," *PNM*, IV/2 (Spring–Summer 1966), 29–46. Twenty-three American composers confront the matter, in as many essays, in "The Composer in Academia: Reflections on a Theme of Stravinsky," *College Music Symposium*, X (1970), 55–98.

after World War II as international leader of progressive trends in Western music. Among other side effects of the emigration of European musicians to America was the stimulus it provided for the establishment of musicology as an accepted discipline in American universities: although a chair of musicology had been created in 1930 for Otto Kinkeldey (1878–1966) at Cornell, it was really the impact of such newly arrived European musicologists of the stature of Alfred Einstein, Curt Sachs, Hans David, Karl Geiringer, Leo Schrade, and others that led to a rapid development of musicological curricula in American universities and to the consolidation of the American Musicological Society (established 1934) and the Music Library Association (1931).

YOUNGER COMPOSERS OF THE PERIOD

If the composer-professors typified the basic conservatism of the 1930–45 period, so did the rise to prominence of fundamentally conservative young composers as opposed to vanguardists. The acknowledged young leaders were probably Samuel Barber, Gian-Carlo Menotti, William Schuman, and an "Eastman School group."

Barber (1910–81) demonstrated a conservative lyricism in his earliest works: songs and choral pieces and an impassioned setting for voice and string quartet of Matthew Arnold's *Dover Beach* (1931; Barber's own performance of 1935, with the Curtis Quartet, is on *NW* 229:s1/1). Tending to write single, masterly examples in each instrumental genre, he applied an easy, cantabile vocal line to works like the Sonata for Violoncello and Piano (1932) and to two orchestral pieces that achieved a *succès d'estime* when, alone among American compositions, they were performed by the ultra-conservative conductor Arturo Toscanini and the NBC Symphony Orchestra: the (first) *Essay for Orchestra* (1937) and an *Adagio for Strings* (1938; adapted from the slow movement of the 1936 String Quartet). Despite some absorption of Stravinskyan textures in a work like *Capricorn Concerto* (1944) and of Schoenbergian chromaticism in a Piano Sonata (1949), Barber's style continued along a neo-Romantic, "expressive" path. One of the most poignant exemplars of that style, partly because of the warm nostalgia of its text by James Agee, is *Knoxville: Summer of 1915* (1948) for voice and orchestra, in a characteristically accessible rondo-like form.

A close associate of Barber from their days together as students at the Curtis Institute was Gian-Carlo Menotti (he was to be the librettist for Barber's elaborately Victorian opera *Vanessa* [1958] and the chamber opera *A Hand of Bridge* [1959]). By the mid-1940s Menotti (b. 1911 in Italy; to America 1927) had successfully bridged the gap between the opera house and Broadway: after modest successes with *Amelia al Ballo* (produced in

1937 in English translation) and *The Old Maid and the Thief* (1939), his intense and spooky short opera *The Medium* (1946), preceded by a curtain-raising skit, *The Telephone*, began in 1947 a durable career as competitor to the spoken dramas of the Broadway playhouses. Menotti combined the theatrical sense of a popular playwright and a Pucciniesque musical vocabulary with an Italianate love of liquid language and a humane interest in characters as real human beings; the result was opera more accessible than anyone else's at the time. Writing his own librettos, Menotti had a knack for choosing timeless themes of human conflict in topical settings. Two other operas that are both cannily full of *coups de thèâtre* are *The Consul* (1950), based on the frustrations of life under a bureaucracy (its powerful, moving climactic *scena*, "To this we've come:/That men withhold the world from men," is on *NW* 241:s2/2), and a Christmastide fantasy, *Amahl and the Night Visitors* (1951), the first opera commissioned for television, became even greater popular successes than *The Medium*. The full-scale grand opera *The Saint of Bleecker Street* (1954), poised on the razor's edge of the human conflict between spiritual and physical desires, won several prizes (among them the Pulitzer for 1955) and has had many productions; Menotti's later works, however, have been less successful.

William Schuman (b. 1910) was mentioned earlier (p. 220) as a participant in the "American Wave" of the 1930s. *American Festival Overture* was followed by other works on American themes, such as the Billings-based *New England Triptych* (1956) built on *Be Glad Then, America, When Jesus Wept,* and *Chester*; the baseball opera *The Mighty Casey* (1953); and the cantata after Walt Whitman, *A Free Song* (1943). Schuman also wrote several big works for wind band, among them *Newsreel (in Five Shots)* (1941) and *George Washington Bridge* (1950). These were a response to the immense proliferation of bands in schools and colleges across the land. The marching band, most often in evidence between the halves of intercollegiate football games, had once again become a major voice of American vernacular-tradition music. This revival of the band's popularity was accompanied, however, by cultivated-tradition ideals of polished performance. An old problem of bands, their uncertain instrumentation, was disappearing as a more or less standardized instrumentation emerged. After the football season the marching bands, often retitled "symphonic wind ensembles," became concert-giving organizations. Good contemporary music was needed for them. Schuman was not alone in helping to fill the demand: among others, Thomson contributed *A Solemn Music* and *At the Beach* (both 1949); Harris, the overture *Cimarron* (1941), *Take the Sun and Keep the Stars* (1944), and *Fruit of Gold* (1949); Barber, a *Commando March* (1943).

More important in Schuman's output were orchestral symphonies, string quartets, and choral works. A pupil of Harris, Schuman shared with him a fondness for rhapsodic or ostinato forms, long chromatic slow themes, and polychordal harmony. Schuman's rhythms, however, tended to be more nervously athletic than Harris's, more clearly related to pop-music origins, and his orchestration brighter, more sharp-edged with brass and metal-percussion instruments. Two excerpts from his *Symphony for Strings* (1943), the first also a part of his *Three-Score Set* for piano (1943), can suggest respectively Schuman's resonant bichordal harmony and his energetic, stuttering fast-movement rhythms (Example 9-5). The Symphony No. 3 (1941)

EXAMPLE 9-5. W. Schuman, *Symphony for Strings* (New York: G. Schirmer, Inc., 1943). Quoted by permission. (a) Second movement, measures 1–4. (b) Third movement, measures 1–11 (First violin part only).

has joined Copland's Third and Harris's Third as a modern classic; the three works are not infrequently programmed together. Critical opinion, however, rates even higher *A Free Song* of 1942, a secular cantata to a text by Whitman, which won the first Pulitzer Prize in music, and the Sixth Symphony (1948), considered by some to be Schuman's masterpiece. Other important scores, by a composer convinced of the power and potential of modern dance, and one for whom the orchestra was the most natural as well as the most important vehicle of his thought, were for dance: Schuman wrote a number of scores for Martha Graham, including *Undertow* (1945; recorded on NW 253:s1) and the Graham masterpiece *Night Journey* (1947).

Several other younger composers of promise in the late 1930s and early 1940s were graduates of the Eastman School of Music at the University of Rochester, under Howard Hanson's direction; they had studied either with Hanson or with Bernard Rogers (1893–1968). This "Eastman Group" included Robert Palmer (b. 1915), Robert Ward (b. 1917), William Bergsma (b. 1921), and Peter Mennin (1923–83). All shared the relatively conserv-

ative, evolutionary attitudes of their mentors; all seemed to share an aim to
write the Great American Symphony by way of the Depression-era overture,
a one-movement piece ten minutes in length or less, with at least one section
of broadly arching, wide-intervalled, mostly diatonic melody supported by
slow-moving, rich harmony. The latter, although functional and directive,
avoided structures like dominant sevenths or ninths and diminished-seventh
chords; non-tertial sonorities replaced them, as did sometimes triads or
added-tone chords derived from diatonic (but not major) modes.

Related to these Eastman composers in his general style, but pos-
sessing the lyric gifts of a Barber as well, was Norman Dello Joio (b. 1913),
a prolific composer on whose works was stamped the impress of his Italianate
background and of his training under Paul Hindemith. Also related to the
Eastman School (if only as a sometime student there) is David Diamond (b.
1915), whose first major orchestral work, *Symphony in One Movement* (1931),
was premiered at Eastman while he was a special student of violin there.
Diamond left the school after a year's study with Rodgers (1933–34) to seek
a more progressive atmosphere. He worked with both Sessions and Boulanger and lived for many years in Florence, Italy (1953–65). A prolific,
professional composer with nine symphonies, ten string quartets, and many
other works in all media to his credit, Diamond had many performances of
works like *Psalm* (1936) for orchestra, *Elegy in Memory of Maurice Ravel*
(1938–39), and—his most frequently performed piece—*Rounds* (1944) for
string orchestra, all in a lyrical, but intense, and finely crafted personal style.

The only strong avant-garde impulse during the period was felt on
the West Coast: there, carrying on where Cowell had begun, younger composers like John Cage and Lou Harrison (b. 1917) interested themselves in
percussion music, non-Western scales, and new means of formal organization; an older one, Harry Partch (1901–74), pursued a lonely path to a whole
new theory of music based on division of the octave into forty-three tones.
Partch codified his theory in detail in the book *Genesis of a New Music*
(1949).

Cage (b. 1912) studied with both Cowell and Schoenberg. In a Fore-
word to a catalogue of his works, he summarized "the various paths my
musical thought has taken"; those of the period before World War II were

> . . . chromatic composition dealing with the problem of keeping repetitions
> of individual tones as far apart as possible (1933–34); composition with fixed
> rhythmic patterns or tone-row fragments (1935–38); composition for the dance,
> film and theatre (1935–   ); composition within rhythmic structures (the whole
> having as many parts as each unit has small parts, and these, large and small,
> in the same proportion) (1939–56); intentionally expressive composition (1938–
> 51). . . .[11]

---

[11] *John Cage* (New York: Henmar Press Inc., 1962), p. 5.

Few people in the period were aware of Cage as an early exponent of Schoenberg's tone-row technique or as a composer who applied rather similar principles to the organization of rhythm. Many more were familiar with Cage's "prepared piano." "Preparation" meant the alteration of the instrument's tonal quality by inserting between the strings various bits of material; the preparation varied depending on the expressive aim. The sonorous result, totally unlike the usual sound of a piano, is like a tiny version of an Indonesian gamelan orchestra of chimes, gongs, and delicate percussion instruments. This ingenious adaptation of the instrument arose out of Cage's work with modern dancers (from 1938 on, first as accompanist for a group in Seattle, where he met the dancer and choreographer Merce Cunningham and they began a long collaboration). "The need to change the sound of the instrument arose through the desire to make an accompaniment, without employing percussion instruments, suitable for the dance . . . for which it was to be composed" is Cage's comment on the first prepared-piano piece, *Bacchanale* (1938).[12] Cage's most extended work for prepared piano, the seventy-minute *Sonatas and Interludes* (1946–48), aims to express the various "permanent emotions" of (East) Indian tradition; his interest in the Orient, later to be decisive in his musical thought, was already apparent (four sonatas and one interlude recorded on *NW 203:s1/4–8*). Two movements for prepared piano flank two all-percussion trios in *Amores* (1943); and Cage's interest in what Varèse had called "sound—any sound" led him to write a number of all-percussion pieces, adding to the more or less conventional instruments such new sound sources as recordings of constant and variable pitch-frequency, sound-generator whines, and other mechanical and electronic devices (*Imaginary Landscape No. 1* [1939] and *Imaginary Landscape No. 3* [1942]).

JAZZ: SWING

Jazz of the 1930s underwent a major change in style from that of the 1920s. For most of the pre-World War II period, in fact, the very term "jazz" implied the earlier style, the "hot jazz" of the 1920s. The newer style was called "swing," a term perhaps deriving from a 1932 recording of Duke Ellington's band with singer Ivie Anderson: *It Don't Mean a Thing if It Ain't Got That Swing*. The swing style was materializing in the late 1920s and early 1930s, but most Americans did not hear it until about 1935. In the intervening years, between the financial crash and the mid-1930s, the strident, earthy music of New Orleans jazz was out of fashion: America in crisis

[12] Ibid., p. 15.

seemed to want rather to be lulled by the soothing sounds of radio crooners, like Rudy Vallee (1901–86) and Bing Crosby (1904–77), and of non-jazz dance bands like Guy Lombardo's and Wayne King's. Some bands, however, found a way to compromise between the large, euphonious, popular dance band and the improvisatory, "swinging" manner of jazz: thus did the new jazz reach the ears of the public (partly through several popular late-evening radio programs, like "Let's Dance" and "The Camel Caravan," the former sponsored by a cracker-manufacturing corporation, the latter by a cigarette company).

The main vehicle for swing was the big band—even bigger than those developed in the later 1920s. As Benny Goodman (1909–86), the clarinetist whose band more than any other helped to popularize swing, explains in his autobiography,

> It was about this time [1934], or maybe just a little earlier, that large bands became standardized with five brass, four saxes, and four rhythm. . . . Ten men . . . used to be considered the limit of even a large dance orchestra. [13]

In the new big-band style, the individual voices of earlier jazz combos were replaced by three "sections," one of brass instruments (trumpets and trombones), one of reeds (saxes, doubling occasionally on clarinets), and one of rhythm instruments (typically guitar, double bass, piano, and drums). Too unwieldy to permit either the casual approach to form or the collective improvisation of early jazz, the big swing band of the 1930s relied on written arrangements. Increasingly, jazz improvisation became a matter of solos set off against an arranged background music. Models for such arrangements were found in the earlier work of Fletcher Henderson and Duke Ellington and in the arrangements for Jimmy Lunceford's band made by Sy Oliver between 1933 and 1939. These men could simulate an improvisatory style in their written-out, repetitive "riffs" for full band. Moreover, the sections did not play the notes exactly as written: through many rehearsals they shaped the written arrangements into an even more improvisatory, swinging style. [14] Partly because of the new necessity to be able to read music, partly because of the richly harmonized ensemble arrangements, and partly because the swing band had to play not only the older jazz "standards" but also the harmonically more sophisticated popular songs, the chordal vocabulary of jazz musicians expanded. This was reflected in more adventurously chromatic solo improvisations.

---

[13] *The Kingdom of Swing* (Harrisburg, PA: Stackpole Sons, 1939), p. 138.
[14] The use of *square* as a term of opprobrium came into existence during the era as a precise description of the way swing was *not* to be played. To the degree that soloists and even whole sections did not round off notated rhythms and pitches in an improvisatory, feelingful way, they were "square."

The rhythmic basis of swing was a strong, even $\frac{4}{4}$ ("solid" was a favorite adjective of the period) as opposed to the tendency of earlier jazz to march along in $\frac{2}{2}$. Swing drummers typically overlaid the regular thumping four-beats-to-the-measure of the bass drum with a slight emphasis on beats 2 and 4 through a conventional pattern (♩ ♪♫ ♩ ♩ ♪♫ ♩ | ♩) played with drumstick or wire brush on a high-hat cymbal, with totally different effect from the accents on beats 1 and 3 of early jazz. One of the first drummers to establish this convention was Chick Webb (1902–39), but it was more closely identified with the Kansas City style of jazz as played by the bands of Bennie Moten and his successor, William "Count" Basie (1904–84). Basie's band, along with Ellington's, was probably the most influential of all in establishing the swing style, but nationally the style was diffused by the bands of white leaders like Goodman, Tommy Dorsey (1905 –56), Artie Shaw (b. 1910), and Glenn Miller (1904– 44), perhaps mainly because discriminatory practices made it difficult for the black bands to get the same degree of exposure to the mass audience.

The swing era seemed to breed virtuosos. Some were dazzling soloists, like the peerless pianist Art Tatum (1910–56); from 1933 on, Tatum made more than six hundred recordings (some with small combos) that display his Harlem stride-based style, enriched with harmonic elaborations, rhythmic and contrapuntal complications, and an almost unbelievable fleetness of hand (cf. his solo performances of *Willow Weep for Me* and *Too Marvelous for Words* on *SCCJ*:s5/1–2). Virtuosos of another sort were a few legendary singers, notably Ella Fitzgerald (b. 1918), who began a very long career with beguiling songs like *A-Tisket, a-Tasket* (1938) backed up by Chick Webb's band (which Fitzgerald joined in 1935) and with scat singing of an immense range of timbres and pitch (from d to c^3), and Billie Holiday (ca. 1912–59), whose singing between about 1936 and 1944, a fresh synthesis based on that of Bessie Smith's blues and Louis Armstrong's improvisatory style, justified claims for her as the pre-eminent jazz singer of the period. Holiday had a special empathetic musical relationship with Count Basie's tenor saxophonist Lester Young (1909–59); among her most celebrated recordings are ones in which they worked together (as in *He's Funny That Way* or *All of Me*, on *SCCJ*:s4/6–7, or *I Can't Get Started with You*, on *NW* 295:s1/1).

Other jazz performers rose to virtuoso status as star soloists who improvised brilliantly over the background riffs of the big bands' "sidemen." Some of the misplaced values of any star system were evident in this development of the swing era, as the star performers seemed to be trying to play as fast or as high, or both, as possible. One thinks of several musicians associated with the Benny Goodman band during this period: the trumpeter Harry James (1916–83), who was celebrated for machine-gun-like velocity in such pieces as *The Flight of the Bumblebee,* and whose high notes were to be exceeded only later by the stratospheric "screech trumpet" of Maynard Ferguson, star soloist with the huge, colorful band of Stan Kenton (1911–79); the drummer Gene Krupa, whose sweat-drenched head and body, behind a blizzard-like flurry of drumsticks flailing an ever-larger battery of instruments, became a familiar swing-era photo image; and the vibraphonist Lionel Hampton (b. 1909), whose natural taste and invention were often left behind in response to his public's demands for sheer virtuosity. Hampton, along with another black, the pianist Teddy Wilson (1912–86), was employed by Goodman to play in small groups that alternated with the big band (and made recordings of their own), thus initiating a breakdown of "segregated" jazz.[15]

One could claim a special kind of virtuosity for Duke Ellington in the late 1930s and 1940s in his virtually unique role as a *composer* in the jazz world. Improvisation, as we have seen, remained crucial to jazz expression (and it continued to be crucial in the Ellington band's work, with the help of such fine improvisers as alto saxophonist Johnny Hodges, trumpeter Cootie Williams, and tenor saxophonist Ben Webster); and composerly skills were required, as we have also seen, in preparing the necessary arrangements for the big bands. But no one before Ellington—and few after him—had such a far-sighted vision of the jazz orchestra (his was a fifteen-piece ensemble by 1940, with six brass, five reeds, and four rhythm) as a challenging, malleable "instrument" with an infinite potential for sonic variety; no one had Ellington's gifts for conceptual creativity; and no one had Ellington's capacity for molding his jazz conceptions into freshly shaped and convincing compositions. As Gunther Schuller has summarized in his *TNGDAM* article on Ellington,

> Ellington is generally regarded as the most important composer in jazz history. . . . The exact number of his compositions is unknown, but is estimated at about 2000. [He] was one of the first musicians to concern himself with composition and musical form in jazz—as distinct from improvisation, tune writing, and arranging.

"Composition," in this context has of course a special meaning: Ellington was celebrated for embodying his conceptions in arrangements that were worked out during rehearsals and not always fully written down and that were inspired by, and expressly intended for, the musicians of his orchestra. And as Schuller writes, "Ellington's relentless productivity makes an over-

---

[15] A good example of the crowd-pleasing, blazing virtuosity discussed in this paragraph is *Flying Home,* a riff-based showcase for improvising soloists by Sid Robin, Benny Goodman, and Lionel Hampton, as recorded in 1942 by Hampton and his own orchestra (*NW* 261:s1/1); note especially the concluding dialogues between Hampton on vibes and the screech trumpet of Joe Newman.

view of his work virtually impossible. [And] serious study of Ellington's oeuvre has also been hampered by an almost total absence to date of his orchestral music in published form." But no one can doubt the composerly mastery of the musician who created such works as *Azure* (1937), *New East St. Louis Toodle-Oo* (1937; on *SCCJ*:s6/5), *Concerto for Cootie* (1940; on *SCCJ*:s6/7), *Ko-Ko* (1940; on *SCCJ*:s7/2), or *Never No Lament* (*Don't Get Around Much Anymore*) (1940).

With such abundant virtuosity, ·of various sorts, on hand, and with a transcontinental popularity bred in radio stations, recording studios, and on the stages of movie houses (where swing bands appeared increasingly "in person"), jazz began to be more than just a functional music to dance to or to drink to: it became a concert music as well. In 1938, Goodman's band appeared in concert at New York's Carnegie Hall; since that time, jazz as concert music has become commonplace and the balance between its use as utilitarian music and as a new kind of art-music has swung increasingly toward the latter.

THE MUSICAL AND THE POP SONG

With the rapid rise of sound films, during the 1930s, to a favored position among public entertainment media, the Broadway musical was threatened by the film musical of Hollywood, which could lavish more money on a single show and thus produce even more star-studded, eye-popping, mind-boggling spectaculars than Ziegfeld had offered in his Follies. Musically, however, the Hollywood musical offered nothing new. Nor did the theater musical of the 1930s immediately strike out on any new paths. Nevertheless, it tended to give increasing emphasis to the dramatic element and to span in its songs a greater range of emotional and psychological expression. And now and then, some of the social preoccupations of other American arts (and music) were visible in it, as in Harold Rome's *Pins and Needles* (1937), the opening number of which (*Sing Me a Song of Social Significance*) ushered onstage a cast drawn entirely from theater classes of the International Ladies' Garment Workers Union. (It became a kind of theme song of the political left during the era).

Among the musical comedy figures to be lured to Hollywood were the Gershwins, who left New York for California after *Porgy and Bess* (see p. 205). They seemed on the way to a series of successful film musicals (beginning with *Shall We Dance* and *A Damsel in Distress*; both 1937) when the composer died of a brain tumor at the age of thirty-eight. (*The Goldwyn Follies*, for which Gershwin had planned to compose a full-scale ballet under the working title of *The Swing Symphony*, was released posthumously in 1938; it included four Gershwin songs, among them the ineffably sweet *Love Walked In*.)

The other top musical comedy team, Rodgers and Hart, maintained their successful collaboration. They began the decade with a score for *Simple Simon* (1930), which included the poignant *Ten Cents a Dance*, about a dime-a-dance "hostess" in a Depression-era public ballroom. Later musicals by them that were outstanding for their songs were *Babes in Arms* (1937), *The Boys from Syracuse* (1983), and—outstanding also for its unwonted dramatic weight and development of character (that of a "perfect heel")— *Pal Joey* (1940).

The 1930–45 period saw the major successes in the lyric theater of Cole Porter (1891–1964). Unlike Gershwin or Rodgers, Porter wrote both the lyrics and music of his songs. A Yale University graduate (and later a student of music at both Harvard and the Schola Cantorum in Paris), a *bon vivant* with an independent income and a fondness for residence in both Paris and Venice, Porter wrote songs with mordantly witty lyrics married to music of often brittle and always sophisticated charm. He was an ironic, sometimes caustic spokesman for the pre-jet-set, *New Yorker*-reading, up-to-the-minute urbanites who knew a good *double entendre* when they heard one—whether verbal (*Let's Do It*, from the show *Paris* of 1928; *Katie Went to Haiti*, from *Du Barry Was a Lady* of 1939) or both verbal and musical (*But in the Morning, No*, also from *Du Barry*; the song is a gavotte, with a wicked quotation of a musical phrase from *The Star-Spangled Banner*). Blues inflections in Porter's earlier songs (*What Is This Thing Called Love?* of 1929) are cast in swing-style rhythms in the later ones (*It's De-Lovely*, from *Red, Hot and Blue* of 1936; *Most Gentlemen Don't Like Love*, from *Leave It to Me* of 1938).

Porter's thorough musical training shows up in various ways in his songs. To point only to his two most famous ones: in *Begin the Beguine* (from *Jubilee*, 1935) it allows him to control a song of extraordinary length (108 measures) and unique form; in *Night and Day* (from *The Gay Divorce*, 1932) it lies behind the unusual chromaticism and tonal plan, the unconventional form, and the cleverly offset repeated-note monotony.[16] At another level, that of the musical as a whole, Porter was to reveal this thorough musical knowledge, along with an innately elegant and witty personality, in his later (and perhaps greatest) musical, *Kiss Me, Kate* (1948), based on Shakespeare's *The Taming of the Shrew*—even though its individual songs did not become classics of the popular genre.

---

[16] Pianist-composer Leo Smit has noted the resemblance between the chorus theme of *Night and Day* and Schumann's song *Die Lotosblume* (and similar echoes of European art-music in other Porter songs) in a provocative little essay on "The Classic Cole Porter," *Saturday Review*, December 25, 1971.

A few other composers deserve mention here as writers of songs or musicals that are striking in one way or another. Harold Arlen (1905–86) is considered by some critics to be in every way the peer of Gershwin.[17] *Stormy Weather* (1933) suggests the flexibility of Arlen's phrase lengths (in a field tyrannized by four-measure fragments); *Over the Rainbow* (from the film *The Wizard of Oz* of 1939) seemed to be tailor-made for the wide-eyed yearning innocence of the young Judy Garland; *Blues in the Night* (from the movie of the same title, 1941) and *That Old Black Magic* (1942) each have unique qualities. Vincent Youmans (1898–1946) has proved to have remarkable staying power: his 1925 hit musical, *No, No, Nanette*, had a successful revival in the early 1970s (see p. 203, footnote 8); *Tea for Two* was its top song. Kurt Weill (1900–50), who had come to the United States as a refugee in the mid-1930s, put his experience in German musical theater to good use in several Broadway musicals, most notably *Lady in the Dark* (1941) and the virtually operatic *Street Scene* (1946). But *Street Scene*—and, no less, a work like Porter's *Kiss Me, Kate*—might never have been possible without a musical of 1943 that set a new standard for the genre. This was *Oklahoma!*, a collaboration between Richard Rodgers and his second partner, Oscar Hammerstein II. It had excitingly original choreography by Agnes de Mille that synthesized ballet movement and square-dance figures. The artfully folkish work brought plot, music, and dance into such a tightly knit whole that some believed themselves witnessing a new form of American vernacular opera.

Another composer identified with musicals of the 1930s (and others earlier and later) must be mentioned here, although he never wrote one. This is Robert Russell Bennett (1894–1981), one of the early students of Nadia Boulanger. Bennett dominated the field of orchestral arrangements of musicals from Kern's *Show Boat* (1927) through Lerner and Loewe's *Camelot* (1960); among some three hundred shows for which he provided adroit orchestrations that set the highest of standards were the Gershwins' *Of Thee I Sing*, *Oklahoma!*, *Kiss Me, Kate*, Rodgers and Hammerstein's *South Pacific*, and Lerner and Loewe's *My Fair Lady*.

BIBLIOGRAPHICAL NOTES

Eric Salzman's "*Modern Music* in Retrospect," *PNM*, II/2 (Spring–Summer 1964), 14–20, analyzes the American musical mood of 1924–46 as revealed in the pages of the lively journal *Modern Music*; the magazine's longtime editor, Minna Lederman, takes us behind the scenes (and includes many substantial

[17] Alec Wilder, *American Popular Song* . . . *1900–1950* (New York: Oxford University Press, 1972).

excerpts from articles) in her memoir *The Life and Death of a Small Magazine: (Modern Music, 1924–1946)*, ISAMm 18 (1983). Copland's *Our New Music* (New York: McGraw-Hill Book Company, 1941) or the relevant chapters in its revision under the title *The New Music 1900–1960* (New York: W. W. Norton, 1968) remains valuable as a view of things looking back from 1941; the anthology edited by Cowell, *American Composers on American Music* (1933; 2nd ed. New York: Frederick Ungar Publishing Co., 1962), is similarly valuable as a view looking forward from 1933. Thomson's *The State of Music* (1939; rev. ed. New York: Vintage Books, 1962) is concerned with the aesthetic and economic ways and means of the American composer.

Thomson's *Virgil Thomson* (New York: Alfred A. Knopf, 1966; repr. New York: Da Capo Press, 1977) is a deliciously written autobiography, superseding the biographical half of *Virgil Thomson: His Life and Music* (New York: T. Yoseloff, 1959) by Kathleen Hoover and John Cage; Cage's incisive analysis of the music remains, however, by far the best account. There is still no convincing monograph on Roy Harris, and the best writing on Marc Blitzstein is by the British author Wilfrid Mellers, in Chapter X of his *Music in a New Found Land* (New York: Alfred A. Knopf, 1966). Mellers is sympathetic to both the art and ideology of Blitzstein; since both are revealing of a major theme of the 1930s, his discussion is especially valuable.

We still await major life-and-works monographs on most of the composers cited in this chapter (among them Sessions, Porter, Douglas Moore, William Schuman, and Ross Lee Finney); Howard Pollack's *Walter Piston* (Ann Arbor: UMI Research Press, 1982) and Dan Stehman's *Roy Harris: An American Pioneer* (Boston: Twayne Publishers, 1984) are exceptions. Sessions's thoughtful and revealing essays on music have been edited by a sometime student and long-time colleague, Edward T. Cone, in *Roger Sessions on Music: Collected Essays* (Princeton, NJ: Princeton University Press, 1979). A fresh and knowledgeable view of Barber as composer is offered by Hans Heinsheimer in "Samuel Barber: Maverick Composer," *Keynote*, IV/1 (March 1980), 7–11; Barbara Heyman is at work on a promising City University of New York Ph.D. dissertation.

Apart from the two surveys of jazz cited in the bibliographical notes of Chapter 8, the literature on jazz of the 1930s and early 1940s, though vast, is very uneven. Frank Tirro's book *Jazz: A History* (New York: W. W. Norton, 1977), severely criticized on some counts, is perhaps strongest on the swing era (and that of the later bop style). The Macmillan Jazz Master Series includes Rex Stewart's *Jazz Masters of the Thirties* (1972) and Ira Gitler's *Jazz Masters of the Forties* (1966). The Smithsonian Collection's four long-playing albums of music by Duke Ellington's orchestra (*Duke Ellington 1938* and similarly titled collections from 1939, 1940, and 1941) include long and exhaustive liner notes by, respectively, Gunther Schuller, James Patrick, Larry Gushee, and Gary Giddins. Lewis Porter's *Lester Young* (Boston: Twayne Publishers, 1985) is a fine style study. Ross Russell's *Jazz in Kansas City and the Southwest* (Berkeley: University of California Press, 1971) is useful.

Richard Rodger's *Musical Stages* (New York: Random House, 1975) is a pleasant autobiography. Robert Kimball's *Cole* (New York: Holt, Rinehart and Winston, 1971) is definitive on the composer's life and lyrics but hardly mentions his music as such; Kimball has also meticulously edited *The Complete Lyrics of Cole Porter* (New York: Alfred A. Knopf, Inc., 1983) and, with Dorothy Hart, *The Complete Lyrics of Lorenz Hart* (New York: Alfred A. Knopf, Inc., 1986).

part four

Since World War II

TEN

THE POST-WAR DECADES: INTO THE 1960S

The period immediately following World War II, like that after World War I, was one of marked progressivism and rapid development in American music, due partly to a rising prosperity that increased the sources of patronage and the audience for music. With the introduction in 1948 of the long-playing microgroove recording, the cost of records diminished and sales boomed; the phonorecord became almost as important a medium for new music as the concert (more important, for some music), and assessment of a composer's "success" tended more and more to be based, not on the number of his or her compositions that were published, but on how many were recorded. Giant philanthropic entities like the Ford and Rockefeller foundations, and smaller music-oriented ones like the Koussevitzky Foundations or the Martha Baird Rockefeller Fund, as well as state, county, municipal, and (by 1965) federal organizations in support of the arts, provided new money for composers' commissions and performance organizations. The audience grew spectacularly: a favorite statistic of the 1950s was one demonstrating that more Americans went to concerts than to baseball games. By the early 1960s, arts centers were being constructed in city after city, the most extensive one being Lincoln Center for the Performing Arts in New York, a complex of buildings housing one major concert hall and several smaller ones; two theaters for drama, ballet, musical comedy, and even opera; a library-museum; and a huge opera house (the new home of the Metropolitan). Despite the advent of television, radio continued to appeal to a large audience, and a 1955 survey revealed that about 1000 radio stations broadcast a weekly total of 13,795 hours of "concert music" (i.e., neither jazz nor pop music), an average of almost fourteen hours per week per station. The number of composers increased dramatically. So did the number of performance organizations: one survey[1] reported that whereas in 1939 there had been about 600 symphony orchestras in the United States, by 1967 there were 1436, more than half of the world's 2000 such orchestras; there were 918 opera-producing groups; there were, in American schools, some 68,000 instrumental music organizations (of which 50,000 were wind bands).

This lively, developing scene in the musical culture at large was reflected in musical composition as well. The post-war period saw various trends of widely diverging character, in rapid evolution.

TWELVE-TONE COMPOSITION AND RELATED METHODS; ELLIOTT CARTER

One striking development was the widespread adoption by many composers of the twelve-tone technique of composition. Viewed before the war as the more or less private method of composers associated directly at one time or another with Arnold Schoenberg, the techniques of organizing music on the basis of a row or series of the twelve chromatic tones now came to be used by a majority of young American composers (like their European contemporaries). Some older ones as well, who before the war had not practiced row technique at all, began to do so in the late 1940s.

Reflecting this trend was the belated recognition of a composer like Wallingford Riegger, who had long utilized serial technique but had to wait until its general adoption before gaining the esteem of the musical community, as embodied in the New York Music Critics Circle prize awarded for his Third Symphony (1948). Typical of the Americans who had grown into twelve-tone technique from other directions than tutelage by Schoenberg, Riegger's application of it, from his earliest examples (*Three Canons for Woodwinds*, 1931, and *Dichotomy*, 1931–32), was anything but doctrinaire. In the Third Symphony, a twelve-tone row is the main source of the first movement's thematic material (Example 10-1; the oboe theme—[b] in

[1] *Concert Music USA, 1968* (New York: Broadcast Music, Inc., 1968).

the example—exposes the entire row), but the development section of the quasi-sonata structure abandons the row, reverting to chromatic clusters of a sort found in many other works by Riegger, e.g., his *Music for Brass Choir* (1948–49). The second movement of the Third Symphony is not row-based at all, and the last movement's passacaglia and fugue subjects are both seven-tone themes, not twelve-tone (although they are ultra-chromatic). A work like the one-movement Woodwind Quintet, or to give it its title as published in Germany, *Bläserquintett*, Op. 51 (1952; recorded on *NW* 285:s1/2), is so accessible in its peppery vigor and its perfectly idiomatic writing, full of a telegraphic chatter especially congenial to wind players, that its being full of rather rigorous canons and serial chromaticism is hardly even noticed.

EXAMPLE 10-1. W. Riegger, Symphony No. 3, first-movement row-based themes. Copyright 1949 Associated Music Publishers, Inc. Used by permission. (a) "Motto," measures 1–4. (b) First-group theme, first statement, measures 4–6. (c) First-group theme, climax, measures 64–68. (d) Recapitulation, "Quasi fugato," measures 213–16.

Two older European-born composers with twelve-tone experience also rose to prominence shortly after World War II: Ernest Krenek (b. 1900) and Stefan Wolpe (1902–72). Though a prolific composer, Krenek's impact on American music was felt more through his teaching and his didactic works, especially the books *Music Here and Now* (originally *Über neue Musik*; English translation published 1939) and *Studies in Counterpoint Based on the Twelve-Tone Technique* (1940). Wolpe, in America from 1938, was to influence a number of young Americans through his music per se, which proposed many new extensions of the tone-row technique. Like that of Webern (with whom he had worked briefly in 1933), Wolpe's music invited a new method of listening based on the perception of intervals rather than melodic "themes" or harmonic "chords," let alone larger-dimension relationships between chords; a fairly brief work that is particularly rewarding along these lines is *Form* (1959) for piano (recorded on *NW* 308:s2/1).

Among the mature Americans who gradually came to incorporate dodecaphonic principles in their music were Roger Sessions, Aaron Copland, Ross Lee Finney, a whole "Stravinsky school," and Hugo Weisgall.

Sessions's increasingly chromatic style of the 1930s and 1940s had led him to the brink of row usage. In the most natural way, he began viewing his ideas as susceptible to tone-row abstraction: "As a result of the fact that the opening theme [of the Sonata for Violin Solo, 1953] contained twelve different tones, and seemed to go naturally on that basis, I caught myself using the twelve-tone system."[2] Thus Sessions's twelve-tone music *sounded* hardly different from his pre-twelve-tone music. It retained the dense texture; the proliferation of contrapuntal filigree-work; the lengthy, non-repetitive and usually non-sequential melodic line; and the traditional Classic-Romantic expressive gestures of his earlier music. It also retained a high seriousness, a loftiness, that proved generally forbidding to audiences and made Sessions more a composers' composer than anyone else of his generation. Perhaps most accessible among his later compositions are *The Idyll of Theocritus* (1954), for soprano and orchestra, and the work many consider his masterpiece, the cantata *When Lilacs Last in the Dooryard Bloom'd* (1970) to Whitman's text responding to Abraham Lincoln's death: the critic Michael Steinberg has written of this work (in an essay accompanying the recording, *NW* 296), "Projecting the poetry now in simple chordal declamation, now in the long, high-arched melodies of which he is the master, [Sessions] conveys wonderfully the feel and variety of Whitman's lines."

Copland first essayed serial technique, tentatively and not without a certain stiffness of effect, in his Piano Quartet (1950), more masterfully in his Piano Fantasy (1952–57). In the Fantasy a ten-note row is the basis; the other two chromatic notes (E, G♯) are reserved for special use as a kind of cadence-interval. In fact, the work may be heard tonally as being in or about E major. Neither the Fantasy nor the Quartet, nor the later *Connotations* for orchestra (1962), make use of folk or popular materials; even so, they are transparently the work of the composer of *Appalachian Spring* and *Rodeo*. In this connection, Copland had some sensible things to say about the impact (or lack of it) of twelve-tone usage on a composer's style and the expressive content of his music:

    [2] Edward T. Cone, "Conversation with Roger Sessions," *PNM*, IV/2 (Spring-Summer 1966), 40.

To describe a composer as a twelve-toner these days is much too vague. . . .
Twelve-toneism is nothing more than an angle of vision. Like fugal treatment,
it is a stimulus that enlivens musical thinking. . . . It is a method, not a style.[3]

Finney had been a student not only of Nadia Boulanger (in 1927–
28) but also (in 1931–32) of Alban Berg, along with Schoenberg and Webern
one of the first twelve-tone composers; not until about 1950, however, did
Finney interest himself in serial technique. I have already mentioned (see
pp. 220) his interest in the American musical past; this was expressed through
a forceful, masculine style in a music distinctly tonal, rhythmically energetic,
and neo-Classic in formal principles. With his String Quartet No. 6 (1950)
Finney began to work with tone-rows, but with the explicit aim of reconciling
them with larger plans of tonal organization, such as architectonic design of
tonal centers and aspects of functional directive harmony. Another of his
concerns in the 1950s was with arch forms and other symmetrical or circular
plans, as in the Sixth and Seventh Quartets. The latter (1955) he thought of
as resembling a figure eight:

> Like a skater, the first movement starts at the mid-point, then circles out,
> returning to the beginning, using the pitches in reverse order but making
> different music with them. The second (final) movement accomplishes figur-
> atively the opposite sweep, and the quartet ends in the center with the theme.[4]

Such "spatial" visions of music, derived perhaps from the various reversible
and invertible, horizontal (linear) and vertical (harmonic) points of view in
twelve-tone method, were becoming increasingly common during the 1950s.
     Among other mature composers who, after many years of lack of
interest in Schoenberg's method, adopted it suddenly and absorbed it into
their individual styles, were some identified as a "Stravinsky school." These
were mainly former pupils of Boulanger and included Louise Talma (b. 1906),
Arthur Berger (b. 1912), Ingolf Dahl (1912–70), and Irving Fine (1914–62).[5]
At the same time that Stravinsky approached row composition (via Renaissance counterpoint) in his *Cantata* (1952) and turned definitively to
dodecaphony in the mid-1950s, these composers began to espouse the twelve-

---

     [3] "Fantasy for Piano," *New York Times*, October 20, 1957.
     [4] The description is by Leslie Bassett (b. 1923), a former pupil and later colleague of
Finney and a Pulitzer Prize-winning composer in his own right, writing in the program booklet
for the University of Michigan School of Music's 1966 Festival of Contemporary Music.
     [5] Two works suggesting the appropriateness of relating these composers to Stravinsky,
stylistically, are the *Concertino a tre* (1946) by Dahl (*NW* 281:s2/2) and the *Childhood Fables
for Grownups* (1954–55) by Fine (four songs from the two sets recorded on *NW* 300:s2/4-7).
The transparent elegance of Dahl's instrumental writing; the convincing if surprising contours
and rhythms of Fine's settings of Gertrude Norman's witty poems; and the biased, off-center
rhythmic torque of both men's music speaks clearly for their admiration and absorption of the
"neo-Classic" Stravinsky.

tone idea. As with Sessions and Copland, its use by them hardly affected their personal idioms although it distinctly reduced their tendency to neo-Classical formal structures.

Twelve-tone procedures and a style akin to the Viennese expressionists were heard in several operas of the 1950s and 1960s by Hugo Weisgall (b. 1912), a former pupil of Sessions. A cultivated litterateur, Weisgall found libretto material in plays by Wedekind (*The Tenor*, 1950), Strindberg (*The Stronger*, 1952), Pirandello (*Six Characters in Search of an Author*, 1956), Yeats (*Purgatory*, 1958), and Racine (*Athaliah*, 1963). Musically, all are intense, densely packed works; *Six Characters*, leavened by wit and melodrama, has the most subtle and penetrating characterization, sensitive balancing of voices and orchestra, and theatrical presence.

Related to the intense, near-expressionist atmosphere of Weisgall's operas is the music of three other composers, all of whom felt the impact of Schoenberg's ideas or his music in significant ways. Leon Kirchner (b. 1919) studied with both Schoenberg and Sessions, and although he did not adopt the twelve-tone method, his music carries on their highly expressive, ultra-chromatic manner. George Rochberg (b. 1918) tended to move with the vanguard stylistically: after works of the 1940s in various neo-tonal manners, the *Twelve Bagatelles* for piano (1952) were twelve-tone pieces; dedicated to Luigi Dallapiccola, they reflect that Italian composer's lyrical and finely ordered style. Ben Weber (1916–79) also wrote a music of lyric grace; characteristic is his *Symphony on Poems of William Blake* (1950), for baritone and orchestra. The work of all three composers during this period suggested that for them the anti-Romantic struggle was over, its issues dead. As Rochberg put it in 1963: "Now that the question arises on all sides: after abstractionism, what next? the answer rings out clearly: the 'new romanticism.' "[6] (As we shall see, this was a prophetic declaration, made a decade or so before the fact.)

By about 1960, the composer whose music, though not twelve-tone, seemed most sovereignly to embody these attitudes of an urgent expressivity; of careful, considered organization of highly chromatic pitch materials; and of high seriousness and even "monumentality" was Elliott Carter (b. 1908). Carter was a "second generation" pupil of Boulanger (from 1932 to 1935) after working under Piston at Harvard. (The mastery of craft he owed to these master teachers is exemplified by his setting, dating from 1937, of Robert Herrick's *To Music*, appropriately reminiscent of English unaccompanied madrigal style; recorded on NW 219:s1/2.) More important in his later development were his close association with Ives and Ives's music, certain procedures in Debussy's music that suggested to him unusual modes

---

[6] Quoted in Alexander Ringer, "The Music of George Rochberg," *MQ*, LII (1966), 414.

of "musical logic" (change, process, evolution), and his unshaken belief in the musical work as *communication* between composer and listener. Writing slowly and fastidiously, Carter first achieved in his Piano Sonata (1945–46) that sense of a work's being *sui generis* that was typical of almost every composition by him thereafter. The sonata is in every way a work for a pianoforte; no transcription is imaginable, nor is any aspect of the piece derived from other instrumental idioms. Even the harmonic materials grow from the piano's special qualities of resonance and its sostenuto-pedal effects. Rhythmic complexities abound; at the time of the sonata's composition, Carter believed these realizable only in a soloist's work, but later he was to find the means to make them playable by ensembles. In two big, subdivided movements, the Piano Sonata is ever developmental; various ideas announced in the introduction (Example 10-2)—the conflict between B and A♯, the material in thirds, the rising arpeggio figure—are re-presented, but in constant flux. The scope of the work sonorously and formally is very grand; no earlier American piano sonata succeeds as well in realizing to the fullest the ideas it proposes.

EXAMPLE 10-2. E. Carter, Piano Sonata (New York: Mercury Music Corporation, 1948), measures 1–7. Quoted by permission.

With each of his major works following the Piano Sonata, Carter's musical conception seemed to grow larger, his mode of expression more commanding. The Sonata for Cello and Piano (1948); the three string quartets (1951, 1959, 1972); the Sonata for Flute, Oboe, Cello, and Harpsichord (1952); the Variations for Orchestra (1955–56); the Double Concerto for Piano and Harpsichord (1961); the Piano Concerto (1965)—all are "masterworks" in concept, aims, and realization. Carter usually took a long time to write a piece of music—there were no works premiered between the last two just mentioned, for instance—but each piece was a major event.

In this period, Carter's music was marked by an increasing richness of texture, an increasing "personalization" of instrumental voices, and an increasing complexity of rhythmic procedures. The Piano Concerto has passages with as many as seventy-two different parts proceeding simultaneously (a degree of density the composer referred to as "swamping"); what a leap from the movement in the earlier *Eight Etudes and a Fantasy* (1949), for woodwind quartet, that is written on one note only (although of course that was only a witty conceit)!

Carter's "personalization" or "personification" of instruments reflects his view that his scores are "scenarios, auditory scenarios, for performers to act out with their instruments." In the Second Quartet, each instrument is "like a character in an opera made up primarily of 'quartets.' The individuals of this group are related to each other in what might be metaphorically termed three forms of responsiveness: discipleship, companionship, and confrontation"; in the Piano Concerto, the solo piano "is in dialogue with the orchestral crowd, with seven mediators—a concertino of flute, English horn, bass clarinet, solo violin, viola, cello, and bass"—who serve as a kind of soothing Greek chorus between the sassy piano and the square orchestra.[7]

The increasing rhythmic complexity in Carter's mature works arose from his dissatisfaction with the limited range and modes of continuity in even the most "advanced" scores of Western music, and from his perception of the broader rhythmic repertory in such other music as Indian *talas*, Arabic *durub*, Balinese "tempi," and drum pieces of the African Watusi. While composing the Cello Sonata he worked out a manner of *evolving* rhythms and tempos, a constant change of pulse, based on a technique called by Richard Franko Goldman metric modulation—"a means of going smoothly, but with complete accuracy, from one absolute metronomic speed to another, by lengthening or shortening the value of the basic note unit."[8] This technique ensures the most precise temporal controls over a music in rhythmic flux while permitting the greatest degree of independence among the separate voices in Carter's favored contrapuntal textures. Example 10-3, from the sixth variation of the Variations for Orchestra, shows one use of the technique. Each six-measure period accelerates gradually from $\quarternote$ = 80 to $\quarternote$ = 240: as the cello breaks into triplet eighth notes at measure 301, the

---

[7] The three quotations of Carter's words are respectively from his "Shop Talk by an American Composer," *MQ*, XLVI (1960), 189–201; jacket notes for the Composers Quartet recording of his First and Second string quartets (Nonesuch H-71249); and an essay in *The Orchestral Composer's Point of View*, ed. R. S. Hines (Norman: University of Oklahoma Press, 1970), pp. 39–61. In the last essay, Carter offers revealing explanations of his techniques, as of the 1960s, for rhythmic and pitch organization.

[8] Richard Franko Goldman, "The Music of Elliott Carter," *MQ*, XLIII (1957), 161. David Schiff, in his masterly study of *The Music of Elliott Carter* (London: Eulenburg Books; New York: Da Capo Press, 1983), p. 26, points out that the term "is slightly misleading, because the metre does not really change," and he says that Carter now prefers the term "tempo modulation."

viola begins the theme again in quarters, at the initial ♩ = 80 tempo. The undulating, fluid effect of wavelike overlappings of voices at different tempos is unique; it suggests Carter's extraordinary rhythmic imagination, apparent in every work. Example 10-3 can also suggest the thoroughgoing chromaticism, not quite twelve-tone in organization, of Carter's mature style and its energetic, strongly directional melodic action, which contributes to the sense of dynamism and "expressivity" in his work.

EXAMPLE 10-3. E. Carter, Variations for Orchestra, measures 295–307. Copyright 1957 Associated Music Publishers, Inc. Used by permission.

Carter's later works continued to extend the boundaries of rhythmic inventiveness, "harmonic" structure (in the sense of plans of structural intervals and more complex simultaneities), and form (breaking down boundaries in that realm—as in the interlocked duos of the String Quartet No. 3 of 1971). They also became seemingly more spontaneous and somewhat more accessible: the textures were more aerated, and with pieces like the song cycle *A Mirror on Which to Dwell* (1975) and the setting of poems by Robert Lowell, *In Sleep, in Thunder* (1981), Carter returned to vocal music for the first time in many years. Bayan Northcott (in his *TNGDAM* article on Carter) summarizes the composer's chief achievement this way:

> His aim [has been] to complement the innovations of the earlier modern masters in the handling of pitch (Schoenberg), rhythm (Stravinsky), and texture (Varèse) with parallel developments in the domain of timing, through the large-scale integration of tempo relationships and harmonic backgrounds. . . . [He displays] a grasp of dynamic form comparable, among 20th-century composers, only with Berg.

SYSTEMATIC SERIAL COMPOSITION; MILTON BABBITT

Schoenberg's "method of composing with twelve tones which are related only with one another," as he called his serial technique of twelve-tone composition, was initially a substitute for the comprehensive principles of pitch organization of Classic-Romantic tonality, in which eleven of the twelve tones were related to the other (the "tonic"). The twelve-tone method sought to acknowledge fully the chromatic vocabulary developed in Western music by ensuring a continued and total chromaticism in the organization of pitch. However, just as tonality had affected aspects of music other than pitch, so did the new "atonal" method. More consciously than Schoenberg, Webern had explored these implications of serial technique. In a work like Webern's Symphony, Op. 21 (1928), the structure of the pitch row affects aspects of rhythm, dynamics, phrase-structure, counterpoint, orchestration, and over-all form; in the second movement, even the choice of row transpositions used in each variation derives from the shape of the pitch row itself. It was this logical extension of the serial principle that made Webern, not Schoenberg, the hero of a whole generation of composers after World War II, the "post-Webernites" of the 1950s, headed in Europe by the French composers Olivier Messiaen and Pierre Boulez and the German composer Karlheinz Stockhausen. However, even before these Europeans began working out the implications of Webern's later works, the American Milton Babbitt (b. 1916) was moving in a similar direction.

A trained mathematician, Babbitt saw not just a "method" in twelve-tone music but a real *system* (a concept denied by Schoenberg), and in the pitch row not just a "series" but an ordered *set*, in the definitive mathematical sense. As early as the mid-1940s, Babbitt was using the serial principle to structure durational and other nonpitch components of his music. He was also addressing himself to control of the two dimensions of pitch, horizontal-linear and vertical-harmonic, in such a way that every note—or to use a newer and more precise terminology, every pitch class (C, E♭, etc., the register not specified)—was not only a member of an unfolding linear set but also of another, related set, governing and in fact creating the vertical dimension. This kind of thinking led him to a study of the structure of twelve-tone sets themselves and to an extension of a principle advanced first by Schoenberg: that of "combinatoriality" (as Babbitt termed it), the combining of various forms of a set without note duplication between simultaneous hexachords (six-note series or half rows), or in short, the production of twelve-tone *aggregates*.

Babbitt developed further Schoenberg's discovery, formulating methods for constructing pitch sets that would be "semi-combinatorial" or "all-combinatorial." A semi-combinatorial set is so constructed that one of its transformations (besides its retrograde) can be transposed so that the first hexachord includes the same notes as the last hexachord of the original set; it can then be combined with that transposed version without destroying the ideal of total chromaticism. The all-combinatorial set is so constructed that *all* of its transformations and one or more of its transpositions achieve the same end. These sorts of sets open up vast possibilities for contrapuntal techniques that still maintain total chromaticism.

The earliest works by Babbitt to be based on these ideas were *Three Compositions for Piano* (1947), *Composition for Four Instruments* (1948), and *Composition for Twelve Instruments* (1948; revised 1954). In the first of the *Three Compositions*, the pitch set is an all-combinatorial set. Four forms only (and their retrogrades) are used; as Example 10-4 shows, various pairs of these may be combined without duplicating the pitch-content of corresponding hexachords (see any pairing of the A and B hexachords in the example). Constant rotation of the chromatic total in the music is ensured not only by consistent aggregate formations but also, in single voices, by

EXAMPLE 10-4. Pitch-set forms used in M. Babbitt, *Three Compositions for Piano,* No. 1.

following one set linearly with another whose first hexachord is the "opposite" of the one just completed: in the lower voice of measures 1-8, for example (see Example 10-5), there appear successively the prime form of the set at the "zero" level (P–O; A–B hexachord order), then the retrograde inversion at the first transposition (RI–1; A–B order), then the inversion at the seventh transposition I–7; A–B order: the order of successive set forms is constantly varied as the composition proceeds.

EXAMPLE 10-5. M. Babbitt, *Three Compositions for Piano* (Hillsdale, NY: Boelke-Bomart, Inc., 1957), No. 1, measures 1–8. Quoted by permission.

In addition to pitch, Babbitt "serializes" other components in this music: duration, dynamics, and the three-note chords characteristic of the work.

The numerical series 5 1 4 2 (= 12, or the number of sixteenth notes in a measure of $\frac{3}{4}$, which is the meter of the piece) is chosen as the prime form of a "durational set"; 2 4 1 5 is its retrograde, 1 5 2 4 its inversion, and 4 2 5 1 its retrograde inversion. The form of the movement, in six sections, is determined by the various uses of this set: in measures 1 through 8, it controls the grouping of even attacks (Example 10-6 [a]); in measures 9 through 18, the articulations between groups of even sixteenths (Example 10-6 [b]); in measures 20 through 28, accents and repeated notes (Example 10-6 [c]); in measures 29 through 48, temporal durations between attack points (Example 10-6 [d]). In measures 49 through 56 an effect of recapitulation is achieved by a return to the manner of measures 1 through 8.

It will be noticed that the "durational set" forms run parallel to those of the pitch set: when for example an RI form of the pitch set appears, it is associated with the 4 2 5 1 (RI) form of the "durational set" (see Example 10-6 [c]).

EXAMPLE 10-6. Use of the "durational set" in M. Babbitt, *Three Compositions for Piano*, No. 1.

Dynamics are also "serialized" in such a way as to reflect and confirm the serial ordering of pitch materials in the piece. The *mezzo piano* of measure 1 is associated with the prime form of the pitch set; *mezzo forte*, with the retrograde; *forte*, with the inversion; and *piano*, with the retrograde inversion. This holds true up to the "recapitulation" of measures 49 through 56, when the "dynamics set" is "transposed."

Finally, the three-note chords—or better, simultaneities (since the very term *chord* implies earlier tonal music)—that appear frequently in the composition reveal a serial approach: the register chosen for the notes of each—that is, the particular pitch assigned to each of the row's pitch classes—is determined by the following scheme:

$$
P = \begin{array}{cccc} 2 & 3 & 8 & 9 \\ 1 & 4 & 7 & 10 \\ 0 & 5 & 6 & 11 \end{array} \qquad R = \begin{array}{cccc} 9 & 6 & 5 & 2 \\ 10 & 7 & 4 & 1 \\ 11 & 8 & 3 & 0 \end{array}
$$

$$
I = \begin{array}{cccc} 0 & 5 & 6 & 11 \\ 1 & 4 & 7 & 10 \\ 2 & 3 & 8 & 9 \end{array} \qquad RI = \begin{array}{cccc} 11 & 8 & 3 & 0 \\ 10 & 7 & 4 & 1 \\ 9 & 6 & 5 & 2 \end{array}
$$

Thus, in measure 11 (Example 10-7) the upper part is an expression of the pitch set I–1 and the vertical ordering of each three-note group follows the I version of the "registral set" scheme just given; the lower part, built from the pitch set RI–1, forms its simultaneities according to the RI version of that scheme.

In his *Composition for Twelve Instruments*, Babbitt went further to integrate the pitch and durational components of his music by deriving a

EXAMPLE 10-7. Serial approach to three-note simultaneities in M. Babbitt, *Three Compositions for Piano*, No. 1, measure 11.

durational set from the pitch set and composing in terms not only of a twelve-*tone* system but of a twelve-*duration* system as well. Example 10-8 shows (a) the prime pitch set, with each note defined by its *order* number and its *pitch* number (the latter measured in semitones up from the first note); (b) the pitch set transposed up two semitones, thus altering the pitch numbers of the tones; and (c) the durational set, based on a sixteenth-note unit that corresponds to pitch set P–2.

EXAMPLE 10-8. Pitch and duration sets in M. Babbitt, *Composition for Twelve Instruments* (1948).

The musical expression in *Composition for Twelve Instruments* is one emphasizing single-impulse events; the pointillistic texture has been likened to a bank of multi-colored lights, of varied wattage, flashing on and off at different rates. Later works by Babbitt have demonstrated that other textures, other expressive qualities, are perfectly possible with his systematic serialism. *All Set*, for instance, written in 1957 for a Brandeis University arts festival, is scored for a seven-piece jazz ensemble and is based metrically, rhythmically, melodically, and even at some points harmonically on the style of the "progressive jazz" of the 1940s. Works for voice tend to have a frankly *espressivo* line, as in the song cycle *DU* (1951); *Two Sonnets*, for baritone, clarinet, viola, and cello (1955); and the *Composition for Tenor and Six Instruments* (1960). In these, duration is not serially organized, Babbitt believing that correct prosody should be the primary rhythmic determinant.

Nevertheless, various linked chains of pitch relationships exist in them, as can be heard in the opening measures of *DU*, which also can exemplify Babbitt's expressive, sensitively rhythmed and contoured vocal line, reminiscent of the lyric art of Webern.

"Wiedersehen," the first song of *DU*, is based on a set that is all-combinatorial and is furthermore an "all-interval" set, in that it can be presented in such a way that every possible interval within an octave occurs once, and only once (Example 10-9). Such a set ensures a variety of interval structures in the music and allows a linear deployment free from built-in symmetries and other form-dictating repetitions.

EXAMPLE 10-9. The all-interval set of M. Babbitt's *DU*.

The singer's first four phrases, each of three notes, expose the prime form of the set (Example 10-10). Each three-note phrase is accompanied by piano music with the nine other chromatic notes; vertical dotted lines in Example 10-10 show the four twelve-tone aggregates thus created. Within each aggregate, three-note interval structures are formed by voice and piano (circled in Example 10-10); they are the *same* structures within each aggregate; in the first aggregate, for example, the four interval structures ("molecules" might be an apposite word for them) are all based on the intervals of a major third (or its inversion, a minor sixth), a minor second (or major seventh), and a perfect fifth (or perfect fourth). Finally, the nature of the accompaniment is such that we hear it as having three "voices": a high-register voice beginning B–F♯–A, a middle-register voice (E–G–D), and a low-register voice (A♭–C♯–B♭). Tracing each of these voices through the excerpt, we discover that each is itself a twelve-tone set, related directly to the prime set of the singer. Moreover, within each of the four chromatic aggregates, each of the accompanying voices is a different form of the singer's three-note phrase: the piano's high-register "voice" is an intervallic retrograde, the middle-register voice an inversion, and the low-register voice a retrograde inversion. These linear relationships have been bracketed in Example 10-10.

Through such extensions of the serial principle, not only to both the horizontal and vertical dimensions of pitch but to other realms as well, Babbitt created music with a staggeringly complex network of inter-relationships. But not only are these relationships complex; they *are* the music. The interlocked components are inseparable, and it is no longer meaningful

EXAMPLE 10-10. M. Babbitt, *DU* (Hillsdale, NY: Boelke-Bomart, Inc., 1957), measures 1–5. Quoted by permission.

to speak of one, or to hear one, separate from the others; the music, approaching "total organization," demands total hearing.[9]

Babbitt has been second only to Schoenberg himself as formulator and codifier of serial concepts. He has also been an influential and much beloved teacher of younger composers, from bases at Princeton University and the Juilliard School. Among those who, taught by both Sessions and Babbitt, constitute what has been called a "Princeton school" are Peter Westergaard (b. 1931), Henry Weinberg (b. 1931), Donald Martino (b. 1931), Benjamin Boretz (b. 1934), and James K. Randall (b. 1929). Of these, Martino—who leavened his Princetonian serialism with Italianate lyricism through two years' study in Florence with Dallapiccola—has the broadest range compositionally; his *Seven Pious Pieces* (1972), a cappella settings of poems

---

[9] Some critics would add ". . . or none at all," claiming that *analyzing* such music is a more meaningful exercise than experiencing it aurally. Babbitt has countered this view in the article "Who Cares if You Listen?" (the title not of Babbitt's coinage), *High Fidelity Magazine*, VIII/2 (February 1958); reprinted under Babbitt's preferred title, "The Composer as Specialist," in *Esthetics Contemporary*, ed. Richard Kostelanetz (Buffalo, NY: Prometheus Books, 1978).

by Herrick (recorded on *NW* 210:s2/3), though atypical in some respects, exemplify his versatility and wit; more characteristic is the work that won him the Pulitzer Prize for 1974, *Notturno* for six players. Boretz distinguished himself as a theorist and editor: he was the prime mover and for many years chief editor of the journal *Perspectives of New Music* (1962–   ), considered by many as essentially a vehicle for the Princetonians' musical ideas.

ELECTROACOUSTIC MUSIC

Babbitt's interest in "total control" over musical materials led him perhaps inevitably to the medium of electroacoustic music, and in the late 1950s he became one of the directors of the first major American electronic music studio, co-sponsored by Princeton and Columbia universities and an outgrowth of the studio established at Columbia in 1953.

Electroacoustic music—music made or altered electrically (as opposed to acoustic music, made by mechanically vibrating or resonating bodies)— had a prehistory from the late nineteenth century and experiments arising out of early telegraphy. Effective composition of such music, however, had to await the development of reliable and easily handled recording techniques; essentially, it was only with the perfection of magnetic tape-recorder technology after World War II that electroacoustic music was of interest to many composers. Pioneers in *musique concrète* (composition from pre-recorded sounds, often sounds of nature or machinery, stored on tape, then electronically manipulated, reassembled, and retaped) were a few French composers, notably Pierre Henry, working in the Paris studios of the French national radio in the late 1940s. Pioneers in *elektronische Musik* (composition from electronically generated sound materials stored on tape, then—as with *musique concrète*—manipulated, reassembled, and retaped) were a few Germans, notably Herbert Eimert and Karlheinz Stockhausen, working in the Cologne studios of the West German national radio in the early 1950s. John Cage was the first American actually to prepare a piece on magnetic tape (*Imaginary Landscape No. 5*, 1951–52), but two other composers began about the same time to work systematically in tape-music composition: Otto Luening (b. 1900) and Vladimir Ussachevsky (b. 1911), both on the faculty of Columbia University.

Working singly and together, Luening and Ussachevsky had produced enough compositions by the fall of 1952 to present the first American tape-music concert (at the Museum of Modern Art in New York City). Luening's first tape pieces were *musique concrète* based on solo flute sounds: *Fantasy in Space, Low Speed*, and *Invention* (all 1952). Ussachevsky's early work culminated in *A Piece for Tape Recorder* (1956), which combined electronically generated sounds with pre-recorded sounds on file in a library of sound-on-tape maintained at the Columbia studio; some of the latter had been used for his earlier pieces *Sonic Contours* and *Underwater Waltz* (both 1952). The two composers collaborated in 1954 in two "concertos" for tape-recorded sounds and orchestra, *Rhapsodic Variations* and *A Poem in Cycles and Bells*, and in other works through the 1960s.

The basic equipment for these composers of early electroacoustic music consisted of two or more tape recorders; an electronic generator of sound signals, whether sine-wave (a fundamental pitch with no overtones), square-wave (fundamental with odd-numbered upper partial tones), or saw-tooth-wave (fundamental with all upper partials); a generator of noise, whether the hissing steam-like sound of "white noise" (an infinite number of signals over the entire range of the audible sound spectrum) or the cloud-like band of sound of "colored noise" (an infinite number of signals within a limited range of frequencies); various sound-filtering and reverberating devices; scissors, razor blade, splicing block, and a supply of magnetic tape. With such equipment the composer was in an extraordinary and unprecedented position—the same as that which painters, sculptors, and writers had always enjoyed—one permitting the artist to create directly and concretely in the desired medium, not having to submit to interpretation, through a different medium, by a performer.

Understandably, Edgard Varèse, who more than thirty years earlier had dreamed of "instruments obedient to [his] thought" and of music invigorated by science, turned enthusiastically to tape music, creating three major works in the new medium before his death. One was *Déserts* (completed 1954), for a group of winds, piano, and percussion instruments alternating with "organized sound" material on tape, in a big ABACABA form—A standing for the sections played by instruments; B for tape music based on raw sounds collected by Varèse in a foundry, a sawmill, and several factories; and C for tape music based on percussion-instrument sounds. The work seems wholly integrated; the electroacoustic interpolations simply broaden the expressive range of Varèse's "sound-mass" techniques of the 1920s, and the music has a power of almost terrifying dimension.

In 1957–58, working together with the architect Le Corbusier for the Brussels World's Fair pavilion of the Philips Corporation (a Dutch radio and electronic firm), Varèse composed *Poème électronique*. Here finally all his ideas of music as spatial, of sound as "living matter," could be realized. The work was planned for tape-recorded performance through some 425 loudspeakers arranged in 15 "tracks" and embedded in the looping curves of the ceiling and walls of Le Corbusier's building; the sound actually swept in great circles around and overhead, at different speeds and along various tracks simultaneously. Varèse composed the piece in a great variety of sounds, including a mysterious frictional sound originating in a tape recording of his rubbing his palms together, and also including the human voice, which lends an awesome presence to the work. In *Poème électronique* even more than in *Déserts*, he approached the realization of his vision for a work never finished (*Espace*)—an apocalyptic sound montage in space: "voices in the sky, filling all space, crisscrossing, overlapping, penetrating each other, splitting up, superimposing, repulsing each other, colliding, crashing together."[10]

At the early Columbia University studio, as elsewhere in the 1950s, electroacoustic-music composition was a tedious task, involving recording and re-recording sounds on magnetic tape, then manually splicing together bits of tape to really "compose" a work. A great step in reducing such laborious techniques was taken with the development by the Radio Corporation of America of an electronic sound synthesizer (originally designed for use in speech synthesis), an advanced model of which, the Mark II, was installed in the Columbia studio in 1959 as the keystone of a Columbia-Princeton Electronic Music Center under the direction of Luening, Ussachevsky, and Babbitt. The RCA Synthesizer allowed Babbitt (and others of his compositional persuasion) to pursue the ideal of a totally organized music, for it made possible the most precise control of not only the pitch components but also those of rhythm, dynamics, and timbre (including such details— seldom of primary concern to earlier composers of non-electronic music— as the "attacks" and "decays" of sounds). The result, in works by Babbitt like *Composition for Synthesizer* (1961) and *Ensembles for Synthesizer* (1964), was a music of great lucidity and unique sonorous and architectonic qualities (in striking contrast to the music of both Luening and Ussachevsky, which seldom lost sight of its non-electronic musical sources, or the music of Varèse, with its cosmic stridency and gestural dynamism).

Other works by Babbitt combined synthesized sound with live performance: *Vision and Prayer* (1961), *Philomel* (1964), and *Correspondences* (1967). In these a new vitality appeared. In *Vision and Prayer*, Dylan Thomas's poem is set against a wholly synthesized accompaniment; the voice moves from recitation through speech-song and back again. *Philomel*, a wondrously musical poem by John Hollander on the transformation into a nightingale of the ravished and speechless Philomela, is set by Babbitt for live voice, taped and electronically altered voice, and synthesized sound. Composed for the remarkable soprano Bethany Beardslee (whose performance is preserved on NW 307:s1), the music of *Philomel* is as precisely ordered and as full of structural subtleties as any of Babbitt's; at another level it is a profoundly moving, "expressive" work. One critic has remarked that Philomela's "final triumphant phrase [Example 10-11], her ultimate recognition of her vocal powers, celebrates Mr. Babbitt's new-found voice as well."[11] The later

[10] Quoted in Chou Wen-chung, "Varèse: A Sketch of the Man and His Music," *MQ*, LII (1966), 151–70.
[11] Richard F. French, in "Current Chronicle," *MQ*, L (1964), 382–88.

EXAMPLE 10-11. M. Babbitt, *Philomel*, conclusion (live voice part only). Copyright Associated Music Publishers, Inc. Used by permission.

Phonemena (1975), for soprano and tape or soprano and piano (both versions recorded on *NW 209*), is a playful encore piece dedicated "to all the girl singers I've known"; the text consists entirely of phonemes—twenty-four consonant sounds and twelve vowel sounds (numbers not haphazardly chosen but obviously related to serial structural concerns).

A grant from the Rockefeller Foundation enabled the Columbia-Princeton Center to invite many composers to use its facilities; in 1969, a survey listed some 225 compositions made at the center by more than 60 composers from 11 countries.[12] A few composers closely identified with the center (besides its directors) rose to special prominence. Walter (later Wendy) Carlos (b. 1939) produced the first "hit" of electronic music, the synthetically recomposed Baroque works on the best-selling recording *Switched-On Bach* (1968). Mario Davidovsky (b. 1934), originally from Argentina, began with some purely electronic studies (1961 and 1962) but then concentrated on an integration of electronic sounds with music for live performers, in a series of eight dialogue-like pieces entitled *Synchronism.* Jacob Druckman (b. 1928) also emphasized live/electronic confrontations in some brilliantly conceived, powerful, almost theatrical works like *Animus I* (trombone and tape; 1966), *Animus II* (female singer, percussionists, and tape; 1968), and *Animus III* (clarinet and tape; 1969). Charles Wuorinen (b. 1938), a virtuoso pianist and conductor (especially as co-director of the Group for Contemporary Music in New York from 1962 into the 1980s) and a prolific composer of non-electronic music, was able easily—like Babbitt—to turn his rigorously serial style to the electronic medium (*Orchestral and Electronic Exchanges*, 1965); his *Time's Encomium* (1968–69), commissioned by Nonesuch Records, won the 1970 Pulitzer Prize in music—the first one awarded to a wholly electronic work, existing only in recorded form.

Even if, as mentioned, the RCA Synthesizer marked a great step forward in reducing the laborious, time-consuming job of electronic com-

---

[12] See the list of "Compositions Created at the Center" in the brochure issued with the album *Columbia-Princeton Electronic Music Center Tenth Anniversary Celebration* (CRI-268; issued 1972).

position in a "classic" studio, it was a super-costly, bulky, and literally unique machine. However, during the mid-1960s, technologists aided by the invention of tiny transistors and solid-state circuitry developed smaller, less expensive, and easier-to-operate synthesizers. These were based on a principle of voltage control and consisted of a group of modules—sound generators, sound modifiers (filters, amplifiers, mixers, reverberators, and the like), control voltage generators, and control voltage processors. The first such modular synthesizers were those of Robert Moog, working in upstate New York, and Donald Buchla, of the San Francisco area; other makes—among them the ARP, the Putney, and the ElectroComp—were soon on the market. It is hard to say whether these small synthesizers came into existence out of composers' needs or whether their invention spurred composers into making electronic music—probably a bit of both. But by the early 1970s electronic-music studios built around Moog or Buchla or other modular equipment were to be found all across the country; electroacoustic-music composition had entered a new phase of widespread practice.

Some composers associated with this development should be mentioned. Morton Subotnick (b. 1933) was one of the founders of the pioneering San Francisco Tape Music Center and directed it from 1961 to 1965. He and other composers in the area—notably Pauline Oliveros (b. 1932) and Larry Austin (b. 1930)—actually collaborated with Buchla in the development of his synthesizer equipment. Subotnick's *Silver Apples of the Moon* (1967) symbolized the new status of electronic music and was in fact a "first": in a happy and (with hindsight) seemingly inevitable marriage of technology, commerce, and art, it was specifically commissioned by the enterprising firm of Nonesuch Records and was planned to fill the two sides of an LP record. A second Nonesuch commission, *The Wild Bull* (1968), and *Touch* (for Columbia Records; 1969) shared with *Silver Apples* Subotnick's fondness for lengthy sequential patterns and multiple ostinatos (arising partly, at least, out of characteristics of the Buchla equipment). The prolific Kenneth Gaburo (b. 1926) turned to the live/electronic medium in a series of compositions aptly entitled *Antiphony* (1958–84); among them *Antiphony III* (1962), composed at the Yale and University of Illinois studios, is a brilliant concerto-like work for sixteen voices and tape. Roger Reynolds (b. 1934), one of a lively group of composers in the San Diego area, moved beyond live/electronic antiphony into multi-media in *Ping* (1968), which calls for slide projections, film, and combined instrumental, *concrète*, and electronic sound in a highly personal realization of a story by Samuel Beckett. Reynolds's *Traces* (1969) is for piano, flute, cello, and six separate channels of taped sound (both *concrète* and electronic), so planned that a rich tapestry of combination tones, difference tones, and other by-products or "residues" (traces) of musical events is woven. The later *From Behind the Unreasoning Mask* (1975; recorded on NW 237:s1/1) suggests how the virtually infinite sonorous and timbral range of the new synthesizers stretched composers' ideas of the possibilities for *live* music: Reynold's piece is scored for only trombonist and percussionist (the latter aided by an assistant) plus four-channel pre-recorded tape, but the variety of the instrumentalists' sounds is immense, and the high incidence of silence among the sounds invites the ear to revel in them just as such.

The late 1950s saw the beginning of the use of digital computers to aid both the recording of music and its composition. Record manufacturers were slow to make commercial use of computers; only in the mid-1970s did some companies begin to put computers to work in the process of making master tapes. The first serious experiments in computer-aided composition were carried out, however, in 1955–56, by the composer-mathematician team of Lejaren Hiller (b. 1924) and Leonard Isaacson, working with an Illiac high-speed digital computer at the University of Illinois. Their first product was a four-movement *Illiac Suite* (1956) for string quartet, each movement entitled "Experiment," intended to show the compositional possibilities of one or another aspect of computer programming. Anything but radical in sound and structure, the *Illiac Suite* was more a technological breakthrough than anything else.

More fruitful than Hiller's approach were those of some other composers who developed methods for actually synthesizing sounds by means of computers. Early work was done at the Bell Telephone Company laboratories in New Jersey, where sound-synthesizing computer programs were developed by Max Mathews in 1957. By the mid-1960s these programs were the basis for computer-music composition in such academic studios as those at Stanford University, where John Chowning (b. 1934) was a pioneer, and Princeton University, where J. K. Randall produced a number of works, including *Quartets in Pairs* (1964), *Mudgett: Monologues by a Mass Murderer* (1965; for voice and computer), and *Lyric Variations* (1968; for violin and computer). The Princeton studio was also where Charles Dodge (b. 1942) composed *Earth's Magnetic Field* (1970), probably the first work of computer music to be commissioned (by Nonesuch Records).

EXPERIMENTAL MUSIC OF CHANCE AND INDETERMINACY; JOHN CAGE

At precisely the same time that composers of electroacoustic and computer music like Babbitt and Ussachevsky, Hiller and Dodge, were increasing the composer's personal control over musical materials and their realization in sound, an apparently opposite impulse was leading other composers in a different direction. In their music the will and determination of the composer were reduced: either they found ways of producing their music by chance or random methods (thus minimizing their role in the choice of the notes to be played or sung) or they produced not the actual note-symbols in ordered relationships but just musical raw material, to be ordered by the performer; for some works, not even the raw material was provided, only suggestions about the physical activity to initiate it or about the environment in which it was to take place.

Several adjectives have been used to define this music: *aleatory, indeterminate, chance, improvisational,* and *random* are some of them. The different connotations of each of these are subsumed, however, under the more general term *experimental,* in the precise meaning defined by John Cage: "An experimental action is one the outcome of which is unforeseen."[13] The "action" here is that of musical composition; the "outcome" is the musical performance. It is in this sense that the music to be discussed in this section is "experimental."

Undisputed leader of such experimental music from the early 1950s was Cage himself. In the summary of his compositional methods partially quoted previously (p. 232), Cage lists the post-war "paths my musical thought has taken" as these:

. . . composition using charts and moves thereon (1951); composition using templates made or found (1952–   ); composition using observation of imperfections in the paper upon which it is written (1952–   ); composition without a fixed relation of parts to score (1954–   ); composition indeterminate of its performance (1958–   ).

Underlying all these means for reducing his dominance over the musical experience and letting the music "happen"[14] was Cage's discovery in 1951 that there is no silence. Previously, he had organized his music on the assumptions that the opposite of sound was silence; that duration was the only characteristic of sound measurable in terms of silence; that therefore any valid musical structure (a work of sounds and silences) must be based not on frequency, as traditionally it had been, but on duration. Then one day Cage entered a soundproof and anechoic chamber, as silent as technologically possible. He heard two sounds, one high, one low; the engineer in charge explained that the high sound was his nervous system in operation, the low sound his blood circulating. Cage's reactions:

[13] "Composition as Process," three lectures given at Darmstadt in September 1958; reprinted in Cage, *Silence* (Middletown, CT: Wesleyan University Press, 1961), pp. 18–55.

[14] Cage's influence on the mixed-media, unmatrixed, often improvisational form of theater called Happenings was very great, following his organization at Black Mountain College in 1952 of an event involving painting, dance, piano playing, poetry, films, slides, phonorecordings, radios, and a lecture by himself. See Michael Kirby, *Happenings* (New York: E. P. Dutton, 1965).

The situation one is clearly in is not objective (sound-silence), but rather subjective (sounds only), those intended and those others (so-called silence) not intended. If, at this point, one says, "Yes! I do not discriminate between intention and non-intention," the splits, subject-object, art-life, etc., disappear, an identification has been made with the material, and actions are then those relevant to its nature, i.e.:

A sound does not view itself as thought, as ought, as needing another sound for its elucidation, as etc. . . .

A sound accomplishes nothing; without it life would not last out the instant.

Relevant action is theatrical (music [imaginary separation of hearing from the other senses] does not exist), inclusive and intentionally purposeless. . . .[15]

The most dramatic, certainly the most famous, application by Cage of these ideas is the work known as *4'33"*, a three-part piece for any instrument or combination of instruments; its score consists of the headings, "I," "II," and "III," each followed by the word "TACET" (for musicians, of course, an instruction to remain silent). In its premiere performance on August 29, 1952, the pianist David Tudor appeared and seated himself at the piano, stopwatch nearby; he indicated the beginning of each part of the piece by closing, the end by opening, the keyboard cover; and he played . . . nothing. (The performance took four minutes and thirty-three seconds, hence the title by which the work is known; it is in fact untitled, or rather, as Cage puts it in the score, "The title of this work is the total length in minutes and seconds of its performance.") But if the performer/s of *4'33"* make/s no intentional sounds, there are other sounds to be heard, and the audience, in the traditional listening situation of a recital, is invited to listen to them. As Tudor puts it, "It is one of the most intense listening experiences one can have. You really listen. You're hearing everything there is. Audience noises play a part in it. It is cathartic—four minutes and thirty-three seconds of meditation, in effect."[16]

Cage could hardly repeat himself as a composer of "silent" music. From the theoretical and philosophical position so vividly dramatized by *4'33"*, and aided by certain ideas of Zen Buddhism and other Oriental and speculative sources, he sought to find other ways to remove himself—his memory, taste, will—from the act of "composition" in a traditional sense. The "charts and moves thereon [and the] templates made or found" that he

[15] From an article of 1955, reprinted as "Experimental Music: Doctrine" in *Silence*, pp. 13–17. The bracketed phrase is Cage's.

[16] Quoted in Harold Schoenberg, "The Far-out Pianist," *Harper's* CXXX (June 1960), 49. The original version of *4'33"*, which shows its relation to earlier (non-experimental) music by Cage and is different from the published "score," is reproduced in *Source*, I/2 (July 1967), 46–55.

mentions were themselves prepared by chance operations, typically by tossing coins and translating the results into visual diagrams according to an
intricate system based on the Chinese *I Ching* (Book of Changes); the diagrams were then translated into conventional notation. Such was the composing
method for *Music of Changes* (1951) for piano (Parts III and IV on *NW*
214:s2). Coin tossing together with notational "decisions" made on the basis
of the inevitable minute imperfections on the surface of music paper provided
the basis for the score of *Music for Piano 21–52* (1955), two groups of sixteen
pieces that may be played alone or together in an indeterminate time span;
the duration and dynamics of individual notes are free.

Another score-producing method was to suggest the notes by dropping an *I Ching*-derived stencilled diagram onto graph paper and then plotting
the result in "graph notation," from which the performer might make any
specific sonorous version he wished. *Music for Carillon [No. 1]* (1952) is an
example: Cage published it in graph notation and also in two different conventionally notated versions. For the *Concert for Piano and Orchestra* (1957–
58) there is no master score; indeed, the work may be realized as a piano
solo (the pianist being "free to play [from a "book" of eighty-four different
kinds of composition] any elements of his choice, wholly or in part, and in
any sequence") or as a chamber work, a piece for symphony orchestra, one
for piano with orchestra, etc. This is a work, in other words, not only "without
a fixed relation of parts to score" but also "indeterminate of its performance."
Together with the *Concert* may be performed an *Aria* (1958), in which Cage
leaves many aspects of performance undetermined. The *Aria* may also be
sung with the tape-music piece *Fontana Mix* (1958), itself experimental in
that the "sound sources, their mechanical alteration, changes of amplitude,
frequency, overtone structure, the use of loops [for continuous repetition of
taped material], special types of splicing, etc. may be determined" by the
producer from graph-notated drawings and point-speckled transparent sheets.
The voice-tape montage "is intended seriously to be fun, to provoke the
audience to audible response, to break down the standard notion of performance in one dimension and an audience confined silently in another
dimension."[17]

With such a conception, Cage had reached that point of indeterminacy
where composer, performer, and listener meet and mingle in producing the
musical experience. The means for obtaining such an experience were refined
in such later works as *Theatre Piece* (1960), and Cage attained his ideal of
non-self-expression as a composer: "I have no desire to improve on creation."[18] The paradox of that sentence is that in it lies perhaps the *most*
creative aspect of Cage's "many paths": a profound humanism aimed at

[17] Peter Yates, "Music," *Arts and Architecture*, LXXVII/7 (July 1960), 4, 32.
[18] Quoted in *Time*, LXXV/12 (March 21, 1960), 46.

Since World War II

freeing human beings by removing the artificial barriers of their own making and permitting them to experience life with reawakened sensitivity. Cage's essential goal is essentially "to introduce us to the very life we are living."

Three composers closely associated in New York with Cage and his experimental-music ideas in the 1950s were Christian Wolff (b. 1934), Morton Feldman (b. 1926), and Earle Brown (b. 1926). Both Wolff and Feldman took up Cage's ideas about setting sounds free, free from *intended* inter-relationships. Wolff spoke of "a concern for a kind of objectivity, almost anonymity—sound come into its own. The 'music' is a resultant existing simply in the sounds we hear, given no impulse by expression of self or personality."[19] In a number of chamber pieces, some indeterminate not only as to duration of tones but as to instrumentation, Wolff developed a notation whereby the players, responding to each other spontaneously—as basketball or hockey players do (if that analogy does not seem too far-fetched)—could seem to *pass* notes to each other, loosing them as an arrow is loosed rather than propelled. (He spoke of a "parliamentary participation" of performers, who responded to each other's "cues.") Typically, Wolff's music in performance includes more "silence" than sound, the notes hovering separately in the air almost as autonomous intelligences.

Feldman, too, developed in the early 1950s new notations for allowing the sounds to be "free," often suggesting through graphic means generalized areas (of register, for instance: high, medium, or low) within which the performer has a free choice of specifics (in 1951 a series of works entitled *Projection*, for various small groups; another similar series of works called *Intersection*; and *Marginal Intersection*, for orchestra). By the 1960s he had achieved "a more complex style in which each instrument is living out its own individual life in its own individual sound world," often by virtue of Feldman's having chosen "intervals that seemed to erase or cancel out each sound as soon as we hear the next" (as in the series of five chamber pieces entitled *Durations*, 1960–61).[20] In *The Swallows of Salangan* (1961), for wordless chorus and instruments, all the performers are given a music of successive notes; no rests are specified; there are precise pitch indications but no rhythmic ones. The conductor initiates the performance with a slow downbeat, then gives no others. Within the general tempo thus cued, the performers move through their parts, determining for themselves the actual durations of the slow, successive tones. The result, different in detail with every performance, is something like a cloud mass, the outlines of which are constantly, almost imperceptibly, shifting from moment to moment but which retains its identity as it moves through space. Although various details

<hr>

[19] Quoted by Cage in "History of Experimental Music in the United States," *Silence*, p. 68.

[20] Feldman, jacket notes for *Durations I-IV* and other pieces on Time 58007/S-8007 (1963).

of Feldman's music of this period were experimental (their exact results unforeseen), he obviously had a clear generalized image of each work. His musical personality was (and remains) a distinctive one as well, tending to favor slow rhythms, very soft dynamics, and what Cage called "tender" sonorities. In some later pieces—one of the first was *Structures* for orchestra (completed 1962)—Feldman returned to notating rhythms and pitches precisely, but in such a way as to create the same kind of ethereal but intense atmosphere, the weightless but clustered density, the non-periodic but fluid rhythmic flow, of his experimental music.

Earle Brown was influenced in his musical ideas by artists, especially the sculptor Alexander Calder and the painter Jackson Pollock. In the mobiles of Calder he saw the possibilities of a work never being the same twice yet always being the same work. In Pollock's "action" paintings he saw possibilities for a work's being spontaneously realized on the basis of graphic cues given by the composer. In a remarkable group of compositions published under the title *Folio* (1952–53), Brown presented his first "open-form" music on the mobile principle: *1953* for piano, a study for the larger *Twenty-five Pages*. The score may be read either side up; the pages may be played in any sequence; the two-stave systems may be read in either treble or bass clef; the duration of each system is to be determined by the performer. Thus in many ways this music is "mobile." The notation, original with Brown, is "time notation": the horizontal length of a note suggests its duration relative to other notes and to the time span determined for each system. *Folio* also includes Brown's first Pollock-like pieces, *MM 87 and MM 135* for piano ("composed very rapidly and spontaneously and . . . in that sense performances rather than compositions"), and the celebrated work *December 1952*, the score of which is reproduced as Example 10-12. "Score" is not quite the word: *December 1952* is a single page of plain paper (Example 10-12 "frames" it in gray) on which are drawn lines and rectangles, both horizontal and vertical, of various lengths and thicknesses. The lines and rectangles may be read as implying direction, loudness, duration, and pitch. This page constitutes either/both score and/or parts for (any) performer(s), who are to "track" their way around the page (which may be held in any position), realizing spontaneously (or under the control of a conductor reacting to the sheet as to a score) the sonorous implications of the markings and the "tracks" chosen. Vaguely reminiscent of an artist's drawing—by someone like Mondrian—*December 1952* has been exhibited as a work of graphic art and is historically significant as the first wholly graphic music (at least since the staffless neumes of the early Middle Ages).

Utilizing various idioms of experimental and non-experimental music and various methods of notation, Brown developed further his mobile, open-form ideas in such works as *Available Forms I* for chamber ensemble (1961) and *Available Forms II* for "large orchestra four hands" (two conductors).

EXAMPLE 10-12. Earle Brown, *December* 1952. Reproduced by permission of Associated Music Publishers, Inc.

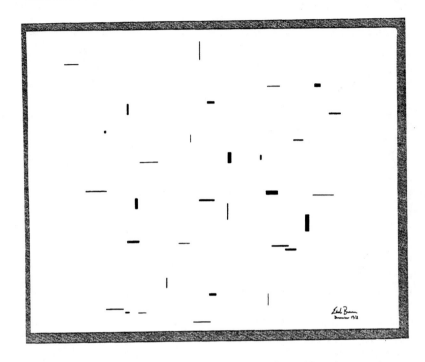

In each of these works, Brown composed a number of brief musical events, sharply differentiated in character. These may be sounded in any order, repeated, combined, cut off in the middle, taken at different tempos, all at the discretion of the conductor—who thereby realizes one version of the work from the "available forms." Such works offer maximum possibilities of transformation and mobility (as with Calder), and they are formed spontaneously in performance (as with Pollock).

MUSIC AS PROCESS AND ACTION

Clearly, the experimental music of Cage and the New York school of the 1950s and early 1960s completely changed the traditional relationships between composers and performers. One critic has put it this way:

Experimental music engages the performer at many stages before, above and beyond those at which he is active in traditional western music. It involves his intelligence, his initiative, his opinions, and prejudices, his experience, his taste and his sensibility in a way that no other form of music does, and his contribution to the musical collaboration which the composer initiates is obviously indispensable. For while it may be possible to view some experimental scores only as concepts, they are, self-evidently, (specific or general) directives for (specific or general) action.[21]

Not only were composer-performer relationships changed; so were those between listeners and performers: in the most extreme instance, Cage's *4'33"*, the listener *is* the performer, is in fact both performer and composer. And the "musical work" itself was a different thing: no longer a kind of *object*, it was a *process*, different from performance to performance.

A number of composers in the late 1950s and 1960s based further developments on these altered relationships, with their implicit redefinition of "music" itself, as well as on Cage's idea that "relevant action is theatrical (music [imaginary separation of hearing from the other senses] does not exist), inclusive and intentionally purposeless." Viewing the future as leading to a sort of *Gesamtkunstwerk*-like Happening, radically anti-establishment, and reminiscent in their mockery and humor of the Dada artists earlier in the century, these composers joined other artists in sound-and-environment events so diverse as to make generalization or categorization almost impossible. New York City was a major center, with an American wing of an international group called Fluxus particularly active, but similar groups existed in Ann Arbor, Michigan (the ONCE group), Seattle ("Dimensions of New Music"), and elsewhere in the country. The subtitle of *An Anthology* (1963) edited by the composer La Monte Young (b. 1935) suggests the "theatrical . . . inclusive and intentionally purposeless" diversity of this music-as-process-and-action movement:

Chance operations / Concept art / Meaningless work / Natural disasters / Indeterminacy / Anti-art / Plans of action / Improvisation / Stories / Diagrams / Poetry / Essays / Dance constructions / Compositions / Mathematics / Music

Among the contributors, who included Cage, Brown, and Wolff, were Joseph Byrd, Toshi Ichiyanagi, Richard Maxfield, Nam June Paik, and James Waring. Young himself included a number of his compositions of 1960. *Composition 1960 #10* is reproduced as follows, in its entirety:

Draw a straight line and follow it.

October 1960

---

[21] Michael Nyman, *Experimental Music: Cage and Beyond* (New York: Schirmer Books, 1974), p. 13.

Composition 1960 #7—" ♩♩♩ to be held for a long time"—was performed in New York in 1961 by a string trio; its duration was forty-five minutes; it evoked a large number of ancillary sounds (mostly audience noises) but also revealed to those who continued to listen a whole inner world of fluctuating overtones in the open fifth as sustained by the players.

Among the ONCE group composers, Robert Ashley (b. 1930) and Gordon Mumma (b. 1935) were the leaders. A typical piece of Ashley's is *Public Opinion Descends Upon the Demonstrators* (1961), for a single operator of complex electronic playback equipment with a large variety of pre-recorded sounds on tape, and an audience. The audience is seated unconventionally so that its members are facing each other and the operator can observe their reactions. The operator determines the sounds of the piece according to audience activity and produces different sound complexes in response to any of the following actions "performed" by a member of the audience: (1) leaving the auditorium, (2) walking around in the auditorium, (3) speaking aloud or laughing, (4) whispering (audibly or noticeably), (5) making any kind of exaggerated gesture, (6) making any kind of secretive gesture, (7) glancing "meaningfully" at another member of the audience, (8) seeking a remote visual diversion (through the windows, about the ceiling, etc.), (9) looking toward a loudspeaker, (10) making an involuntary physical gesture (yawning, scratching, adjusting clothing, etc.), (11) showing an enforced physical rigidity (waiting it out). Things get lively as soon as the audience members begin to understand that in some mysterious way *they* are creating the piece: exhibitionists, angry resenters, and shrinking violets all contribute to a lively interaction between "audience" and "performer" in which traditional roles are thoroughly confused and in which no one is certain who the "composer" really is.

Like Ashley, Mumma was concerned with activating the musical experience: *Meanwhile, A Twopiece* (1961) for two performers (of a piano, percussion instruments, and "another instrument on which one of the performers is proficient") and pre-recorded tape is written in a notation that indicates only the physical gestures to be made by the performers, with cues for them to move from instrument to instrument at certain points. In speaking of the ideology of such a piece, Mumma suggested that there may have been other reasons than Cage's ideological ones for the rise of "music as process and action." The physicality, free choice of sounds, and interaction between performers in *Meanwhile* were partly a reaction to the impact of the new recorded-sound technology: "With the widespread use of 'canned' music (radio, phonograph, and tape playback in serious music, commercial popular music, jazz, and electronic music) the visual or theatrical aspect of the performance of music has lost much of its significance."[22] In *Meanwhile* and in

---

[22] Private communication, February 23, 1962.

other similar works like *Gestures II* for two pianos (1962), Mumma vehemently re-asserted such significance, as did Ashley and other composers of process and action music.

JAZZ: THE EMERGENCE OF BOP

The onset of World War II tended to inhibit the free development of various kinds of American music, but perhaps especially jazz, as the nation tightened its collective belt to some degree, and nightlife diminished accordingly. Another kind of inhibition was a very real and practical one: in August 1942 James C. Petrillo, head of the powerful musicians' union, the American Federation of Musicians (AFM), called a strike banning AFM members from making any recordings until the record manufacturers agreed to pay a fee to the union for every recording they made. The strike not only created a vacuum between jazz musicians and listeners; more important, it eliminated a major source of communication among jazz players themselves: the phonorecording that had in effect served as text and teacher to the jazz community. Decca Records signed an agreement with the AFM late in 1943, but not until the fall of 1944 did RCA Victor and Columbia, the other two giants in the record manufacturing industry, capitulate. When jazz recordings began to reappear, and especially when the end of World War II in 1946 brought a lifting of restrictions on the use of materials needed for record manufacture, a new species of jazz seemed to burst on a public unaware of the developments that had in fact been going on—almost underground, it seemed.

Some of these developments could be viewed as reactions to certain aspects of pre-war jazz in the swing era, especially the very bigness of the big bands and the pressures on such bands to cater to public and commercial taste. The development of a concert culture for jazz meant a broadening of its base of patronage; but just as in the development of a concert culture in art-music a century or more earlier, one result was a growing lag between the musical thought of the advanced performer and the public. After-hours "jam sessions," in which jazz musicians played for each other rather than for the public, became important proving grounds for new jazz expression. The most lastingly important of these—engaged in almost exclusively by black jazz musicians—reflected another sort of reaction: resentment and anger on the part of blacks against commercial exploitation (whites consistently being paid more than blacks and, typically, under more stable contractual terms) and social discrimination (being relegated to "colored" hotels and boarding houses; their families and friends often not able to gain entrance to the very nightclubs and dance halls in which they were applauded); at the same time, blacks saw jazz being even more highly esteemed as a self-sufficient music, and one that they viewed (not entirely wrongly) as a music of *their* invention and propulsion. Out of such feelings as these arose, among some black musicians' experimentation in after-hours sessions, the initially exclusive and selfconsciously progressive style of "bebop" (or simply "bop"), which developed in New York early in the 1940s and emerged to public consciousness by about 1945.

Among the leaders in the crystallization of bop were the alto saxophonist Charlie Parker (1920–55)—with Armstrong and Ellington one of the most supremely inventive musicians in the history of jazz—the trumpeter Dizzy Gillespie (b. 1917), and the drummer Kenny Clarke (1914–85).

Gillespie contributed much to an expansion of the harmonic language of early bop. In such a work as his famous recording of the popular ballad *I Can't Get Started with You* (reissued on *SCCJ*:s7/5), he can be heard almost forcing the other members of the combo into uncharted terrain with chord substitutions and distant excursions from the song's basic harmonies; and the wicked but humorous harmonic surprises of *Shaw 'Nuff* (1945; reissued on *SCCJ*:s7/6 and *NW* 271:s1/3), in which he and Parker display a dazzling virtuosity in unison duets, are probably of his invention.

Parker, on the other hand, burst on the jazz scene with an unprecedented improvisatory flair and melodic virtuosity, in a style that was asymmetrically phrased, full of chromatic surprises, and built up by unpredictable combinations of the briefest ejaculatory motifs and very long, very fast, looping lines. Despite the aggressive novelty of his language, Parker's art was rooted in jazz tradition: a large number of his recordings, no matter what their titles are, are twelve-bar blues; most others are based on jazz "standards" (tunes, and their basic harmonic progressions, known to all jazz musicians) or the harmonies of a few popular songs, especially Gershwin's *I Got Rhythm* (for example, the *Shaw 'Nuff* just mentioned, which is credited jointly to Parker and Gillespie) or *How High the Moon*, on which is based Parker's celebrated *Ornithology* of 1946.

Bop drummers like Clarke and Max Roach (b. 1924) gave up the incessant four-beat bass-drum thudding of the swing style, reserving that instrument for occasional "bombs" dropped irregularly into a new ride-cymbal-dominated, shimmering background beat.

One of the most common conceits of bop musicians was to base a piece on the harmonies of a well-known song but substitute for its original melody a new one in bop style and then retitle the work. Thus, only the really knowledgeable would recognize Gillespie and Parker's *Anthropology* as a reworking of Gershwin's *I Got Rhythm*, or Gillespie's *Groovin' High* as the old popular song *Whispering* (1920) without the original melody. Example 10-13 shows the beginning of *Whispering* and of its bop derivative, *Groovin' High*, transcribed from the 1945 recording of Gillespie and Parker. The curt two-note figure that opens *Groovin' High* is a characteristic bop motif; some say that the term *bebop* originated as a verbalization of such a figure.

 A revival of the Dixieland style of early jazz also occurred in the 1940s. This began on the West Coast, where the Yerba Buena band of Lu Watters (b. 1911) made some recordings in faithful imitation of the early discs of Louis Armstrong. Actually, the New Orleans jazz revival was only one of many signs of a growing American nostalgia for the 1920s: before long, young Americans were once again dancing the charleston and getting their parents' raccoon coats out of mothballs, enthusiastically acting out their rosy imaginings of life in the prosperous, "secure" 1920s.

EXAMPLE 10-13. A bop-style melody and its source. (a) W/M John Schonberger, Richard Coburn, and Vincent Rose. Copyright 1920 Miller Music Corporation, New York, NY. Copyright renewal 1948 Miller Music Corporation and Fred Fisher Music Co., Inc., for the United States and Canada. Rights throughout the rest of the world controlled by Miller Music Corporation. Used by permission. (b) Dizzy Gillespie, *Groovin' High*. After a transcription of Rondolette recording A-11 by Frank Tirro.

Note: In Gillespie's performance, ♩♩ = approximately ♩♩, more precisely ♪♪

THE REVOLUTION IN POPULAR MUSIC: FROM POP TO ROCK

If jazz underwent rapid changes in the three decades after World War II, an even more violent upheaval occurred in American popular music. With the exception of a continuing undercurrent of sweet, romantic, conservative, virtually "traditional" song—heard from such older performers as Lawrence Welk (b. 1903), Bing Crosby, Perry Como (b. 1912), and Frank Sinatra (b. 1915)—American popular music was transformed entirely, from "pop" to "rock."

As had happened before in popular-music development, one main source of the transformation was the music of blacks, this time the "rhythm-and-blues" of black dance music on recordings.[23] Actually, the term covered several kinds of music American blacks were making and enjoying in the post-war years: big- and small-band jazz, essentially in the swing style; urban blues; and the songs of small vocal groups, most of them all-male quartets.

The strong-rhythmed dance music of big bands, rooted in the Kansas City swing style (Andy Kirk, Jay McShann, Erskine Hawkins, and above all Count Basie), was important as a source of rhythm-and-blues. But the union-musicians' recording ban of 1942–44 and the increasing economic constraints on maintaining big bands had led to a greater importance for the small "jump" bands, with one or two rhythm players backing up one or two melody leads. One of the most successful of these was the Timpany Five, led by the singer and sax player Louis Jordan; their *Choo Choo Ch'Boogie* (1946; reissued on *NW* 261:s1/6) was Jordan's first big hit. Another group that helped the "race" music of blacks cross over into national popularity was the King Cole Trio, led by the creamy-voiced Nat "King" Cole (1917–65), whose early jazz work was eclipsed in popularity by such novelty songs as *Straighten Up and Fly Right* (1943; reissued on *NW* 261:s1/4) and such smooth ballads as *It's Only a Paper Moon* (1943) and *The Christmas Song* (1946).

Another type of music identified with rhythm-and-blues was urban blues, both that of band-backed showmen in big-city dance halls and auditoriums (Chicago being a major center) and of soloists on small-group recordings. Their roots were of course the deep-South rural blues and the recordings of such songsters as Charley Patton from Mississippi and Blind Lemon Jefferson from Texas, and later Leroy Carr, Bukka White, and Robert Johnson. Traditional black bluesmen like T-Bone Walker (1910–75), who traveled

---

[23] "Rhythm-and-blues" was a name coined in the late 1940s by the record industry; the popular-entertainment magazine *Billboard* proposed it as a substitute for "race music," which with the growing social consciousness of the post-war period came to be viewed as offensive. Two decades later, "soul" superseded it, and finally, in the 1980s, simply "black music."

widely in the South and West in the 1930s and 1940s, gradually shifted from acoustic to electric guitar. In Walker's case the specific source is known— the solid-body electric instrument developed and played by Les Paul. Walker's classic *Call It Stormy Monday* (1947; reissued on *NW* 261:s1/7) shows his assimilation of the more powerful and versatile amplified instrument, which was to become standard for rhythm-and-blues groups. Muddy Waters (1915–83) was another rural bluesman who traveled north—to Chicago in 1943. Not particularly identified with rhythm-and-blues, he nevertheless had an enormous influence on its style of performance with pieces like *Hoochie Coochie Man* (1952; reissued on *NW* 261:s2/7).[24] Most of these blues singers were men, but a few women came to prominence as rhythm-and-blues singers, among them Willie Mae "Big Mama" Thornton (1926–84)— who had to wait, however, for national recognition until Elvis Presley recorded in 1956 his version of *Hound Dog: her* version (1952; reissued on *NW* 261:s2/4) was obviously Presley's model. (She was later to be the model for another white star: Janis Joplin.)

Yet another wing of rhythm-and-blues was occupied by small vocal groups—"sidewalk singers," they have been called—whose formation was encouraged both by the instrumental recording ban of the 1940s and the growing popularity of black gospel music, which had a considerable tradition of male "quartets (actually varying in numbers of performers). An early prototype was The Mills Brothers, who began singing in the 1920s, made successful recordings in the 1930s, and then had a spectacular national hit in 1943 with *Paper Doll*. Similar to them stylistically were The Ink Spots, who had risen to national fame in 1939 with *If I Didn't Care*. Less close to white popular-music styles were other groups, many formed originally as gospel-music quartets. One was The Golden Gate Quartet, which easily gained a secular audience with the irresistible (and danceable) drive and precision of songs like *The Sun Didn't Shine on Calvary* (1941; reissued on *NW* 261:s1/3). Several others were "bird" groups, among them The Ravens and The Orioles.

If black rhythm-and-blues, in its various guises, was one major source of the new American popular music, the other was the "hillbilly" music of southern upland whites—or as it would be called when it became known more widely, "country-and-western" music (or "country-western," or just "country"). Originally a folk music rooted in the Anglo-American songs and dances of the nineteenth century, country music was viewed as a commercially viable music from the early days of radio and the rise of the recording

[24] Don Heckman's liner notes for this album are exceptionally helpful. His characterization of *Hoochie Coochie Man* is matchless; it can serve as a good description of the mature rhythm-and-blues style: ". . . whining treble electric-guitar fills around the melody; a slurring, muttering, shouting delivery of the lyric; rolling drum rhythms underpinned by a near-contrapuntal bass line and a call-and-response riff pattern; a beat that socks away unmercifully."

industry, in the 1920s. The songs of Hollywood's cowboy heroes—Gene
Autry, Roy Rogers, Tex Ritter—were related in style to the southeastern
up-country music and "put the 'western' into country-and-western music."[25]
World War II turned it from a music of wide but mainly rural appeal into
a national phenomenon. The first great star of this "new" popular music was
Hank Williams (1923–53), known especially for a mournful, forlorn singing
style that somehow touched people's hearts. An especially poignant example
is the slow waltz *I'm So Lonesome I Could Cry* (1949; reissued on *SCCCM*:s10/
8); 1949 was also the year Williams had his first hit, *Lovesick Blues* (reissued
on *SCCCM*:s10/9), a gently rolling song projected by Williams with an appealing
self-mockery underscored by swooping yodels.

    At about the same time, a sub-genre of country music—bluegrass—
was being defined by Bill Monroe and his Blue Grass Boys; it was in fact
named after the group. Bluegrass was a livelier music than most country,
and more predominant in it was a rollicking, hell-bent-for-leather instrumental undergirding; syncopated banjos and mandolins added a sparky twang
to the softer plucked-string sound of acoustic guitar and bass; instrumentalists
often vied with each in jazz-like exchanges. *Why Did You Wander* of 1946,
from the first recording session of Monroe's group (reissued on *NW* 225:s1/
1), typifies the style; the spectacular three-finger banjo-picking of Earl Scruggs
(b. 1924)—who with the mandolinist-singer Lester Flatt broke away from
the Blue Grass Boys in 1948 to form the Foggy Mountain Boys—is heard
to even better advantage in *Earl's Breakdown* (1951; reissued on *SCCCM*:s13/
3) or *Randy Lynn Rag* (*NW* 235:s2/8).

    These two kinds of music—rhythm-and-blues and country-and-west-
ern—had some stylistic characteristics in common that made their marriage
a potentially happy one. They both emphasized a highly personal, grass-
roots earthiness of vocal style; they both were based rhythmically on a
powerful and danceable instrumental background; and they both tended to
favor the guitar, whether the electrically amplified guitar of the urban blues
singers, the natural "acoustic" guitar (long prominent as a rural, folkish
instrument) of country blues and bluegrass, or the steel guitar, sometimes
amplified, of country-and-western music.

    The transformation of American popular music through the marriage
of black rhythm-and-blues and white country-and-western was owed primarily to a new phenomenon in American society: a self-conscious, self-
aware, and economically strong "youth culture" of rebellious teenagers—
that generation of Americans born just before World War II or during the
baby boom immediately after it, raised in the post-war economic boom, and
come to adolescence in the 1950s. It was during that decade that rhythm-

    [25] As Bill Malone remarks, in his extensive and illuminating liner notes for *SCCCM*,
which include not only commentary on individual pieces of music, but also a "Personal Rem-
iniscence" that is in effect a capsule history of the genre.

and-blues records began to attract white teenagers, especially as a music for dancing. A few alert disc jockeys began to program the records for a general audience, not just for the black community; one of them, Alan Freed, broadcasting in Ohio during the early 1950s, was instrumental in popularizing the name "rock 'n' roll" for this music.[26] Soon record manufacturers were marketing rhythm-and-blues/rock-and-roll recordings generally, not just to blacks. And soon they were employing white musicians to "cover" black hits—to perform them in their own versions, usually smoother-edged, somewhat diluted, and generally more successful commercially than the black originals—or were searching for white musicians whose styles were based on, or close to, black music. White rock-and-roll hits in turn awakened interest in the black music and musicians they imitated. Before long, much American popular music was moving in the direction of rock-and-roll.

The first indication at the national level of the change in popular-music taste was the appearance in 1953 of a rock-and-roll song on the weekly "chart" of best-selling popular-music recordings published in *Billboard* magazine: it was *Crazy Man Crazy*, by Bill Haley and his Comets (a white group). Haley (1925–81) was even more successful the following year with *Shake, Rattle and Roll* (a cover for black Joe Turner's recording of it earlier in 1954, which is reissued on *NW* 249:s1/1); but neither of the earlier songs approached the success of Haley's *Rock Around the Clock* in 1955. Used as theme music for the movie *Blackboard Jungle*, which dealt with juvenile delinquency, it came to be identified with youthful rebellion.

Haley's was primarily a northern style based on the heavy rolling beat of rhythm-and-blues (and its powerful "backbeats" on notes 2 and 4 of a $\frac{4}{4}$ measure), with, however, a slight twang of guitars from country-and-western. The opposite balance typified the songs of his successor in popularity (and in fact the most spectacularly successful rock-and-roll star of the 1950s and early 1960s), Elvis Presley, born in 1935 in Mississippi. Presley sang (and played guitar to) a music blending a dash of rhythm-and-blues with large amounts of country-and-western—some called the style "rockabilly," others "country rock." He recorded first for Sun Records, a Memphis firm, and built a reputation as the nation's most promising country musician; in mid-1955 he reached No. 1 on *Billboard*'s country-music chart for the first time with *Mystery Train* (reissued on *NW* 207:s1/9), an infectious blues. In early 1956, now under contract to RCA Victor, he recorded the song *Heartbreak Hotel*; the company arranged for television appearances and put together an LP album by him, partly from material recorded earlier.[27] Within

---

[26] Freed did not invent the term, although he claimed to have done so and has been credited with it. See Charlie Gillett, *The Sound of the City*, 2nd ed. (New York: Dell Publishing Company, 1972), p. 9.

[27] The album's songs clearly reveal Presley's models: *Blue Suede Shoes* (based on an original by the white country-and-western singer Carl Perkins), *I Got a Woman* (originally

a few weeks, both the single of *Heartbreak Hotel* and the LP album were leading *Billboard*'s pop-music chart. A few months later, a disc with Presley's cover of Big Mama Thornton's *Hound Dog* on one side rose to the No. 1 position not only on the pop chart but also on those of rhythm-and-blues and country music. Presley had reached the top; for eight years, into 1963, he was to remain there.

If Presley and other early white rock-and-roll stars—notably Pat Boone (b. 1934), Jerry Lee Lewis (b. 1935), and Buddy Holly (1938–59)—were the national favorites, some black musicians were more inventive. One whose originality, power, and wit can be measured by his enormous impact on later musicians was Chuck Berry (b. 1926). His first record, *Maybellene* (1955; reissued on *NW* 249:s1/6), was about sex and speed; others spoke directly to, and for, the youth culture, like *School Day* (1957), *Sweet Little Sixteen* (1958), and *Almost Grown* (1959) (". . . Don't bother me, leave me alone,/Anyway I'm almost grown"). In *Roll Over Beethoven* (1956), Berry opted for popular as opposed to high culture (". . . Roll over, Beethoven, and tell Tchaikowsky the news") in an unconscious echo of earlier American vernacular-culture champions (see p. 115). He sounded other notes of protest in his songs, and with his powerful shouting-blues voice, the brassy sounds of his amplified guitar, and his drummer's bombshell backbeats he helped to confirm rock-and-roll as a music of the rebellious youth culture.

Bo Diddley (b. 1928), Fats Domino (b. 1928), Sam Cooke (1931–64), and Little Richard (b. 1935) were other blacks who, although heard mainly within the black community during the 1950s, were to provide material for nationally—even internationally—popular covers later. (Many in the black community complained bitterly about this cultural, and economic, robbery.)

More versatile than they, able to adapt to a variety of styles (popular ballads, gospel songs, and jazz as well as rock-and-roll) and thus able to win a national audience more easily, was Ray Charles (b. 1930), a versatile, blind singer and pianist who along with Presley dominated the pop-music field in the early 1960s with a style of song and singing often so heavily tinged with the idioms of black gospel music that it invited a new categorization—"soul" music. A performance like his 1959 version of Hank Snow's *I'm Movin' On* (reissued on *NW* 249:s2/7) owes as much to church practices—for example, the furious tempo, the ecstatic vocalization, the backup singing group (in this case The Raelets) urging the soloist on—as to the country-music origins of the song or to rhythm-and-blues in general. This aspect of Charles's art was immensely influential among younger black pop singers of the later

---

recorded in 1955 as a rhythm-and-blues number by the black Ray Charles), *Tutti Frutti* (a recent rock-and-roll hit—his first—by another black, "Little Richard" Penniman), and *Money Honey* (originally recorded in 1954 by the black gospel-influenced group The Drifters); in addition, there were rockabilly-tinged slow ballads and even a version of Rodgers and Hart's *Blue Moon.*

1960s such as Aretha Franklin, Stevie Wonder, Steve Winwood, and James Brown.

By the late 1950s a new trend in popular music—by no means unrelated to rock-and-roll—was visible. This was an increased interest in folk music, especially that of the American past, and in folkish songs newly written. Pete Seeger (b. 1919) and The Weavers, strongly influenced by the leftist, Depression-era folk singing of Woody Guthrie (1912–67), turned *Goodnight, Irene*—which had been recorded in 1943 by the country-blues singer Huddie Ledbetter, known as Leadbelly (1885–1949)—into a hit as early as 1950. But it was not until several years later that folk music, or folk-derived music, began to rival rock-and-roll in national popularity; The Kingston Trio's *Tom Dooley* (1958), based on a late nineteenth-century ballad, was a landmark. By the middle 1960s, the folk-music revival had progressed so far that perhaps the most universally well-known song in the country was an earlier labor-movement song with a tune of uncertain origins, its words adjusted by Pete Seeger and others to the major socio-political drives of the time for civil rights and world peace: *We Shall Overcome* (Example 10-14).

EXAMPLE 10-14. *We Shall Overcome.* New Words and Music Arrangement by Zilphia Horton, Frank Hamilton, Guy Carawan & Pete Seeger. TRO © Copyright 1960 and 1963, Ludlow Music, Inc., New York, NY. Used by permission. Royalties derived from this composition are being contributed to The Freedom Movement under the trusteeship of the writers.

Among the leading figures in the folk revival were Harry Belafonte (b. 1927), who popularized the calypso style of the West Indies in 1957; Joan Baez (b. 1941), who came to prominence in 1960 with her first LP album (including *Donna, Donna* and *House of the Rising Sun*); the trio of Peter, Paul, and Mary, whose first hit album (1962) included *Cruel War* (by Peter [Yarrow]) and a version of Pete Seeger's *Where Have All the Flowers Gone?*; and a young man known as Bob Dylan.

Dylan (b. 1941 as Robert Zimmerman) began his career as a New York coffee-house balladeer in 1961. His model was Woody Guthrie; he sang in a high, harsh, somewhat tuneless voice that sounded very "old-timey," very "country," and he played an acoustic guitar, sometimes punctuating his songs with wails on a harmonica hung on a frame around his neck. He had a unique poetic sensibility, and a number of his songs stated unforgettably some major themes of the 1960s—at least those of the disillusioned, alienated youth, sick of the country's domination by a military-industrial complex, its undeclared wars, and its racial strife. Some of these were *Blowin' in the Wind* (1963), against racial prejudice; *A Hard Rain's a-Gonna Fall* (1963), against the nuclear bombing threat; *It Ain't Me Babe* (1964), about superficial boy-girl relationships; *Mr. Tambourine Man* (1965), about alienation; and *Subterranean Homesick Blues* (1965), about the absurdity of it all.

Among many others influenced by Dylan was the team of Paul Simon and Art Garfunkel (both born in 1941). They treated topics as timely as Dylan's, if in a less poetically unique and musically uncompromising and individualistic way, in such songs as *The Sounds of Silence* (1964), *Scarborough Fair/Canticle* (1966), and *Mrs. Robinson* (from the film *The Graduate* of 1968).[28] In fact, one of the most striking things about the new popular songs of the later 1960s was the quality and significance of their lyrics: they spoke of serious matters both timely and timeless, and in a more poetically artful way than had the popular songs of a generation earlier.

Ironically, the team of musicians that most clearly personified the intersections of black and white, urban and country, folk and pop, and pop and art in American "popular" music of the later 1960s—a team that even surpassed Presley in popular success—was not American at all but British: The Beatles (John Lennon, Paul McCartney, George Harrison, and Ringo Starr). Early in 1964 their recording of *I Want to Hold Your Hand* reached No. 1 on the *Billboard, Cashbox*, and *Variety* charts; during one week in March the top five recordings were all by them; and for the whole period from February to July songs by them led all others. This fantastic popularity, absolutely without historical precedent, was maintained by The Beatles for years, in fact virtually until the group dissolved in 1970; it was due to several factors, among them the inventiveness of Lennon and McCartney as songwriters; canny management and promotion of the group; and its studied eclecticism, always seeming to be one step ahead of the expanding stylistic range of rock-and-roll.

---

[28] Hollywood was slow to adopt the new pop music: Columbia made *Rock Around the Clock* with Bill Haley and the Comets in 1956, but thereafter, other than the many films with Elvis Presley as the male lead, beginning with *Love Me Tender* (1956), few Hollywood products used rock-and-roll on their soundtracks until the late 1960s. The first film with an all-rock score was Richard Lester's *A Hard Day's Night* (1964), a British production starring The Beatles (and their music).

BIBLIOGRAPHICAL NOTES

The music discussed in this chapter (and the following two) is also treated extensively, in the broader context of Western music in general, in Eriz Salzman's companion volume *Twentieth-Century Music: An Introduction*, 3rd ed. (Englewood Cliffs, NJ: Prentice-Hall, Inc., 1988). More narrowly focused on techniques of composition in concert music is David Cope's *New Directions in Music*, 4th ed. (Dubuque, IA: Wm. C. Brown, 1984). Leonard B. Meyer's *Music, the Arts, and Ideas* (Chicago: University of Chicago Press, 1967) is an important critical-aesthetic contribution.

Riegger's life and music are briefly but authoritatively discussed in Stephen Spackman's *Wallingford Riegger: Two Essays in Musical Biography* (ISAMm 17 [1982]).

Elliott Carter's many published articles and essays have been edited by Else Stone and Kurt Stone in *The Writings of Elliott Carter* (Bloomington: Indiana University Press, 1977). They may best be complemented, concerning Carter's music, by the "authorized" study of his former pupil David Schiff (see footnote 8).

The issues of *PNM*, from the first on, have been especially sympathetic to serial composition and its composers, especially Milton Babbitt. "Sounds and Words: Milton Babbitt at 60" is the title of a double volume of *PNM* (XIV/2–XV/1; Spring-Summer/Fall–Winter 1976) dedicated to him and including a complete list (to 1976) of his important theoretical writings. Pages 10–128 of *PNM*, XXIV/2 (Spring-Summer 1986), are a follow-up entitled "Milton Babbitt: A 70th Birthday Forum, Part I"; this includes an important, closely argued, and refreshing essay by Joseph N. Straus on behalf of Babbitt's *music*, its music examples recorded on an accompanying cassette. The most significant recent addition to Babbitt's writings is *Milton Babbitt: Words About Music (The Madison Lectures)*, eds. Stephen Dembski and Joseph N. Straus (Madison: University of Wisconsin Press, 1987). For most readers, Babbitt's essays are extremely difficult; they are in effect summarized, in a very clearly written practical manual, by Charles Wuorinen, in his *Simple Composition* (New York: Longman, Inc., 1979). One of the best entrées into Babbitt's music remains that of Elaine Barkin, in her too modestly entitled "A simple approach to Milton Babbitt's semi-simple Variations," *Music Review*, XXVIII/4 (November 1967), 316–22. (The *Semi-Simple Variations* [1956] and all the other piano music of Babbitt, including the epochal *Three Compositions* of 1947–48, are recorded by Robert Taub on Harmonica Mundi HMC-5160; released 1986.)

Otto Luening speaks from a position of authority in Chapter 24 ("Electronic Music 1906 to Present") of his generous, fascinating autobiography, *The Odyssey of an American Composer* (New York: Charles Scribner's Sons, 1980). Elliott Schwartz's *Electronic Music: A Listener's Guide* (New York: Praeger Publishers, 1973), though outdated now, remains a sympathetic introduction.

More up to date is Barry Schrader's *Introduction to Electro-Acoustic Music* (Englewood Cliffs, NJ: Prentice-Hall, Inc., 1982); it includes interviews with the composers Berio, Oliveros, Subotnick, Jean-Claude Risset, and Mumma, each centered on one of their works.

Hiller and Isaacson's *Experimental Music: Composition with an Electronic Computer* (New York: McGraw-Hill Book Company, 1959) relates in detail the problems and progress of early computer composition; a good summary account, with an extensive bibliography, is John Strawn's *TNGDAM* article "Computers and Music."

Cage's own essays and lectures are unparalleled sources for his ideas on the experimental music of chance and indeterminacy; the books that contain them are listed definitively (along with much other material) in *A John Cage Reader*, compiled and edited by Peter Gena and Jonathan Bent, supplemented by Don Gillespie (New York: C. F. Peters, 1982). The German journalist Walter Zimmerman has edited a massive collection, *Morton Feldman Essays* (Kerpen, Ger.: Beginner Press, 1985), containing three essays and an epilogue about Feldman and twenty-three pieces of writing *by* him (plus a list of his works and a bibliography).

La Monte Young's *An Anthology* [*etc.*, *etc.*, *etc.*] (see p. 271) is difficult to find but worth the search, for examples of the Fluxus-inspired music of process and action. Only slightly less elusive, unfortunately, are the issues of the West Coast periodical *Source* (1967–77), which tend to be multi-media productions themselves, with recordings, templates, scores, and other bits of material (fur, for example) as well as essays and articles. Michael D. Williams has produced a helpful annotated list of the contents of *Source*, with cumulated indices, as No. 19 of the Music Library Association's Index Series (Canton, MA: Music Library Association, 1978).

An early analyst of bop was Leonard Feather, in *Inside Be-Bop* (New York: J. J. Robbins, 1949; repr. 1972 as *Inside Jazz*). Ira Gitler's *Jazz Masters of the Forties* (New York: Macmillan, Inc., 1966) is excellent; more subjective— often provocatively so—is the criticism of Martin Williams in his collection *Jazz Masters in Transition 1957–69* (New York: Macmillan, Inc., 1970).

For rhythm-and-blues, turn first to Charles Keil, *Urban Blues* (Chicago: University of Chicago Press, 1966), and Arnold Shaw, *Honkers and Shouters: The Golden Years of Rhythm & Blues* (New York: Macmillan, Inc., 1978). Country-and-western music is definitively chronicled in Bill C. Malone's *Country Music U.S.A.*, rev. ed. (Austin: University of Texas Press, 1985). Besides *The Rolling Stone Illustrated History of Rock & Roll*, ed. Jim Miller, rev. ed. (New York: Random House/Rolling Stone Press, 1980), the best books on rock-and-roll and later rock are Greil Marcus's *Mystery Train: Images of America in Rock 'n' Roll Music* (New York: E. P. Dutton, 1975) and Ed Ward, Geoffrey Stokes, and Ken Tucker's *Rock of Ages: The Rolling Stone History of Rock & Roll* (New York: Rolling Stone Press/Summit Books, 1986); Charles Hamm's *TNGDAM* entry on "Rock" provides further bibliography.

ELEVEN

INTERSECTIONS, INTERACTIONS, PROJECTIONS: FROM THE 1960S TO THE MID-1970S

Each of the suggestive nouns in the title of this chapter might be found as a heading for a musical work of the 1960s or early 1970s. The first decade or so after World War II had seen extraordinary activity in American music, along widely divergent lines; beginning in the 1960s, however, it seemed there might be some new syntheses developing—or if that term suggests too strongly mergers wholly completed, at least some "intersections" and "interactions" among different kinds of music; and perhaps these "projected" some syntheses lying ahead. In all the areas of American music— jazz, popular music and musical theater, concert music—one of the most striking trends of the later 1950s and 1960s was the intermingling of musical techniques, languages, and even worlds that had seemed separate before. The titles themselves say something, too, about the period: abstract, cool, detached, anti-expressionist and anti-romantic in implication, they bespeak a kind of "laid-back" acceptance of the ups and downs and absurdities of modern life. As one composer-critic of the period put it, "For the younger composers, and many of the older ones, the barriers are down, the categories destroyed. . . . Any kind of statement is possible."[1]

POST-BOP JAZZ AND THE "THIRD STREAM"

In jazz, three principle types of the period—cool jazz, hard bop, and free jazz—arose from interactions of attitude and intersections of style.

The beginnings of cool jazz are often identified with a famous series of recordings made in 1949–50 by a nonet led by the trumpeter Miles Davis (b. 1926). Based on sophisticated arrangements, many of them by Gil Evans, this was chamber jazz of great musical elegance, but also of great restraint expressively, compared to the contemporaneous bop style.[2] The ruminative, often gutturally soliloquizing trumpet of Davis and the thin, pale tone of alto saxophonist Lee Konitz (b. 1927) were characteristic. Pianist in the performances of *Venus de Milo* by Gerry Mulligan (b. 1927) and in his own *Rouge* was John Lewis (b. 1920). In 1952, Lewis founded the Modern Jazz Quartet; its light sound (piano, vibraphone, bass, and drums) and a style including contrapuntal niceties like canon and fugue (*Versailles*, 1956; *Concorde*, 1963) and such unusual source materials as Elizabethan harpsichord music (*The Queen's Fancy*), music by Johann Sebastian Bach (*Vendôme*), and old English carols (*God Rest Ye Merry, Gentlemen*) made it the epitome of cool jazz.

Related to the Modern Jazz Quartet in breadth of style sources was the music of a quartet headed by the pianist Dave Brubeck (b. 1920), who had studied with Milhaud; it featured the improvisatory brilliance of the alto saxophonist Paul Desmond (1924–77). Typical of their work is a version of *Perdido*, recorded in 1953 during a concert at Oberlin College, which includes witty and apparently spontaneous quotations from a 1928 Broadway show tune (*Crazy Rhythm*), a popular song of 1935 (*The Music Goes Round and Round*; cf. NW 248:s2/1) and Stravinsky's *Petrushka*, plus a fugal exposition in the manner of Baroque-era music. Brubeck also broke out of the traditional $\frac{4}{4}$ meter of jazz with such pieces as *Take Five* (in $\frac{5}{4}$) and *Blue Rondo à la Turk* (in $\frac{9}{8}$, the eighths divided 2 + 2 + 2 + 3).

---

[1] Salzman, *Twentieth-Century Music*, 2nd ed. (Englewood Cliffs, NJ: Prentice-Hall, Inc., 1974), p. 200.

[2] The collaboration between Evans (b. 1912) and Davis was exceptionally fruitful: following the nonet recordings (reissued as the Capitol album *Birth of the Cool*) came the albums *Miles Ahead* (1957), *Porgy and Bess* (1958), and *Sketches of Spain* (1959–60). In *Miles Ahead*, Davis plays both trumpet and flugelhorn; the album also includes early examples of "modal jazz," to some degree a conception owed to Evans. *Porgy and Bess*, derived from songs in Gershwin's opera, includes a remarkable transformation, at Evans's hands, of *Summertime* (reissued on *SCCJ*:s10/2).

Even more eclectic, sophisticated, and intellectualized was the work of the pianist-composer Lennie Tristano (1919–78), noted as a teacher of vanguard jazz style in the 1950s. His *Crosscurrent* of 1949 (reissued on *SCCJ*:s8/8) exemplifies the melody-dominated style of his recording groups, this one displaying amazing unison playing by Konitz and the tenor saxophonist Warne Marsh; in the same year Tristano's quartet "stretched almost to the breaking point" the harmonic underpinning of Jerome Kern's *Yesterdays* (as Gunther Schuller puts it in the liner notes of the reissue on *NW* 216:s1/3).

Perhaps in reaction to such a cultivated chamber jazz, there emerged in the mid-1950s a hard, harsh, leather-lunged style sometimes called "hard bop" or "funky" jazz. The latter term, an old colloquialism for "smelly" or "dirty," with sexual implications like the original ones of "jazz" itself, suggested the back-to-the-roots quality of the style. As conceived by Horace Silver (b. 1928), pianist and co-director of the Jazz Messengers with the drummer Art Blakey (b. 1919), by Blakey himself, and by the alto saxophonist Cannonball Adderley (1928–75), hard bop combined the chromaticism, the asymmetrical phrases, and the sharp punctuation of the bop style with the old earthiness of New Orleans jazz, plus an accessible intensity related to black rhythm-and-blues. The result was a tough, angular, honking music as complex harmonically as bop and cool jazz but also as expressively fervent and powerfully communicative as the early jazz of the 1920s. Well-known and widely successful examples of hard bop include Silver's *Stop Time* (1954; reissued on *NW* 271:s2/6) and *Nica's Dream* (1956; reissued on *NW* 242:s1/3) and Benny Golson's *Blues March* (originally recorded by the Jazz Messengers; re-recorded in 1960 by the Jazztet, co-led by Golson and Art Farmer; the latter reissued on *NW* 242:s2/1).

Two musicians related to hard bop but so independent and inventive that they resist classification were Charlie Mingus and Thelonious Monk. Mingus (1922–79) was an extraordinary double-bass player and a visionary composer. In the mid-1950s he organized a Jazz Workshop with which to develop his ideas—a four- to eleven-piece band usually including the drummer Dannie Richmond and often the vanguard alto-sax player Eric Dolphy (as in the angry political satire *Original Faubus Fables* of 1959, referring to Orville Faubus, the segregationist governor of Arkansas; a 1960 recording including the sneering text is reissued on *NW* 242:s2/4). Mingus's visionary concepts sometimes led him to a music difficult to claim as jazz in any traditional sense—for example, *Eclipse* (1953; reissued on *NW* 216:s1/5), with its unconventional contrapuntal use of unconventional instruments (flute, cello) in an unconventional form, with unconventional lyrics appearing (unconventionally) to begin and end the piece. On the other hand, he could inspire a group to a roaring, ripsnorting riot of tradition-based riffs and solos, such as *Hora Decubitus* (1963; reissued on *SCCJ*:s10/5), which also exemplifies his fondness, as a composer, for dense textures, low-pitched ensembles, and acrid dissonance.

Monk (1917–82) had been one of the architects of the bop style in New York in the mid-1940s but almost immediately veered off on a purely personal path, highly influential if also almost inimitable—as can be heard in such early works as the blues transformation *Misterioso* (1948; reissued on *SCCJ*:s9/4) and the original version of *Evidence* (recorded on the same day; reissued on *SCCJ*:s9/6). Monk's mature piano style was so iconoclastic in its spare, spastic, broken-rhythmed, angular melody, often seeming at odds with the harmony (itself full of strangeness and surprise), and the whole feigning a kind of uncertain awkwardness, that many listeners and critics were deceived into thinking that he couldn't really play the piano. Ultimately, however, his absolute mastery was acknowledged universally. One leading jazz critic, thinking of such unique re-creations as Monk's coruscating, awesomely original solo on the blues-based *Bags' Groove* (recorded by Miles Davis's All Stars in 1954; reissed on *SCCJ*:s10/1) or his 1957 recording of the ballad *I Should Care* (reissued on *SCCJ*:s9/8), has written,

> His compositions and his playing were of a piece. His improvisations were molten Monk compositions, and his compositions were frozen Monk improvisations. . . . His medium- and up-tempo tunes are stop-and-go rhythmic structures [which] move irregularly through sudden intervals and retards and broken rhythms. His balladlike tunes are altogether different. They are intense and graceful art songs, which move slowly and three-dimensionally. . . . He filled us with his noble, funny, generous music. . . .[3]

With the appearance in the late 1950s of the saxophonists John Coltrane (1926–67) and Ornette Coleman (b. 1930) and the pianist Cecil Taylor (b. 1933), some jazz approached the ultra-chromatic, atonal style of certain concert music. This free jazz ("the new thing," "atonal jazz," "the new wave" were other attempts to name it) gave up the traditional basis of jazz in a pre-existent "tune" (or the progression of harmonies underlying a tune) and a steady, even beat, turning instead to an almost wholly spontaneous, rhapsodic, and passionately expressive style—"speechlike cries, squawks, moans, and cackles . . . slurring, burring, braying, crying" was one early critical response—in which the players almost seemed to rely on extrasensory perception to follow each other's ideas.[4] Coleman's dirge-like *Lonely Woman*

---

[3] "Notes and Comment," *The New Yorker*, March 1, 1982, pp. 37–38 (an obituary article, unsigned but most probably by Whitney Balliett).

[4] The quotation is from Nat Hentoff, "The New Jazz—Black, Angry, and Hard to Understand," *New York Times Magazine*, December 25, 1966, pp. 10, 36–39. Only much later would analyses make clear the strong structural foundations of some so-called free jazz. See especially Lewis Porter, "John Coltrane's Music of 1960 through 1967: Jazz Improvisation as Composition" (Ph.D. dissertation, Brandeis University, 1983), notably the analysis of "Giant Steps," recorded May 5, 1959 (in *Giant Steps*, Atlantic 1311).

(1959; reissued on *SCCJ*:s12/1) reveals an almost Ivesian dissociation between the soloists (Coleman on alto sax, Don Cherry on trumpet) and the backup bass and drums; his *Free Jazz* of 1960 (partially reissued on *SCCJ*:s12/3) is an extraordinary thirty-six-minute achievement in collective free improvisation by a double quartet. The aims of such music were related to ideals of personal freedom and self-expression: the players sought to "speak" instrumentally with each other, and to their listeners. In *Alabama* (1963; reissued on *SCCJ*:s12/4) Coltrane ruminates meditatively on a speech by the black leader Martin Luther King, Jr.; in the fourth part ("Psalm") of one of his most celebrated works, the suite *A Love Supreme* (1964), he "recites" with his tenor sax a prayer (printed on the record jacket, Impulse AS-77 [reissued as MCA 29017]).

Some free-jazz musicians, notably the saxophonists Albert Ayler (1936–70) and Archie Shepp (b. 1937), identified the searing expressionism of free jazz with the struggles of American blacks and with the militant black nationalism of the 1960s. Ayler commented, "It's not about notes anymore. It's about feelings!" The poet and playwright LeRoi Jones (who later took the Black Muslim name Imamu Amiri Baraka) said, "You hear . . . poets of the Black Nation."[5] One of Shepp's early pieces had the title *Rufus*; this was an abbreviation for *Rufus Swung His Face at Last to the Wind, Then His Neck Snapped*, and the idea behind the piece was a lynching.

As a vanguard music, free jazz eluded the popularity or even the acceptance of other jazz. This was especially true of the music of free jazz's most determined, uncompromising, conceptually "far-out" exponent, the pianist Cecil Taylor (b. 1933). His unprecedently energetic, intense, violent, percussive, asymmetrical, and unpredictable performances brought him critical acclaim but few jobs. Even repeated hearings of recorded works such as the thirty-minute-long *Holiday en masque* (NW 201:s2) or the almost hour-long *3 Phasis* (NW 303, entire) leave most listeners, not excluding jazz aficionados, bemused.

Several composers of the period moved freely from jazz to concert music or the reverse. Gunther Schuller (b. 1925) saw in the intersection of these two mainstreams of American music possibilities for a "third stream," a term he coined in the late 1950s. There had been plenty of interaction between contemporaneous vernacular- and cultivated-tradition music during the twentieth century, from Ives and his ragtime pieces through Carpenter and Copland to Blitzstein and even Babbitt—and in the opposite direction, from Joplin and his ragtime opera and ballet scores through Gershwin to Duke Ellington. Schuller's perception, however, was that post-war jazz had achieved a sophisticated language and freedom of form that made it possible to imagine, if not a true fusion, at least a happy marriage between jazz and

[5] Both quotations are from the jacket notes of *The New Wave in Jazz (Impulse A-90)*.

non-jazz. His *Transformation* (1957; reissued on NW 216:s2/3), for an eleven-piece jazz-like ensemble, "begins as a straight twelve-tone piece . . . and is gradually transformed into a jazz piece . . . only to succumb to the reverse process."[6] *Conversations* and *Concertino* (both 1959) set a jazz quartet (with the makeup of the Modern Jazz Quartet) against, respectively, string quartet and symphony orchestra. In these works the two styles are kept discrete; they intersect but are not fused. In other works, like *Seven Studies on Themes of Paul Klee* (1959), his First Symphony (1965), and the opera *The Visitation* (1966), Schuller moved closer to a real synthesis.

A number of other composers also utilized jazz elements. Their incentive seemed to spring not from any "Americanist" ideal, nor from pursuit of the third-stream ideal envisioned by Schuller. Some of them, practicing jazz musicians themselves, simply found the repertory of jazz idioms and inflections to be natural, viable foundations for more formal composition. Among these were Hall Overton (1920–72) and Francis Thorne (b. 1922); the latter's witty chamber work punningly entitled *Six Set Pieces* (1967) combines jazz-derived ideas easily and convincingly with serial techniques, even in two helter-skelter movements based on the idea of "jam sessions" (and so titled). Salvatore Martirano (b. 1927) first came to notice as a conventionally schooled twelve-tone composer (*Mass*, for double chorus, 1952–55; recorded on NW 210:s1/1–3, 2/1–2) but began to exploit his background as a jazz keyboardist in the late 1950s—as in his *Ballad*, for an amplified singer working over popular songs of the 1930–50 period; or *O, O, O, O, That Shakespeherian Rag* (1958), the title from T. S. Eliot, the text from Shakespeare, and the music, for chorus and instrumental ensemble, a "so elegant, so intelligent" commentary on the verses.

Another composer well versed in ragtime and jazz as a pianist, and a connoisseur of American popular music in general, was William Bolcom (b. 1938). This orientation influenced much of his career. He and the mezzo-soprano Joan Morris achieved both critical and popular success with recitals and recordings of American popular songs of the Tin Pan Alley era, in serious, stylish, "period" presentations. Bolcom also helped to spark a ragtime revival in the early 1970s, as a performer and composer of new piano rags like *Seabiscuits* (1967) and the poignant *Graceful Ghost* (1970). Together with William Albright he wrote *Brass Knuckles* (1969), a rollicking rag studded with cluster-chord crashes. Bolcom's works in larger forms reveal a cheerful, purposeful eclecticism, beginning with his first major composition, *Dynamite Tonite* (1963), a "cabaret opera for actors," and perhaps culminating in his massive setting of forty-six poems by William Blake, *Songs of Innocence and of Experience* (1956–84) for soloists, choruses, and orchestra—itself culminating in a blues-tinged Jamaican *reggae*-derived finale, over a swinging

---

[6] Schuller, jacket notes for *Mirage: Avant-Garde and Third-Stream Jazz* (NW 216).

ostinato, on Blake's *A Divine Image* ("Cruelty has a Human Heart/And Jealousy a Human Face"). Albright (b. 1944) himself contributed a number of rags to the repertories of both pianists and organists, notably his *Dream Rags* for piano (1970)—one of them the grand panoramic *Nightmare Fantasy Rag—A Night on Rag Mountain*—and several witty *Organbooks*.

THE ROCK ERA RAMPANT

By the late 1960s, variants of rock-and-roll were multiplying so fast, each seeming another step removed from the ultimate source (rhythm-and-blues/country-and-western), that the new pop music came to be called simply "rock," plus one of any number of qualifying adjectives. There was folk rock (The Byrds, The Band, Country Joe & The Fish, The Mamas and the Papas, and especially the work since the mid-1960s of Bob Dylan and Neil Young). There were blues rock (Ike and Tina Turner, The Righteous Brothers), soft rock (James Taylor, Bread, The Carpenters), and hard rock (The Doors, The Jimi Hendrix Experience). There was acid rock (or psychedelic rock) from San Francisco groups like Jefferson Airplane and The Grateful Dead. (The adjectives referred to LSD and other hallucinatory drugs; to songs that spoke positively of such drugs—*White Rabbit*, by the singer Grace Slick—or hinted at their use; and to the delirious experience of rock concerts, which combined ear-splitting, mind-numbing amplification, hypnotically repetitive rhythms and static or constantly revolving harmonies, and bizarre, kaleidoscopic "light-shows.") There were southern-white rock (The Allman Brothers, Lynyrd Skynyrd) and northern-black rock ("Motown"—the rock-related black popular style named after Berry Gordy's publishing and recording company in Detroit and typified by Diana Ross and the Supremes, Martha and the Vandellas, Marvin Gaye, and Stevie Wonder). There were Bach rock (*A Whiter Shade of Pale*, by the British group Procol Harum) and Renaissance rock (*Pavan for My Lady*, by the short-lived American one, Ars Nova). In reaction to the "British invasion" in the later 1960s of groups like The Beatles, The Rolling Stones, and The Who, there was self-consciously raw, raunchy, violence-tinged punk rock (The Ramones, Black Flag, X). There was a rock of artistic pretensions dubbed art rock (The Velvet Underground, later the "new wave" group Talking Heads). There was even rock that was not—or as one critic described it, "unpopular pop": the complex, Varèse- and Stravinsky- and Cage-influenced music of Frank Zappa (b. 1940) and his group, The Mothers of Invention;[7] their early concerts were precursors of the cynical

---

[7] The characterization is that of Lawrence Gushee, in an unpublished paper of 1972. David Walley implies the same thing in the title of his biography of Zappa, *No Commercial Potential* (New York: Outerbridge & Lazar, Inc., 1972).

grotesqueries of rock called variously rock-'n'-rouge, deca-rock (for "deca-dent"), or glitter rock: the homoerotic, sado-masochistic, chaotic unisex spectacles of performers like David Bowie and Alice Cooper (both males).

Rock was diffused primarily by recordings and air-play (on the radio). It also became a major kind of concert music, for a huge and almost exclusively youthful audience all across the country. Especially after The Beatles filled the giant Shea Stadium in New York in the fall of 1966, rock concerts and festivals became a commonplace, in both outdoor arenas and immense interior halls ("rock palaces") like Fillmore Auditorium in San Francisco and Fillmore East in New York. The peak of rock-concert productions occurred in a field near Woodstock, New York, in the summer of 1969, when more or less 450,000 young people gathered for a three-day "festival of love" and music; perhaps the nadir was reached later that year at Altamont Speedway, east of San Francisco, when many members of an audience of 300,000 experienced bad drug "trips," violence, and rioting (with a few deaths).

By the mid-1970s, it seemed that this glut of rock in all its variant versions might be presaging the decline of the genre and the dawn of a new cycle of American popular music. One critic forecast a renaissance of melodious lyricism, seeing worthy successors to the songs of Gershwin, Kern, and Rodgers in those of Joni Mitchell (in the albums *The Circle Game, Clouds, The Ladies of the Canyon*), Carly Simon (*Anticipation, No Secrets, You're So Vain*), Carole King (*Now That Everything's Been Said, Writer, Tapestry*), and Randy Newman (*Randy Newman, 12 Songs, Sail Away*).[8] And perhaps this lyric renaissance would come out of the musical, which had finally begun to reflect the transformation of American popular music.

THE MUSICAL

The rock revolution had effected a diffusion of the geographical centers (in performance, recording, and publishing) of popular music: Nashville, New Orleans, Memphis, Detroit, and San Francisco were as important breeding grounds and distribution centers as New York. The American musical comedy, however, with its center of gravity at Broadway and Times Square, remained dominated by New York's tendency to a narrow if sophisticated insularity and for a long time tended to maintain the aesthetic and the style of pre-World War II musical theater. Only in 1967, in *Hair* (music composed by Galt MacDermot), did the popular lyric theater begin to catch

    [8] Don Heckman, "You Like to Recognize the Tune? You Will," *New York Times*, September 24, 1972.

up with the new pop music. *Hair*, although not the revolutionary work it seemed at first to be (partly because of one semi-nude scene), was at least perceptibly tinged with rock, in such songs as *Aquarius* and *Good Morning, Starshine*, and with rock's themes of protest from the youth culture.

At least one brilliant new composer of musicals (as well as other kinds of works) had appeared in the immediate post-war years: Leonard Bernstein (b. 1918). A Harvard graduate with prodigious gifts as a pianist, conductor, and composer, Bernstein moved easily from one to another of America's worlds of music, "classical" and popular. His Second Symphony, "The Age of Anxiety" (1949), includes a lengthy jazz-tinged piano solo; his ballet score *Fancy Free* was amplified into a musical, *On The Town* (both 1944). With a style that might be described as "by Copland out of Stravinsky" and with complete fluency in popular-music idioms, Bernstein created in *West Side Story* (1957) the freshest musical of the post-war period. A recasting of the Romeo and Juliet story in terms of the ethnic melting pot of Manhattan's upper west side, *West Side Story* was an evocative portrait of post-war urban America; its finely balanced interaction between drama and ballet owed much to the choreographer Jerome Robbins (who had also conceived the dances of *Fancy Free*). And with *Mass* (composed for the opening in 1971 of the Kennedy Center for the Performing Arts in Washington, DC) Bernstein wrote a work that had some relationship, at least, with avant-garde impulses toward a new, "third music theater" (see p. 303).

The only other post-war musical to rival (and even outdo) the success of *West Side Story* was *My Fair Lady* (1956), composed by Frederick Loewe (b. 1901) to the book and lyrics of Alan Jay Lerner (1918–86) after Shaw's *Pygmalion*. Perhaps the American audience that responded by the millions to this near-operetta was identifying with the guttersnipe-turned-lady of the heroine; musically speaking it had little to identify with, for like all the other musicals of the late 1950s and most of the 1960s, *My Fair Lady* shared in no way in the popular-music revolution.

By the early 1970s, another figure seemed especially promising as a composer of musicals: Stephen Sondheim (b. 1930). Sondheim had written the lyrics for Bernstein's *West Side Story* and Jule Styne's *Gypsy* (1959). Later he went on independently to write both the lyrics and music for a series of musicals of high inventiveness and artistry (*A Funny Thing Happened on the Way to the Forum, Company, Follies*), which seemed to culminate in a fresh and elaborate work, *A Little Night Music* (1972). Its unique score— with every song in one or another type of triple meter (especially waltzes), a rich harmonic language evocative of Strauss's *Der Rosenkavalier*, contrapuntal duets and trios, a quartet, and even a double quintet—suggested once again (as with *Oklahoma!* almost thirty years earlier) that the American musical might be aspiring to a new high-mindedness. This turned out not to be true, but Sondheim himself was to go on to an even more ambitious, virtually operatic musical-theater work in *Sweeney Todd, the Demon Barber of Fleet Street* (1979) and to an experimental, developmental score for *Sunday in the Park with George*, which won the 1985 Pulitzer Prize for drama.

THE NEW VIRTUOSITY

Virtuosity had long had a role in American music—but virtuosity of a circumscribed and conventionalized sort. This was especially true in concert music, where the very term *virtuoso* connoted simply a performer who had a more spectacular technical command than most over traditional methods of vocal or instrumental production. But much of the new concert music put brand-new demands on performers: the post-Cage process-and-action music called for improvisatory skills and a new responsiveness to the situation at hand; serial music, obeying the dictates of intervals, rows, sets, and subsets, often simply disregarded the assumed limits of performer capabilities (especially in melodic contour, dynamics, range, and articulation, each of which tended not only to be extremely varied but also to change with unprecedented rapidity). Electroacoustic music had stretched all the boundaries of traditional music—and in doing so had affected composers' ideas of what they might try to get out of *live* performers. And the intersections and interactions among various kinds of music, coupled with the increasing range of musical experience possible to get from recordings (not just music of the Western tradition but folk and traditional music from all over the world), had stimulated the imaginations of both composers and performers.

One result was that composers were demanding more and different things of performers; another was that performers were demonstrating to composers that more and different things were possible. And out of this development came a new virtuosity, displayed dazzlingly by specialist singers and instrumentalists (and a few conductors)—and counted on by composers. Among the singers, pre-eminent were Bethany Beardslee (b. 1927), Cathy Berberian (1928–83), Jan DeGaetani (b. 1933), Paul Sperry (b. 1934), Phyllis Bryn-Julson (b. 1945); Susan Davenny Wyner (b. 1945), and Joan La Barbara (b. 1947); among the instrumentalists, the flutist Harvey Sollberger (b. 1938); clarinetist William O. Smith (b. 1926); trumpeter Gerard Schwarz (b. 1947); trombonist Stuart Dempster (b. 1936); cellist Fred Sherry (b. 1948); double-bassist Bertram Turetzky (b. 1933); percussionist Max Neuhaus (b. 1939); and pianists David Tudor (b. 1926), Paul Jacobs (1930–83), Robert Miller (1930–81), Frederick Rzewski (b. 1938), and Ursula Oppens (b. 1944). Rzewski was also an organizer of one of the many new-music chamber ensembles that developed to meet the challenge of the new virtuosity (Musica Elettronica Viva, founded in Rome in 1966 to specialize in live/electronic music);

among others were the Contemporary Chamber Players (Chicago, 1954–   ), the ONCE Group (Ann Arbor, 1961–69), the Group for Contemporary Music (New York, 1962–   ), Speculum Musicae (New York, 1971–   ), Parnassus (New York, 1974–   ), the New Music Consort (New York, 1975–   ), and similar groups in almost every substantial city and university—not to mention string quartets that specialized in the new-music repertory, such as the Juilliard, Composers, Concord, Emerson, and Kronos quartets. Some conductors, too, won acclaim as specialists in new music, among them Gunther Schuller, Thomas Nee (b. 1920), Ralph Shapey (b. 1921), Arthur Weisberg (b. 1931), Dennis Russell Davies (b. 1944), and Michael Tilson Thomas (b. 1944).

A number of leading younger composers of the period were identified with one or another of the new-music ensembles, often as organizers or conductors, and usually performers as well. Charles Wuorinen, for example, co-founded with Sollberger the Group for Contemporary Music and has often served as its pianist and/or conductor. As a composer, he is a serialist, and temperamentally and intellectually inclined to "a very detailed structuring of events [in a composition] down to a very small scale, as well as on a very large scale" (thus adhering to Babbitt's serial approach); on the other hand, he believes that "since even the most detailed score still represents an assemblage of generalities . . . it should always be possible to reinterpret compositions"[9]—thus coming down on the side of the interpretive performer. The overwhelming majority of Wuorinen's works have been for live performers, especially for virtuoso soloists; it was ironic, then, that his Pulitzer Prize (see p. 262) was awarded to an all-electronic composition. More characteristic are the *Piano Variations* (1964), several chamber concertos with different solo instruments (cello, flute, oboe, and others), the one-act opera *The Politics of Harmony* (1966–67), and the *Bassoon Variations* (1972). The last-named (recorded on *NW* 209:s2/3) is particularly accessible and attractive sonorously, the bassoon being "accompanied" by an unusual duo—harp and timpani. Wuorinen writes a music sometimes of ferocious intensity and furious activity, sometimes of complex lacy delicacy, that both responds to and demands more of the new virtuosity, approaching at times the outer limits of interpretative possibility and perception.

The response of composers to the new virtuosos' unimagined capabilities is well illustrated by such works as *Inflections I* (1969) by Robert Hall Lewis (b. 1926) and *General Speech* (1969) by Robert Erickson (b. 1917). Lewis writes,

> I was reluctant at first to attempt a composition for an instrument I had considered rather limited [the double-bass]. . . . When I received a tape from

[9] Quoted in Benjamin Boretz, "Conversation with Charles Wuorinen," *Contemporary Music Newsletter*, III (November-December 1969), 4–8.

Bert [Turetzky], however, on which he demonstrated more technical possibilities and resources than I had known existed, my imagination was awakened. . . .[10]

Lewis went on to write a ten-minute work of staggering virtuosity for unaccompanied double-bass, usually considered one of the most recalcitrant of instruments (and seldom thought attractive or interesting enough sonorously to hold its own all alone). Erickson's piece was commissioned by Stuart Dempster; it is a "setting" for unaccompanied trombone of General Douglas MacArthur's retirement speech in which the trombonist must "merge his playing of precisely notated (and often difficult) musical events with the verbal articulation into the instrument of a phoneticized version of [the] speech." The result is not only a marvel of virtuosity but a savage parody, turning MacArthur's "Duty! Honor! Country! . . ." oratory into belching, growling, howling gobbledygook. (Recall that in 1969 American sentiment against the country's involvement in the Vietnam War was at a peak.)

Equally demanding of performers' virtuosity but more accessible is the music of George Crumb (b. 1929), whose early works were so well received that he was unquestionably the most highly acclaimed "young" American composer of the early 1970s; already by 1968 he had won the Pulitzer Prize, for the orchestral piece *Echoes of Time and the River*. A large number of Crumb's earlier works are settings of the picturesque image-laden Spanish poems of Federico García Lorca, among them four books of *Madrigals* (1965–69); *Songs, Drones and Refrains of Death* (1968); *Night of the Four Moons* (1969); and *Ancient Voices of Children* (1970). Later Crumb turned to cosmic images, as in *Makrokosmos I* and *II* (1972, 1973), each a set of "Twelve Fantasy-Pieces after the Zodiac for Amplified Piano," and *Star-Child* ("A Parable for Soprano, Antiphonal Children's Voices, and Large Orchestra"; 1977) All these reveal an extraordinarily subtle and adventuresome tonal imagination, a unique "ear," especially for tiny and delicate shades of timbre.

To realize his sonorous visions, Crumb called on an immense range of new performance techniques: humming into wind-instrument mouthpieces, vocalizing into undamped (and amplified) piano strings, whispering, shouting, "bending" of pitch microtonally (by, for example, turning the tuning pegs of a double-bass), and so forth. And from the world of popular music he borrowed many instruments: banjo, mandolin, toy piano, jew's harp, musical saw, cowbells, electric guitar, and other amplified instruments. *Black Angels* ("1970, *in tempore belli*" is the composer's dating, referring to the war in Vietnam) is for electric or amplified acoustic string quartet; *Vox Balaenae* (1972) is for flute, cello, and piano, all amplified. In the latter work,

---

[10] This and the following quotation are from the liner notes to NW 254, on which both works discussed here are recorded.

the players are to wear black half masks; the depersonalization of the human components eerily increases the "personalization" (à la Carter) of the music.

Another, older composer who came to new prominence in the 1960s after building an earlier reputation as a neo-Classic *Wunderkind* was Lukas Foss (b. 1922). In 1957, inspired by the improvisatory vitality of jazz, Foss organized an Improvisation Chamber Ensemble in Los Angeles, hoping to develop principles of non-jazz improvisation. This ensemble had a marked effect on the music that he composed. *Time Cycle* (1959–60), four songs on texts having to do with time, clocks, or bells, appeared in two different versions, one of them for soprano and orchestra with improvisatory interludes between the songs (the other without them).

The score of *Echoi* (1961–63), for piano, percussion, clarinet, and cello (the instruments in Foss's improvisation ensemble), includes not only conventionally "precise" notation but also "proportional" notation, which, barless and beatless, requires the performers to view the entire score and to follow each others' playing; it also includes passages of "no coordination" and free reordering of given pitches; passages with random, aperiodic assortments of dynamics, articulations, and pitches; and passages with headless notes—stems and beams only—suggesting the general contour of a line but not specifying pitches or, for the percussionist, which instruments to strike or the order in which to strike them. Toward the end of *Echoi*, two pre-recorded but uncoordinated tape tracks, one of clarinet music, the other of cello music, are turned on, and the live clarinetist and cellist are to echo in a free manner the taped sounds of their own instruments. There are other aspects of choice and chance in *Echoi* (no two performances will ever be the same), but the composer's ideas dominate throughout. Example 11-1 suggests some of the aspects of notation I have mentioned: the notation is proportional; large notes stand for longer time, small notes for shorter; dotted lines show the moments of coordination among performers; "*c. 1s.*" (in the piano part) represents a rest of "about one second"; headless notes in the vibraphone staff indicate general melodic contour but no specific pitches.

COLLAGE, MIXED MEDIA, AND MUSIC THEATER

Intersection and interaction are by definition the common ground among several other kinds of works that became increasingly important in the post-war period: collage pieces (from the French word for "pasteup"), mixed-media productions, and a new kind of music theater closely related to mixed media. Although many influences conjoined to stimulate the rise of such works, they were all to some degree indebted to precepts and examples offered by John Cage.

EXAMPLE 11-1. L. Foss, *Echoi*, first movement excerpt. © Copyright 1964 by Carl Fischer, Inc., New York. Reproduced by permission.

In composing—or, rather, giving directions for—such a work as his *Imaginary Landscape No. 4* (1951) for twelve radio receiving sets (twenty-four performers), Cage effectively set the stage for a collage piece. The musical "found objects" to be "pasted up"—comparable to the bits of wood, newspaper, ribbon, and whatnot in a collage by Picasso or Braque (or more relevant to Cage, his contemporary and friend Robert Rauschenberg)—are the bits of broadcast sound picked up by the various radios from different stations. Like the musical quotations in works of Ives (who must be considered the American ancestor of collage technique) or the pre-recorded materials of a *concrète* piece, these sonorous "objects" make for a double level of perception: one experiences a new work but at the same time is invited—or *made*, willy-nilly—to perceive or remember others.

One of the first major collage-technique works of the post-war era—a drastic and startling one—was the third movement of *Sinfonia* (1968) by Luciano Berio (born in Italy in 1925 and a musically influential American resident from early in the 1960s until 1972). Against a playing of the scherzo of Gustav Mahler's Second Symphony, countless fragments of other music proliferate—some spoken or sung, some played—by Bach, Schoenberg, Debussy, Ravel, Strauss, Berlioz, Brahms, Berg, Hindemith, Beethoven, Wagner, Stravinsky, Boulez, Stockhausen, Ives, Berio himself, and others. Berio remarked that the movement could be considered "a documentary on an *objet trouvé* recorded in the mind of the listener."[11] The surrealist effect

---

[11] From jacket notes by the composer for the Columbia recording (MS-7268).

of *Sinfonia* is common also to Foss's *Baroque Variations* (1967), based on material "found" in Handel, Bach, and Scarlatti; he described its third variation, "Phorion" ("booty," "spoils," even "stolen goods"), as "torrents of baroque semiquavers, washed ashore by ocean waves, sucked in again, returning. . . ." Foss's *Geod* (1969) is also based on *objets trouvés* in that depending on the location of the particular performance, different patriotic/national source materials are to be borrowed.

More subtle is the collage technique in a work like Crumb's *Ancient Voices of Children*, where evocative fragments of other music—flamenco, *Bist du bei mir* from the Notebook for Anna Magdalena Bach, a bit of Mahler—emerge from the matrix of the composition like flickerings of memory, and in a number of works by Michael Colgrass and Jacob Druckman. Colgrass (b. 1932) broke from strict serialism in 1966 with *As Quiet As*, an orchestral work using a theme from a sonatina by Beethoven transformed in manners reminiscent, successively, of Haydn, Stravinsky, Webern, and Count Basie. The very titles of Colgrass's *Déja vu* (1977) and *Flashbacks* (1979) suggest collage; the former (recorded on *NW* 318:s1) is a brilliant quarter-hour-long piece for four percussion soloists and orchestra that transforms a single borrowed phrase into various styles (including big-band jazz). Both the title and the contents of Druckman's *Delizie contente che l'alme beate* (1973), for woodwind quintet and tape, derive from an aria by the seventeenth-century opera composer Francesco Cavalli, who provided similar source material for *Lamia* (1975), for soprano and orchestra. Druckman's Pulitzer Prize-winning *Windows* (1972) is mosaic-like, with "fragments of 'old music'—galant dances, wisps of chorale, hints of waltz—cunningly placed"[12]; another orchestral work, *Aureole* (1979; recorded on *NW* 318:s2/1), is described by the composer as centered on a "constant but shifting, shimmering melody from which all the music springs"—the "Kaddish tune" from Bernstein's Third Symphony.

Related to musical collage is another post-war approach to structure explored by some American composers—musical "spatialization," so to speak. Traditionally, Western music has been thought an exclusively temporal art: time is the only continuum in which music has generally been considered to exist. However, some post-World War II composers have conceived of music as spatial as well as temporal. (Ives had such a vision; so had Varèse.)

In some works, physical space itself is crucial, as in Carter's Second String Quartet (1959), where the players are to be more widely separated than usual, or Crumb's *Ancient Voices of Children*, with its placement of a boy soprano offstage. In several imaginative works by Roger Reynolds, including *The Emperor of Ice Cream* (1962; rev. 1974) and *Blind Men* (1966), not only

---

[12] Andrew Porter, in a *New Yorker* review of February 10, 1975, reprinted in his *Music of Three Seasons: 1974–1977* (New York: Farrar Straus Giroux, 1978), p. 92.

is the spatial distribution of the performers specified but also the scores show their movement from one area of the stage to another; some later pieces by Reynolds, notably several in a series of compositions called *Voicespace* (late 1970s), are composed on separate tape tracks (at least four) to be played through different speakers widely separated around the perimeter of the hall.

In other works, however, the "spatialization" is a matter of *composition*, not performance procedures. The musical discourse is not shaped according to principles of harmonic continuity or of underlying omnipresent "beat" but is essentially one of discrete sounds, or blocks of sounds, shaping time rather than being shaped by it. The result is an effect of sound in space more than in time, for the whole perception of time's passing is altered and attenuated by the discreteness of the sonorous events. Some composers no longer even speak of "sonorities" (let alone "chords" or "harmonies") but of "densities," "sound structures," or "sound objects"; and their ideas of musical form often rest on the intersection and interaction of such sound structures or on the equally spatial images of textures thick or thin, fluctuating or constant, combined or opposed. High-low contrasts are planned or emphasized in spatial terms, as are timbral shifts.

Symptomatically, an older composer like Henry Brant (b. 1913), who had been interested for a long time in the separation and spatial disposition of instrumentalists and singers in halls, auditoriums, and even the out-of-doors, achieved new recognition for such works as *Antiphony I* (1953; rev. 1968), for five orchestral groups; *The Grand Universal Circus* (1956), a theater piece calling for eight solo voices and thirty-two choristers; *Fire in Cities* (1961), for choruses and instrumental groups; and *Voyage Four* (1963), a "total antiphony," with musicians not only onstage but also against side and back walls and beneath the floor. *Verticals Ascending* ("After the Rodia [Watts] Towers"; 1967) is for double wind ensemble; for the recording on NW 211:s1/3, the two bands were placed back-to-back on opposite sides of the stage, separated by a sound wall and 50 feet of space, and led by two conductors.

Ralph Shapey (b. 1921) has similarly divided performers into subgroups and disposed them in spatially separated positions. Thus his *Ontogeny* (1958) divides a full orchestra into seven sub-orchestras, repositioned on stage. Another orchestral work, *Rituals* (1958), is similarly conceived, and one critic spoke of its conveying "not what is called organic growth, but rather . . . a sense that the whole piece exists at once and that a listener's (and the performers') progress through it in time is kin to viewing central, unchanging images from different aspects, under different lights, against different backgrounds."[13] There is a similar quality even in slighter works

    [13] Andrew Porter, "Musical Events: Affirmation," *The New Yorker*, July 9, 1979, pp. 76–78.

by Shapey that do not call for spatial separation of the players, such as the duo for flute and piano, *Configurations*, of 1964 (recorded on *NW* 254:s2/ 1). In speaking of his *Incantations* (1961) for soprano and ten instruments, Shapey articulated his spatial concept of music as being made of "sound-objects":

music as an object in Time and Space

aggregate sounds structured into concrete sculptured forms

images existing as a totality from their inception, each
    a self-involved unit of individual proportions

related, inter-related, and unrelated images organized into an organic whole

permutations occurring only within each self-contained unit. . . .[14]

Both the collage technique and the compositional idea of "sounds structured into concrete sculptured forms" are naturally inviting ones for live/electronic music, especially because it lends itself so well to a kind of abstract musical drama: juxtaposition of discrete elements can easily suggest dramatic opposition and conflict. Man-against-machine is embodied in the last movement of Foss's *Echoi*, when the live performers struggle against pre-recorded tapes of their own performance. Man-against-machine is also the theme of Druckman's *Animus I* (see p. 262); the composer describes the dramatic result:

> . . . After the first splitting off of the tape and the ensuing dialogue the [trombone] player sits while the electronic sounds move too quickly for him to compete. The man begins again with angrier, more animal-like material; the tape again enters . . . this time driving him off the stage. The tape exhausts itself, the man reenters, the two finish in a tenuous balance.[15]

Like collage in purposeful juxtaposition of discrete, disparate materials, but extended beyond sound to other media, are mixed-media productions. The term came into existence as a generalization for amalgamations of several art forms other than the traditional ones of, say, opera or ballet. Some mixed media had origins in the Happenings of the 1950s and early 1960s and in the action-and-process music of the ONCE, Fluxus, and other such groups. Some also reflected, or at least paralleled, the multiple bombardment of the senses of a rock concert. Some were probably an attempt, if unconscious, to make up for the loss of the visual and human elements in electroacoustic music. And of course some flowed from Cage's dictum that "relevant action is theatrical (music [imaginary separation of hearing from the other senses] does not exist)."

---

[14] Quoted in "Music Programs and Notes," University of Illinois 1965 Festival of Contemporary Arts, p. 23.

[15] Jacket notes for *Electronic Music III* (Turnabout TVS-34177; released 1967).

Cage himself was co-producer with Lejaren Hiller of one of the most spectacular mixed-media events, *HPSCHD* ("harpsichord" in a six-letter form convenient for computer coding), which was premiered at the University of Illinois in May 1969. The production lasted about five hours; it involved seven harpsichordists; computer-generated sounds on fifty-one different tapes; projections from fifty-two slide projectors; a battery of colored spotlights; and an audience of several thousand who sat, stood, danced, or wandered through the environment. The sound materials of the work, and their organization, were an extraordinary mix. Three of the (amplified) harpsichordists played material based on the *Introduction to the Composition of Waltzes by Means of Dice*, attributed to Mozart; another played any Mozart music of his choice; two others began with material by Mozart and moved on through music by Beethoven, Chopin, Schumann, Gottschalk, Ives, Schoenberg, Cage, and Hiller; the seventh played a computer-generated repertory of materials in equal-tempered twelve-tone tuning. Meanwhile, on the fifty-one tapes were sounds based on *different* equal-tempered divisions of the octave, from five to fifty-six tones (but excluding the conventional one of twelve). When *HPSCHD* was recorded—a twenty-minute segment of it, at least—a further nicety was added: along with the recording (Nonesuch H-71224; released 1969) came a computer printout, which enabled the listener to "perform" (at least to transform) the work by manipulating the knobs and buttons of the record-playing equipment. (This acknowledgment and utilization of the added "medium" of the piece in its recorded form was a brilliant and genial idea of Cage and Hiller.)

The West Coast seemed to encourage multi-media work. (Cage, of course, came from there originally, as did Partch, whose invented instruments have an awesome physical presence, calling attention to themselves visually as well as sonorously.) Two figures mentioned previously (p. 263) as San Francisco tape-music composers—Morton Subotnick and Pauline Oliveros—went on to compose intriguing multi-media works. In the mid-1960s Subotnick wrote a series of diverse pieces entitled *Play!*; each combined live-music performance with tape-music performance, often with other media as well—films, slides, other props, and sometimes actors—and usually with the musicians performing unusual physical activities (lowering their heads, raising their arms, turning to each other as if in surprise or questioning). In *An Electric Christmas* (1967), Subotnick organized one of the most unusual mixed-media presentations of the late 1960s. Evocative of a rock concert in its setting and format, *An Electric Christmas* was an evening-long event that mingled medieval music played by the New York Pro Musica (an early-music ensemble), rock by a group called Circus Maximus, Subotnick's own electronic music (mostly composed and "played" by him, on an onstage synthesizer), film projections, and a light show; it culminated in a joyous, semi-improvisatory version by the whole crowd of the fourteenth-century love song *Douce dame jolie*, by Guillaume de Machaut. In that same decade of the 1960s, in which mixed media peaked as a compositional ideal, Oliveros organized similar productions. One was *Valentine for SAG* (1968), the acronym referring to the Sonic Arts Group, which developed out of ONCE; this production is based on a game of hearts played onstage, with the four players' heartbeats amplified, while at the same time a narrator discusses the history of card games, two carpenters build a picket fence downstage, a croquet player hits a few balls, and projections of giant playing-cards are displayed.

Robert Ashley (see p. 272) turned almost entirely to mixed media and continued to be a leading-edge vanguardist into the 1980s, working not only with dramatic live/electronic combinations—as in *The Wolfman*, in which Ashley himself, heavily miked, shouts "with maximum amplification against a deafening electronic roar"—but also with advanced video projection, instrumental and vocal music, lecture-like narration, and various graphic enhancements—as in *Perfect Lives (Private Parts)*.[16]

Obviously, there is an element of theatricality in virtually all the works we have been considering here. The composer-critic Eric Salzman (b. 1933) has claimed that they tend toward a "third music theater—neither opera nor musical—that [is] in the process of finding itself[:] a primarily non-verbal art integrating sound, movement, image, music, language, idea, thinking, feeling."[17] Salzman himself pursued this vision by organizing in 1970 a music-theater group called Quog to perform such works as his own *The Nude Paper Sermon* (1968–69), "tropes" for actor, Renaissance consort, chorus, and electronic music. He later collaborated with Michael Sahl (b. 1934) in small-scale music-theater pieces, of which *Civilization and Its Discontents* (1980) was especially well received. In these works, just as media are mixed, so are musical styles, in a dramatic (and theatrical) response to the experimental situation, when everyone has access through modern technology to a virtually limitless range of musics. As Salzman put it,

> Multi-track, multi-layer experience becomes the norm: Ravi Shankar, John Cage, the Beatles, Gregorian chant, electronic music, Renaissance madrigals and motets, Bob Dylan, German *Lieder*, soul, J. S. Bach, jazz, Ives, Balinese gamelan, Boulez, African drumming, Mahler, *gagaku*, Frank Zappa, Tchaikowsky, Varèse . . . all become part of the common shared experience.[18]

---

[16] The quotation is from the sympathetic chapter on Ashley in John Rockwell's *All American Music* (New York: Alfred A. Knopf, Inc., 1983), pp. 96–108.

[17] *New York Times*, December 12, 1972.

[18] From the composer's jacket notes for *The Nude Paper Sermon* (Nonesuch H-71231; released 1969). The same point, put in almost the same way, had been made by the composer Ben Johnston in a thoughtful essay, "On Context," *Source*, II/2 (July 1968), 44–45: ". . . Machaut, the Beatles, Wagner, Ravi Shankar, Pete Seeger, Bach, and Xenakis meet . . . only as far from me as my record player."

THE NEW EXPRESSIONISM

One of the most powerful, if paradoxical, effects of the new ideas of time and space in music, of "concrete sculptured forms," of the new virtuosity, and also of the music involving chance and performer choice in a context of composer-controlled image of sound, is a new expressionism. Unlike the post-Romantic expressionism of a Strauss or a Schoenberg, it is not the composer's feelings that seem to be loosed but in part those of the performers, and even more potently and extraordinarily, those of the *sounds themselves*. Not only do the performers seem more alive, flexible, and responsive to each other, but also in a peculiarly palpable way the music itself takes on an unprecedented sentience, personalization, and vitality. Hear Lukas Foss, speaking of the second movement of *Echoi*:

> . . . vibraphone shadowing clarinet (close canon at the unison) sticks to him like glue. clarinet should make futile attempts to escape its own shadow, like an insect trying to extricate itself from a spider web. cello joins in the pursuit. . . . pitchless percussion also shadowing, imitating. everyone wanting to get in on the act.[19]

Or hear Chou Wen-chung (b. 1923)—a former pupil of Varèse whose Chinese origins allow him to relate what seems new in American music to some very old Oriental ideas—speaking of his orchestral works *All in the Spring Wind* (1953) and *And the Fallen Petals* (1954):

> . . . a tonal brushwork in space—with ever-changing motion, tension, texture, and sonority. . . . The ancient Chinese musician believed that each single tone or aggregate of tones is a musical entity in itself and a living spark of expression as long as it lasts. Therefore, it was also believed that the meaning in music lies intrinsically in the tones themselves, that maximum expressiveness can be derived from a succession of tones without resorting to extraneous procedures.[20]

Or think of the abstract musical drama in Druckman's *Animus I* (see p. 301), when the tape drives the trombonist offstage but then "exhausts itself," or of the musical self-commentary inherent in quotation and collage techniques.

Many present-day American composers are building a whole new musical aesthetic on an assumption of the potential *liveliness*—in a literal sense—of sounds themselves. This is especially true of those working in

---

[19] "Work-Notes for *Echoi*," *PNM*, III/1 (Fall-Winter 1964), 54–61.
[20] "Towards a Re-Merger in Music," *Contemporary Composers on Contemporary Music*, eds. Elliott Schwartz and Barney Childs (New York: Holt, Rinehart and Winston, 1967), pp. 309–15.

electronic or *concrète* music, who no longer have to think, and who choose not to think, in terms of twelve-tone equal temperament, Classic-Romantic or "neo-" tonalities, metrical rhythm, traditional instruments, standardized instrumentation, or even "performance." Suggestive in this connection is a set of hints to beginning electronic-music composition students for shaping their works, a guide written by Laurie Spiegel (b. 1945), who as a young composer was teaching even younger composers. She suggested working toward any of four "forms"—static, evolutionary, climactic, and dialog. "Dialog form" she defined as "two or more distinctly separate sounds or textures brought into interaction." This interaction can be realized in different ways; some that she suggested are the following (and note the personalization):

a.   they [the sounds] begin as separate but eventually merge into one, or find some relationship to each other;
b.   one of several equals [sounds again] eventually dominates over others;
c.   one texture breaks up into several components which exhibit increasing individuality;
d.   a sound originally by itself begins to be accompanied (or possibly attacked) by another. . . .[21]

MINIMALISM

The 1960s saw the beginning of an important new movement in American music—*minimalism*, a term borrowed from art critics, who from the mid-1960s applied it to works by such artists as the painter Frank Stella, the sculptor Donald Judd, and the versatile Robert Morris. Most of the composers called minimalists reject the term, but they are in the same position as Schoenberg, who rejected the term *atonal* for his music: they are stuck with it.

In the background of minimalism were various musical trends of the 1950s. In both the serialist and aleatoric camps, certain *reductive* tendencies were important—for example, the post-Webern composers' fondness for isolating single tones and giving them a microcosmic identity all their own (also true of Wolff's music, as we have noted), or among the New York school composers, Feldman's unchanging, uninterrupted, murmuring low-level volume and slow-motion rhythms. Also important was Cage's having wiped the slate clean, so to speak, with 4′33″ and its invitation to listeners simply to *listen*—to anything in the environment that caught their attention. The insistent, powerful pulse and the cyclical, variation-like structure of most

[21] ". . . Some Possible Shapes for Sound Composition . . ." (unpublished). I am grateful to Laurie Spiegel for permission to quote from this material.

jazz were also important. Technology, too, counted for a lot—the technology that had reduced much of the world to a non-stop jet flight and that led to the long-playing disc and magnetic tape as new recording media—for it made available an unprecedented range of exotic music, distant or ancient, much of it based on very different principles of structure and continuity from those of the Western art-music tradition; it also made it possible for composers to work directly with the materials of composition and to manipulate, alter, repeat, and adjust them at will.

Interest in third-world cultures—on the rise during the 1960s, among musicians as among the general public—also fed into the minimalist aesthetic. Cage had emphasized the impact of Zen Buddhism on his thought and had used the Chinese *I Ching* to guide his composition. The great Indian sitarist Ravi Shankar had toured widely in the United States in the 1950s and moved here in the 1960s. The development, by Cowell and younger composers, of all-percussion music had stimulated interest in Indonesian gamelan groups and North African drumming. Yoga was newly popular; so was meditation, and also mind-altering drugs, used partly as aids in inducing meditative states.

Additionally, an increasing disillusionment with the predominant compositional method espoused within the musical "establishment"—the twelve-tone technique, which though challenging intellectually to composers remained resolutely incomprehensible to listeners—contributed to the rise of minimalism in the 1960s. The early leaders, all in their thirties, were La Monte Young, Terry Riley, Steve Reich, and Philip Glass.

Young (see p. 271) began in the mid-1950s to introduce into his serial compositions unusually long-held notes and lengthy silences; his Trio for Strings (1958) goes further: a fifty-minute work, it is based on only four notes (for instance, G, C, C♯, and D), a "dream chord" (Young's term) that he had heard singing in telephone wires. By 1960, influenced by Cage's radical ideology, Young was making such apparently neo-Dada statements as *Composition 1960 #7* and *Composition 1960 #10* (see p. 272), which were typically realized as "static" drone-based pieces. But as suggested earlier, to anyone who really listened, they were not in fact static: like "real" music, they pulsed and "moved" with a strange inner life of minutely shifting timbres arising from the slight variations of overtone structure in the tone(s) sounded— as, for example, when a violinist's bow moves across the string with very slight changes of pressure not willed by the performer but simply the result of human "imperfection."

Young made other drone-like pieces that revealed a different bent— a growing preoccupation with just intonation and non-tempered tuning systems (confirmed by lengthy study later, in the 1970s, with the Indian master Pandit Pran Nath). One example is the drone piece entitled *The Second Dream of the High-Tension Line Stepdown Transformer*, from *The Four*

Dreams of China (1962). Its pitch material is simply four tones, in the frequency ratios 36:35:32:24. Example 11-2 (a) gives two possible pitch realizations of the tones; the interval 36:35 is smaller than a semitone, hence the arrows in the example. Example 11-2 (b) illustrates the just-intoned second (36:32 = 9:8), fourth (32:24 = 4:3), and fifth (36:24 = 3:2) that are produced between three pairs of the tones. In performing the composition, strict rules dictate which tones may be sounded together; otherwise, each tone may enter or exit at will. A "harmonic" music results, harmonic in the sense of the intervals formed—not only between the basic tones but also between their upper partials—and of the combination tones produced when these simple fundamental tones are dwelt on. Example 11-2 makes the piece look static—this is *music?*—but to the degree that the performers develop an acute sensitivity for the resultant "harmonies," and the listener does also, the music is not at all static; a strange, hypnotic, dream-like succession of delicate sound-images unfolds in shimmering, floating procession.

EXAMPLE 11-2. Basis of L. M. Young's *Second Dream of the High-Tension Line Stepdown Transformer* (1962). (a) Pitches to be sounded (approximate; just intonation is to be used). (b) Interval ratios produced.

Terry Riley (b. 1935) was an associate of Young on the West Coast and later in New York; he, too, became a student of Pran Nath. In the early 1960s he supported himself partly as a jazz pianist, and his background in jazz fed into one of the seminal minimalist works, his *In C* (1964). This is a work for any number of musicians, playing any melodic instruments, each musician running in order through a series of fifty-three very brief melodic figures—repeating each figure, however, as many times as he or she wishes before moving on to the next one.[22] The total length of *In C* and its moment-to-moment details (and as mentioned, its instrumentation) are variable, which suggests a Cage-derived aleatory randomness. But this factor is offset by the repetitive element and by a strictly controlled rhythm, governed by a continuous, metronomic pulse (heard nakedly at the very beginning of the recording, drummed on the top two C's of a piano); these latter aspects are jazz-related.

---

[22] All these figures are printed on the jacket of the recording of *In C* (Columbia MS-7178; released 1968).

Steve Reich (b. 1936) also became interested in music based on the
repetition of brief modular patterns (when he, like Riley, was working at
the San Francisco Tape Music Center in the mid-1960s). Reich was especially
intrigued by the possibilities of "phase-shift" patterns—created when identical, repeated phrases, at first played simultaneously, gradually get out of
phase ("out of sync") as one part moves ever so slowly ahead of the other.
These he had noticed by chance in the minute differences in speed of two
tape recorders. Capitalizing on his discovery, he composed the *concrète*
works *It's Gonna Rain* (1965) and *Come Out* (1966), each based on a single,
short spoken phrase, and both built up from endless repetitions of their
basic phrases, with multi-track tape techniques used to create pileups of the
gradual phase shifts. The resultant pulsation of out-of-phase tape tracks produces a kind of rhythmic combination-tone effect: as the parts, initially in
phase, gradually go out of phase, and as the number of tracks increases to
four, then eight, a thick tapestry of multiple pulsations is perceived, as
hypnotic and euphoric rhythmically as Young's music is harmonically.

Reich developed techniques for live performance of such phase-shift-
based music in *Piano Phase*, for two keyboardists (1967); *Four Organs*, for
electric organs and maracas (1970); and *Phase Patterns* (also 1970), for four
or more identical keyboards. Example 11-3, the opening of *Piano Phase*, can
suggest the principle involved: player 1 repeats a one-measure figure throughout
the piece (except at the very end, a coda), maintaining an absolutely steady

EXAMPLE 11-3. Steve Reich, *Piano Phase* (1967), beginning (basic module and first
three phase shifts). Copyright © 1980 by Universal Edition (London), Ltd., London.
All rights reserved. Used by permission of European American Music Distributors
Corporation, sole U.S. agent for Universal Edition.

tempo; player 2 repeats the same figure but, after repetitions of measure 1, gradually accelerates until he or she is one-sixteenth note ahead of player 1 (but back in phase, at measure 3). The same gradual phase shift occurs after the in-phase repetitions of measure 3, and so on throughout the piece.

Philip Glass (b. 1937) had a conventional but thorough musical training in this country and in France (with Nadia Boulanger). In Paris in 1965 he had an especially significant encounter with Indian music, through Ravi Shankar and the tabla player Allah Rakha; this profoundly affected his musical thought and set him on the so-called minimalist path. Like Riley and Reich, Glass also began building pieces by repetition of melodic cells—varying the repetitions, however, by occasional additions or subtractions of units within them, as in *Strung Out* (1967), for amplified violin, and *Two Pages* (1968), for two amplified keyboard instruments. An excerpt (Example 11-4) from *Music in Fifths* (1969) can suggest the principle: each numbered figure is to be repeated as many times as the players wish; at an agreed-upon cue they move to the next figure, which is a variant of the first; after similar repetitions of that figure, on to the next, which is yet another minutely varied version of the basic figure; and so on through the piece.

EXAMPLE 11-4. Philip Glass, *Music in Fifths* (1969), modules 13–19. © Dunvagen Music Publishers. Reproduced by permission.

The radicalism of Glass's works lay not only in their emphasis on repetition but in their rejection of polyphony (in favor of monophony or two-note parallelism), their rejection of harmony, and their diatonic melodic vocabulary; they sound superficially like five-finger exercises.

The early minimalist music of these composers had a number of things in common: (1) radical reduction of the compositional material for each work; (2) extensive repetition of such material (accepting, in Young's case, a drone as repetition carried to the nth degree), and moreover, repetition with virtually unchanging timbre, pitch, pace, and level of volume; (3) static, euphonious, non-modulatory harmony (if any at all); (4) lack of "drama"—

that is, lack of contrast, opposition, argument, climax, patterns of tension and release. As a result of all these factors, the music has an *apparent* accessibility, lack of complexity, denial of intellectuality, and lack of expressiveness or emotionality. Moreover, as one critic pointed out, one might claim that "the concept of [the musical] *work* [is] replaced by the notion of *process*."[23] Reich, especially, was interested in this idea: in his essay "Music as a Gradual Process" (1968), he said, ". . . I do not mean the process of composition, but rather pieces of music that are [themselves], literally, processes"; Glass said somewhat similarly that in his work of this period he "took rhythmic structure and made that more or less the subject of the work."[24]

The works of the 1960s by these composers were greeted with incredulity, hostility, and disdain. The academic serialists accused the minimalists of artistic nihilism; the aleatoric avant-garde accused them of aesthetic fascism. The critics largely ignored the music—and could afford to, at least during the 1960s and early 1970s, since it was performed most often in nonestablishment performance spaces (artists' lofts, art galleries, museums) and unknown even to most musicians, let alone the general public. Its early supporters were mainly visual artists who shared the minimalist aesthetic and who collaborated enthusiastically with their musical counterparts. Not until the mid-1970s, in fact, did the existence of musical minimalism rise to public consciousness; two landmarks were Glass's opera *Einstein on the Beach* (1976), which sold out two performances at the Metropolitan Opera House (rented for the occasion), and Reich's *Music for 18 Musicians* (also 1976), the 1978 recording of which (ECM/Warner Bros. 1-1129) sold more than 20,000 copies within a year. By then, the so-called minimalist pioneers had moved on stylistically to a music that no longer seemed "minimal" at all.

BIBLIOGRAPHICAL NOTES

One of the best writers on the jazz discussed in this chapter is Gary Giddins; his criticism (mostly from *The Village Voice*) is collected in *Riding on a Blue Note* (New York: Oxford University Press, 1981). Out of the dissertation cited in footnote 4, Lewis Porter developed the important article "John Coltrane's *A Love Supreme*: Jazz Improvisation as Composition," *Journal of the American Musicological Society*, XXXVIII (Fall 1985), 593–621. The authoritative work

[23] Wim Mertens, *American Minimal Music* (New York: Alexander Broude, 1983), p. 88.
[24] Reich's essay was first printed in his *Writings About Music* (Halifax: Press of the Nova Scotia College of Art and Design; New York: New York University Press, 1974), pp. 9–11. Glass is quoted in Robert Palmer, "Philip Glass Comes to Carnegie Hall—At Last," *New York Times* (May 28, 1978), Arts and Leisure, pp. 13, 15.

to date on free jazz is Ekkehard Jost's *Free Jazz* (Graz, Aus.: Universal Edition, 1974).

Third-stream music is discussed, along with many other topics, in Gunther Schuller's collection *Musings: The Musical Worlds of Gunther Schuller* (New York: Oxford University Press, 1985).

Rock to the mid-1970s is perhaps most sensibly discussed in the second edition of Charlie Gillett's *The Sound of the City: The Rise of Rock n' Roll* (New York: Dell Publishing, 1972) and Robert Christgau's *Any Old Way You Choose It: Rock and Other Pop Music* (New York: Penguin Books, 1973), as well as Greil Marcus's *Mystery Train: Images of America in Rock n' Roll Music* and *The Rolling Stone Illustrated History of Rock & Roll* (both cited in the bibliographical notes for Chapter Ten; see p. 284).

Although critical literature of substance on the American musical is quite thin, the books by Gerald Bordman cited earlier (see p. 215) are reliable; see also Andrew Lamb's *TNGDAM* article "Musical." Stephen Sondheim has been the subject of several dissertations; John Rockwell adroitly discusses him in context in the chapter "Urban Popular Song, the Broadway Musical, the Cabaret Revival & the Birth Pangs of American Opera" in his *All American Music* (New York: Alfred A. Knopf, Inc., 1983).

Two representatives of the new virtuosity, Charles Wuorinen and Frederick Rzewski, write authoritatively (and interestingly) on "Performance" in the *Dictionary of Contemporary Music*, ed. John Vinton (New York: E. P. Dutton, 1974). George Crumb is well served by his publisher in *George Crumb: Profile of a Composer*, ed. Don Gillespie (New York: C. F. Peters, 1986).

The background and continuing tradition of American vanguard music are well sketched by John Rockwell in his *TNGDAM* article "Experimental Music." Stephen Husarik discusses not only *HPSCHD* but other collage pieces (including Cage's *Musicircus* of 1967) in "John Cage and LeJaren [sic] Hiller: HPSCHD, 1969," *American Music*, I/2 (Summer 1983), 1–21. The new music theater is a special interest of Eric Salzman; this is reflected in his *Twentieth-Century Music: An Introduction*, 3rd ed. (Englewood Cliffs, NJ: Prentice-Hall, Inc., 1988).

The early minimalist leaders are discussed in Wim Mertens' *American Minimal Music: La Monte Young, Terry Riley, Steve Reich, Philip Glass*, trans. J. Hautekiet (New York: Alexander Broude, 1983). A uniquely thorough and authoritative study of Reich's work into the 1970s is K. Robert Schwarz's "Steve Reich: Music as a Gradual Process," *Perspectives of New Music*, XIX/1 & 2 (Fall-Winter 1980/Spring-Summer 1981), 373–92; XX/1 & 2 (Fall-Winter 1981/Spring-Summer 1982), 225–86.

TWELVE

OUR PLURALISTIC POST-MODERN ERA:
SINCE THE MID-1970S

As we have seen, the period immediately following World War II was one of seemingly simple dualities in American music: from the mid-1940s to the mid-1960s, new music appeared to center on pairs of opposite camps—twelve-tone music and serialism vs. the music of chance and indeterminacy; bop vs. swing; rock-and-roll vs. pop. The period that followed, from about the mid-1960s to the mid-1970s, was one of intersections and interactions that promised new syntheses. But instead, from the mid-1970s to the mid-1980s, things moved in different directions—lots of them. Multiplicity and cross-currents, diversity of aesthetic aims and practical means, confusion and profusion seemed to reign. One type of music was termed "new age," but the era was hardly one that prized newness as such; instead, it embraced both the new and the old, the close and the distant, the high-artistic and the popularesque, often in startling juxtapositions. Lines once clearly drawn in American music between conservative and radical, between avant-garde and traditional, between modernist and mainstream, were sketchy at best. It was a period of pluralistic *post-modernism*.

One young composer, in describing his new opera, wrote,

This music is Postmodern in the sense [in which] the term is applied to architecture. . . . Postmodernism debunks inevitability or unity of voice—all moments in history, [including] the present as well, exist with equal weight, share equal value, can rub shoulders with each other. . . . The timeliness of the music does not lie in its Modern elements but in the juxtaposition—and, hopefully, balance and reconciliation—[of] a range of elements drawn from the continuity of our present-into-past.[1]

Noah Creshevsky (b. 1945), whose works include a considerable number in the *musique concrète* tradition, spoke rather similarly of his entertaining potpourri of a piece, *Drummer* (1986):

Drummer's familiar Times Square sounds . . . have been compositionally manipulated to form the happy deception of intentionality. [The work] is a kind of sleight of hand, insisting on making order where there is none. Which of us has not hoped that . . . the evident chaos around us is a pattern whose order eludes us?

Creshevsky's *Strategic Defense Initiative* (1986)—its title, of course, borrowed from the official name for President Reagan's proposed "Star Wars" space-based defense program—is also built up by extreme and unpredictable juxtapositions of sonic source materials; at first seeming funny, reminiscent of the musical satires of Spike Jones (1911–65), it eventually projects, in the course of ten minutes, an eerie, uncomfortable atmosphere of a world in torment (an atmosphere contrived by the composer, of course, in exquisitely precise details and timings).

The composer-conductor Lukas Foss found something of the same sort of unmodulated, hard-edged adjacencies in William Bolcom's *Songs of Innocence and Experience* (see p. 290):

When we [modernist composers] use something borrowed we feel we have a duty to transform it, which we call "making it our own." But [Bolcom] puts each style in its own ambiance. Melting pot does not quite describe it, because the ingredients are not melted. . . .[2]

Note that there is no suggestion here of a *synthesis* of styles but rather a pluralistic juxtaposition and co-existence. (Perhaps not surprisingly, the American composer whose work had first seemed to celebrate such juxtapositions—Charles Ives—reached a new, and still unsurpassed, popularity in the mid-1970s, symbolized by the international festival-conference orga-

---

[1] Conrad Cummings, "Notes on the Music of 'Eros and Psyche' " (unpublished typescript, ca. 1983).
[2] Quoted in Will Crutchfield, "Bolcom Sets Blake to Several Kinds of Music," *New York Times*, January 9, 1987.

nized in 1974 around his music.) George Rochberg sized up the situation more generally; in an essay on his Third String Quartet (1971) and his shift to a neo-tonal style, he wrote,

> . . . We can no longer live with monolithic ideas about art and how it is produced. . . . On the contrary, the twentieth century has pointed . . . toward a difficult-to-define pluralism, a world of new mixtures and combinations . . . replete with juxtapositions of opposites (or seeming opposites) and contraries.[3]

POST-MINIMALISM

The radical minimalism of the late 1960s and early 1970s, as produced by Young, Riley, Reich, Glass, and others, had far-reaching influence on various kinds of music of the later 1970s and 1980s. The early minimalists themselves, however (with the exception of Young, who maintained a singularly pure and constant ideal), changed with the times: perhaps they too were caught up, to some degree, in the pluralistic currents that were washing over so much of American culture. Thus, although their music remained unmistakably rooted in the minimalist aesthetic, it developed a greater complexity, wider range of expression, and swifter rate of change—which made it seem hardly minimalist any more. If *maximalist* is too strong a term for it, *post-minimalist* may serve.

Terry Riley seemed to disappear for a time, having gone to both Europe and India (where he studied with the master singer Pandit Pran Nath, as did Young); he increasingly emphasized improvisatory performances, and he recorded only on obscure European labels. However, with the CBS album *Shri Camel* (released in 1980; the music composed in 1975–76) he reasserted his presence in American musical life. All four compositions on the album are performed by Riley himself, on an electric organ (a Yamaha YC-45-D) partially retuned in just intonation to permit the subtlest of India-influenced shadings of pitch; thus they have a new complexity of intonation. A different kind of complexity arises from multiple-track recording techniques, with as many as sixteen digital-delay channels allowing a rich tapestry-like improvisatory interaction as well as an exceptionally broad range of polyphonic voices and dynamic levels. In a number of later works, especially a series for string quartet commissioned by the Kronos Quartet, Riley returned to tempered tuning and wrote for acoustic instruments performing in real time (as in *Cadenza on the Night Plain* of 1984).

---

[3] "On the Third String Quartet," in George Rochberg, *The Aesthetics of Survival*, ed. William Bolcom (Ann Arbor: University of Michigan Press, 1984), pp. 239–42.

Steve Reich's phase-shift and process-driven music had already begun to expand and become more variegated and complex in the early 1970s; characteristic was *Drumming* (1971)—a sort of giant étude based on the single rhythmic phase

(on different-pitched drums, suggested by the stemming) but with changing timbres and instrumentation (including wordless voices) supporting its ninety-minute length and delineating a big four-section structure. *Music for Mallet Instruments, Voices, and Organ* (1973) introduced even sharper contrasts—of timbres, of sustained notes against pulsatile repeated ones, of accelerating patterns superimposed on decelerating ones—and for the first time in his career, Reich used harmonic shifts both gradual and abrupt as a structural element. With the hour-long *Music for 18 Musicians* (1976) these tendencies peaked in a multi-layered, colorful work of immense attractiveness (as was confirmed in the extraordinary success, for a piece of new "classical" music, of its 1978 recording).

Yet another phase in Reich's career began with *Tehillim* (1981), in which for the first time since his student days he set words to music. *Tehillim* is a four-movement work for voices and chamber group (adapted also for full orchestra) on Hebrew psalm texts. ("Tehillim" is Hebrew for "Psalms.") The post-minimalist expansions of Reich's music of the 1970s are here extended not only to medium (texted voices and polychromatic instrumental ensemble) but also to melody—no longer short-breathed, modular, and repetitive but arching, varied in phrase shapes, and fully responsive to both the structure and the meaning of the psalm verses; the work ends with a jubilant blaze of hallelujahs. The percussive background, however, maintains a typical Reichian pulse.

Even more ambitious and tending even more to "mainstream" modes of expression (including chromatic, cyclic harmony) are *The Desert Music* (1983), a five-movement setting, for a twenty-seven member chorus and an instrumental ensemble of eighty-nine players, of parts of poems by William Carlos Williams, and *Three Movements for Orchestra* (1986), scored for conventional symphony orchestra (but with prominent mallet-instrument and piano parts).

The music of Philip Glass after the mid-1970s followed a rather similar curve in the direction of greater variety, complexity, and accommodation to traditional modes of thought and expression, but in forms and media different from those favored by Reich—specifically operas, works for dance, and film scores. Glass's meeting in 1974 with the experimental-theater writer and director Robert Wilson, who shared his interest in expanded time-scales and means for altering the perception of time's passing, led to their unique theater work *Einstein on the Beach* (1976)—termed by Glass and Wilson

an opera but perhaps better described as an unprecedented combination of
mime, dance, and abstract music, with a few incidental spoken texts. The
four-act piece (five hours long, and without intermissions) is basically plot-
less, though images and objects related to Albert Einstein and his epochal
discoveries are the basis for the sets, props, lighting, and stage action. Five
substantial interludes for instruments and wordless chorus serve as inter-
mezzi—prelude, entr'acte pieces, and postlude—which are connective and
articulative tissue (Glass called them "knee plays") and also provide the main
musical substance of the work. There are no solo singers, and the twelve-
member chorus, prominent throughout, enunciates only numbers or solfège
syllables, *describing* its music by counting the beats and pulses or naming
the pitches. A man costumed and made up as Einstein (touseled white hair,
droopy mustache, sloppy shirt, suspenders, baggy pants) sits on a platform
between the pit and the stage, playing a violin (as Einstein actually did).
The "orchestra" consists of the Philip Glass Ensemble, made up of amplified
woodwinds and keyboards plus wordless solo voice. The audience looks past
the old man to see visions of "the thoughts, theories, technological wonders,
and moral dilemmas which emanated from the mind of this scientific thinker,
as well as the earth-shaking effects of his discoveries, all presented in a post-
surrealist stage idiom."[4]

    Einstein's artistic success in Europe and the United States turned
Glass definitively in the direction of theatrical and cinematic works. It became
the first in a trilogy of operas, each centered on a historical figure of outstanding importance in world history, the three figures representing different
arenas of human action. *Einstein on the Beach* represents, of course, science,
especially the terrifying scientific advances of the nuclear age ("on the beach"
evoking Nevil Shute's apocalyptic novel of that title); *Satyagraha* (1980),
subtitled "M. K. Gandhi in South Africa 1893–1914," revolves around racial
and ethnic politics; *Akhnaten* (1984), named for the Egyptian pharaoh who
was the first leader to espouse monotheism, explores themes of religion. If
Einstein is primarily a work of mime and dance, *Satyagraha* is one of solo
and choral song undergirded by a relatively modest orchestra of woodwinds,
strings, and organ; *Akhnaten* one of singing by soloists, two small vocal
ensembles, and a large chorus, with a full orchestral component. Thus the
progression is one of increasing conventionality of forces—also of drama-
turgy, for *Einstein* is essentially timelessly surreal; *Satyagraha* moves back
and forth among past, present, and future; and *Akhnaten* proceeds in a
straight-line conventional chronology.

    [4] Leslie Lassetter, "The Operatic Trilogy of Philip Glass: *Einstein on the Beach*, *Satya-
graha*, and *Akhnaten*" (M. Mus. thesis, College-Conservatory of Music, University of Cincinnati,
1985), p. 51. Glass himself offers a detailed discussion of the structural and motivic basis of the
music of *Einstein* in the booklet accompanying the recording (Tomato TOM-101; released 1979),
which also includes a perceptive essay by Robert Palmer.

The minimalist composers' first supporters and enthusiasts had been "downtown" artists. (The term connoted initially an area of Manhattan south of Greenwich Village, where after World War II there was an especially heavy concentration of artists living and working in low-rent lofts in ex-industrial buildings; later it developed a connotation of "experimental" or "vanguard" as opposed to the more conventionally shaped and supported art of the "uptown" galleries, museums, and concert venues north of 42nd Street.) By the late 1970s, however, the minimalists had developed remarkably large audiences among others as well—especially young people more comfortable with rock than with "serious" music. Glass, especially, had a fruitful relationship with rock musicians, notably David Byrne and the group Talking Heads. Among the most unusual of his slighter works of the 1980s was the recorded song cycle *Songs from Liquid Days* (1986), for which he commissioned lyrics from Byrne and other popular or crossover artists (such as Paul Simon and Laurie Anderson); set them with an expanded version of the Philip Glass Ensemble as accompaniment; and recorded them with a variety of specially chosen singers, some from the popular-music world (Linda Ronstadt, the female trio The Roches), some not (Douglas Perry, who had created the role of Gandhi in *Satyagraha*). Although the recording was immensely successful, with sales that put it on *Billboard* magazine's "charts" of best sellers, critics remained puzzled and wrote quizzically about the hybrid character of the cycle.[5] A similar reaction greeted American productions of portions of a new collaboration by the makers of *Einstein on the Beach*—the twelve-hour-long, five-act (plus prologue) operatic extravaganza *the CIVIL warS; a tree is best measured when it is down* (begun in 1983), which achieved sold-out houses but befuddled critics.

The number of composers who have been described as minimalists by one critic or another, at one time or another, in connection with one work or another, is very large indeed. The term has served as a catch-all for many kinds of reductive compositions: for the works by Alvin Lucier (b. 1931) that explore the acoustic characteristics of physical spaces, such as *I Am Sitting in a Room* (1970) or *Music on a Long Thin Wire* (1977); for the works by Jon Gibson (b. 1940) that combine modular structures with improvisation, such as *Cycles* (1973) for pipe organ; for the burbling semi-improvisatory cyclic works, such as *The Continuing Story of Counterpoint* (1976–83), of David Borden (b. 1938) and his ensemble Mother Mallard's Portable Masterpiece Co.; for self-defining works by Tom Johnson (b. 1939) such as *An Hour for Piano* (1971), *The Four-Note Opera* (1972)—on A, B, D, and E, for five voices and piano—or *Nine Bells* (1979), and his purely visual com-

---

[5] One conscientious reviewer, in concluding his uncertain critical comments, wrote resignedly, "Oh, what the hell, go ahead and buy it. You'll hate yourself in the morning, but so what?" (A[ndrew] S[tiller], in *Opus*, III/2 [February 1987], 17).

positions produced by a music typewriter (*Symnmetries* of 1981); for the
early open-structure works of Harold Budd (b. 1936), such as *The Candy-
Apple Revision* (1970), which may be played by any instrument(s) and consists
solely of a D♭ major triad; for the visually oriented "eyescores" of William
Hellerman (b. 1939), such as *To the Last Drop* (1974; reproduced as Fig.
23 in the *TNGDAM* article "Notation"); for some of the "political" works of
Frederick Rzewski, such as two inspired by the 1971 prisoners' revolt at
Attica (New York) State Prison, *Coming Together* and *Attica* (both 1972);
for the "sonic meditations" of Pauline Oliveros; for the Amerindian- and
Mexican-music-influenced works of Peter Garland (b. 1952), such as the set,
for two violins and gourd rattles, of six *Matachin Dances* (1980–81); for
almost all the compositions of Phill Niblock (b. 1933).

  The younger composer who by the mid-1980s seemed most strongly
to represent *post-minimalist* sensibilities, and seemed to have found, more
successfully than others, ways to bridge the gap between minimalist and
more traditional styles and aesthetics, was John Adams (b. 1947). He combined a driving, pulsatile, minimalist rhythmic sense with a rich harmonic
palette and carefully planned, through-composed structures expressed typically through conventional instrumental forces with more than a hint of
influence from the Classic-Romantic concert-music tradition. The sympathetic critic Michael Walsh, writing of such works as *Phrygian Gates* (1977)
for piano; *Shaker Loops* (1978) for string septet; *Harmonium* (1980) for chorus
and orchestra; and *Grand Pianola Music* (1981–82) for two pianos, two
singers, and chamber ensemble, described the result:

> Adams' music represents less of a conscious break with the past than either
> Reich's or Glass's; instead [he] draws inspiration from composers like Bee-
> thoven, Mahler, Sibelius and Stravinsky. His works have a lushness and emotional
> depth largely absent in the ascetic though fundamentally cheerful sounds of
> Reich or the giddy, explosive rhythms of Glass. . . . Adams has forged a big,
> strong, personal style, expressed in complex forms that employ a more exten-
> sive use of dissonance than other minimalists.[6]

New-Age Music

Related to minimalism and hovering on the edge of the pop-music world
was new-age music, a phenomenon that rose to prominence in the late 1970s

  [6] "Music[:] The Heart is Back in the Game," *Time*, September 20, 1982, pp. 56–58.
Another critic had a less sympathetic view; referring primarily to such later works as *Harmo-
nielehre* and *Light Over Water* (both 1984–85), Edward Rothstein wrote, ". . . John Adams'
sole accomplishment is to join the Minimalist audience with the mainstream, offering conde-
scendingly accessible works that speak to both. . . . I think, though, that Mr. Adams is important
far beyond his achievements: he marks, in a peculiar way, the end of Minimalism. . . . Philip
Glass's 'Satyagraha' and Steve Reich's early works were its apotheoses. Mr. Adams marks its
demise," ("Edward Rothstein on Music[:] The Trashing of Minimalism," *The New Republic*,
December 2, 1985, pp. 26–28.)

and early 1980s. Its name derived from an organic-food and naturopathy magazine called *New Age*, and it had close connections with the increased American interest in such Asiatic traditions as yoga and meditation. Almost exclusively a recorded music drawing on the latest in high-tech sonic clarity and nuances, new-age music was an improvisatory, modal or microtonal, open-ended, tensionless, climaxless, trance-like, essentially amorphous music that was strangely becalming—"music from the hearts of space," as the title of one popular late-evening radio program put it. Much of it was based on piano or acoustic guitar or gentle synthesized sounds; all of it was quiet and faceless. Some have claimed that the earliest new-age record album was *Music for Zen Meditation* (1964), improvisations by the clarinetist Tony Scott (b. 1921) aided by two Japanese classical musicians; but not for another decade or more did the genre reach significant dimensions. Then, however, dozens of minor new-age-music composers and composer-performers were recorded by such specialist labels as Windham Hill and Private Music; perhaps best known were the pianist George Winston (b. 1949), whose 1982 album *December* was an immense success; the keyboardist Steven Halpern, who produced a series of albums collectively titled *The Anti-Frantic Alternative* ("music for relaxation, meditation, and pure listening pleasure"); the Swiss harpist Andreas Vollenweider (*Down to the Moon*, 1986); and the Japanese electronic-music composer known as Kitaro (real name Masanori Takahashi), who by 1986 had issued no fewer than seventeen albums of new-age music, eight of them from his sound tracks for the long-running Japanese television series *Silk Road*.

THE NEW ACCESSIBILITY

The composer George Rochberg was quoted earlier (p. 248) as having cried out in 1963, "Now that the question arises on all sides: after abstractionism, what next? the answer rings out clearly: the 'new romanticism.'" He was looking back at a past dominated by the intellectualism of serial composition and the formalism of neo-Classicism. But he was also speaking, with extraordinary prescience, of the future: exactly twenty years later a major festival of new music was centered on the theme "Since 1968, a New Romanticism?" This was Horizons '83, the first of a series of annual festivals organized under the auspices of the New York Philharmonic by the orchestra's composer-in-residence at the time, Jacob Druckman; in the program book of the festival Druckman wrote,

. . . During the mid-1960s the tide [shifted, in] a gradual change of focus, of spirituality and of goals.

> . . . One can discern a steady re-emergence of those Dionysian qualities [of] sensuality, mystery, nostalgia, ecstasy, transcendency.

Druckman's use of the term "New Romanticism" has been widely applied to much American music of the past decades. For many, however, his purposely general definition has been too narrowly redefined: "New Romanticism" immediately suggests the nineteenth century—the age of Beethoven, Schumann, Liszt, Wagner, Mahler. But the qualities cited by Druckman inform other music than that of the nineteenth-century Romantics, and thus the term "New Romanticism" is not a comfortable one. Let us seek another.

Co-existent with minimalist, post-minimalist, and new-age music were, of course, other types of American music, some conceived along more "traditional" lines, some pursuing a post-Cageian path of experimentalism, some moving into technological no-man's lands. No one could lump all these under such a term as "New Romanticism." But a great deal of this otherwise variegated and widely differentiated music shared one aspect: accessibility. The anti-modernist tendencies of post-modernism were expressed in various ways, but almost all of them shared a new warmth, emotionality, revival of traditional tonal harmony, and—especially—accessibility. It was as if, in an age of technological revolution, of social and racial unrest, of dire poverty amid unprecedented plenty, of the threat to all of nuclear annihilation, artists were reaching out to audiences rather than communing only with themselves, secure in the certainty that posterity would understand their message. Thus a major trend of the period might be termed "the new accessibility."

Neo-Romanticism and Neo-Mannerism

Some of the music of "the new accessibility" does indeed merit the term *neo-Romantic*, in that it overtly relates to, and sometimes even quotes or is based on, music of the Romantic era. Druckman's dating of the dawn of a possible neo-Romanticism—1968—was probably chosen in recollection of a key work of that year, *Sinfonia* by Luciano Berio (who was living in the United States at the time), the premiere of which by the New York Philharmonic on October 10 had an immense and immediate impact. Not only was the collage technique of the third movement startling (see p. 298), with its basis in Mahler's Second Symphony and quotations from many other composers' music; even more of a surprise—and this was true of all the movements—was the *accessibility* of Berio's musical language. *Dans le sable* (1967–68; arranged for large orchestra 1970), by the West Coast composer Loren Rush (b. 1935), had prefigured Berio's work in its obsessive references to earlier music (in this case Barbarina's cavatina "L'ho perduto," in Mozart's *Le nozze di Figaro*) and in its accessibility. Similarly, George Rochberg's return to tonality (mentioned earlier, p. 314) was accomplished with many explicit references to such composers as Beethoven and Mahler, not only in the Third Quartet but in later works as well, such as the "Concord" quartets (nos. 4–6, 1977–78); their musical language of tonal design, harmony, and rhythm justifies the term "neo-Romantic."

More important than mere quotation of themes or reinterpretation of earlier harmonic/rhythmic language was the adoption of an immense expressive and gestural *range*, evocative of the nineteenth century, in works not only by Rochberg but also by a number of others. This is the main characteristic of the music of the 1970s and 1980s by Druckman, especially a series of orchestral works—following the Pulitzer prize-winning *Windows* of 1972—including *Incenters* (1973) and two works relating to the dramatic myth of Medea, *Lamia* (1974) and *Prism* (1980). Many works by others share this broad gestural expansiveness, such as the birdsong-inspired orchestral *Auroras* (1982) of Robert Erickson; the ballet score *Ulysses' Bow* (1983) of John Harbison (b. 1938); the Clarinet Concerto (1977) and the *Three Hallucinations* (1981) of John Corigliano (b. 1938); the orchestral *Sequoia* (1981) and the Piano Concerto "Homage to Beethoven" (1985) by Joan Tower (b. 1938); the *Adagio for Oboe and String Orchestra* (1977) by Tison Street (b. 1943); the symphonic poem *Aftertones of Infinity* (1979) by Joseph Schwantner (b. 1943); a number of compositions by Ellen Taaffe Zwilich (b. 1939), including her Symphony No. 1 (Three Movements for Orchestra; 1983); and the symphony *RiverRun* (1984) by Stephen Albert (b. 1941). (The last three works cited won Pulitzer Prizes, Zwilich's—which has a "Mahlerian glow and intensity [and a] mystery-laden slow movement"[7]—being the first ever awarded to a woman.)

Some of Frederic Rzewski's works, too, move far from a minimalist-narrow range of expression—notably the fifty-five-minute-long set of variations for piano on an anti-totalitarian Chilean popular song, *The People United Will Never Be Defeated!* (1975), of which the critic John Rockwell wrote, "The overall idiom suggests romantic piano writing, with an idiomatic felicity in that writing that has warmed the hearts of piano buffs and provides some rattling virtuoso passages. But this is not just a romantic resurrection."[8] The pervasiveness of the aesthetic of the new accessibility is suggested in the music of one young composer trained by three modernists (Wuorinen, Carter, and Babbitt): Tobias Picker (b. 1954), who combines thoroughgoing serialist structural techniques (mostly unheard) with an exuberant, eclectic audible surface in such works as his Violin Concerto of 1981; Symphony of 1982; and *Keys to the City* (Piano Concerto No. 2; 1983), a celebratory piece for the centennial of the Brooklyn Bridge.

---

[7] As put in a review by Andrew Pincus in the *New York Times*, October 12, 1986.

[8] *All American Music: Composition in the Late Twentieth Century* (New York: Alfred A. Knopf, Inc. 1983), p. 86, in a chapter centered on Rzewski entitled "The Romantic Revival & the Dilemma of the Political Composer."

Some older composers whose music had been criticized in the modernist era as being out of step with musical evolution, old-fashioned in its
conservative tonal language, rhythmic simplicity, and traditional forms and
expressive gestures—in short, anachronistic—achieved a new regard and
respect in the context of the new accessibility. Samuel Barber, who had
been seen as a"maverick," a throwback, an impossible neo-Romantic, suddenly emerged as a prophet; his works, always successful with audiences,
now got favorable notices from the critics as well. (Too late, said some
sympathizers who claimed that the critics' savaging of the Metropolitan
Opera premiere of Barber's *Antony and Cleopatra* in 1966 had led to a deep
depression and a swift decline on Barber's part.)

Others who had similarly been quietly working away as competent
"conservative" composers—and doing so quite successfully in terms of publication, performance, and recording, though not in terms of critical acclaim—
were belatedly acknowledged. This was true, for example, of Ned Rorem
(b. 1923), who, though hailed regularly as a first-rate (and saucily forthright)
diarist—*The Paris Diary* (1966), *The New York Diary* (1967), *The Final
Diary* (1974)—and composer of many grateful songs, was thought to be a
minor musical conservative until the 1970s. Then he began to be recognized
as an elegant and versatile composer, even something of a proto-post-mod-
ernist in such works as the symphonic poem *Lions* (1963), with its hallucinatory
evocations (by a supplementary onstage jazz combo) of the pop-song style
of Billie Holiday and the swing era. Robert Starer (b. 1924) similarly emerged
from the shadows of critical neglect into a sunny glade of recognition, after
many years of turning out shapely, broadly expressive works with the versatility and assuredness possible only to an artist thoroughly in command of
his craft. Like Rorem, Starer was applauded most as a composer of vocal
music—particularly after initiating a series of works to texts by the novelist
Gail Godwin, including *Journals of a Songmaker* (1975); the opera *Apollonia*
(1978); and the poignant, powerful monodrama *Anna Margarita's Will* (1979).[9]

One composer whose name is inevitably mentioned in connection
with the New Romanticism, new tonality, new accessibility, or whatever
term the writer prefers, is David Del Tredici (b. 1937), especially in relation
to a long series of big works inspired by Lewis Carroll's *Alice's Adventures
in Wonderland* and *Through the Looking Glass*. Composed over some eighteen years (1968–86), with perhaps more to come in the series, most of this

---

[9] Lingering resentment of the years of critical neglect is not hard to find in such
composers' writings. Rorem snapped, "Now that the American mode of the moment is accessibility, erstwhile hellions like Del Tredici and Rochberg are lauded for returning to the tonal
corral, while I, never a prodigal son, am shunned for having written such music before it was
stylish." (From a 1980 article in *Christopher Street* magazine; reprinted in Rorem's *Setting the
Tone* [New York: Coward-McCann, 1983], pp. 165–71. My thanks to Carol Oja for this reference.) See also Starer's candid and illuminating autobiography, *Continuo: A Life in Music*
(New York: Random House, 1987), especially the chapter on "Mr. X."

Alicead is scored for amplified soprano (who both sings and declaims), "folk group" (saxophones, mandolin, banjo, and accordion) or rock group, and extremely large orchestra.[10] Del Tredici's handling of these forces is virtuosic, reminiscent of Strauss or Mahler. Those composers, and Wagner, are also the sources of the harmonic style, which is straightforwardly tonal, as well as of the basic melodic materials and, to some degree, their pervasive, transformational usage. But in such a work as *Final Alice* (which won the Pulitzer Prize for 1976), as in Wonderland itself, all is skewed, distorted, exaggerated, unbalanced, full of weird juxtapositions and dizzying tangential swoops. Fragments of melody repeat themselves obsessively, crazily; long, ardent, arching vocal phrases also appear—but often are placed so high in tessitura, against such a welter of instruments, that the soprano can only bawl them out. The vocal range demanded of her is immense, and now and then she has to traverse its entirety in a sudden, surprising bel-cantoesque burst of virtuosity; crescendos rise, over great stretches of time, to feverish, hysterical climaxes, maintained long after their emotional peak can be sustained.

The first few measures of the "Simple Alice" song of *In Memory of a Summer Day* (1980) shows how Del Tredici suddenly skews a promissory antecedent-consequent phrase structure in foursquare metrical shape by dropping or adding a beat (Example 12-1 [a]); in the same work, a luscious altered-seventh chord on E, scored for strings and harp—a chord termed by the composer the "Chord of Rapture"—turns into one of "Regret" with the addition of a "stingingly dissonant F natural in stopped horns" (Example 12-1 [b]) in a "two-measure distillation of the sentiment of the entire piece."[11] A private, semi-secret self-reference concludes *Final Alice*, when over a sustained A, which grows ever softer until *it* concludes with the orchestral oboe's "tuning A" that began the work, the singer counts slowly to twelve in Italian and adds a whispered "tredici" (i.e., thirteen).

This handling of historical style elements in a readily recognizable but purposefully distorted, imbalanced, and private way—turning common practice into an involuted, highly personal language—is more neo-Mannerist than neo-Romantic (using the former term as art historians do in reference to, say, mid-sixteenth-century Italian art vs. the Renaissance classicism of the early sixteenth-century—Pontormo and Bronzino vs. Leonardo da Vinci and Raphael). Thus it would seem more appropriate to term works like the

---

[10] "Alicead" is Andrew Porter's witty term; see his collection of criticism, *Music of Three Seasons: 1974–1977* (New York: Farrar Strauss Giroux, 1978), pp. 558–63. Porter unravels the tangle of Del Tredici's Alice pieces in a helpful listing (with dates and places of first performances and approximate timings) in "Musical Events[:]Child Mabel," *The New Yorker*, June 16, 1986, pp. 109–13.

[11] From liner notes by Del Tredici for the recording of *In Memory of a Summer Day* (Nonesuch 9-79043-4 G; released 1983).

EXAMPLE 12-1. David Del Tredici, *In Memory of a Summer Day* (1980) (*Child Alice*, Part I). (a) Song, "Simple Alice." (b) Chord of Rapture and Regret. © Copyright 1980 by Boosey & Hawkes, Inc. Reprinted by permission.

Alice pieces of Del Tredici "New Mannerism" than "New Romanticism"; the distinction is worth making. Similarly, most of the pieces in a set of *25 Waltzes by Contemporary Composers*, compiled in 1976–78 by Robert Moran (b. 1937)—by such diverse composers as Babbitt, Cage, Glass, Harrison, Sessions, Tower, and Moran himself—are better described as neo-Mannerist than neo-Romantic, despite their obvious roots in waltz styles from Schubert to Ravel.

CONSERVATISM AND NOSTALGIA IN THE POPULAR-MUSIC WORLD

Not surprisingly, the currents of accessibility that led to stylistic retrospection in the concert-music world also affected popular music and jazz. There were various retrenchments in rock, away from the angry, snarling "punk rock" (of, for example, the New York Dolls or the Ramones) and the cynical "glitter rock" of the mid-1970s and its "heavy metal" successors (Blue Oyster Cult, Grand Funk Railroad, Aerosmith), toward simpler, smoother types. Older performers (Frank Sinatra, Willie Nelson, Barbra Streisand) continued to maintain a toehold on the "charts." There even arose, by the 1980s, a counterrevolutionary pop nostalgia resurrecting older styles, such as rockabilly, big-band jazz, and pre-rock pop songs, as in the albums *What's New* (1983) and *Lush Life* (1984) by Linda Ronstadt (b. 1946) and the sensuous renderings of "standards"—*Star Dust, When You Wish Upon a Star*, and the like—on the album *Hot House Flowers* (1984) by Wynton Marsalis (b. 1961). Reissues of earlier recordings proliferated: in 1976, of almost 700 "new" jazz recordings, nearly half were reissues; and within a few years rock-record manufacturers also were re-pressing "golden oldies" (e.g., a twelve-album Capitol Record set of 1985 tracing rock-and-roll from the early 1950s through the early 1970s) and biographies of dead stars (e.g., the Hopkins-Sugerman 1980 biography of Jim Morrison [of The Doors] and Albert Goldman's *Elvis* of 1981).

Broadway, in the late 1970s and early 1980s, seemed host to almost more revivals than new musicals (despite Sondheim's continued innovative efforts)—such as Rodgers and Hammerstein's *Oklahoma!* (revived 1979) and Rodgers and Hart's *On Your Toes* (revived 1983)—and to revues built around songs of older composers, such as *Ain't Misbehavin'* (1976; music mainly by Fats Waller), *Eubie* (1978; Eubie Blake), and *Sophisticated Ladies* (1981; Duke Ellington).

Country music, never inaccessible, reflected the new mood in its own ways. On the one hand, the identity of much country music became blurred, its edge and bite softened, by submission to the influence of rock, particularly the electronic technology of rock; crossover successes—country-music hits also rising to the top of the rock charts—were not infrequent. On the other hand, there was at the same time a nostalgic return to simple soulful songs eschewing the backup strings and vocal choruses that had come to characterize the "Nashville sound" of the nationally popular country-and-western repertory. One older leader of the revisionist rebels was Willie Nelson (b. 1933), who achieved immense crossover success in the mid-1970s with giant rock-like festivals and such albums as *Red Headed Stranger* (1975), which included the most popular country-music song of the year, *Blue Eyes Crying in the Rain* (reissued on *SCCCM*:s16/8). Younger figures who resisted the country-pop style in favor of a more traditional hard-core rural and honkytonk approach included Moe Bandy (b. 1944), with such songs as *It Was Always So Easy (to Find an Unhappy Woman)* (1974; reissued on *SCCCM*:s16/5), and Ricky Skaggs (b. 1954), in such songs of the early 1980s as *Crying My Heart Out Over You* and *Heartbroke*.

JAZZ AND ROCK

Even if there were currents of nostalgia, revivalism, and retrospection in various areas of jazz, rock, and pop, these strands were not at a standstill, and the period from the mid-1970s to the mid-1980s saw important other developments.

The free jazz of the 1960s seemed almost to go underground in the next decade, overwhelmed by the rock revolution; and it never became the major voice of jazz. It did, however, lead to such exciting music as that of the Association for the Advancement of Creative Musicians (AACM), a loosely organized, Chicago-based cooperative, founded in 1965 by the pianist Muhal Richard Abrams (b. 1930). And out of the AACM came the important and long-lived Art Ensemble of Chicago (AEC), which produced some twenty albums in as many years, that of early 1985 being called *The Third Decade*. Though centered on a traditional core of saxophones, trumpet, double bass, and drums, the AEC played also on literally hundreds of other instruments, from many cultures, and burst the traditional boundaries of jazz in appearing in costumes and makeup; offering dance, mime, and theater skits; and drawing on a huge repertory of black music, old and new. Also from the Middle West, and branching out from free jazz into eclectic individual styles, were the woodwind player and composer Anthony Braxton (b. 1945) of Chicago and the saxophonists Oliver Lake (b. 1942), Hamiet Bluiett, and Julius Hemphill (of the Black Artists Group of St. Louis), who joined with the Californian David Murray to form the World Saxophone Quartet in 1976.

In something like a spirit of "If you can't lick 'em, join 'em," large numbers of jazz musicians borrowed ideas and instruments from rock, and the most striking general development in jazz of the 1970s and early 1980s was the music known as "jazz-rock," "electric jazz," or "fusion." Throbbing rock rhythms, heavy amplification, and the use of electric piano and keyboard synthesizers typified this brand of jazz, which had been forecast as early as the late 1960s by Miles Davis (in the albums *In a Silent Way* and *Bitches Brew*). Jazz-rock of the 1970s was led primarily by musicians associated at one time or another with Davis, especially Herbie Hancock (b. 1940) in such albums as *Headhunters* (1973); the group Return to Forever led by Chick Corea (b. 1941); and Weather Report, a group formed in 1970 around the keyboardist Joe Zawinul (b. 1932) and the saxophonist Wayne Shorter (b. 1933).

Influences flowed in the opposite direction, too, in the 1970s, for several strands of rock borrowed from jazz and the blues, especially "hard rock," but also to some degree "heavy metal" and "art rock." Hard rock, as typified by the group Lynyrd Skynyrd (centered on the singer Ronnie Van Zant), was essentially electrified blues with a pile-driving southern-rock beat. Even more aggressive was heavy metal, characterized by one critic as "blues chords plus high-pitched male tenor vocals singing lyrics that ideally combined mysticism, sexism, and hostility," the performers "decking themselves out in leather and studs, growling and grimacing for all they were worth, turning concerts into exercises in high-decibel rants."[12] Heavy-metal's prototype was the British group Led Zeppelin, which was sedulously imitated by such American bands as Aerosmith (*Dream, Walk This Way*; both 1976),

---

[12] Ken Tucker, in Ed Ward, Geoffrey Stokes, and Ken Tucker, *Rock of Ages: The Rolling Stone History of Rock & Roll* (New York: Rolling Stone Press, 1986), p. 485.

Blue Oyster Cult (*Agents of Fortune*, 1976), and Grand Funk Railroad (*All the Girls in the World Beware*, 1975; *Born to Die*, 1976).

Art rock, as the name implies, had aesthetic pretensions higher than other types; its pedigree went back not only to the first "concept album" of the Beatles, *Sgt. Pepper's Lonely Hearts Club Band* (1967), and the self-conscious artiness of another British group, Emerson, Lake & Palmer, but also to such American bands as Frank Zappa's Mothers of Invention and The Velvet Underground. The latter bands were independently establishing an art-rock tradition at about the same time, one which perhaps peaked with Zappa's response to a commission from Pierre Boulez: *The Perfect Stranger*, a seven-movement set of "preposterously non-modern" pieces (recorded in 1984 for EMI Records by Boulez, conducting the Ensemble InterContemporain of Paris and the Barking Pumpkin Digital Gratification Consort—Zappa's group under a mockingly "arty" new name).

Several sub-genres of rock sputtered into existence in the 1970s, were exploited furiously on rock-oriented radio stations and recordings, and then fell victim to their own over-commercialization.

"Disco" took its name from discothèques—the nightclubs, popular since the 1960s, where patrons danced to recorded music. It was a relentlessly rhythm-dominated, designed-for-dancing music; in its background were the black soul music of the Detroit-based Motown recording company (the songs, for instance, of the Temptations, Diana Ross and the Supremes, Smokey Robinson and the Miracles, Stevie Wonder, and the Jackson Five) and the pop-soul issues of Philadelphia International Records, like Motown a black-owned firm. There were musicians who rode to stardom on the disco wave—notably Donna Summer (b. 1948) with the erotic *Love to Love You Baby* (1975) and The Bee Gees' soundtrack recording from the movie *Saturday Night Fever* (1977)—but the real star of disco was the disc jockey: using two turntables to segue seamlessly from one record to another, the deejay built "sets" that rose inexorably in tension and excitement until they peaked climactically. This development led, in New York in the late 1970s, to the even more creative deejays' "scratching"—backspinning records by hand and using other collagist techniques to create a harsh, percussive background for the incredibly athletic, solo "break dancing" or for the improvisatory streetwise rhyming dialogue called "rapping." A landmark in the early recorded history of rap was the album *Run-D.M.C.* (1984) by the pair of hip-hoppers who called themselves just that.

By about 1979 the fad for disco had peaked and passed, giving way to a grittier species of black-inspired rock: funk. That term, as we have seen (p. 287), had been applied to some jazz of the 1950s; it was also used to describe the harsh, howling athleticism of the 1960s soul music of James Brown (b. 1933). Now it served to describe a rock style considerably more intricate rhythmically than disco, and in fact inspired in part by African polyrhythms (as well as call-and-response techniques). A number of funk groups emerged in the wake of Sly and the Family Stone, a group headed by Sly Stone (b. 1944), among them Kool and the Gang; the Ohio Players; and Earth, Wind and Fire. But the prototypical funk artist was George Clinton (b. 1940), who headed a constantly changing cast of rock musicians under the group names The Parliaments and Funkadelic, producing wild extravaganzas, three and four hours long, marked by songs with such titles as *Maggot Brain, America Eats Its Young,* and *Free Your Ass and Your Mind Will Follow*—musical equivalents of the contemporaneous belittlings of American white-dominated society by the black actor and comedian Richard Pryor. Highly successful albums by "P-Funk" included *Tear the Roof Off the Sucker* and *Mothership Connection* (both 1976) and *Funkentelechy vs. the Placebo Syndrome* (1977).

By the mid-1970s, rock was the principal dialect of American popular music (having even affected the folkish speech of country music) and was no longer identified with rebellious youth or a counterculture; it was, in fact, the mainstream of the establishment's popular music. Perhaps inevitably, this led to a nonconformist reaction from within the ranks: punk rock. In the hands of such groups as the New York Dolls and the Ramones (and in the lyrics and voice of Patti Smith), this was a deliberately outrageous, primitive, raw, raunchy, revisionist rock. It in turn gave way to a less ragged but still lean and hard-edged rock termed "new wave," typified by the group Talking Heads, led by the versatile David Byrne (b. 1952). Self-consciously artistic (the original group had formed as students at the Rhode Island School of Design) but drawing deep from the well of black soul and even African music (though they themselves were all white), Talking Heads issued a series of albums produced by the sophisticated recording-studio technologist Brian Eno (like Byrne, British born)—*Talking Heads '77, More Songs about Buildings and Food* (1978), *Fear of Music* (1979), and *Remain in Light* (1980)— which, surprisingly in view of their uncompromisingly non-commercial eccentricity, turned into successes.

Elaborate studio productions also helped a rock artist who emerged as a figure as olympian and summarizing for the 1970s as Elvis Presley had been for the 1950s (and the Beatles for the 1960s): the singer-songwriter Bruce Springsteen (b. 1949). His album *Born to Run* (1975) catapulted him to national prominence, which he not only maintained but even exceeded a decade later, when *Born in the U.S.A.* (1984) sold more than 7 million copies in a year. The opposite side of the Springsteen coin in the 1980s was Michael Jackson (b. 1958), who broke out of a collaborative role in Motown's Jackson Five with the super-hit albums *Off the Wall* (1979) and *Thriller* (1982). As the critic Ken Tucker put it,

> Ultimately, the ascendance of Springsteen and Michael Jackson summons up the spirit of Elvis Presley. . . . In Springsteen, we could hear and see Presley's

heroic humility, his regular-guy sense of humor, his implied spokesmanship for the American lower middle class. In Jackson, we could observe Presley's smoldering sexuality, his artful, sometimes disturbing eccentricity, his gospel-music roots, and his enduring love for the florid pop ballad. Together, they offered . . . rock music imbued with a sense of history, but invigorated by fresh innovation.[13]

TIMBRAL, TONAL, TEMPERAMENTAL, AND TECHNOLOGICAL OUTREACH

The title of this section is intended to suggest areas in which American composers have been extending the musical boundaries of sound—the quality or color of sounds (*timbre*) and the repertory of sounds—especially in terms of different tuning systems (which involve *tonal* divisions, including microtones, and systems of *temperament*, or alterations of acoustically perfect intervals to form musically viable scales). Significant work in these areas goes back to Ives (his quarter-tone pieces), Cowell (his "string piano" pieces), Varèse (*Ionisation* and other pieces with predominant percussion), and Partch (his pieces based on a forty-three-note scale and newly invented instruments), but in the last decade or so other remarkable advances have been made. Many of these have connected with—and in most instances been made possible by—new *technology* (especially the electronic technology behind synthesizers and computers, in addition to tape recorders). Above all, a more ecumenical attitude toward musical possibilities has proved inspiriting and fruitful.

The "new virtuosity" (see pp. 294–97) has been important in broadening concepts of what is possible sonically, whether in music produced by the human voice or acoustic instruments alone or by electronic transformations. A second generation of the "new virtuosos" has been characterized by a more personal, often theatrical approach to performance and by the composer-performers of "performance art." Thus, although Joan La Barbara gained an early reputation as a virtuoso singer who both inspired and interpreted music by others, she went on to compose music for herself as soloist, most often live/electronic music with tape. More boldly theatrical is the work of Diamanda Galas (b. 1955), who exploits stunning and startling costuming, lighting, makeup, and onstage behavior, together with her operatic voice (extended electronically to super-human limits, either by live signal-processing or pre-recorded tape), to produce a gabbling, babbling, roaring turmoil of female vocalization. The titles of such works as *Wild Women with Steak Knives* (1981) and *The Litanies of Satan* (1982) suggest accurately her aura

[13] Ibid., pp. 612–13.

of "a demonic soul in torment" (as one critic wrote); she has said that she attempts to illuminate the outer limits of human emotions, "driving to the extremes of incandescent beauty and unmitigated ghastliness . . . extremes encroaching upon [each] other within microseconds."[14]

The epitome of the performance artist of the late 1970s and 1980s was Laurie Anderson (b. 1947), a winsome, deceptively fragile- and innocent-looking woman of great versatility: poet, sculptor, photographer, singer, storyteller, violinist, composer, lyricist, and electronic high-tech wizard. Her way with rock-like "songs" (with texts that are apt to deal, however glancingly, with cosmic matters), which she performs with the panache and the split-second timing of a great stand-up comedian, brought her abruptly to international attention in 1981; in that year her recording of *O Superman* (backed by *Walk the Dog*) became a pop hit in England and won her a national tour in the United States. These two songs and almost eighty others— plus a dizzying variety of little narratives, skits, comic turns, Chaplinesque shuffling and robotic dance steps, giant backdrops with slide projections, and other visual props—she stitched together into an extravagant four-part, two-evening-long "solo opera" called simply (if grandly) *United States* (1983). A few years later she had moved on, to make the feature-length film *Home of the Brave* (released 1986), a strangely compelling, episodic concert-like work in which, as she put it,

> . . . there are no plots. The strategy of this film is to use technology to criticize itself. Machines are the fall guys. Animals are the straight men. The people are everyone else.[15]

Closely related to performance art are "text-sound compositions"— works that hover on the borderline between literature and music, their "sound" being primarily manipulated "text"; the term "lexical music" is also sometimes used. Among the important makers of text-sound compositions are Jackson Mac Low (b. 1922), Beth Anderson (b. 1950), and Charles Amirkhanian (b. 1945). Mac Low combines verbal, musical, and visual elements— taking what he calls a "multilevel approach to language, sound, and action"— in such works as *Musicwords (for Phill Niblock)* (1978) and *Unstructured Meditative Improvisation for Vocalist and Instrumentalist on the Word "Nucleus"* (1982). Anderson's text-sound compositions (the words of which she writes herself) include *Torero Piece* (1973), *I Can't Stand It* (1976), and *Yes Sir Ree* (1978). Many of Amirkhanian's pieces teeter on the edge of the humorous or ironic—for example, *Church Car* (1980–81), in which two

    [14] Quoted in K. Robert Schwarz, "Young American Composers: New York's 'Downtown' Music," *Music and Musicians*, July 1985, pp. 10–11. See also Galas's own comments, "Intravenal Song," *PNM*, XX/1 (Fall-Winter 1981), 59–62.
    [15] Laurie Anderson, " 'Hi, We Need \$1 Million for a Film,' " *New York Times* April 20, 1986.

speaking vocalists tangle in increasingly complex counterpoint as they pile up repetitions of such minimal phrases as "Church car," "box car," and "auto-bump car" (all spoken very fast), or *Maroa* (1981), with its playful offsetting of liquid words (like the title) with a jazzy hard-edged drum-synthesizer background.

Text-sound composition arises from a fascination with, and exploration of, the compositional possibilities of individual sounds—from the sentence and phrase level down to the most minimal syllables, vowels, consonants, and phonemes. A similar fascination and exploration had led in the late 1960s to instrumental *multiphonics*—the production of two or more notes simultaneously on a single wind instrument—which quickly became one of the resources of the new virtuosity. In the 1970s, the singer-composer David Hykes (b. 1953) found means for achieving *vocal* multiphonics. Inspired by the *hoomi* ("throat") singing of western Mongolians and the resonant chanting of Tibetan Buddhists, Hykes trained himself and a half-dozen other singers (whom he named the Harmonic Choir) in similar "harmonic singing" and in fact raised it to new levels of subtlety, variety, and precise control. His *Hearing Solar Winds* (1977–83), *Current Circulation* (1983–84), and other works are partially improvisatory and made up of wordless, shimmering streams of groaning fundamentals; eerie flute-like upper partials; and long "chordal" glissandos swooping slowly up, down, and around—not exactly performance art, but for obvious reasons best experienced live in large resonant spaces like the giant Cathedral of St. John the Divine in New York, where the Harmonic Choir has been in residence.

Hykes's group produces its unearthly vocal multiphonics by virtue of an acoustically pure just intonation. In this it shares with a small but growing community of American performers and composers an interest in tuning systems other than twelve-note equal temperament, which has dominated Western music for several hundred years. Some have been inspired by exotic music (especially Asiatic) based on other tunings; some have been freed by electroacoustic means of sound production from any *necessity* to think in terms of "12-equal" temperament; and some have been attracted to other possibilities out of sheer musical curiosity.

After Partch, a pioneer in just intonation and alternative tuning systems was Lou Harrison. His interest in Asiatic music arose naturally from residence on the West Coast, tutelage by Cowell, and early involvement with Cage. In the early 1960s he studied traditional music in both Korea and Taiwan; later, collaborating with the instrument maker William Colvig, he built many instruments and even entire gamelan ensembles based on those of Indonesia. For gamelan groups and varied combinations of unusual instruments, Harrison has produced a large body of work, much of it stylistically inspired by Asiatic or ancient music, and has been extremely influential as a teacher. Some compositions for hybrid ensembles of both Eastern and

Western instruments lie on the borderline between the exotic and Western worlds, such as the charming couple *A Joyous Procession and a Solemn Procession* (1962), for wordless high and low voices, trombones, tambourines, handbells, great gong, and bass drum. Each of these processional pieces is based on a different heptatonic mode in just intonation; according to the published score, a facsimile of Harrison's exquisite calligraphy, they may be used for "different celebrations by various religious and civic groups, but may not be used by the military." Harrison has also written more conventional music, to which he brings an extraordinarily refined ear and masterly orchestration (as in the *Concerto on G* of 1961 and the brief tone poem *At the Tomb of Charles Ives* of 1964, both for orchestra, and the Concerto for Organ with Percussion Orchestra of 1973). The Concerto for Piano and Orchestra (1985), though conventional enough in structure and expression, is based on a 12-*unequal* tempered scale known as "Kirnberger II" after the disciple of J. S. Bach who invented it; in his program notes for the concerto, Harrison writes,

> This astonishing tuning contains almost the whole history of "Western Music" from Babylonian times to the middle of the last century, because its flat series produces perfectly tuned fourths and fifths (the whole Middle Ages) and the white keys are, with the exception of a very slightly raised pitch A, in perfect Renaissance and Baroque just intonation.

Ben Johnston (b. 1926) has also written extensively in just intonation, but usually for traditional Western instruments (some of which—the piano, for instance—must of course be retuned). His *Sonata for Microtonal Piano* (1965; recorded on NW 203:s2/1–4) demands a retuning of the instrument in chains of just-tuned non-tempered triads which leave only seven of the eighty-eight piano keys with octave equivalents—in other words, there are eight-one different sounds available (not just twelve, as on the usual keyboard).

Equal temperaments other than 12-equal have interested some composers. The Hiller-Cage extravaganza *HPSCHD* included, as we saw (p. 302), tapes based on almost fifty different alternative equal temperaments. Tui St. George Tucker (b. 1924) has written a number of works in quarter tones (24-equal), among them *Little Pieces for Quarter Tone Piano* (1972), *Quartertone Recorder Duets* (1973), and *Indian Summer* (1983) for two baritones and large ensemble. Easley Blackwood (b. 1933) took advantage of the tuning potential of a synthesizer in his set of twelve *Microtonal Etudes* (1982) for keyboard synthesizer, each étude based on a different division of the octave, from 13-equal to 24-equal. John Eaton (b. 1935) uses not only quarter tones but just intonation and 12-equal temperament in his opera *Danton and Robespierre* (1978).

One composer who has been increasingly involved with non-Western music—without, however, turning to alternative tuning systems—is Alan Hovhaness (b. 1911). Since the 1940s, when he first became interested in Armenian music (he is of Armenian and Scots descent), and especially since about 1960, when Far Eastern elements began to infuse his music, Hovhaness has produced a staggering number of works, primarily instrumental. (Cage has been qoted as saying that Hovhaness is "a music tree who, as an orange or lemon tree produces fruit, produces music.") By the summer of 1986 his production of symphonies alone had reached No. 61 (the "Mount St. Helens" symphony), and his total oeuvre numbers well over 400 compositions, all determinedly tonal; accessible; and though typically tinged with a personal mysticism, just as typically rather insubstantial.

The upsurge of interest in non-Western music and in alternative tuning systems has meant an expansion of instrumental possibilities—not only the importation of third-world folk and traditional instruments but also the adaptation of conventional instruments (new fingerings, for example, for wind instruments; extra valves for brass; extra keys for keyboards) and the invention of others (those of Partch, for instance, or the thirty-one-tone just-tuned zoomoozophone of his former student Dean Drummond). A very special case is that of Conlon Nancarrow (b. 1912), who since the late 1940s has composed almost exclusively for player piano (in conventional twelve-equal temperament). Frustrated by the difficulty of finding performers able to execute his rhythmic ideas, Nancarrow taught himself to punch piano rolls, note by note, and has written—for one or both of a pair of modified uprights in his Mexico City studio—a unique series of more than forty one-movement "studies." The principal structural basis of these is canon, each voice of the canon usually proceeding at its own rate of speed. The character of Nancarrow's studies is well described in Philip Carlsen's *TNGDAM* article on the composer:

> [They] fully exploit the player piano's potential for rhythmic complexity and textural variety; they are showpieces of virtuosity far beyond the capabilities of human performers, with extremely fast arpeggios, trills, and glissandos, effortless leaps, widely spaced block chords, and complex contrapuntal activity. . . . [Nancarrow's] music testifies to his great skill at breathing life into the instrument, and many of the studies have an elegance and spontaneity that belie their mechanical origins.

Without question, the most overwhelmingly significant element in virtually every kind of the new American music of the past quarter-century has been *technology*. Technology has affected the musical experience of virtually everyone—composers, performers, and listeners alike. Radio, recordings, television, and especially electronic and computer technology

have altered the very perception of what music is or can be—in the direction
of limitlessness, of unbounded choice, of cosmic possibilities. John Cage
foresaw this development with astonishing clarity as early as 1937, when he
began a lecture called "The Future of Music: Credo" with these words:

> I believe that the use of noise to make music will continue and increase until
> we reach a music produced through the aid of electrical instruments which
> will make available for musical purposes any and all sounds that can be heard.
> Photoelectric, film, and mechanical mediums for the synthetic production of
> music will be explored. . . . The present methods of writing music, principally
> those which employ harmony and its reference to particular steps in the field
> of sound, will be inadequate for the composer, who will be faced with the
> entire field of sound.[16]

In view of the unparalleled importance of technology to our time, musically
speaking, it seems appropriate to conclude this book with a consideration
of some composers who have been leaders in exploiting (in some cases
actually developing) newly available technology.

Although Cage and a few other composers—among them Ussachevsky, Luening, Varèse, and Subotnick—foresaw the compositional
possibilities of electronic and recording technology fairly early (in the 1950s),
the world of popular music had long capitalized on it and continued to do
so most progressively and aggressively. Early commercial radio and the
budding recording industry of the 1920s thrived on popular music, including
hillbilly music and "race records" for the black community. The crooners of
the 1930s such as Rudy Vallee and Bing Crosby, and even more the great
jazz vocalists (Mildred Bailey, Billie Holiday, Ella Fitzgerald, and especially
Sarah Vaughan), revolutionized popular-song vocalism by special microphone techniques that gave them an extraordinary range of vocal timbres,
in live performance as well as on radio and recordings. Electrically amplified
guitars were available in the early 1930s, and when major artists such as the
jazz guitarist Charlie Christian (1916–42), the blues singer and guitarist
Muddy Waters (1915–83), and the country guitarist Les Paul (b. 1915) began
to use them—Paul actually inventing in 1941 a prototype of the solid-body
electric guitar—the door was opened for a popular-music revolution centered squarely on technology. Jazz of all eras, rhythm-and-blues, rock-and-
roll, later rock, disco, country pop, and other popular-music subgenres are
unthinkable without electronic reproduction, amplification, and other technological components. Television has now and then been host to concert

---

[16] As printed in John Cage, *Silence* (Middletown, CT: Wesleyan University Press,
1961), pp. 3–6. The lecture was first printed in the brochure accompanying the recording,
produced by George Avakian, of Cage's twenty-five-year retrospective concert at Town Hall,
New York, in May 1958 (Avakian JC-1/JCS-1; released 1960).

music and opera—a landmark being NBC-TV's 1951 commission from Menotti of *Amahl and the Night Visitors*—but the only new television-music genre to have emerged is the music-video short, great numbers of which have been produced by rock and pop artists for broadcast over twenty-four-hour-a-day music-video cable channels (such as MTV [Music Television] and VH-1 [Video Hits One]) and even regular network channels.

A few visionary concert-music composers have, however, turned to "video art," which beckons as one of the least-explored new media. One pioneer was Nam June Paik (b. 1932), who since the mid-1960s has experimented with videotape, often in notorious collaboration with the occasionally topless cellist Charlotte Moorman (b. 1933), to produce such works as *Opéra sextronique* (1967), *TV Cello* (1971), and *Global Groove* (1973).

Another major figure is Robert Ashley, whom we met earlier as one of the founders of the ONCE group (see pp. 271–73). From the beginning, much of Ashley's work was theatrical, and beginning in the 1970s, while heading the Center for Contemporary Music at Mills College in Oakland, California (he later moved to New York), Ashley has concentrated on mixed-media performance-art and video-art projects. One is the totally unconventional video opera *Perfect Lives (Private Parts)*, begun in 1977 and finally completed in 1983; although broadcast several times in England and Europe (and one interlude from it, *The Lessons*, here as well), it has yet to be viewed in its entirety in the United Sates. *Perfect Lives* is the central opera in a triptych; the first is *Atalanta (Acts of God)* (1982), which also has been produced in Europe but not yet in the United States; still in progress is *Now Eleanor's Idea*, itself a set of four sub-operas (each about an hour-and-a-half long). Ashley also generously documented the personalities and work of a group of fellow composers in the set of video portraits *Music with Roots in the Aether* (1976), considered by the composer to be as much a "piece" as anything else he has done; it is focused successively on David Behrman, Philip Glass, Alvin Lucier, Gordon Mumma, Pauline Oliveros, Terry Riley, and (breaking the alphabetical ordering) Ashley himself.

The technological tool whose potential for composers and performers of all kinds—and for that matter, ultimately listeners—is greater than any other, but one that has only begun to be realized (even though it was being experimented with as early as the mid-1950s, as we saw on p. 264), is the digital computer. By the mid-1980s, the authors of a major guide to the world of so-called computer music could begin their preface this way:

> Computer music activity has proliferated in recent years. It has grown from its somewhat specialized origins as an interdisciplinary subfield of electronic music, digital signal processing, and experimental music to occupy an increasingly central position in the technologies of professional recording and home audio, as well as electronic music synthesis and composition. The expanded

use of digital electronics in music is likely to continue; what we are now experiencing may be only the beginning of an era in which computer technology predominates in all aspects of the reproduction and synthesis of music.[17]

My phrase "so-called computer music" is intended to downplay the implications that music is actually *composed* by a computer. That is possible, but so far the results have been of limited interest—to practitioners and public alike. Much more significant, at least to the present, have been various uses of the computer as an *aid* to composition of electroacoustic music, as a particularly effective source of synthetic sounds, and of course as a necessary resource for "digital recording" (which made possible, beginning in 1983, the commercial production of compact discs—"CDs"—and their flawless reproductive sound quality).

A major problem for composers attempting to use early digital-computer programs was the difficulty with which they could actually hear the results of their work, or alter, amend, and edit it. This was solved by about 1970 with the development of digital synthesizers; these combined the sound-generating and -processing capabilities of such analog synthesizers as the Moog and Buchla instruments (see p. 263) with the progammability of digital computers. Most recently, high-speed computer technology has made possible astonishing uses of computers in real-time musical performance.

Pioneer work in developing computer programs for the synthesis of musical sound was done by Max Mathews (b. 1926) at the Bell Telephone Laboratories in New Jersey. Other early program developers were Godfrey Winham (1934–75), J. K. Randall, and Hubert S. Howe, at Princeton University, and John Chowning who has directed the Computer Music and Acoustic Group (1966–74) and the Center for Computer Music Research and Acoustics (since 1975) at Stanford University.

Among the composers to have concentrated more recently on computer music with critically acclaimed results are J.K. Randall, Barry Vercoe, Roger Reynolds, and Charles Dodge.

Randall's music is the product of a fierce intelligence combined with rarefied sensibility, as is apparent in such works as *Lyric Variations for Violin and Computer* (1968; recorded on Vanguard Cardinal VCS-10057, released 1969) and the atmospheric, unobtrusive, silence-studded sound-track for the feature-length film *Eakins* (1972; recorded on CRI SD-328, released 1974).

Barry Vercoe (b. 1937) has written interestingly about composing his *Synapse for Viola and Computer* (1976) at the M.I.T. Experimental Music Studio (which he established in 1971): the two computers there

---

[17] Charles Dodge and Thomas A. Jerse, *Computer Music: Synthesis, Composition, and Performance* (New York: Schirmer Books, 1985), p. ix.

. . . are capable of synthesizing a large orchestra-like sound. The composer controls this performance by communicating with the computer in traditional musical terms. Thus, when he "plays" a section of his score at the keyboard, the computer will "listen" and then display those notes in music notation on a screen. The composer can . . . make modifications as he or she goes. Upon request, the computer will synthesize and play back any segment of that score, and can print copies of the score and parts for individual players. . . . I wrote about two-thirds of *Synapse* at home, away from the piano. As each section was completed, I would take it to the studio and "orchestrate" it for synthesized sound. . . . I would listen to the computer performance, add a touch of color here, restore a note there, and so on, until good ensemble was achieved.[18]

Reynolds, whose searching musical mind we have met earlier (see p. 299), first added computer technology to his arsenal of compositional resources in a series of quadraphonic tape-music works collectively titled *Voicespace*—*Still* (1975), *A Merciful Coincidence* (1976), *Eclipse* (1979), and *The Palace* (1980)—realized variously at the Center for Music Experiment (founded by Reynolds) at the University of California, San Diego (UCSD), and at the Stanford University center. He said,

Electronics—at first analog, later digital systems—offered rather precise control over auditory space (a particular sound's size, location, distance, the character of the host space in which it was heard. . . . The four works . . . share a concern with the potential of auditory imaging. . . . They attempt to create a personal theater through the mind's ear.[19]

The "personal theater" that results is one of uncommon richness, resonance, and compelling expression. One can describe these pieces factually as settings of texts by, respectively, Coleridge, Beckett, a group of writers (from whose works a collage of fragments is drawn), and Borges; but "settings" is a meager term for the extraordinary reshapings, the virtuosic manipulations, the consummate technological mastery (in the service of expressive aims) with which Reynolds builds the compositions. Such a piece as *The Palace*, (*Voicespace IV*) might be termed "auditory opera" employing a single voice reciting and singing—some of the vocal materials being performed live (but amplified), some pre-recorded and reverberated, some still natural but "enhanced," and some thoroughly transformed electronically—and the processing capability of a computer music system. The third *Voicespace* (*Eclipse*) approaches more conventional music theater in that it was planned as a collaborative work with the video artist Ed Emshwiller (b. 1925), and its premiere included videotape, film, and placard-picture components. Central

---

[18] Jacket notes for a recording including *Synapse* (CRI SD-393, released 1979).
[19] Jacket notes for *Voicespace* (Vital Records VR-1801/2, released 1982).

to Reynolds's conception was the virtuosity—the singular "new virtuosity"—of the singers whose voices inform the *Voicespace* series, notably Philip Larson and other members of the Extended Vocal Techniques Ensemble organized at the Center for Music Experiment at UCSD. Reynolds went on, in such works as *Archipelago* (1982) and *Transfigured Wind II* (1984), to even more sophisticated usage of computers in the compositional process—and with *Vertigo* of 1986 to another collaboration with Emshwiller reflecting their common involvement in digital processing and generation of imagery, both sonic and visual.

Charles Dodge, working at Columbia and Princeton and later in the Center for Computer Music at Brooklyn College (which he founded), was one of the pioneers in computer synthesis of musical sound. For a number of years, beginning in the early 1970s, he concentrated on compositional applications of *speech synthesis* by computer, producing works that some have likened—not very accurately—to text-sound compositions. In an impressively varied series of pieces—beginning with *Speech Songs* (1972), *The Story of Our Lives* (1974), *In Celebration* (1975), and *Cascando* (1978)—Dodge formed the entire fabric of compositions from computer-synthesized voices. These compositions all originated with texts being "read" into a computer (by means of an analog-to-digital converter); the computer was then used to analyze in infinitesimal detail the vocal sounds, in order to define very precisely each of their many attributes ("parameters") in time segments as brief as milliseconds. Dodge could then alter—independently—any parameter he wished, to put together ("compose") a synthetic voice or texture of voices, and to combine or repeat or manipulate them in any imaginable way. Finally, after editing (right in the computer, no longer needing "hard copy"), he transferred, by means of a digital-to-analog converter, the finished composition with its resynthesized vocal sounds onto audio tape.

The first three works just cited have texts by the poet Mark Strand. The four little *Speech Songs* are amusing études, and *In Celebration* transforms a single speaker's reading into multiple voices, composed into a work full of dark surprises. *The Story of Our Lives* and *Cascando* (originally a radio play by Samuel Beckett) are dramatic dialogues; in both, a non-human "character" in the drama (a book in *The Story of Our Lives*, "Music" in *Cascando*) is made by Dodge to "speak"—in eerie, unforgettably unique sonorities, which nevertheless relate to the resynthesized human vocal sonorities, thanks to the analytic/synthetic precision of Dodge's computer-music techniques. Similar relationships are literally built into the exquisite live/electronic piece *The Waves* (1984), for soprano and tape, based on the first paragraph of Virginia Woolf's novel of that title. Composed for Joan La Barbara, *The Waves* has a synthesized accompaniment derived from computer-aided acoustical analysis of La Barbara's voice reading the Woolf text and using extended vocal techniques. Thus, in the work as performed—at least, if by La Barbara herself (she recorded it on an M.I.T. compact disc, YHDS-16)—the live voice and the tape accompaniment are ineluctably related to each other.

Dodge's virtuoso mastery of computer usage in composition is put at the service of a keen sense of humor in *Any Resemblance Is Purely Coincidental* (1980). An early recording of Enrico Caruso singing "Vesti la giubba" from *Pagliacci* was fed into the computer, stripped of its orchestral accompaniment (in an amazing technological tour de force), analyzed and resynthesized, and then composed into a hilarious search for an appropriate response to a new accompaniment—provided by a live pianist, who waits onstage in vain for the appearance of the incorporeal soloist.

Few composers working in computer-aided composition are as skillful as those just discussed in "humanizing" their work, in being able to overcome the tendency of electronically generated sounds to seem abstract, lacking in sentience and vitality, machine-made—in short, dehumanized. And just as with earlier electroacoustic-music composers, many composers of "computer music" have combined synthetic sound with live performers, in a perhaps half-unconscious attempt to guarantee such humanization. With the most recent technology, computers operate so swiftly that there is virtually no time lag between instructing the computer and hearing the results; the computer's output can thus be used directly in concert performance. Such computers have been termed "real-time digital synthesizers." Understandably, some composers have leaped at the opportunity to exploit such instruments, putting them onstage and, with the composer "playing" them, having them interact instantaneously with live musicians. Two pioneers in such real-time performance electronics are Morton Subotnick and Daniel Lentz.

Subotnick was of course one of the first composers to work extensively with analog synthesizers (see p. 263). Later, in a series of works beginning with *Two Life Histories* (1977), he explored the possibilities of real-time electronics—especially as such electronics could be used to relate to, interact with, and actually transform the sounds of live performers—in what he called "ghost" works. Reynolds commented on the technique and implications of these:

[The "ghost" element] allows physical gesture (the flow of exhaled breath, for example) to be translated into spatial or other musical dimensions. A pre-recorded and composed set of control gestures, played back during performance in coordinated ways, allows the musical sounds produced by the instrumentalist on stage to be transformed by more elemental and large-scale gestural impulses. A "ghostly" influence extends the impact of what musicians on stage are able to accomplish with traditional means. Subotnick [thus] continues the exploration of ways in which electronic devices can elaborate upon and enlarge our most human of endeavors.[20]

Subotnick's *Two Life Histories* is for male voice, clarinet, and electronic sounds produced in real time; *The Last Dream of the Beast* (1978) is a female counterpart, later revised for soprano, chamber ensemble, and real-time electronics. *The Double Life of Amphibians* (1982–84) deepens the electronic involvement: it is scored for pairs ("doubles") of amplified acoustic instruments (cellos, clarinets, trombones, percussion, pianos) and real-time digital synthesizer, which is in fact controlled by the cellos and is wholly dependent on what *they* do for its own manner of "performance." Sonically, as the piece unfolds, the relationship between "instrumental" and "synthetic" sounds becomes more and more symbiotic, until by the end (as the composer explains in the score) "the two become a single homogeneous texture." Similar subtle and changing relationships underlie *The Key to Songs* (1985), "music for an imaginary ballet" for two pianos, viola, cello, two mallet percussionists, and a real-time digital synthesizer—the YCAMS (Yamaha Computer Assisted Musical System).

A number of works by Daniel Lentz (b. 1942) sound superficially close to minimalist music, and some even to new-age music: they contain very little harmonic and rhythmic variety; much repetition of perpetual-motion motifs (often arpeggios) in foursquare phrase structures; very slow changes of texture; very little sense of "development" or motion toward climax; and hardly any sense of contrast, tension, rivalry, or struggle. Yet usually by the end of a work by Lentz one realizes that something considerable *has* happened, that a piece has evolved, materialized, *become* a piece. This has been, in fact, an aesthetic ideal of Lentz's—to shape his music in what he calls "spiral forms," with the musical material kept in a spiraling, additive state of *becoming* rather than in a static state of *being*, in which one musical idea, completed, moves on to another, which is then completed, and so on, to result in the block-form structures characteristic of so much earlier music. This has been especially true of Lentz's vocal works, which often reveal their full texts very slowly, sometimes only at the very end of the piece, after having been introduced partially, in tiny fragments (often only single phonemes), which are instantly repeated together with different, dovetailing fragments, and those re-repeated with still other fragments added until finally—like a jigsaw puzzle—the entire text is spread out before the ear. Along the way, interesting, unpredictable verbal and sonic juxtapositions, configurations, and even meanings not present in the full text emerge.

---

[20] Roger Reynolds, "Extending Our Reach," in the program book of *The Pacific Ring Festival, April 29–May 9, 1986* (La Jolla: University of California, San Diego, 1986), pp. 15–17.

An early example is *O-Ke-Wa (North American Eclipse)* (1974), a thirteen-minute piece for twelve solo singers (with handbells), rasps, and drums. (The Amerindian title is the Seneca word for the tribe's dance for the dead, and Kit Tremaine's brief text is a nostalgic lament for the "dark murmuring Indians," occupants now of "wispy hidden graves.") Each singer has her or his own melodic line and selection of text fragments. The singers introduce the fragments additively in repetitive cycles—text fragment/singer 1, then text fragments/singers 1 + 2 together, then text fragments/singers 1 + 2 + 3 together, and so on, until all twelve voices are sounding and the text is complete. (The ritualistic repetitive cycles are especially apt, given the nature of the text; and ideally the piece is to be performed in darkness, with the singers moving around the audience in a slow shuffle.) Example 12-2 shows the fourth cycle: singer 4 enters; singers 1–3 repeat their phrases as before; singers 5 and 6 hum (▲) and singers 7–12 whistle (△) in heterophonically supportive accompaniment; handbells, rasps, and drums are to be understood.

There is a limit to which such procedures are possible, or effective, in live-only performance, a limit that Lentz perhaps reached in *O-Ke-Wa*. But electronic technology is perfectly suited to them, and Lentz was already in the early 1970s exploring its possibilities, especially analog echo systems (familiar to rock keyboard-synthesizer players), which would free the live performers of the necessity to produce their own repetitive echoes and permit Lentz to build larger structures with broader expressive ranges. In his *Missa Umbrarum* ("Mass of Shadows") of 1973, for example, Lentz has an eight-voice chorus (SSAATTBB) unfold the five sections of the Latin Mass text fragmentarily and in repetitive echo cycles, dovetailing new fragments with the repetitions ("sonic shadows") of ones already introduced, by means of a multiple tape-loop process. The work has other unusual, provocative aspects—among them its instrumentation, which consists solely of wine glasses of various shapes and sizes, held by the singers; these are filled by the conductor (in symbolic substitution for the liturgical celebrant) to begin the performance, and are tapped, tipped (to bend their pitch), struck, stroked, and sipped from (to change their pitch). A similar record-and-repeat-with-tape-delay technique is used for the single reciting voice in the brief *Song(s) of the Sirens* (1975), accompanied by clarinet, cello, and piano. This is based on the voluptuous sirens' song in the *Odyssey* ("Listen to our voices,/Listen to the music which sounds from our lips, sweet as honey/ . . ."); the ambiguous plural in Lentz's title implies the ten cycles of replays-with-additions required for the "song" text to materialize in its entirety. *Three Pretty Madrigals* (1976)—"Slow Motion Mirror," "Midnight White," and "Solar Cadence"—are especially attractive studies, for a few voices and electric pianos, in analog echo-system techniques, applied to Lentz's spiral-form text-building methods. The instrumental *Point Conception* (1981) is a big

EXAMPLE 12-2. Daniel Lentz, *O-Ke-Wa* (1974), cycle No. 4. Reproduced by permission.

piece (thirty-seven minutes long) for big forces (nine pianos), but with an eight-part "cascading echo system" (Lentz's term) in action, a single pianist suffices.

More sophisticated computer/synthesizer technology underlies Lentz's later work, such as *On the Leopard Altar* (1983–84), *Wild Turkeys* and *Time's Trick* (both 1985–86), and *The Crack in the Bell* (1986). For these, he employs his own ensemble of one or more vocalists—notably the agile soprano Jessica Lowe—and several electric keyboardists playing such synthesizers as Yamaha DX-7s or KX-88s; he himself sits at a small (but very powerful) real-time digital processor and mixing console (an Akai MG-1212, at the time of this writing), which is hooked up to the other performers. Using half-inch tape, he can record on more than sixty tracks and mix down, in real time, with uncanny speed and accuracy. In effect, he has right there at his disposal an electroacoustic- and computer-music studio, and a recording studio as well, and he acts as composer, music editor, producer, and recording engineer— all virtually at the same time, on the spot.

On the Leopard Altar expands on the plan of *Song(s) of the Sirens*: from a matrix text, six brief "songs" are lifted, then performed in spiral-form additive fashion, until with the sixth "song" the entire matrix text is unveiled. *Wild Turkeys* (for keyboardists alone) is an étude-like work built from a reservoir of myriads of modular figures (based exclusively on fifths, hence the title), all related to a basic rapid pulse, which are looped repetitively and successively. The keyboardists have precise scores to realize, but many aspects of their realizations—aspects of timbre, register, partial structure, octave doublings, relative intensity of "simultaneities," and others—are governed by Lentz at the console. Despite the heavy reliance on technology and "recording," the resulting piece has all the vitality and spontaneity of "wholly live" music (no two performances are ever quite the same) and is potent, powerful, and propulsive—sheets of kicky-rhythmed, pulsatile, postminimal patterns that flicker and surge and are almost literally electrifying in their effect.

Larger in aims and conception are *Time's Trick* and *The Crack in the Bell*. *Time's Trick* is a witty sketch (part of a musical drama in progress) in which the solo singer must utter staccato phonemes, different ones in each of a number of successive cycles; in each cycle she performs against tape-delay repetitions of the earlier cycles, gradually building the "actual" (matrix) text. The cycles are of considerable length, and during the times when the computer is "searching" for the beginnings of their repetitions, "live only" music (unprocessed, unrecorded, unstored in the computer) is performed by the ensemble—lending, of course, a new textural and sonic quality and a new subtlety of design.

The Crack in the Bell is based on E. E. Cummings's sonnet "next to of course god america i/love you land of the pilgrims' oh"; it was Lentz's response to a commission from the remarkable West Coast music patron Betty Freeman (b. 1921) for the Los Angeles Philharmonic New Music Group. Two versions exist, one for the Lentz Ensemble and performers from the Philharmonic, the other for the Lentz Ensemble alone. Again, Lentz's text-analytic penchant, together with a strain of black humor and healthy cynicism, results in a provocative and lively work, slyly satirical but also deeply felt—like Cummings's verses themselves, and their ambiguous "heroic happy dead/who rushed like lions to the roaring slaughter."

It seems appropriate, in this time of the bicentennial celebration of the U.S. Constitution, roughly a decade after that of the American Revolution, to call attention to such pieces as *O-Ke-Wa, Missa Umbrarum, Wild Turkeys,* and *The Crack in the Bell.* Not only do they share with the other music discussed in this chapter the vivaciously pluralistic post-modernism of the present era; not only do they relate to post-minimalism and text-sound composition and represent the new accessibility; not only do they represent the most recent phase of the new virtuosity and relate, in their real-time spontaneity, to jazz's improvisatory approach to music making. They also call up the past of the United States, both historically (*The Crack in the Bell*) and musically (the Amerindian rasps of *O-Ke-Wa*; the Benjamin-Franklinesque musical glasses of *Missa Umbrarum*); and they touch on grave concerns of the present. Finally, in their spirited interaction between human performers and products of technology, they reaffirm that today, as always in the past, man and machine can make vital music together.

BIBLIOGRAPHICAL NOTES

John Rockwell's panoramic but sharply focused *All American Music: Composition in the Late Twentieth Century* (New York: Alfred A. Knopf, Inc., 1983) is especially valuable in connection with the material in this chapter (and has helpful bibliographical and discographical notes following the text). Eric Salzman's companion volume in the Prentice-Hall series *Twentieth-Century Music: An Introduction,* 3rd ed. (Englewood Cliffs, NJ: Prentice-Hall, Inc., 1988), John Schaefer's *New Sounds: A Listener's Guide to the New Music* (New York: Harper & Row, 1987)—which has more on new-age music than any other source—and Elliott Schwartz's *Music Since 1945: Issues, Materials and Literature* (New York: Schirmer Books, in preparation) are essential reading, though by definition treat much other music besides American. Two books based on interviews are noteworthy: Walter Zimmermann's *Desert Plants: Conversations with 23 American Musicians* (Vancouver, Can.: Zimmermann and A.R.C. Publications, 1976) and Cole Gagne and Tracy Caras's *Soundpieces: Interviews with American Composers* (Metuchen, NJ: Scarecrow Press, 1982).

As of this writing, besides the works cited in footnote 4, the literature on minimalist music is thin. K. Robert Schwarz's double essay on Reich (cited in the bibliographical notes for Chapter 11) is, however, excellent, and he has written the best accounts to date of the work of John Adams: "Young American Composers: John Adams," *Music and Musicians*, March 1985, pp. 10–11, and "John Adams: Music of Contradictions," *New York Times*, January 11, 1987, sect. 2, p. 25.

Stephen Holden was one of the first to note the phenomenon of "Pop Nostalgia: A Counterrevolution," *The New Republic*, April 1985, pp. 121–22; Bill C. Malone touches on it in the revised edition (1985) of his masterly *Country Music U.S.A.* (Austin: University of Texas Press), which is complemented by his *Southern Music/American Music* (Lexington: University Press of Kentucky, 1979).

As usual, writings on jazz, pop, and rock of the last decade and a half are plentiful but exceedingly variable in quality and trustworthiness. Gary Giddins is knowledgeable in, and affectionate toward, recent developments in jazz; besides his *Riding on a Blue Note: Jazz and American Pop* of 1981 (cited at the end of Chapter Eleven), see also his *Rhythm-a-ning: Jazz Tradition and Innovation in the '80s* (New York: Oxford University Press, 1986). (We still await the second volume of Gunther Schuller's jazz history, following *Early Jazz* [up to the mid-1930s] of 1968; it is promised.) Impressive in its comprehensiveness is the Ward-Stokes-Tucker collaborative history of rock cited in footnote 10 (though it completely lacks any bibliography and has an unhelpful index). Ken Emerson writes a thoughtful essay on the leader of the Talking Heads, in "David Byrne: Thinking Man's Rock Star," *New York Times Magazine*, May 5, 1985, pp. 54–57, 74, 77–78, 94–96. Steven Hager's *Hip Hop: The Illustrated History of Break Dancing, Rap Music, and Graffiti* (New York: St. Martin's Press, 1984) is very lively and indeed illustrated, generously. Soul is the subject of Gerri Hirshey's well-written, enthusiastic *Nowhere to Run: The Story of Soul Music* (New York: Times Books, 1984).

Laurie Anderson is discussed by Don Shewey in "The Performing Artistry of Laurie Anderson," *New York Times Magazine*, February 6, 1983, pp. 26–27, 46–47, 55, 59, and by John Rockwell in Chapter 10 of his *All American Music*.

The rising interest in microtones and alternative tuning systems is reflected in the new journal *Pitch: for the International Microtonalist*; I/1 is dated Autumn 1986. Douglas Leedy's *TNGDAM* article "Tuning Systems" is a superb account. The ideas of one influential microtonalist are to be found in Lou Harrison's delightful *Music Primer* (New York: C. F. Peters, 1971).

The most penetrating study of Conlon Nancarrow's studies is Philip Carlsen's *The Player Piano Music of Conlon Nancarrow* (ISAMm; 1987). Also valuable are Roger Reynolds's "Conlon Nancarrow: Interviews in Mexico City and San Francisco," *American Music*, II/2 (Summer 1984), 1–24, and Peter Garland's "Conlon Nancarrow: Chronicle of a Friendship," in his *Americas: Essays in American Music and Culture* (Sante Fe, NM: Soundings Press, 1982). Garland's Soundings Press has been systematically publishing Nancarrow's studies—that is, the staff-notated scores he painstakingly writes out (even though technically they are "useless" since they cannot be "read" by his player pianos).

Robert Ashley's fourteen-hour video piece *Music with Roots in the Aether* may become available for viewing; it is also to be hoped that his book with the same title, but comprised of statements by younger composers about the seven portrayed in Ashley's video portraits, will come onto the public market. The original piece is discussed and described by Norbert Osterreich in *PNM*, XVI/1 (Fall-Winter 1977), 214–28.

The authoritative book cited in footnote 15 includes many bibliographical citations and discusses some of the music by Vercoe, Reynolds, Subotnick, and Dodge touched on here. Harold W. Whipple's "Beasts and Butterflies: Morton Subotnick's Ghost Scores." *MQ*, LXIX (1983), 425–41, is not easy to read but worth the try. Roger Reynolds writes a fascinating account of his own philosophy and procedures in *A Searcher's Path: A Composer's Ways* (ISAMm; 1987).

Daniel Lentz has not been well served by critics, historians, or lexicographers; an especially lurid and irresponsible misrepresentation is that in *Baker's Biographical Dictionary of Musicians*, 7th ed. (New York: Schirmer Books, 1984). Joseph Kerman, however, discusses Lentz's *Song(s) of the Sirens* (1973) perceptively and sympathetically in his textbook *Listen*, 3rd ed. (New York: Worth Publishers, 1980), pp. 479–82.

INDEX